A HANDBOOK ON T
TRIPS AGREEM

C000079808

This handbook describes the historical and legal background to the TRIPS Agreement, its role in the World Trade Organization (WTO) and its institutional framework, and reviews the following areas: general provisions and basic principles; copyright and related rights; trademarks; geographical indications; patents; industrial designs, layout-designs, undisclosed information and anti-competitive practices; enforcement of intellectual property rights; dispute settlement in the context of the TRIPS Agreement; TRIPS and public health; and current TRIPS issues. It contains a guide to TRIPS notifications by WTO Members and describes how to access and make use of the official documentation relating to the TRIPS Agreement and connected issues. Furthermore, it includes the legal texts of the TRIPS Agreement and the relevant provisions of the WIPO conventions referred to in it, as well as subsequent relevant WTO instruments.

ANTONY TAUBMAN is Director of the Intellectual Property Division of the WTO Secretariat.

HANNU WAGER is a senior officer in the Intellectual Property Division of the WTO Secretariat.

JAYASHREE WATAL is a senior officer in the Intellectual Property Division of the WTO Secretariat.

A HANDBOOK ON THE WTO TRIPS AGREEMENT

Edited by
ANTONY TAUBMAN, HANNU WAGER
and
JAYASHREE WATAL

CAMBRIDGE
UNIVERSITY PRESS

CAMBRIDGE UNIVERSITY PRESS
Cambridge, New York, Melbourne, Madrid, Cape Town,
Singapore, São Paulo, Delhi, Mexico City

Cambridge University Press
The Edinburgh Building, Cambridge CB2 8RU, UK

Published in the United States of America by Cambridge University Press, New York

www.cambridge.org
Information on this title: www.cambridge.org/9781107023161

First published 2012

Printed in the United Kingdom at the University Press, Cambridge

A catalogue record for this publication is available from the British Library

Library of Congress Cataloging-in-Publication Data

A handbook on the WTO TRIPS Agreement /
edited by Antony Taubman, Hannu Wager, and Jayashree Watal.
p.   cm.
ISBN 978-1-107-02316-1 (Hardback) – ISBN 978-1-107-62529-7 (Paperback)
1. Intellectual property (International law) 2. Agreement on Trade-Related Aspects of
Intellectual Property Rights (1994) 3. Foreign trade regulation. I. Taubman, Antony.
II. Wager, Hannu. III. Watal, Jayashree.
K1401.H365 2012
346.04'8–dc23

2011042620

ISBN 978-1-107-02316-1 Hardback
ISBN 978-1-107-62529-7 Paperback
ISBN WTO 978-1-107-66327-5 Paperback

CONTENTS

FIGURES

BOXES

TABLES

PREFACE

At the heart of the World Trade Organization (WTO), as an international organization, is a set of rules that regulate trade between nations: a body of agreements which have been negotiated and signed by governments of the majority of the world's trading nations, with the aim of promoting transparency, predictability and non-discrimination in trading relations. These agreements, covering trade in goods, trade in services and trade-related aspects of intellectual property rights, help to define and inform the multiple roles of the WTO, in administering the trade agreements, providing a forum for trade negotiations, handling trade disputes, monitoring national trade policies, providing technical assistance and capacity building for developing countries, and cooperating with other international organizations. Understanding these agreements and their practical, policy and legal contexts therefore provides significant insights into the WTO as an institution, its activities and international role, its partnerships with other organizations, and the way in which WTO Member governments identify and pursue their national interests through this intergovernmental forum.

When, in 1994, at the end of the Uruguay Round of trade negotiations, governments settled on the cluster of agreements that created and defined the WTO, the Agreement on Trade-Related Aspects of Intellectual Property Rights, or the TRIPS Agreement, was part of the package. The TRIPS Agreement was not negotiated as a stand-alone treaty, and did not enter into legal force on its own, but is one of the multilateral trade agreements (MTAs) that are integral to the overarching Marrakesh Agreement Establishing the World Trade Organization. This status means that when the TRIPS Agreement entered into force in 1995, it was as part of a composite set of trade agreements that are together binding on countries that choose to join the WTO as Members. The WTO Agreement also made disputes between Members about trade and intellectual property subject to the same dispute settlement mechanism as is used for a wide range of trade issues. But the TRIPS

Agreement also incorporated significant elements of the established multilateral intellectual property agreements administered by the UN specialized agency for intellectual property, the World Intellectual Property Organization (WIPO). Hence the TRIPS Agreement has a dual character – an important element of international trade law, it also draws heavily on, and builds upon, the established heritage of international intellectual property (IP) law.

The TRIPS Agreement has also come to the fore in a wide range of international policy discussions – ranging over public health, biodiversity, the environment, and human rights, and other debates concerning policy settings for innovation, knowledge-based economic growth and technology diffusion. The need for a practical knowledge of TRIPS, its provisions and its institutional context therefore extends beyond the traditional circle of trade negotiators and IP lawyers, and this *Handbook* has been prepared to serve the needs of this wider community of legislators, diplomats, policy-makers, other government officials, representatives of civil society and industry, practitioners, journalists, students and other interested parties in the general public.

This publication is the latest in a series of WTO *Handbooks*, aimed at providing a non-technical overview of key elements of the WTO system. As a *Handbook* on the TRIPS Agreement, it provides a general account of the Agreement itself, and describes its objectives, principles and other provisions. The TRIPS Agreement has not been a static document since its entry into force in 1995, and the *Handbook* reflects the evolving context of TRIPS, in particular:

- While the *Handbook* is not a legal textbook, and it does not explore questions of legal interpretation, it does describe some of the experience in analysing and interpreting the TRIPS Agreement in the context of dispute settlement.
- The *Handbook* provides an overview of the institutional framework within the WTO that administers the TRIPS Agreement, in particular the TRIPS Council.
- And the *Handbook* gives an update of some of the key developments, such as the Doha Declaration on the TRIPS Agreement and Public Health and the ensuing amendment to TRIPS, and ongoing negotiations and policy discussions within the WTO.

The *Handbook* is up to date at the time of writing, but readers should be aware that some of the processes it describes are dynamic, and several passages have been highlighted as areas where further developments may potentially have occurred since mid-2011.

For reasons of space and brevity, the *Handbook* concentrates on the text of the TRIPS Agreement and on TRIPS-related developments within the WTO itself and does not describe in detail the important discussions and debates in other international policy processes and organizations that have dealt with TRIPS; a very brief description is provided to assist the reader to understand this broader context of TRIPS, but this is not intended to give authoritative guidance, which can instead be obtained from the organizations concerned.

Prospective readers should not pick up this *Handbook* expecting close legal analysis of TRIPS provisions, nor authoritative statements about the implications or impact of the TRIPS Agreement, nor extensive descriptions of the complex policy debates that surround the TRIPS Agreement. There is a vast academic, policy and legal literature concerning the TRIPS Agreement, its interpretation, and these related issues; this *Handbook* does not venture into this territory that has been widely explored and mapped by many expert authors. Instead, this *Handbook* seeks to give the reader an accessible, non-technical overview of the Agreement, and describes how to access and make use of some of the key official documentation that relates to the TRIPS Agreement and related issues. The initiative to publish this *Handbook* responds to the practical feedback received from countless active participants in technical cooperation, and readers are encouraged to provide further feedback to the address ipd@wto.org for possible use should there be a future decision to produce a revised and updated edition.

Antony Taubman
Director
Intellectual Property Division, WTO Secretariat

ACKNOWLEDGEMENTS

Preparation of the *Handbook* was undertaken by the WTO Intellectual Property Division, drawing on years of practical feedback from technical assistance and training programmes prepared and delivered by the Division, in particular the material prepared for the TRIPS module of WTO eTraining in 2007. The former director of the Division, Mr Adrian Otten, substantively reviewed and enhanced earlier versions of this material. The *Handbook* is a collective production by the Division, but the following individuals contributed particularly to certain chapters:

Chapter I: Hannu Wager and Jayashree Watal
Chapter II: Hannu Wager
Chapter III: Wolf Meier-Ewert
Chapter IV: Thu-Lang Tran Wasescha
Chapter V: Jayashree Watal
Chapter VI: Wolf Meier-Ewert, Xiaoping Wu, Robert Anderson and Pierre Arhel
Chapter VII: Roger Kampf
Chapter VIII: Hannu Wager
Chapter IX: Roger Kampf
Chapter X: Antony Taubman
Appendices 1–2: Hannu Wager

The joint editors Antony Taubman, Hannu Wager and Jayashree Watal express thanks to all contributing authors and to those involved in the production process, particularly Karla Brepsant and Karyn Russell.

ACRONYMS AND ABBREVIATIONS

AOC	appellation d'origine contrôlée
AOP	appellation d'origine protégée
BATF	Bureau of Alcohol, Tobacco and Firearms
CBD	Convention on Biological Diversity
CESCR	United Nations Committee on Economic, Social and Cultural Rights
CMO	collective management organization
CTM	Community trademark
DSB	Dispute Settlement Body
DSU	Dispute Settlement Understanding
FDI	foreign direct investment
FTA	free trade area
GATT	General Agreement on Tariffs and Trade
GATS	General Agreement on Trade in Services
GI	geographical indication
GSPOA	Global Strategy and Plan of Action on Public Health, Innovation and Intellectual Property
ICESCR	International Covenant on Economic, Social and Cultural Rights
INAO	Institut National d'Origine et de la Qualité
IP	intellectual property
IPIC	Intellectual Property in Respect of Integrated Circuits
IPR	intellectual property right
LDC	least-developed country
MFN	most-favoured-nation
MTA	multilateral trade agreements
MTO	Multilateral Trade Organization
PDO	Protected Designation of Origin
PGI	Protected Geographical Indication
R&D	research and development
RTA	regional trade agreement
TK	traditional knowledge
TRIPS	Trade-Related Aspects of Intellectual Property Rights
UNCTAD	United Nations Conference on Trade and Development

UNDESA   United Nations Department of Economic and Social Affairs
UNDP   United Nations Development Programme
UNEP   United Nations Environment Programme
UNESCO   United Nations Educational, Social and Cultural Organization
UNFCCC   United Nations Framework Convention on Climate Change
UPOV   International Union for the Protection of New Plant Varieties
WCT   WIPO Copyright Treaty
WGTCP   Working Group on the Interaction between Trade and
            Competition Policy
WHA   World Health Assembly
WHO   World Health Organization
WIPO   World Intellectual Property Organization
WPPT   WIPO Performances and Phonograms Treaty
WTO   World Trade Organization

I

Introduction to the TRIPS Agreement

A   Introduction

1   General

This chapter provides an overview of the TRIPS Agreement. It first explains the historical and legal background of the Agreement and its place in the World Trade Organization (WTO). It then turns to the general provisions and basic principles, as well as other provisions and institutional arrangements, that apply to all the categories of intellectual property rights (IPRs) covered by TRIPS. Chapters II to VII then discuss each of these categories in more detail.

However, in order to understand the TRIPS Agreement it is important to first review the background to the intellectual property (IP) system: what the main forms of IPRs are, why these 'rights' are recognized, and how they are protected. These questions have been at the core of IP policy discussions since the adoption of the earliest IP laws, and continue to spark active debate. This chapter attempts neither to summarize various relevant legal and economic theories, nor to survey the range of views presented in the debate, but merely highlights some of the general concepts and approaches.

IPRs can be characterized as rights given to persons over the creations of their minds. They usually take the form of a limited 'exclusive right' granted under national law to a creator over the use of the creation for a certain period of time. Such a right allows the creator to exclude others from using the creation in certain ways without the creator's authorization. The right holder can then extract economic value from the IPRs by using them directly or by authorizing others to do so.

IPRs are territorial rights, which means that they are valid only in the jurisdiction where they have been registered or otherwise acquired.

IPRs are customarily clustered into two categories: copyright and industrial property.

Copyright can usefully be divided into two main areas:

1. Copyright (or 'authors' rights' in some systems) refers to the rights of authors of literary and artistic works (such as books and other writings, musical compositions, paintings, sculptures, computer programs and films). Authors, or those who derive the right from authors (such as publishers), have the right to determine how their works are used for a minimum period of time after the death of the author.
2. Copyright in a wider sense also includes related rights (sometimes called 'neighbouring rights'), especially the rights of performers (e.g. actors, singers and musicians) over their performances, producers over phonograms (sound recordings), and broadcasting organizations over broadcasts. These rights are also limited in time.

Industrial property can be divided into two fields:

1. The first is the protection of distinctive signs, in particular trademarks (which distinguish the goods or services of one undertaking from those of other undertakings) and geographical indications (GIs, which identify a good as originating in a place where a given characteristic of the good is essentially attributable to its geographical origin). Trademark protection may last indefinitely, provided the sign in question continues to be distinctive; use of the trademark is also often a requirement. A GI can also be protected indefinitely, provided it continues to identify the geographical origin.
2. Other types of industrial property are protected primarily to recognize and stimulate technological innovation and industrial design, and to provide the legal framework for the creation of new technologies and products. In this category fall inventions (protected by patents; although, in a number of countries, innovations that could embody lesser technical progress than patentable inventions may be protected by utility models), industrial designs and trade secrets. The protection is usually given for a finite term (now typically twenty years in the case of patents), although trade secrets can be protected as long as they remain secret. Industrial property also includes legal means to suppress acts of unfair competition.

The intellectual property (IP) system is a tool of public policy: generally, it is intended to promote economic, social and cultural progress by stimulating creative work and technological innovation. More specifically, the main social purpose of protection of copyright and related rights is to encourage and reward creative work. It gives an opportunity for authors and artists to earn their living from creative work. Other than serving as an incentive to authors, copyright essentially provides an economic foundation for cultural industries and the market for cultural products once the rights are licensed or assigned to publishers and producers. Similarly, patents and certain other industrial property rights are designed to provide protection for innovations resulting from investment in research and development (R&D), thus giving the incentive and means to finance applied R&D.

These standard policy objectives are supported by the economic theory that suggests that works and information resulting from creative work and innovation have characteristics of public goods in the sense that they are 'non-excludable' and 'non-rivalrous' in consumption – in other words, once created, absent specific measures, none can be excluded from 'consuming' them. In addition, one's use of a work or an invention does not deprive another of its use and it can be freely used by anyone (unless there are specific legal constraints), unlike physical property such as land that can be fenced off. Therefore, in the absence of IP protection, it is difficult for creators to extract economic value from or 'appropriate' the financial returns from their work, or indeed to influence how they are utilized. Thus, from the society's perspective, there is a risk of 'market failure', that is, underinvestment in socially beneficial creative and innovative work. The IP system also allows market-driven decentralized decision-making, where products are created and technology developed in response to demand. The IP system offers a range of options, but does not preclude the need for other forms of financing mechanisms, in particular in areas where the market alone may not provide adequate incentives (for example, contemporary concert music or cures for neglected diseases).

Another objective of IP protection is the transfer and dissemination of technology. A well-functioning IP regime should, other things being equal, facilitate the direct and indirect transfer of technology, by means such as foreign direct investment (FDI), trade and licensing. The legal titles provided by the IP system are used to define and structure the distinct rights and responsibilities in technology partnerships, such as research cooperation or technology sharing or transfer arrangements. One of the purposes of the patent system is to disseminate technological information by requiring inventors to disclose new technology in their patent applications rather than attempt to keep it secret, so that new technology can become part of the common pool of knowledge of mankind and be freely used once patents expire. Improved information technology tools that facilitate, for example, the availability of patent information on the Internet means that this 'teaching' function of the patent system is becoming increasingly more effective and accessible in practice compared to earlier days.

Trademarks, GIs and other distinctive signs are protected so as to inform consumers and prevent consumer deception. In addition, these forms of IP help to ensure fair competition among producers. They provide an incentive for companies to invest in their reputation through the provision of quality products and services. An equally important objective is to enable consumers to make informed choices between various goods and services.

Reflecting their role as tools of public policy, IPRs are not absolute and unlimited, but are generally subject to a number of limitations and exceptions that aim to balance the legitimate interests of right holders and users. These limitations and exceptions, together with the carefully defined scope of protectable subject matter and a limited term of protection, are intended to maintain an appropriate balance between competing public policy interests so that the system as a whole can be effective in meeting its stated objectives.

2   Historical and legal background to TRIPS

The World Trade Organization (WTO) is the legal and institutional foundation for the administration and development of trade relations among its 153 Members, at the multilateral level. It aims to provide fair and stable conditions for the conduct of international trade with a view to encouraging trade and investment that raises living standards world-wide. It is the successor to the former General Agreement on Tariffs and Trade (GATT 1947), a multilateral trade agreement that was concluded in that year. Further trade liberalization was pursued under the auspices of the GATT through 'trade rounds' aiming at further tariff cuts and strengthened rules. The Uruguay Round was the eighth round of trade negotiations and by far the most comprehensive. These negotiations were launched in 1986 and completed in 1994.

The main results from the Uruguay Round included a further major reduction of customs tariffs worldwide, and the liberalization of, and development of better rules governing trade in textiles and agriculture – two areas previously largely excluded from the GATT. The trading system was also extended into new areas of trade relations not previously dealt with, notably trade in services and IP. This reflected the growing economic importance of these two areas and their increased share of international trade. Furthermore, the results included the development of a reinforced and integrated dispute settlement system, which is applicable to any agreements covered by the WTO. The Uruguay Round also resulted in the creation of a new organization – the WTO – to administer the agreements. The Marrakesh Agreement Establishing the World Trade Organization ('the WTO Agreement') entered into force on 1 January 1995. The 'GATT' now refers to an updated agreement on trade in goods, dubbed 'GATT 1994' to distinguish it from the earlier GATT, which is only one of a number of agreements annexed to the WTO Agreement.

GATT 1947 included several provisions that made reference to IPRs. For instance, GATT 1947 confirmed that Contracting Parties could have rules on IPRs provided that they were consistent with principles of non-discrimination. Article III:4 requires treatment for imported products that is no less favourable than that accorded to like products of national origin in respect of all laws, regulations and requirements; this includes IP laws. More specifically, Article XX(d) allows a general exception to the application of GATT obligations with respect to compliance with laws and regulations that are not inconsistent with GATT provisions, including those that deal with patents, trademarks and copyrights and the prevention of deceptive practices. Additionally, Article IX:6 contains a positive obligation on Contracting Parties to cooperate with each other to prevent the use of trade names in a manner that would misrepresent the true origin of a product, or that would be to the detriment of distinctive regional or geographical names of products protected in other parties' territories by national legislation.

In the Tokyo Round of multilateral trade negotiations (1973 to 1979), the one immediately preceding the Uruguay Round, there was a proposal to negotiate rules on trade in counterfeit goods resulting in a draft Agreement on Measures to Discourage the Importation of Counterfeit Goods. However, negotiators did not reach agreement and this subject was not included in the results of the Tokyo Round when it concluded in 1979. Instead, in 1982, pursuant to a work programme agreed by trade ministers,[1] a revised version of a draft agreement on trade in counterfeit goods

---

[1] 'The CONTRACTING PARTIES instruct the Council to examine the question of counterfeit goods with a view to determining the appropriateness of joint action in the GATT framework on the trade aspects of commercial counterfeiting and, if such joint action is found to be appropriate, the modalities for such action, having full regard to the competence of other international organizations. For the purposes of such examination, the

was submitted. This draft was referred to a group of experts in 1984, which submitted its report a year later. The group met six times in 1985. It produced a report on Trade in Counterfeit Goods that recommended that joint action was probably needed, but could not decide on the appropriate forum. It left it to the GATT Council to make a decision.

During the early 1980s, negotiators worked on a mandate for negotiations for a new Round, including on aspects of IP. Trade ministers met at Punta del Este, Uruguay, in September 1986, and adopted a decision on future trade negotiations, which included the following mandate under the title 'Trade-related aspects of intellectual property rights, including trade in counterfeit goods':

> In order to reduce the distortions and impediments to international trade, and taking into account the need to promote effective and adequate protection of intellectual property rights, and to ensure that measures and procedures to enforce intellectual property rights do not themselves become barriers to legitimate trade, the negotiations shall aim to clarify GATT provisions and elaborate as appropriate new rules and disciplines.

> Negotiations shall aim to develop a multilateral framework of principles, rules and disciplines dealing with international trade in counterfeit goods, taking into account work already undertaken in the GATT.

> These negotiations shall be without prejudice to other complementary initiatives that may be taken in the World Intellectual Property Organization and elsewhere to deal with these matters.

A negotiating group on 'trade-related aspects of intellectual property rights', or TRIPS, was formed to pursue this mandate. From 1986 to April 1989, the group mainly discussed whether there was a mandate to negotiate rules on IPRs in general, or only on their trade-related aspects. For the developing countries, such 'trade-related aspects' only included trade in counterfeit goods or anti-competitive practices in relation to IPRs. However, in the mid-term review of the overall Uruguay Round negotiations, undertaken in April 1989, a decision was adopted that gave the negotiating group on TRIPS a full mandate.[2] This decision is the basis for the current structure of the TRIPS Agreement.

CONTRACTING PARTIES request the Director-General to hold consultations with the Director-General of WIPO in order to clarify the legal and institutional aspects involved.'

[2] The following is an extract from the mandate: '3. Ministers agree that the outcome of the negotiations is not prejudged and that these negotiations are without prejudice to the views of participants concerning the institutional aspects of the international implementation of the results of the negotiations in this area, which is to be decided pursuant to the final paragraph of the Punta del Este Declaration.

Between the spring of 1989 and the spring of 1990, several detailed proposals were submitted by all the major players: EC, United States, Switzerland, Japan and a group of fourteen developing countries (Argentina, Brazil, Chile, China, Colombia, Cuba, Egypt, India, Nigeria, Pakistan, Peru, Tanzania, Uruguay and Zimbabwe). A composite text, based on these submissions, was prepared by the Chairman of the Negotiating Group in June 1990. From then until the end of the Brussels ministerial meeting in December 1990, detailed negotiations were conducted on every aspect of this text. There were six Chairman's drafts of the agreement between July and November 1990. A revised TRIPS text was then sent to the Brussels Ministerial Conference (MTN.TNC/W/35/Rev.1). There was commonly agreed language for large parts of the agreement, but differences continued on the forum for lodging the agreement and on dispute settlement, as well as on some twenty-five other outstanding issues, mainly relating to some provisions on patents and undisclosed information, copyright, GIs and transition periods. Work continued at Brussels until a sudden breakdown of negotiations in the overall Round due to the failure to reach an understanding on agriculture.

Progress was made on the patent provisions, particularly in autumn 1991 – including on the scope and timing of rights, exceptions from patentability, compulsory licensing/government use, exhaustion of rights, term of protection, protection of test data, transition periods,

---

4. Ministers agree that negotiations on this subject shall continue in the Uruguay Round and shall encompass the following issues:

(a) the applicability of the basic principles of the GATT and of relevant international intellectual property agreements or conventions;
(b) the provision of adequate standards and principles concerning the availability, scope and use of trade-related intellectual property rights;
(c) the provision of effective and appropriate means for the enforcement of trade-related intellectual property rights, taking into account differences in national legal systems;
(d) the provision of effective and expeditious procedures for the multilateral prevention and settlement of disputes between governments, including the applicability of GATT procedures;
(e) transitional arrangements aiming at the fullest participation in the results of the negotiations.

5. Ministers agree that in the negotiations consideration will be given to concerns raised by participants related to the underlying public policy objectives of their national systems for the protection of intellectual property, including developmental and technological objectives.

6. In respect of 4(d) above, Ministers emphasise the importance of reducing tensions in this area by reaching strengthened commitments to resolve disputes on trade-related intellectual property issues through multilateral procedures.'

and the protection of existing subject matter. The question of forum was resolved with the decision to encapsulate the results of the negotiations within a Single Undertaking, which would also establish a new organization, the Multilateral Trade Organization (MTO)/WTO. A Draft Final Act (MTN.TNC/W/FA) was released by the then Director-General of GATT, Arthur Dunkel, on 20 December 1991, and came to be known as the Dunkel Text. Only two changes were made to TRIPS provisions between the 1991 Draft Final Act and the 1993 Final Act: first, introducing the text on the moratorium on so-called 'non-violation complaints' in dispute settlement cases (Article 64.2–3); and, second, to limit the scope of compulsory licensing of semi-conductor technology (Article 31(c)).

3   Place of TRIPS in the World Trade Organization

The TRIPS Agreement is Annex 1C of the Marrakesh Agreement Establishing the World Trade Organization ('WTO Agreement') of 15 April 1994, which entered into force on 1 January 1995. The TRIPS Agreement is an integral part of the WTO Agreement, and is binding on each Member of the WTO from the date the WTO Agreement becomes effective for that country. However, the TRIPS Agreement gave original WTO Members transition periods, which differed according to their stages of development, to bring themselves into compliance with its rules (see section D1 of this chapter for transition periods). The Agreement is administered by the Council for TRIPS, which reports to the WTO General Council. The place of the TRIPS Council in the WTO can be seen from Figure I.1.

The Ministerial Conference is the highest decision-making body in the WTO. Its sessions are to take place at least once every two years, during which sessions all matters under the WTO Agreements may be addressed. The General Council constitutes the second tier in the WTO structure. It comprises representatives from all Member countries, usually Ambassadors/Permanent Representatives based in Geneva. It meets some five times in a year. It may adopt decisions on behalf of the Ministerial Conference when the Conference is not in session. The General Council has authority over the Trade Negotiations Committee, which is currently charged with the negotiations mandated by the Doha Development Agenda. The General Council also meets as the Trade Policy Review Body, with its own Chairperson, to carry out trade policy reviews as mandated by the Trade Policy Review Mechanism (Annex 3 of the WTO Agreement), and the Dispute Settlement Body (DSB), with its own

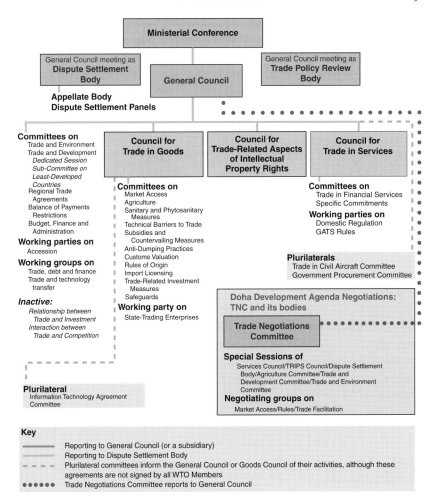

Figure I.1   WTO organizational structure

Chairperson to administer the rules in the Understanding on Rules and Procedures Governing the Settlement of Disputes.

The Council for TRIPS is one of the three sectoral (i.e. subject area) Councils operating under the General Council, the other two being the Council for Trade in Goods and the Council for Trade in Services. It is the body, open to all Members of the WTO, responsible for the administration of the TRIPS Agreement and in particular for monitoring the operation of the Agreement. The Council meets in Geneva formally three to four times a year as well as informally as necessary.

The WTO Agreement serves as an umbrella agreement for the TRIPS Agreement and the other trade agreements annexed to it. It includes provisions on the structure and operation of the WTO. Section E of this chapter explores some of these institutional aspects, namely the cross-cutting decision-making and amendment procedures in the WTO Agreement, and discusses the work of the Council for TRIPS.

4   Overview of TRIPS provisions

The TRIPS Agreement is a comprehensive multilateral agreement on IP. It deals with each of the main categories of IPRs, establishes standards of protection as well as rules on administration and enforcement of IPRs, and provides for the application of the WTO dispute settlement mechanism to resolve disputes between Members concerning compliance with its standards. The following is a brief introduction to the various parts of the Agreement.

(a)   General provisions and basic principles

Part I of the TRIPS Agreement sets out general provisions and basic principles of the Agreement, such as national treatment and most-favoured-nation (MFN) treatment, and exhaustion of IPRs. These general provisions and basic principles are discussed in section B of this chapter.

(b)   Standards concerning the availability, scope and use of intellectual property rights

Part II of the Agreement sets out the minimum standards of IP protection to be provided by each Member in the following fields:

(1) copyright and related rights (i.e. the rights of performers, producers of sound recordings and broadcasting organizations);
(2) trademarks, including service marks;
(3) GIs;
(4) industrial designs;
(5) patents, including the protection of new varieties of plants;
(6) the layout-designs of integrated circuits; and
(7) undisclosed information, including trade secrets and test data.

Part II also contains provisions on the control of anti-competitive practices in contractual licences. These areas of IP and control of anti-competitive practices will be discussed in Chapters II to VI of this *Handbook*.

In respect of each of these fields of IP, the main elements of protection are defined:

- the subject matter eligible for protection;
- the scope of rights to be conferred;
- permissible exceptions to those rights; and,
- where applicable, the minimum duration of protection.

The TRIPS Agreement sets these standards firstly by requiring compliance with the substantive obligations of the main conventions of the World Intellectual Property Organization (WIPO), the Paris Convention and the Berne Convention in their most recent versions. With the exception of the provisions of the Berne Convention on moral rights, all the main substantive provisions of these two conventions are incorporated by reference and thus become obligations between WTO Members under the TRIPS Agreement, separately from the obligations they mostly have to one another directly under those conventions. The relevant provisions are to be found in Articles 2.1 and 9.1, which relate, respectively, to the Paris Convention and to the Berne Convention.

The TRIPS Agreement then adds a substantial number of additional obligations on matters where the pre-existing conventions were silent or were seen as being inadequate. The TRIPS Agreement is thus sometimes referred to as a 'Berne-plus' and 'Paris-plus' agreement. As explained later in Chapter II, the TRIPS provisions on related rights contain certain references to the Rome Convention. The Section on the protection of layout-designs of integrated circuits, explained in Chapter VI, incorporates most of the substantive provisions of the Treaty on Intellectual Property in Respect of Integrated Circuits (IPIC Treaty). Article 2.2 of the TRIPS Agreement contains a safeguard clause, according to which the provisions of the Agreement cannot be understood to derogate from the existing obligations that Members may have to each other under the Paris Convention, the Berne Convention, the Rome Convention or the IPIC Treaty.[3]

---

[3] Unless otherwise indicated, in this *Handbook*, 'Paris Convention' refers to the Paris Convention for the Protection of Industrial Property (the Stockholm Act of 14 July 1967); 'Berne Convention' refers to the Berne Convention for the Protection of Literary and Artistic Works (the Paris Act of 24 July 1971); 'Rome Convention' refers to the International Convention for the Protection of Performers, Producers of Phonograms and Broadcasting Organizations, adopted at Rome on 26 October 1961; and the 'IPIC Treaty' to the Treaty on Intellectual Property in Respect of Integrated Circuits, adopted at Washington on 26 May 1989.

(c)   Enforcement

Part III of the TRIPS Agreement deals with domestic procedures and remedies for the enforcement of IPRs. The Agreement lays down certain general principles applicable to IP enforcement procedures. In addition, it contains provisions on civil and administrative procedures and remedies, provisional measures, special requirements related to border measures and criminal procedures. These provisions specify, in a certain amount of detail, the procedures and remedies that must be available so that right holders can effectively enforce their rights and also provide for safeguards against the abuse of such procedures and remedies as barriers to legitimate trade. These provisions are discussed in Chapter VII.

(d)   Certain other matters

Part IV of the Agreement contains general rules on procedures related to the acquisition and maintenance of IPRs, particularly concerning how applications for IP protection are administered and the kind of appeals or reviews that should be available. These rules are explained below in section C of this chapter.

Part V of the Agreement deals with dispute prevention and settlement. The Agreement makes disputes between Members about the respect of obligations contained in it, whether in the field of substantive standards or in the field of enforcement, subject to the WTO's dispute settlement procedures. Dispute prevention and settlement are discussed in Chapter VIII.

Part VI of the Agreement contains provisions on transition periods, transfer of technology and technical cooperation. Part VII deals with institutional arrangements and certain cross-cutting matters such as the protection of existing subject matter. These two Parts are covered below in section D of this chapter.

B   General provisions and basic principles of the TRIPS Agreement

1   Objectives and principles

The general goals of the TRIPS Agreement are set out in its Preamble, and include reducing distortions and impediments to international trade, promoting effective and adequate protection of IPRs, and ensuring that measures and procedures to enforce IPRs do not themselves become barriers to legitimate trade. The Preamble is largely drawn from the Uruguay Round mandates given to the negotiators of the TRIPS Agreement in the 1986 Punta del Este Declaration (reproduced on p. 6) and in the April 1988 mid-term review decision (relevant extract in footnote 2).

The general goals contained in the Preamble of the Agreement should be read in conjunction with Article 7, entitled 'Objectives'. Article 7 reflects the search for a balanced approach to IP protection in the societal interest, taking into account the interests of both producers and users. IP protection is expected to contribute not only to the promotion of technological innovation, but also to the transfer and dissemination of technology in a way that benefits both its producers and users and that respects a balance of rights and obligations, with the overall goal of promoting social and economic welfare.

Article 8, entitled 'Principles', recognizes the rights of Members to adopt measures for public health and other public interest reasons and to prevent the abuse of IPRs, provided that such measures are consistent with the provisions of the TRIPS Agreement.

The Preamble and Articles 7 and 8 express the general goals, objectives and principles of the Agreement. As recognized by WTO dispute settlement panels, they are to be borne in mind when the substantive rules of the Agreement are being examined. The 2001 Doha Declaration on the TRIPS Agreement and Public Health provides (in paragraph 5(a)) that '[i]n applying the customary rules of interpretation of public international law, each provision of the TRIPS Agreement shall be read in the light of the object and purpose of the Agreement as expressed, in particular, in its objectives and principles'.

2 Minimum standards agreement

As discussed above, the TRIPS Agreement sets out minimum standards of protection to be provided by each Member. Article 1.1 makes it clear that Members may, but are not obliged to, implement in their law more extensive protection than required by the Agreement, provided that such protection does not contravene its provisions. For example, Members may provide for longer terms of protection than that mandated by the TRIPS Agreement but they are not required to do so; however, they cannot do this in a way that conflicts with TRIPS provisions. For instance, in light of the principle of non-discrimination, longer protection could not be made available only to nationals of one country.

Article 1.1 further clarifies that Members are free to determine the appropriate method of implementing the provisions of the TRIPS Agreement within their own legal system and practice.

Given the long history of international cooperation on IP matters, the national laws in this area are often fairly similar. However, to establish how the law applies in any concrete practical situation, the applicable national law will have to be consulted.

3   Beneficiaries

As in the main pre-existing IP conventions, the basic obligation on each Member is to accord the treatment in regard to the protection of IP provided for under the Agreement to right holders and users of other Members. Article 1.3 defines who these persons are. They are referred to as 'nationals' but include persons, natural or legal, who have a close attachment to a Member without necessarily having the nationality of that Member. The criteria for determining which persons must thus benefit from the treatment provided for under the Agreement are those laid down for this purpose in the pre-existing IP conventions of WIPO referred to in the Agreement, applied of course with respect to all WTO Members whether or not they are party to those conventions. The following clarifies who the beneficiaries are for industrial property rights and for copyright and related rights, as the rules differ slightly between these categories.

(a)   Industrial property

Pursuant to Articles 2 and 3 of the Paris Convention, protection is granted in the case of industrial property to natural or legal persons who:

- are nationals of a Member;
- are domiciled in a Member; or
- have real and effective industrial or commercial establishments in a Member.

Pursuant to Article 5 of the IPIC Treaty, similar criteria for determining eligible beneficiaries are applied in relation to layout-designs of integrated circuits.

(b) Copyright

Pursuant to Articles 3 and 4 of the Berne Convention, protection is granted to authors of literary or artistic works who:

- are nationals of a Member;
- have their habitual residence in a Member;
- have their works first (or simultaneously) published in a Member;
- are authors of cinematographic works the maker of which has his headquarters or habitual residence in a Member; or
- are authors of works of architecture erected in a Member or of other artistic works incorporated in a building or other structure located in a Member.

(c) Performers

Pursuant to Article 4 of the Rome Convention, protection is granted to performers whose:

- performance takes place in another Member;
- performance is incorporated in a phonogram as defined below; or
- performance is covered by a broadcast as defined below.

(d) Producers of phonograms

Pursuant to Article 5 of the Rome Convention, protection is granted to producers of phonograms:

- if the producer is a national of another Member;
- if the first fixation of sound (i.e. recording) was made in another Member; or
- if the phonogram was first published in another Member.

In accordance with the provisions of Article 5(3) of the Rome Convention as incorporated into the TRIPS Agreement, a Member may declare that it does not apply either the criterion of fixation or that of publication. The criterion of nationality, however, may not be excluded.

(e) Broadcasting organizations

Pursuant to Article 6 of the Rome Convention, protection is granted to broadcasting organizations:

- whose headquarters are situated in another Member; or
- when the broadcast was transmitted from a transmitter in another Member.

In accordance with the provisions of Article 6(2) of the Rome Convention as incorporated into the TRIPS Agreement, a Member may declare that it will protect broadcasts only if both relevant conditions are met, i.e. that the headquarters of the broadcasting organization are situated in another Member and the broadcast was transmitted from a transmitter situated in the same Member.

4   National treatment and most-favoured-nation treatment

A key principle in the WTO is that of non-discrimination. It applies to trade in goods, trade in services and IPRs. It has two components: national treatment, and most-favoured-nation (MFN) treatment. As regards IPRs, the fundamental rules on national and MFN treatment of foreign nationals can be found in Articles 3 to 5 of the TRIPS Agreement. These rules are common to all categories of IP covered by the Agreement. These obligations cover not only the substantive standards of protection but also matters affecting the availability, acquisition, scope, maintenance and enforcement of IPRs as well as those matters affecting the use of IPRs specifically addressed in the Agreement. While the national treatment clause forbids discrimination between a Member's own nationals and the nationals of other Members, the MFN treatment clause forbids discrimination between the nationals of other Members.

Article 3 of the TRIPS Agreement on national treatment requires each Member to accord to the nationals of other Members treatment no less favourable than that it accords to its own nationals with regard to the protection of IP. With respect to the national treatment obligation, the exceptions allowed under the four pre-existing WIPO treaties (Paris, Berne, Rome and IPIC) are also allowed under TRIPS.

An important exception to national treatment is the so-called 'comparison of terms' for copyright protection allowed under Article 7(8) of the Berne Convention as incorporated into the TRIPS Agreement. If a Member provides a term of protection in excess of the minimum term required by the TRIPS Agreement, it does not need to protect a work for a duration that exceeds the term fixed in the country of origin of that work. In other words, the additional term can be made available to foreigners on the basis of 'material reciprocity'. For example, if Member A provides its own nationals with a copyright term of seventy years, instead of fifty years as required by Article 12 of the TRIPS Agreement, while Member B provides for fifty years, Member A need not protect works from Member B for more than fifty years.

With respect to performers, producers of phonograms (sound recordings such as CDs) and broadcasting organizations, the national treatment obligation applies only with respect to rights provided under the TRIPS Agreement. Therefore, the obligation is confined to the protection provided in the Agreement, and does not cover other rights that holders of related rights may have under domestic laws or other international agreements.

Exceptions can be allowed to the national treatment principle for judicial and administrative procedures – for instance, foreign applicants for IP protection may be required to provide an address for service or a local agent in that jurisdiction. But Article 3.2 of the Agreement requires that such exceptions be necessary to secure compliance with laws and regulations which are consistent with the TRIPS Agreement and that such practices not be applied so as to constitute a disguised restriction on trade.

While the pre-existing multilateral IP conventions also provide for national treatment, they do not contain obligations on MFN treatment. In these conventions, national treatment is an across-the-board obligation with relatively minor exceptions. Given that the same treatment has to be given to nationals of other convention members as to a member's own nationals, it would normally follow that the same treatment would be given to the nationals of each of the other members. This leaves little scope for discrimination between the nationals of other members of those conventions. However, during the TRIPS negotiations, suggestions for the incorporation of an MFN provision into the Agreement were made since some countries had agreed to give, as a result of bilateral negotiations, more favourable protection to IPRs of the nationals of one or more of their trading partners than they gave to their own nationals. As a result, MFN treatment was incorporated into the Agreement.

Article 4 on MFN treatment requires that, with regard to the protection of IP, any advantage, favour, privilege or immunity granted by a Member to the nationals of any other Member shall be accorded immediately and unconditionally to the nationals of all other Members. For example, if Member A decides to recognize and enforce the patents granted in Member B from a certain date in the past irrespective of whether the inventions covered meet the novelty criterion or not, Member A must extend the same advantage to nationals of other Members.

Where exceptions to national treatment allow material reciprocity, a consequential exception to MFN treatment is permitted under Article 4(b) and 4(c). Limited exceptions to MFN are also allowed under Article 4(a) concerning international agreements on judicial assistance or law enforcement of a general nature.

Furthermore, Article 4(d) exempts from this obligation advantages deriving from international agreements related to the protection of IP that entered into force prior to the entry into force of the WTO Agreement, i.e. before 1 January 1995. This is subject to the conditions that such agreements are notified to the Council for TRIPS and do not constitute an arbitrary or unjustifiable discrimination against nationals of other Members. On the other hand, there is no such exemption for advantages deriving from international agreements that entail higher standards than required by the TRIPS Agreement that enter into force after 1 January 1995 – this means that any such higher standards must be available to nationals of all WTO Members.

In addition, Article 5 of the TRIPS Agreement provides that national and MFN treatment obligations do not apply to procedures provided in multilateral agreements concluded under the auspices of WIPO relating to the acquisition or maintenance of IPRs. This Article recognizes that certain WIPO agreements, such as the Patent Cooperation Treaty, the Madrid Agreement Concerning the International Registration of Marks and the Protocol to that Agreement, and the Hague Agreement Concerning the International Registration of Industrial Designs, provide for a system of international applications only open to persons that are nationals or residents of signatory countries or have a real and effective industrial or commercial establishment in those countries. The exception in this Article only applies in respect of procedures relating to the acquisition and maintenance of rights, not to the substantive standards of protection themselves. The exception contained in Article 5 is not limited to pre-existing WIPO agreements.

5   Exhaustion

The term 'exhaustion' refers to the generally accepted principle in IP law that a right owner's exclusive right to control the distribution of a protected item lapses after the first act of distribution. In many countries, once the item has been put on the market by or with the consent of the right owner, the exclusive distribution right is 'exhausted' (which is why the principle is referred to in some jurisdictions as the 'first-sale doctrine') and further circulation of that item can no longer be controlled by the right holder. In simple terms, exhaustion describes the fact that once one has legitimately obtained an item incorporating protected IP, for instance a copyright-protected DVD or a patented mobile phone, one is then free to further sell, transfer or otherwise distribute it without further authorization from the right holder. This entitlement does not, of course, affect any other exclusive rights the right holder may enjoy, for example, the right to authorize activities such as reproduction or communication to the public – so the entitlement to distribute a legitimately purchased CD does not in itself extend to an entitlement to make reproductions or public performances of the recorded music.

While it is generally accepted that IPRs are exhausted within the jurisdiction where the first sale took place, are such rights exhausted when the first sale takes place outside the jurisdiction in question? The answer to this depends on whether a country applies a regime of national or international exhaustion and thereby prevents or allows so-called 'parallel importation'.

National exhaustion means that right owners' distribution rights are only considered exhausted once they put the protected item on the market in that country. Distribution rights would not be considered exhausted with regard to protected items that were only put on the market in another country, so that right holders can still control the sale or import of such items into the first country. For example, in a country with a national exhaustion regime, for copyright and related rights right holders can prevent the importation into that country of DVDs that they have sold in other countries. Thus, parallel imports of products first sold on other markets are illegal in a country with a national exhaustion regime.

In contrast, if a country has an international exhaustion regime, this means that the right owner's distribution right in that country is exhausted regardless of where the first act of distribution took place. Thus, right holders cannot use IPRs to prevent the importation and sale of DVDs that they have sold in another country. Therefore, in countries with an international exhaustion regime for copyright and related rights, parallel imports are legal. A country may, in principle, adopt different exhaustion regimes for different categories of IPRs.

Note that the products imported as parallel imports are not counterfeit or pirated goods, but genuine original products that have been sold in other countries with the authorization of the right holder; they do not infringe IPRs in the country of origin.

An alternative approach is taken in some free trade areas (FTAs) or customs unions, namely regional exhaustion: in this case, the right holder's IPRs are exhausted once the first sale takes place anywhere within the specified region.

It is generally understood that national exhaustion favours market segmentation as well as differential pricing, product differentiation and differing release dates, whereas international exhaustion facilitates parallel importation of the same product sold at lower prices in other countries.

During the Uruguay Round negotiations, Members negotiated a text that left them considerable discretion as to how to regulate the question of exhaustion. Article 6 provides that, for the purposes of dispute settlement under the TRIPS Agreement, nothing in the Agreement shall be used to address the issue of the exhaustion of intellectual property rights, provided that the national and MFN treatment obligations are complied with. This proviso was clarified in the 2001 Ministerial Declaration on the TRIPS Agreement and Public Health. It confirmed that the effect of the TRIPS provisions relevant to exhaustion of IPRs was to leave each Member free to establish its own regime for exhaustion without challenge, subject to the MFN and national treatment provisions of Articles 3 and 4. This Declaration will be discussed further in Chapter IX.

C   Procedures for the acquisition and maintenance of intellectual property rights

The TRIPS Agreement does not deal in detail with procedural questions concerning the acquisition and maintenance of IPRs. However, Part IV contains general rules on these matters. The essential goal is to ensure that unnecessary procedural difficulties in acquiring or maintaining IPRs are not employed to impair the protection required by the Agreement. Certain more specific rules are to be found in the sections of Part II dealing with individual categories of IPRs and in the provisions of the Paris Convention and the IPIC Treaty, which are incorporated by reference into the TRIPS Agreement.

Part IV consists of a single article, Article 62. It allows Members to require, as a condition of the acquisition or maintenance of rights related to trademarks, GIs, industrial designs, patents and layout-designs, compliance with reasonable procedures and formalities (paragraph 1).

Where the acquisition of an IPR is subject to the right being granted or registered, the procedures must permit the granting or registration of the right within a reasonable period of time so as to avoid unwarranted curtailment of the period of protection (paragraph 2).

Paragraph 4 of Article 62 requires that procedures concerning the acquisition or maintenance of IPRs and, where a Member's law provides for such procedures, administrative revocation and *inter partes* procedures such as opposition, revocation and cancellation, must be governed by the general principles concerning decisions and review set out in paragraphs 2 and 3 of Article 41 of the Agreement. These general principles require that procedures be fair and equitable. They are discussed further in Chapter VII.

Final administrative decisions in such procedures must generally be subject to review by a judicial or quasi-judicial authority (paragraph 5 of Article 62).

D   Transitional arrangements and other matters

1   Transition periods

The TRIPS Agreement gave all Members transition periods so that they can meet their obligations under it. The transition periods, which depend on the level of development of the country concerned, are contained in Articles 65 and 66. Except for LDC Members, these transition periods have already expired.

(a)   Developed countries and non-discrimination
(all Members)

Developed country Members have had to comply with all of the provisions of the TRIPS Agreement since 1 January 1996. Moreover, all Members, including those availing themselves of the longer transition periods, have had to comply with the national and MFN treatment obligations since 1 January 1996 (Article 65.1).

(b)   Developing countries and economies in transition

For developing countries, the general transition period was five years, i.e. until 1 January 2000 (Article 65.2). The same transition period was available for countries in transition from a centrally planned into a market economy, provided they met certain conditions (Article 65.3).

The TRIPS Agreement provided special transition rules in the situation where a developing country did not provide product patent protection in a given area of technology on 1 January 2000. This provision was especially relevant to pharmaceutical and agricultural chemical inventions. According to Article 65.4, a developing country could delay the application of the TRIPS obligations on product patents to such areas of technology until 1 January 2005.

However, in the situation where a country did not provide patent protection for pharmaceutical and agricultural chemical products commensurate with the TRIPS provisions on scope of patentable subject matter as of January 1995, some additional transitional arrangements apply. In accordance with the 'mail-box' provision contained in Article 70.8, the country concerned is required to provide a means by which patent applications for such inventions can be filed. These applications do not need to be examined for their patentability until the country starts applying product patent protection in that area. However, when that time comes, the application has to be examined by reference to the prior art that had been disclosed when the application was first filed (i.e. the invention has to be assessed whether it was 'new' as of that earliest date). If the application is successful, product patent protection would then have to be granted for the remainder of the patent term counted from the filing date of the application.

If a product that is the subject of such a mail-box patent application in a Member obtains marketing approval before the decision on the grant of the patent is taken, there is an obligation under Article 70.9 to grant exclusive marketing rights for a period of up to five years or until the patent is granted or rejected, whichever is shorter. This is subject to a number of conditions: subsequent to the entry into force of the WTO Agreement, a patent application must have been filed, a patent granted and marketing approval obtained in another Member for the product in question.

These provisions were addressed in reports adopted by the Dispute Settlement Body in cases *India – Patents I* and *II* (DS50 and 79).

(c)   Least-developed countries

The TRIPS Agreement contains a number of specific provisions for LDCs, reflecting the recognition in the Preamble of their 'special needs ... in respect of maximum flexibility in the domestic implementation of laws and regulations in order to enable them to create a sound and viable technological base'. For the purposes of determining the LDC status of a country, the WTO uses the UN list of LDCs.

Article 66.1 originally provided LDC Members a transition period until 1 January 2006, with an extension upon a duly motivated request.

Pursuant to the Doha Declaration on the TRIPS Agreement and Public Health, the TRIPS Council decided in 2002 to extend the transition period for LDCs for certain obligations with respect to pharmaceutical products until 1 January 2016. This Decision can be found in document IP/C/25. Supplementing this Decision, the General Council adopted a waiver for the same period in respect of the obligations of LDC Members under Article 70.9 concerning so-called exclusive marketing rights. Thus, LDC Members availing themselves of the extended transition period are required to provide a 'mail-box' if they do not already provide patent protection for pharmaceutical products, but the obligations in respect of exclusive marketing rights for such products have been waived until 1 January 2016. This decision can be found in document WT/L/478.

In 2005, upon a request of LDCs, the TRIPS Council extended the transition period for LDCs for the application of all other provisions of the TRIPS Agreement, except for Articles 3 to 5 on non-discrimination, until 1 July 2013. It also set up a process to help them implement TRIPS within their national IP regimes. The Council called on LDCs to identify their priority needs for technical and financial cooperation, which developed countries are to help to effectively address. It also called for the WTO to enhance its cooperation with WIPO and other relevant international organizations. Furthermore, the decision provides that LDC Members will ensure that any changes in their laws, regulations and practice made during the additional transition period do not result in a lesser degree of consistency with the provisions of the TRIPS Agreement. It is without prejudice to the earlier extension with respect to pharmaceutical products and to the right of LDC Members to seek further extensions. This Decision is contained in document IP/C/40. Technical cooperation for LDCs is further discussed in Chapter X.

(d)   Acceding countries

Any transition periods for acceding countries are set out in their protocols of accession. Apart from LDCs that join the WTO, newly acceded countries have generally agreed to apply all relevant provisions of the TRIPS Agreement as of the date of entry into force of their membership in the WTO.

2   Protection of existing subject matter

(a)   Application of the rules

An important aspect of the transition arrangements under the TRIPS Agreement are the provisions relating to the treatment of subject matter existing at the time that a Member starts applying the provisions of the Agreement (e.g. already existing works, inventions or distinctive signs). These rules are contained in Article 70.

As provided in Article 70.2, the rules of the TRIPS Agreement generally apply to subject matter existing on the date of the application of the Agreement for the Member in question (i.e. at the end of the relevant transition period) and which is protected in that Member on that date, or which is still capable of meeting the criteria for protection (e.g. undisclosed information or distinctive signs not yet protected as trademarks).

The interpretation of Article 70.2 was addressed in reports adopted by the Dispute Settlement Body on *Canada – Patent Term* (DS170).

(b)   Additional requirements in respect of pre-existing works and phonograms

In respect of copyright and the rights of producers of phonograms (sound recordings) and performers in existing phonograms, there is an additional requirement to comply with Article 18 of the Berne Convention, not only in respect of the rights of authors but also in respect of the rights of performers and producers of phonograms in phonograms (Articles 9.1, 14.6 and 70.2 of the TRIPS Agreement). Article 18 of the Berne Convention includes the so-called 'rule of retroactivity', according to which the Agreement applies to all works which have not fallen into the public domain either in the country of origin or the country where protection is claimed through the expiry of a term of protection. The provisions of Article 18 allow some transitional flexibility where a country is, as a result, taking subject matter out of the public domain and putting it under protection, to safeguard the interests of persons who have in good faith already taken steps on the basis of the material in the public domain (for example, a film producer that has already invested in the making of a film using a work that is brought under copyright). The application of Article 18 of the Berne Convention to the rights of producers of phonograms and performers in existing phonograms was addressed in two dispute settlement complaints in *Japan – Measures Concerning Sound Recordings* (DS28 and 42). Both cases were settled bilaterally without panel reports.

3   Transfer of technology

Article 7 of the TRIPS Agreement recognizes that the protection and enforcement of IPRs should contribute to the transfer and dissemination of technology (see section A4(a) above).

Article 66.2 of the TRIPS Agreement requires developed country Members to provide incentives to enterprises and institutions in their territories for the purpose of promoting and encouraging technology transfer to LDC Members in order to enable them to create a sound and viable technological base.

In 2003, pursuant to instructions given by ministers at the Doha ministerial meeting, the Council adopted a decision on 'Implementation of Article 66.2 of the TRIPS Agreement' that put in place a mechanism for ensuring the monitoring and full implementation of the obligations in question. Under this Decision, developed country Members shall submit annually reports on actions taken or planned in pursuance of their commitments under Article 66.2. To this end, they are to provide new detailed reports every third year and, in the intervening years, provide updates to their most recent reports. These submissions are reviewed by the Council at its end-of-year meeting each year. The review meetings are intended to provide Members an opportunity to, *inter alia*, discuss the effectiveness of the incentives provided in promoting and encouraging technology transfer to LDC Members in order to enable them to create a sound and viable technological base.

The precise nature of such incentives has not been further elaborated upon in the TRIPS Agreement. The annual reports submitted by developed countries to the TRIPS Council contain examples of available incentives. The subject of technology transfer is discussed further in Chapter X.

The Council Decision on technology transfer referred to above can be found in document IP/C/28. Annual reports submitted pursuant to it are available on the WTO Documents Online database. Further information on how to access these reports can be found in Appendix 1 to this *Handbook*.

Transfer of technology to LDC Members is also addressed in the 2003 Decision on Implementation of Paragraph 6 of the Doha Declaration on the TRIPS Agreement and Public Health and the 2005 Protocol Amending the TRIPS Agreement. This is discussed further in Chapter IX.

4   Technical cooperation

Article 67 of the TRIPS Agreement requires developed country Members to provide, on request and on mutually agreed terms and conditions, technical and financial cooperation in favour of developing and least-developed country Members. According to this provision, the objective of such cooperation is to facilitate the implementation of the Agreement. The Article specifies that such assistance shall include assistance in the preparation of laws and regulations on the protection and enforcement of IPRs as well as on the prevention of their abuse, and support regarding the establishment or reinforcement of domestic offices and agencies relevant to these matters, including the training of personnel.

In order to ensure that information on available assistance is readily accessible and to facilitate the monitoring of compliance with the obligation of Article 67, developed country Members present descriptions of their relevant technical and financial cooperation programmes and update them annually. For the sake of transparency, intergovernmental organizations, such as WIPO and the World Health Organization (WHO), have also presented, upon the invitation of the Council, information on their activities. The information from developed country Members, intergovernmental organizations and the WTO Secretariat on their technical cooperation activities in the area of TRIPS is available on the WTO Documents Online database.

The TRIPS Council has agreed that each developed country Member should notify a contact point for technical cooperation on TRIPS, in particular for the exchange of information between donors and recipients of technical assistance. These notifications are made available on the WTO Documents Online database. Further information on how to access the reports and other information referred to above can be found in Appendix 1 to this *Handbook*.

5   Security exceptions

In line with other WTO Agreements, Article 73 stipulates that the TRIPS Agreement cannot be construed to require a Member to furnish information or to take action against essential security interests, nor to prevent action in pursuance of obligations under the United Nations Charter for the maintenance of international peace and security.'

E   Institutional arrangements

The WTO Agreement serves as an umbrella agreement for the TRIPS Agreement and the other trade agreements annexed to it. It includes provisions on the establishment, scope, functions and structure of the WTO. It defines the WTO relationship with other organizations, its secretariat, budget and contributions, legal status, and decision-making and amendment procedures. Additionally, it presents information on the definition of original Members, accession, non-application, acceptance, entry into force and deposit, denunciation and final provisions. The subsection below focuses on the decision-making procedures as regulated in the WTO Agreement. The following sub-section discusses the work of the Council for TRIPS.

1 Decision-making procedures

The cross-cutting rules on decision-making and amendment procedures are contained in the WTO Agreement. It provides that the Ministerial Conference has the authority to take decisions on all matters under any of the multilateral trade agreements, including the TRIPS Agreement, if so requested by a Member, in accordance with the specific requirements for decision-making in the WTO Agreement and in the relevant multilateral trade agreement (Article IV:1). In the intervals between meetings of the Ministerial Conference, its functions are conducted by the General Council (Article IV:2). Given this, a reference to the Ministerial Conference/General Council is used below where appropriate.

According to the general rules on decision-making, the WTO continues the practice of decision-making by consensus (Article IX:1). Where a decision cannot be arrived at by consensus, the Article provides for the possibility of deciding a matter by voting. In these circumstances, decisions concerning authoritative interpretations and waivers can be taken by specific qualified majorities that differ as indicated below. Similarly, decisions to submit a proposed amendment to the Members for acceptance is to be taken by consensus, failing which there is the possibility of deciding it by qualified majority (Article X). In the absence of specific rules, decisions of the Ministerial Conference and the General Council can be taken by a majority of the votes cast but, as of the date of writing, all decisions in the WTO have been agreed by consensus. The practice has been that where a body has failed to reach consensus on a matter, it has held further consultations with a view to seeking consensus.

The rules on authoritative interpretations are set out in Article IX:2 of the WTO Agreement. It provides that the Ministerial Conference and the General Council have the exclusive authority to adopt interpretations of the WTO Agreement and of the multilateral trade agreement; this authority must be exercised on the basis of a recommendation by the Council overseeing the functioning of the relevant agreement, i.e. in the case of the TRIPS Agreement on the basis of a recommendation by the TRIPS Council. If a decision concerning interpretation cannot be arrived at by consensus, the decision by the Ministerial Conference or the General Council to adopt an interpretation requires a three-fourths majority of WTO Members. This procedure cannot be used in a manner that would undermine the amendment provisions set out in Article X. In other words, the validity of an authoritative interpretation that goes so far as to effectively amend provisions of WTO Agreements could be challenged on this basis.

To date, no such formal interpretation of the TRIPS Agreement or any other multilateral trade agreement has been adopted.

It should be noted that, for the purposes of resolving a specific dispute, dispute settlement panels and the Appellate Body may need to clarify the provisions of the TRIPS Agreement, but without adding to or diminishing the rights and obligations in the Agreement. The outcome of a dispute does not bind other Members, although the clarifications made in dispute settlement are widely referred to for guidance on understanding the relevant provisions of the TRIPS Agreement. For discussion of the dispute settlement system, see Chapter VIII.

Paragraphs 3 and 4 of Article IX of the WTO Agreement provide the Ministerial Conference/General Council with authority to waive an obligation imposed on a Member by the WTO Agreement or any of the multilateral trade agreements, including the TRIPS Agreement. It may exercise this authority 'in exceptional circumstances'. A request for a waiver must be submitted initially to the Council overseeing the relevant agreement; thus a request for a waiver concerning the TRIPS Agreement must be submitted initially to the TRIPS Council. After the relevant Council has considered a draft waiver, it forwards it to the Ministerial Conference/General Council for consideration pursuant to the practice of decision-making by consensus. If the latter does not reach consensus, any decision to grant a waiver requires a three-fourths majority of the Members. The usual practice is that once the relevant sectoral Council has approved a draft waiver by consensus, the General Council adopts it by consensus without further substantive discussion. Any waiver granted for a period of more than one year is to be reviewed by the Ministerial Conference not later than one year after it is granted, and thereafter annually until the waiver terminates. In each review, the Ministerial Conference/General Council is to examine whether the exceptional circumstances justifying the waiver still exist and whether the terms and conditions attached to the waiver have been met. The Ministerial Conference/General Council, on the basis of the annual review, may extend, modify or terminate the waiver.

By May 2011, 208 decisions on waivers had been taken under Article IX of the WTO Agreement. Most of them concern the Harmonized Commodity Description and Coding System (usually referred to as the 'Harmonized System') and regional trade agreements. Two of them have concerned the TRIPS Agreement. One of them supplements a TRIPS Council decision to extend the LDCs' transition period for certain obligations with respect to pharmaceutical products by waiving the obligations concerning so-called exclusive marketing rights (see section D1(c) of this chapter). The other waiver provides additional flexibility for access to medicines by establishing a system that enables production and export of pharmaceutical products under compulsory licence to meet the needs of countries with inadequate domestic manufacturing capacity (the so-called Paragraph 6 System, see Chapter IX).

The procedure for amending the multilateral trade agreements, including the TRIPS Agreement, is laid down in Article X of the WTO Agreement. The TRIPS Council can initiate the procedure for amendment of the TRIPS Agreement by submitting to the Ministerial Conference a proposal to amend the Agreement. Also any Member may submit to the Ministerial Conference/General Council a proposal to amend the TRIPS Agreement. The Ministerial Conference/General Council then decides whether to submit the proposed amendment to the WTO Members for acceptance. As mentioned above, the WTO continues the practice of decision-making by consensus, although Article X:1 also foresees the possibility of voting if consensus is not reached. Individual Members then separately notify their formal acceptance of an agreed amendment. The amendment enters into force once two-thirds of Members have notified their acceptance. If the amendment alters the rights and obligations of Members, then it only enters into force for those Members that have accepted it; otherwise, it comes into effect for all Members after two-thirds have accepted it.

The process for amending WTO Agreements has to date been used only once – the amendment to the TRIPS Agreement that makes the waiver decision providing the Paragraph 6 System referred to above a permanent part of the Agreement (see Chapter IX). Following a recommendation by the TRIPS Council, the decision on the amendment was taken by the General Council acting with the authority of the Ministerial Conference.

A specific amendment scenario is set out in Article 71.2 of the TRIPS Agreement – it refers to amendments 'merely serving the purpose of adjusting to higher levels of protection of intellectual property rights achieved, and in force, in other multilateral agreements and accepted under those agreements by all Members of the WTO'. The TRIPS Council may refer consensus proposals for such amendments to the Ministerial Conference, which may adopt the amendment without any further acceptance process. This provision has not been used so far.

2   The work of the Council for TRIPS

The main forum for work on the TRIPS Agreement is the Council for TRIPS ('TRIPS Council') itself, which was created by the WTO Agreement to 'oversee the functioning' of the TRIPS Agreement. The basic provision on the role of the TRIPS Council is contained in Article 68 of the TRIPS Agreement. It should be read together with the provisions of the WTO Agreement concerning the structure and operation of the WTO.

In its regular sessions, the TRIPS Council mostly serves as a forum for discussion between governments of WTO Members on key issues – this work is often facilitated by the collection of information about the comparative approaches taken by Members in their national laws and policies through the notification process and through more specific surveys and questionnaires. Some of the main functions and working methods of the TRIPS Council in regular session are described below and in Appendix 1 to this *Handbook*.

Currently, the TRIPS Council also meets in special sessions. The Trade Negotiations Committee was set up by the Doha Ministerial Declaration, which in turn assigned it to create subsidiary negotiating bodies to handle negotiations for different topics, among them the special sessions of the TRIPS Council. These special sessions serve as a forum for negotiations on the establishment of a multilateral system for notification and registration of GIs for wines and spirits, as mandated by the Doha Ministerial Declaration and Article 23.4 of the TRIPS Agreement (see Chapter X).

The regular and special sessions of the TRIPS Council are both open to all WTO Member governments. They are convened under separate chairs, but their meetings are usually held back-to-back.

Beyond the TRIPS Council, other mechanisms can be used to promote dialogue between WTO Members, such as the consultations on TRIPS implementation issues that have been convened directly by the Director-General of the WTO, in line with a mandate given by the Hong Kong Ministerial Declaration (see Chapter X).

In addition, the Trade Policy Review Mechanism undertakes regular reviews of the trade policies of WTO Members, and this process regularly looks at IP policies as one of a wide range of policy fields covered.

(a)   Notifications

The TRIPS Agreement obliges Members to make certain notifications to the Council for TRIPS. These notifications facilitate the Council's work of monitoring the operation of the Agreement and promote the transparency of Members' laws and policies on IP protection. In addition, Members wishing to avail themselves of certain flexibilities provided in the Agreement that relate to the substantive obligations have to notify the Council.

Article 63.2 of the TRIPS Agreement requires Members to notify the laws and regulations by which they give effect to the Agreement's provisions. The Article specifies that the purpose is to assist the TRIPS Council in its review of the operation of the Agreement. The Council has agreed that laws and regulations should be notified without delay as of the time that the corresponding substantive TRIPS obligation has effect. Any subsequent amendments should also be notified without delay. Given the difficulty of examining laws and legal procedures relevant to many of the enforcement obligations in the TRIPS Agreement – especially since much relevant material is often found in general civil and criminal law, not in IP legislation – Members have undertaken, in addition to notifying legislative texts, to provide information on how they are meeting these obligations by responding to a Checklist of Issues on Enforcement (document IP/C/5).

As seen in B3 above, Articles 1.3 and 3.1 allow Members to avail themselves of certain options in regard to the definition of beneficiary persons and national treatment, provided that notifications are made to the TRIPS Council.

As seen in B4 above, Article 4 on MFN treatment provides that, with regard to the protection of intellectual property, any advantage, favour, privilege or immunity granted by a Member to the nationals of any other country shall be accorded immediately and unconditionally to the nationals of all other Members. There are certain exceptions to this obligation. According to subparagraph (d) of that Article, exempted from this obligation is any advantage, favour, privilege or immunity accorded by a Member deriving from international agreements related to the protection of IP which entered into force prior to the entry into force of the WTO Agreement, provided that such agreements are notified to the TRIPS Council and do not constitute an arbitrary or unjustifiable discrimination against nationals of other Members.

As seen in D4 above, Article 69 of the Agreement requires Members to establish and notify contact points in their administrations for the purposes of cooperation with each other aimed at the elimination of trade in infringing goods.

A number of notification provisions of the Berne and Rome Conventions are incorporated by reference into the TRIPS Agreement but without being explicitly referred to in it. A Member wishing to make such notifications has to make them to the Council for TRIPS, even if the Member in question had already made a notification under the Berne or the Rome Convention in regard to the same issue.

All of the notifications referred to above are circulated in the IP/N-series of documents, which are available at the WTO Documents Online database. The easiest way to access this documentation is through the WTO TRIPS transparency toolkit webpage, which provides access to various notifications and other reports from Members, and related formats, guidelines and background materials.[4] Notified laws and regulations are also available on the WIPO Lex search facility for national laws and treaties on intellectual property, which can be accessed through the WIPO GOLD online database.[5]

Appendix 1 to this *Handbook* contains a more detailed guide to TRIPS notifications. Notifications pursuant to Article 6*ter* of the Paris Convention as incorporated into the TRIPS Agreement will be discussed below.

(b)   Review of national laws and regulations

A key mechanism for monitoring implementation of the TRIPS Agreement is the examination of each Member's national legislation by other Members, in particular at the end of its transition period. The notifications made pursuant to Article 63.2 discussed above form the basis for these reviews. The procedures for these reviews provide for written questions and replies prior to the review meeting, with follow-up questions and replies during the course of the meeting. At subsequent meetings of the Council, an opportunity is given to follow up points emerging from the review session that delegations consider to have not been adequately addressed. The records of these reviews are circulated in the IP/Q– series of documents, which are available on the WTO Documents Online database.

(c)   Forum for consultations

The TRIPS Council constitutes a forum for consultations on any problems relating to the TRIPS Agreement arising between countries, as well as for clarifying or interpreting provisions of the Agreement.

---

[4] From the WTO homepage, follow the links 'trade topics' and 'intellectual property'. From this TRIPS gateway page, follow the link 'Notifications – members' transparency toolkit'.
[5] WIPO GOLD can be accessed at www.wipo.int/wipogold/en/.

Members occasionally bring such issues before the Council for the purposes of sharing information, clarification or discussion. To the extent they involve differences between Members, the aim is, whenever possible, to resolve them without the need for formal recourse to dispute settlement.

(d) Forum for further negotiation or review

The WTO constitutes a forum for negotiations among its Members concerning their multilateral trade relations in the area of IP, as in other areas covered by the WTO Agreement. Certain specific areas of further work are called for in the text of the TRIPS Agreement. These areas include:

- the negotiation of a multilateral system of notification and registration of GIs for wines;
- the review of Article 27.3(b) (which concerns the option to exclude from patentability certain plant and animal inventions); and
- the examination of the applicability to TRIPS of non-violation complaints under the dispute settlement process.

Apart from these specific reviews that will be discussed in Chapter X, Article 71.1 includes a provision for a general review of the implementation of the Agreement in the year 2000, and each two years after that date. The Council may also undertake reviews 'in the light of any relevant new developments which might warrant modification or amendment' of the Agreement. In effect, these review provisions have led to a regular item appearing on the agenda of the TRIPS Council since 2000. No proposals on issues to be taken up under this item are being pursued. The Doha Declaration mentions the Article 71.1 review in the context of the TRIPS Council's broader work programme, and refers to work on the issues of the relationship between the TRIPS Agreement and the Convention on Biological Diversity, the protection of traditional knowledge (TK) and folklore, and other relevant new developments raised by Members pursuant to Article 71.1 (paragraph 19 of WT/MIN (01)/DEC/1).

The Doha Ministerial Declaration and the Declaration on the TRIPS Agreement and Public Health, both adopted in 2001, and certain subsequent ministerial declarations have given specific tasks to the Council's regular and special sessions. Past and ongoing work on such matters will be discussed in the subsequent chapters in the context of the substantive area concerned.

(e)   Cooperation with the World Intellectual Property Organization

To facilitate the implementation of the TRIPS Agreement, the WTO concluded with WIPO an agreement on cooperation between the two organizations, which came into force on 1 January 1996. As explicitly set out in the Preamble to the TRIPS Agreement, the WTO aims to establish a mutually supportive relationship with WIPO. The Agreement provides for cooperation in three main areas, namely (1) notification of, access to and translation of national laws and regulations; (2) implementation of procedures for the protection of national emblems; and (3) technical cooperation.

As regards notification of, access to and translation of national laws and regulations, the WTO Secretariat transmits to the WIPO Secretariat copies of the laws and regulations it has received from Members under Article 63.2 of the TRIPS Agreement.[6] The International Bureau of WIPO places such laws and regulations in its collection and makes them available to the public through the WIPO Lex search facility, which can be accessed through the WIPO GOLD online database.[7] In 2010, the two organizations established a WIPO–WTO Common Portal that allows countries to simultaneously electronically submit texts of IP laws and regulations to the two organizations. WIPO also makes available to developing countries assistance for translation of their laws and regulations.

As regards the implementation of procedures for the protection of national emblems under Article 6*ter* of the Paris Convention for the purposes of the TRIPS Agreement, the cooperation agreement provides that the procedures relating to communication of emblems and transmittal of objections under the TRIPS Agreement shall be administered by the WIPO Secretariat in accordance with the procedures it applies under Article 6*ter* of the Paris Convention. Article 6*ter* of the Paris Convention, as incorporated into the TRIPS Agreement, provides for the communication of emblems and of objections thereto among Members. The TRIPS Council has decided to recognize that their

---

[6] Parties to the Paris and Berne Conventions are required to notify their relevant laws to the WIPO Secretariat. The Assemblies of the Paris and Berne Unions have decided that the requirements under these conventions to communicate national laws to the WIPO Secretariat can be fulfilled by communication of such laws through the WTO Secretariat.
[7] WIPO GOLD can be accessed at www.wipo.int/wipogold/en/.

communication through the WIPO Secretariat would be considered as communications for the purposes of the TRIPS Agreement.

As regards technical cooperation, the agreement provides that the WIPO and WTO Secretariats enhance cooperation in their legal–technical assistance and technical cooperation activities relating to the TRIPS Agreement for developing countries, so as to maximize the usefulness of those activities and ensure their mutually supportive nature. The assistance they make available to the members of their own organization will be made available also to the members of the other organization.

An example of this cooperation is the WIPO–WTO Joint Initiative on Technical Cooperation for Least-Developed Countries that was launched in 2001. It is aimed at helping LDC Members of the WTO comply with their obligations under the TRIPS Agreement and make best use of the IP system for their economic, social and cultural development. It is open to other LDCs as well. The TRIPS Council Decision on the extension of LDCs' transition period discussed above calls upon the WTO to seek to enhance its cooperation with WIPO and other relevant international organizations. The two organizations also run a number of annual joint technical cooperation activities, notably the Colloquium for University Teachers of IP and the Advanced Course on IP for government officials.

II

Copyright and related rights

A   Introduction

1   General

Part II of the TRIPS Agreement sets out the substantive standards for the protection of IP that WTO Members should follow. This chapter outlines the provisions of Section 1 of Part II (running from Article 9 to Article 14), which sets out the protection that Members must make available for literary and artistic works, performances, phonograms (or sound recordings) and broadcasts.

This section has to be read, like all other sections in Part II, together with the relevant provisions of certain pre-existing treaties in the area of international IP law that are incorporated by reference into the TRIPS Agreement. In the case of copyright, the relevant treaty is the Berne Convention; and on related rights, there are certain references to the Rome Convention. The relationship between the TRIPS Agreement and these Conventions is explained in section C3 below.

A note of caution: the provisions of the TRIPS Agreement stipulate the minimum level of protection that Members have to provide to nationals of other Members. In other words, they determine the obligations that such countries have towards each other. Given the long history of international cooperation on copyright matters, the national laws in this area are often fairly similar. However, to answer any question the reader may have on how the law applies in any practical situation, the applicable national law will have to be consulted.

2   What are copyright and related rights?

As set out in Chapter 1, the term 'copyright' in its narrow sense usually refers to the rights of authors in their literary and artistic works. In civil law jurisdictions, the term 'authors' rights' is sometimes used.

In the wider sense, copyright also includes 'related rights'. The TRIPS Agreement covers in Article 14 three categories of such related rights. These are the rights of performers, producers of phonograms and broadcasting organizations. These rights are discussed in this chapter in section C below.

In common law jurisdictions, the term 'copyright' is sometimes used in a broad sense, extending also to related rights. In civil law jurisdictions, the term 'neighbouring rights' is sometimes used for these rights.

The main social purpose of protection of copyright is to encourage and reward creative work. The income generated by copyright may allow authors to dedicate themselves to creative work and can help to justify the considerable upfront investment often entailed in the creation of certain types of works, such as films. Authors often exploit their works by licensing them to publishers and producers. Copyright is thus the economic backbone of cultural industries. Another rationale for copyright, as in other IPRs, is equity, a sense that it is fair that an author would draw some benefit from others using the fruits of his or her creative efforts.

Performers are also protected for their creative work. Protection of phonogram producers and broadcasting organizations safeguards the investments required to produce sound recordings or the financial and organizational resources needed to bring a broadcast to the public.

Historically, the original domain of copyright was literature, art and other cultural activities. More recently, it has provided protection to new areas such as computer programs and databases and the economic importance of copyright has greatly increased in knowledge-based economies.

3   What is the relationship of the TRIPS Agreement with the pre-existing provisions of the Berne and Rome Conventions?

During the Uruguay Round negotiations, it was recognized that the Berne Convention standards for copyright protection were adequate for the most part. Thus it was agreed that the point of departure for TRIPS negotiations should be the existing level of protection under that Convention as it was last revised in Paris in 1971, namely under the Paris Act of 1971 of the Convention. In the area of copyright, therefore, the TRIPS Agreement confines itself to clarifying or adding obligations on a number of specific points. The Agreement accordingly has a so-called 'Berne-plus' structure. Hence TRIPS Article 9.1 obliges Members to comply with the substantive provisions of the Berne Convention, namely Articles 1 through 21 and its Appendix. There is one exception: TRIPS does not create rights or obligations in respect of moral rights conferred under Article 6*bis* of that Convention. See further discussion at B2(f) below.

The relevant provisions of the Berne Convention deal with questions such as subject matter to be protected, rights to be conferred and permissible limitations to those rights, minimum term of protection, and protection of pre-existing works. The Appendix to the Berne Convention allows developing countries, under certain conditions, to make some limitations to the right of translation and the right of reproduction.

As the WTO dispute settlement panel in *US – Copyright Act* (DS160) stated, through their incorporation, these substantive rules of the Berne Convention have become part of the TRIPS Agreement and, as provisions of that Agreement, have to be read as applying directly to Members as part of their WTO obligations. The panel also used the negotiating history of these provisions, as reflected in the records of the various diplomatic conferences adopting and revising the Berne Convention, as a relevant source for their interpretation even in the TRIPS context.

The relationship of the TRIPS Agreement with the Rome Convention differs from that with the Berne Convention with respect to related rights. The TRIPS Agreement creates no general obligation to comply with the provisions of the Rome Convention. The level of protection it requires is in some respects higher and in other respects lower than that under the Rome Convention. However, despite these differences, the provisions of TRIPS Article 14 on related rights are clearly inspired by the Rome Convention, and the TRIPS Agreement directly refers to certain provisions of that Convention. For example TRIPS Article 1.3 incorporates the relevant provisions of the Rome Convention dealing with the criteria for eligibility of performers, producers of phonograms and broadcasting organizations for protection of their related rights, as discussed in Chapter I. TRIPS Article 14.6 provides that Members may provide for conditions, limitations, exceptions and reservations in respect of related rights to the extent permitted by the Rome Convention. For these reasons it is important to be aware of the relevant Rome provisions, and how those provisions are understood in the context of that Convention.

Two more recent multilateral treaties on copyright and related rights were adopted after the TRIPS Agreement was concluded, namely the WIPO Copyright Treaty (WCT) and the WIPO Performances and Phonograms Treaty (WPPT). They are not incorporated into the TRIPS

Agreement but build on it, and in some respects, they require a higher level of protection than TRIPS standards on copyright. They are sometimes referred to as the WIPO 'Internet treaties' because they address a number of questions that have arisen in the context of the use of protected materials on the Internet. Since their provisions do not form part of the TRIPS Agreement, they are not discussed here. More information on them and other WIPO-administered treaties is available on the WIPO website at www.wipo.int/treaties/en/.

B   TRIPS provisions on copyright

The obligations of Members with respect to standards concerning the availability, scope and use of copyright are given in Articles 9 to 13 of Section 1 of Part II of the TRIPS Agreement, including in the substantive provisions of the Berne Convention incorporated into the Agreement by the reference in Article 9.1.

1   What is the subject matter to be protected?

(a)   'Literary and artistic works'

Article 2.1 of the Berne Convention as incorporated into the TRIPS Agreement obliges Members to protect 'literary and artistic works'. This expression includes 'every production in the literary, scientific and artistic domain, whatever may be the mode or form of its expression'. Article 2.1 contains a non-exhaustive list of such works. Examples of works covered by copyright include books, newspapers, other writings, musical compositions, films, photographs, paintings and architecture.

Article 10 of the TRIPS Agreement clarifies two areas of subject matter that should be protected.

(i)   **Computer programs**   Article 10.1 provides that computer programs, whether in source or object code, shall be protected as literary works under the Berne Convention. This provision confirms that computer programs must be protected under copyright and that those provisions of the Berne Convention that apply to literary works shall be applied also to them. This means that only those limitations that are applicable to literary works may be applied to computer programs. It also confirms that the general term of protection for literary works applies to computer programs, which means that the shorter terms that may apply to photographic works and works of applied art cannot be used for this subject matter.

Article 10.1 further confirms that the form in which a computer program is, whether in source or object code, does not affect the protection. This means that a program is protected irrespective of whether it is in a form designed for a person to understand and work upon ('source code') or in its machine-readable form, for example as it will be stored on a computer hard-disk and actually executed by the computer ('object code' or 'machine code').

(ii)   Databases   Article 2(5) of the Berne Convention as incorporated into the TRIPS Agreement provides that collections of literary and artistic works such as encyclopaedias and anthologies that, by reason of the selection and arrangement of their contents, constitute intellectual creations are to be protected as such. This does not affect the protection of individual works included in the compilation. For example, a personal selection of poems in an anthology may demonstrate originality and thus deserve protection; however, each poem contained in the collection remains separately protected.

Article 10.2 of the TRIPS Agreement clarifies that databases and other compilations of data or other material shall be protected as such under copyright even where the databases include individual pieces of data that are not protected under copyright. Databases are eligible for copyright protection provided that they, by reason of the selection or arrangement of their contents, constitute intellectual creations. The provision also confirms that databases have to be protected regardless of what form they are in, i.e. whether in machine-readable or other form. Furthermore, the provision clarifies that the protection of databases shall not extend to the data or material itself, and that it shall be without prejudice to any copyright subsisting in the data or material itself.

(b)   Derivative works

Stemming from Article 2(3) of the Berne Convention as incorporated into the TRIPS Agreement, Members' obligations extend to the protection of so-called 'derivative works', such as a translation of a book into a different language, an arrangement of a song for an orchestra, and a film adaptation of a play. Both the original work and the derivative work are protected. For example, a publisher who wishes to publish a translation of a novel into a different language would need to seek authorization from both the author of the novel and the translator.

(c) Certain other categories of works

Pursuant to Article 2(4) of the Berne Convention as incorporated into the TRIPS Agreement, Members are free to determine whether or not to protect official texts of a legislative, administrative and legal nature, and official translations of such texts. It is widespread practice not to have restrictions on reproducing such official texts.[1]

Works of applied art and industrial designs can span the borderline between copyright and industrial property. Pursuant to Article 2(7) of the Berne Convention as incorporated into the TRIPS Agreement, Members are free to determine the extent of the application of their copyright laws to works of applied art and industrial designs, as well as the conditions under which such works and designs are protected. However, such productions should always be protected, either as copyright works or industrial designs, or both. For example, textile designs can be protected by copyright or by industrial designs, or by both means.

(d) Certain principles governing eligibility
for copyright protection

(i) **Idea/expression dichotomy** Article 9.2 of the TRIPS Agreement provides that copyright protection shall extend to expressions and not to ideas, procedures, methods of operation or mathematical concepts as such. In other words, copyright protection does not cover any information or ideas contained in a work; it only protects the original way in which such information or ideas have been expressed. Thus everyone is free to use the information contained in a work, including for the purpose of creating new works. For example, the idea behind a detective novel is not protected as such but an unauthorized reproduction of that novel that is an expression of the idea is prohibited.

This principle, commonly referred to as the 'idea/expression dichotomy', has always been present in copyright doctrine, although it had not been explicitly set out in the provisions of the Berne Convention. Article 9.2 of the TRIPS Agreement is therefore the first explicit confirmation of the principle in multilateral IP law.

(ii) **Originality** Another principle present in copyright doctrine is the requirement for originality: an expression is protected only to the

---

[1] In some common law jurisdictions, governments claim crown copyright or government copyright in legal texts, but may choose to permit widespread reproduction in any case.

extent that it reaches the necessary level of originality (which varies between jurisdictions). Although this principle is not specifically addressed by the provisions of the TRIPS Agreement or the Berne Convention, the legislative history of the Berne Convention indicates that the term 'works' has been understood to refer to original, intellectual creations. In other words, they are original creations of the human mind such as literary works, songs and films.

The meaning of the term 'works' is made clear also in Article 2(5) of the Berne Convention in respect of collections such as encyclopaedias and anthologies, where it is stated that the condition of protection is that such collections should be 'intellectual creations'. Similarly, Article 10.2 of the TRIPS Agreement refers to 'intellectual creations' in respect of compilations of data or other material.

Article 2(8) of the Berne Convention clarifies that the Convention does not apply to news of the day or to miscellaneous facts having the character of mere items of press information. To illustrate this, take as an example a bulletin of a sports club that has a news item on the results of a recent tennis tournament. If the item merely contains the results without any original expression, the bare recounting of the facts may not be considered an original work and could be copied in its entirety. (However, note that the level of the originality requirement is very low in some jurisdictions, and need not display literary or artistic creativity.) If the item can be considered as an original intellectual creation, for example if it analysed the results of the tournament or described significant passages of the games, then copying it would require an authorization from its author. However, anyone would still be free to use the information contained in that item, such as the scores, the sequence of games, and the identities of players, without prior permission.

(iii) **Automatic protection**   A key feature of the Berne Convention and thus also of the TRIPS Agreement is that copyright protection – unlike most other forms of IPRs – may not be subject to any formality of registration, deposit, or the like. This principle is contained in Article 5(2) of the Berne Convention that has been incorporated into the TRIPS Agreement.

This principle is also reflected in Article 62.1 of the TRIPS Agreement. It allows Members to require, as a condition of the acquisition or maintenance of IPRs provided for under Sections 2 through 6 of Part II of the Agreement, compliance with reasonable procedures and formalities. These Sections concern the protection of trademarks, GIs, industrial designs, patents and layout-designs of integrated circuits. However, Article 62.1 does not refer to Section 1 on copyright and related rights.

(iv)   Independence of protection   Article 5(2) of the Berne Convention as incorporated into the TRIPS Agreement further provides that the enjoyment and exercise of the rights in the country where protection is claimed are independent of the existence of protection in the country of origin.

2   What are the rights to be conferred on authors?

(a)   General

This section describes the rights that Members have to confer on authors; the following section discusses permissible limitations and exceptions to these. In order to have a full picture of copyright protection in any jurisdiction, both the rights and limitations available under the applicable law will need to be considered. Since the TRIPS Agreement is a minimum standards agreement and provides various flexibilities, the level of protection may vary between different Member countries.

The rights under copyright are divided into two main categories:

- economic rights, which allow authors to extract economic value from the utilization of their works; and
- moral rights, which allow authors to claim authorship and protect their integrity; as explained below, Members do not have any rights or obligations under the TRIPS Agreement in respect of moral rights.

Highlighted below are the main aspects of economic rights, although this is not an exhaustive review of all economic rights provided under the TRIPS Agreement. These can be categorized into four groups of exclusive rights:

- reproduction right;
- rental right;
- right of public performance, broadcasting and communication to the public; and
- translation and adaptation right.

The basic TRIPS rules on the economic rights are those stemming from the provisions of the Berne Convention as incorporated into the TRIPS Agreement. In addition, the Agreement requires Members to provide rental rights as explained below.

(b)   Reproduction right

This most basic right is reflected in the term copyright. Authors have an exclusive right of authorizing the reproduction (or copying) of their works 'in any manner or form' (Article 9.2 of the Berne Convention). This includes, for example, reproducing a novel in the form of a book or reproducing a song on a sound recording. The reproduction right covers any forms of technology, including photocopying of a book or copying the contents of a CD onto a computer hard-disk (although, as outlined later, exceptions are permitted for reproduction in certain cases, for instance for some forms of personal use).

Authors normally license the reproduction right to publishers and producers, and it thus becomes the legal basis of many commercial forms of exploitation of works.

(c)   Rental right

TRIPS Article 11 provides that authors shall have in respect of at least computer programs and cinematographic works (or films) the right to authorize or to prohibit the commercial rental to the public of originals or copies of their copyright works. Such rental rights are not covered by the provisions of the Berne Convention.

This Article provides two exceptions. First, with respect to cine-matographic works, the exclusive rental right is subject to the so-called 'impairment test': a Member is excepted from the obligation unless such rental has led to widespread copying of such works which is materially impairing the exclusive right of reproduction conferred in that Member on authors and their successors in title. Second, in respect of computer programs, the obligation does not apply to rentals where the program itself is not the essential object of the rental. This might be the case, for example, when one rents a television that includes some software to control it. However, if such software is rented separately from such a device, the exclusive rental right would apply.

The TRIPS Agreement, including the Berne provisions incorporated into it, does not require authors to be provided a general right of distribution. However, in many jurisdictions, the rental right is regulated as a part of a general distribution right.

(d)   Rights of public performance, broadcasting and communication to the public

Authors enjoy an exclusive right of authorizing the public performance of their works (Article 11 of the Berne Convention). For example, on the basis of this right, the author of a play may authorize or prohibit the performance of his or her play at a theatre. Or songwriters can authorize live performances of their music in restaurants, or recorded performances of their music in discothèques or retail outlets. The right covers only public performances and no authorization is required for a private performance.

Exclusive rights also cover the right of broadcasting of works or communication thereof to the public by other wireless means, and the right of communication to the public by wire (e.g. by cable) or by rebroadcasting of broadcast works as well as the right of public communication by loudspeaker and similar means of broadcast (Article 11*bis*(1) of the Berne Convention).

The application of some of these provisions was reviewed in a panel report on *US – Copyright Act* (DS160), which is discussed below.

In practice, when music is being played in public, the number of right holders involved is so great that it is impracticable for users to seek permission from each of them. That is why in many countries right holders in musical works have authorized so-called 'collective management organizations' (CMOs) to license restaurants, retail outlets, broadcasting organizations and other users to perform their music on their behalf. There is normally one CMO for each country managing a certain type of use of works. Through reciprocal agreements, each of them can license the entire world repertoire for users in their country. They distribute the collected revenues, after the deduction of administration costs, to individual right holders.

So if a performance is to be organized at a restaurant, does one need to contact all the relevant composers and lyricists? No. Normally, the restaurant has an agreement with the local CMO that allows it to perform music against a lump-sum payment. On the basis of the information that the CMO receives from the restaurant and other users on what pieces have been performed, it distributes royalties to the concerned right holders.

(e) Rights of translation and adaptation

Authors have the exclusive right of authorizing the translation of their works into another language (Article 8 of the Berne Convention). They also enjoy the exclusive right of authorizing adaptations, arrangements and other alterations of their works, such as turning a novel into a film script (Article 12 of the Berne Convention). As noted before, translations and adaptations are protected under copyright. Therefore, the use of a translation or an adaptation requires permissions both from the original author and the author of the translation or adaptation.

(f) Moral rights

Under Article 6*bis* of the Berne Convention, the author shall have the right, independently of his economic rights, to claim the authorship of the work and to object to any distortion, mutilation or other modification of, or other derogatory action in relation to, the said work, which would be prejudicial to his honour or reputation.

TRIPS Article 9.1 provides that Members do not have rights or obligations under the TRIPS Agreement in respect of the rights conferred under Article 6*bis* of that Convention. Moral rights were explicitly excluded from the TRIPS Agreement on the grounds that these rights that protect the personal link between the author and his or her work are not trade-related.

However, this does not affect the obligations of those Members that are also parties to the Berne Convention to protect moral rights. This is made even clearer in Article 2.2 of the TRIPS Agreement, which contains a safeguard clause, according to which the provisions of the Agreement cannot be understood to derogate from the existing obligations that Members may have to each other under the Berne Convention.[2]

3   What are the permissible limitations and exceptions?

The provisions of the Berne Convention incorporated into the TRIPS Agreement allow Members to provide limitations and exceptions to the exclusive rights of authors in respect of particular acts of exploitation. In addition, Article 13 of the TRIPS Agreement contains a general clause on exceptions and limitations.

The limitations that Members may provide pursuant to the provisions of the Berne Convention that have been incorporated into the TRIPS Agreement are of two types:

- free use (that is, use of protected works without the obligation to ask for authorization and to pay any remuneration); and
- non-voluntary licences (allowing use of protected works without authorization but with the obligation to pay equitable remuneration to right holders).

---

[2] Moral rights are also provided under the WCT, and their application has been extended to performers under the WPPT.

Free use of copyrighted works is allowed for some specified purposes, subject to certain conditions. Examples of such uses include quotations, illustrations for teaching purposes, and reporting of current events (Articles 10 and 10*bis* of the Berne Convention).

Under Article 9(2) of the Berne Convention, countries may provide limitations to the reproduction right in certain special cases, provided that such reproduction does not conflict with a normal exploitation of the work and does not unreasonably prejudice the legitimate interests of the author.

In addition to the limitations explicitly mentioned in the text of the Berne Convention, there was express agreement at various conferences to revise the Convention to allow countries to provide 'minor exceptions' to the right of public performance. As confirmed by the panel report on *US – Copyright Act* discussed below, such 'minor exceptions' are also permitted under the TRIPS Agreement. Examples of minor exceptions given in the revision conferences include performances of music in religious ceremonies, by military bands, or in the context of education.

Many national laws have detailed provisions on permitted exceptions, for example allowing free private or personal use of works. Several countries, however, have introduced a compensation system to counterbalance the prejudice to copyright owners created by the widespread private reproduction of audiovisual works and phonograms in the form of a levy on blank recording material and/or recording equipment. Schemes for exercising the right of reproduction in respect of photocopying or at least for granting compensation for such copying have also been introduced in several countries on a legislative or a contractual basis. In addition to specific free uses, the laws in common law jurisdictions often recognize the notion of 'fair use' or 'fair dealing', which covers various free uses allowed under international law.

The Berne provisions allow the use of non-voluntary licences in certain situations. These are licences granted by the authorities in a Member and not voluntarily by the right holder. Such licences can be applied in respect of broadcasting of works and the communication to the public of broadcast works (Article 11*bis* of the Berne Convention). The same is true in respect of recording of musical works and any words pertaining thereto, but only if the right holder has already authorized an earlier recording (Article 13 of the Berne Convention). The Appendix to the Berne Convention allows developing countries, subject to certain conditions, to make use of compulsory licensing in respect of the rights

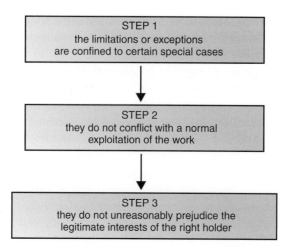

Figure II.1   Three-step test

of translation and reproduction for educational purposes. Given that the provisions of the Appendix have been incorporated into the TRIPS Agreement, these possibilities are also available under the Agreement.

Article 13 of the TRIPS Agreement, entitled 'Limitations and Exceptions', is a clause governing limitations and exceptions generally. It sets out the so-called 'three-step test' (Figure II.1). It permits limitations or exceptions to exclusive rights only if three conditions are met: (1) the limitations or exceptions are confined to certain special cases; (2) they do not conflict with a normal exploitation of the work; and (3) they do not unreasonably prejudice the legitimate interests of the right holder.

The language used in Article 13 of the TRIPS Agreement has its origins in the similar language used in Article 9(2) of the Berne Convention, although the latter only applies in the case of the reproduction right. Article 13 was applied in the dispute settlement case *US – Copyright Act* (DS160) (Box II.1).

4   *Term of protection*

According to the general rule contained in Article 7(1) of the Berne Convention as incorporated into the TRIPS Agreement, the minimum term of protection shall be the remainder of the life of the author and fifty years after his or her death, or more simply 'life plus fifty years'.

BOX II.1 US – COPYRIGHT ACT[3] (DS160)			
PARTIES		**_AGREEMENTS_**	**_TIMELINE OF THE DISPUTE_**
Complainants	EC	Articles 11*bis* (1)(iii) and 11(1)(ii) of the Berne	Establishment of Panel	1 February 1999
			Circulation of Panel report	15 June 2000
Respondent	United States	Convention as incorporated into the TRIPS Agreement by its Article 9.1, and Article 13 of the TRIPS Agreement	Circulation of Appellate Body report	NA
			Adoption	27 July 2000

(a) Measures at issue

Section 110(5) of the US Copyright Act permitted, under certain conditions, the playing of radio and television music in public places such as bars, restaurants and shops, without the payment of a royalty:

- Section 110(5)(A) contained the so-called 'homestyle exemption' which allowed small restaurants and retail outlets to amplify music broadcasts without authorization by the owner of copyright in the musical works and without the payment of a fee, provided that they used only homestyle equipment (i.e. equipment of a kind commonly used in private homes).
- Section 110(5)(B) contained the so-called 'business exemption' which allowed the amplification of music broadcasts, without authorization by the owner of copyright and without the payment of a fee, by food service and drinking establishments and by retail establishments, provided that their size did not exceed a certain square footage limit. It also allowed such amplification of music broadcasts by establishments above this square footage limit, provided that certain equipment limitations were met.

---

[3] *United States – Section 110(5) of the US Copyright Act.*

BOX II.1 *(cont.)*

(b) Summary of key Panel findings

The findings of the Panel in this case (document WT/DS160/R) provide an important discussion of the scope and application of exceptions and limitations under the TRIPS Agreement:

- The Panel considered that the exceptions in the US law implicated two exclusive rights in artistic works provided under the provisions of the Berne Convention as incorporated into the TRIPS Agreement: principally, the right to authorize the public communication of a broadcast by loudspeaker or analogous instrument in Article 11*bis*(1)(iii), but also the right to authorize the communication to the public of the performance of works in Article 11(1)(ii).
- The Panel concluded that the incorporation of these two Articles into the TRIPS Agreement included the entire *acquis* of these provisions under the Berne Convention, in other words their full legal background and not merely the bare text: this background included the possibility of providing so-called 'minor exceptions' to the respective exclusive rights. The panel then applied TRIPS Article 13 three-step test to clarify and articulate the standards applicable to permissible minor exceptions.
- The panel found that the 'business exemption', *inter alia*, covered a substantial majority of eating and drinking establishments and close to half of retail establishments and affected a major potential source of royalties. It did not meet the requirements of Article 13.
- On the contrary, the 'homestyle exemption', given that it covered a comparably small percentage of users and could not acquire economic or practical importance of any considerable dimension, satisfied the requirements of Article 13.

There are two categories of works, namely photographic works and works of applied art, for which the minimum term is shorter, namely twenty-five years from the making of such works.[4]

These Berne provisions are supplemented by Article 12 of the TRIPS Agreement, which provides that whenever the term of protection of a work, other than a photographic work or a work of applied art, is calculated on a basis other than the life of a natural person, such term

---

[4] A number of countries provide a longer general term of protection for literary and artistic works than required under the TRIPS Agreement, for example the life of the author plus seventy years after his or her death.

shall be no less than fifty years from the end of the calendar year of authorized publication or, failing such authorized publication within fifty years from the making of the work, fifty years from the end of the calendar year of making. This could be relevant, for example, in cases where the copyright is vested from the outset in a legal entity rather than a natural person. For example, where copyright originally vests under domestic law with a company in respect of a computer program developed by it, the rights should not end before fifty years from the end of the calendar year in which the computer program was published.

C   TRIPS provisions on related rights

The obligations of Members with respect to related rights are given in Article 14 of Section 1 of Part II of the TRIPS Agreement. As discussed in section A2 of this chapter, the provisions of the Rome Convention have not been incorporated into the Agreement. However, there are certain references to that Convention. For example, the limitations and exceptions applicable to related rights have been regulated by such a reference.

Article 14 deals with three categories of holders of related rights, namely performers (such as musicians, actors and dancers), producers of phonograms (or sound recordings such as CDs) and broadcasting organizations. What is common to all of them is that they bring their own contribution in making literary and artistic works available to the public. For example, a performer brings his or her skill and creativity into a performance of a musical composition. Technical skill and investment is needed from a phonogram producer to put the performance on a sound recording. And a broadcasting organization brings its financial resources and organizational capacity to transmit the performance of the song to the public. They all need protection against acts such as bootlegging, piracy and signal misappropriation so as to be able to dedicate their resources to this process.

Article 14 is drafted in a way that recognizes the differences between the civil law and common law systems in their approach to the protection of related rights (civil law systems have traditionally laid more emphasis on the recognition of distinct, personal rights over protected subject matter, whereas the common law approach typically included a wider range of remedies for unauthorized uses). The Agreement leaves Members free to implement their obligations under Article 14 within their own legal traditions and to employ a range of legal means for that purpose.

1   Relevant rights under the TRIPS Agreement

(a)   Performers

According to Article 14.1, performers shall have the possibility of preventing the unauthorized fixation of their performance on a sound recording, for example a CD. The fixation right required under the TRIPS Agreement covers only audio, not audiovisual recordings or fixations. This means that musicians must have the possibility of preventing an unauthorized sound recording of their concerts (e.g. bootlegging), but actors need not be given a similar possibility of preventing the unauthorized filming of their theatre performances. Performers must also be in position to prevent the reproduction of such fixations.

Performers must also have the possibility of preventing the unauthorized broadcasting by wireless means and the communication to the public of their live performance.

(b)   Producers of phonograms

In accordance with Article 14.2, Members have to grant producers of phonograms an exclusive reproduction right. In addition to this, they have to grant, in accordance with Article 14.4, an exclusive rental right at least to producers of phonograms. The provisions on rental rights apply also to any other right holders in phonograms as determined in national law. This right has the same scope as the rental right in respect of computer programs. Therefore it is not subject to the impairment test as in respect of cinematographic works. However, it is limited by a so-called 'grandfather clause', according to which a Member, which on 15 April 1994 (the date of the signature of the Marrakesh Agreement) had in force a system of equitable remuneration of right holders in respect of the rental of phonograms may maintain such a system provided that the commercial rental of phonograms does not lead to the material impairment of the exclusive rights of reproduction of right holders.

(c)   Broadcasting organizations

Broadcasting organizations shall have, in accordance with Article 14.3, the right to prohibit unauthorized fixation, the reproduction of fixations, and the rebroadcasting by wireless means of broadcasts, as well as the communication to the public of their television broadcasts.

However, it is not necessary to grant such rights to broadcasting organizations, if owners of copyright in the subject matter of broadcasts are provided with the possibility of preventing these acts, subject to the provisions of the Berne Convention. For example, in some common law jurisdictions those who hold the copyright in respect of the content of a broadcast have such rights and therefore broadcasting organizations do not have a separate right in the signal.

2 Limitations and exceptions

Article 14.6 provides that any Member may, in relation to the protection of performers, producers of phonograms and broadcasting organizations, provide for conditions, limitations, exceptions and reservations to the extent permitted by the Rome Convention.

Such limitations provided under the Rome Convention and thus applicable also under the TRIPS Agreement include, for example, private use; use of short excerpts in connection with the reporting of current events; and use solely for the purposes of teaching or scientific research. In general, the Rome Convention also permits a country to provide for the same kinds of limitations as it provides for in its domestic law in respect of literary and artistic works.

3 Term of protection

The term of protection available to performers and producers of phonograms shall last at least until the end of a period of fifty years computed from the end of the calendar year in which the fixation was made or the performance took place.

The term of protection granted to broadcasting organizations shall last for at least twenty years from the end of the calendar year in which the broadcast took place (Article 14.5).

III

Trademarks

A   Introduction

1   General

This chapter explains the provisions of Section 2 of Part II of the TRIPS Agreement entitled 'Trademarks'. This Section contains seven articles, from Article 15 to Article 21, and deals with the protection that Members have to make available for trademarks.

This section has to be read, like other sections in Part II of the TRIPS Agreement that cover standards of IPRs, together with the relevant provisions of pre-existing treaties in the area of international IP law which are incorporated by reference into the TRIPS Agreement. In the case of trademarks, the relevant treaty is the Paris Convention. The relationship between the TRIPS Agreement and the Paris Convention is explained below (see section A3 below).

This chapter will also have to be read in conjunction with other relevant provisions of the TRIPS Agreement that are explained in other chapters. Wherever appropriate, cross-references are made to other chapters.

As seen in Chapter I, the TRIPS Agreement stipulates the minimum level of protection that Members have to provide to nationals from other Members. In other words, they determine the obligations that Members have *vis-à-vis* each other. Given the long history of international cooperation on IP matters, the national laws in this area are often fairly similar. However, as is the case for all IPRs, to establish how the law applies in any concrete practical situation, the applicable national law will have to be consulted.

2   What is the role of trademarks?

A trademark is a sign or a combination of signs that is used to distinguish the goods or services of one enterprise from those of another.

The owner of a trademark has the exclusive right to use it in the market-place to identify certain goods or services, or to authorize (or license) others to use it in return for payment or other benefits.

The trademark system thus serves to protect producers against unfair competition from other producers seeking to free ride on the goodwill and positive reputation earned by the trademark owner. By providing a certain guarantee that a trademarked product or service originates from or is authorized by the trademark owner, trademark protection also facilitates consumers' choices when purchasing certain products or using certain services. Consumers often rely on trademarks to indicate the source company and to distinguish the product from similar goods that are produced by other enterprises. Trademarks therefore help consumers to reliably identify and purchase a product or service which they prefer because of its taste, quality or other characteristic that consumers have come to expect on the basis of previous purchases or through advertising or word-of-mouth recommendation. Thus, trademarks protect an undertaking's goodwill, as well as the consumers, against confusion and deceptive practices. The registration system was developed over time as a way of clarifying the existence and scope of trademark rights, and as a way of putting other traders on notice about those rights.

In the past, trademarks were mainly registered and protected for goods. The registration of trademarks for services ('service marks') was optional under the Paris Convention, and few countries provided for registration of such marks. However, with the rise of the service economy and the resulting importance of trademarks in distinguishing services, the TRIPS Agreement stipulated that service marks should be protected in the same way as trademarks for goods. Where the provisions on trademarks apply equally to marks identifying goods and services, the term 'products' will be used in this chapter to denote both goods and services.

In general, trademarks are registered and protected with respect to certain products, which are described in detail in the trademark registration (e.g. 'FedEx' for document delivery services, 'Toyota' for automobiles and related services and 'Samsung' for consumer electronics).[1] The owner generally only enjoys the exclusive right of use of the registered trademark with respect to the same or similar products for which it

---

[1] Detailed classification systems of goods and services for the purposes of trademark registrations have been agreed to in the Nice Agreement and the Vienna Agreement, which are administered by the World Intellectual Property Organization (WIPO).

is registered. For example, a trademark registered for hairdressing services would not, normally, be enforceable against use of the mark on a new range of irrigation equipment.

While trademark rights are typically acquired by the *registration* of a sign as a trademark, some countries make these rights available without registration simply on the basis of use. In some jurisdictions, such unregistered trademark rights are referred to as *common law trademarks*. The TRIPS Agreement only obliges Members to accord rights to the owner of registered trademarks. However, it explicitly recognizes in Article 16.1 Members' entitlement to make trademark rights available without registration on the basis of use. And it requires protection for well-known marks that are not registered.

Trademark rights, like other IPRs, are territorial, which means that they are in principle valid only in the jurisdiction where they have been registered or otherwise acquired.[2] To be protected in different countries, therefore, a mark needs to be registered in each individual jurisdiction. To go through separate procedures for trademark registration in many countries can be expensive and administratively complicated. A number of international treaties dealing with aspects of national and international registration have therefore been concluded under the auspices of WIPO, to facilitate and harmonize registration in multiple jurisdictions.[3]

3   What is the relationship of the TRIPS Agreement with the pre-existing provisions of the Paris Convention?

As discussed in Chapter I, during the Uruguay Round negotiations it was recognized that, for the most part, the Paris Convention already provided important basic standards of industrial property protection.

---

[2] The protection for well-known marks required by Article 6*bis* of the Paris Convention and Article 16.2 and 16.3 of the TRIPS Agreement is an exception to that rule.

[3] The Trademark Law Treaty and the Singapore Treaty harmonize national and regional registration procedures, the Madrid Agreement and the Protocol relating to the Madrid Agreement facilitate multiple registrations in a number of jurisdictions, and the Nice Agreement and the Vienna Agreement establish international classification systems relevant to trademarks. These international treaties concluded under the auspices of WIPO have not been incorporated into the TRIPS Agreement. Furthermore, Article 5 of the TRIPS Agreement exempts procedures relating to the acquisition and maintenance of IPRs that are contained in WIPO's multilateral treaties from TRIPS national treatment and MFN obligations.

It was therefore agreed that the point of departure should be the existing standards under the latest Act, the Stockholm Act of 1967, of that Convention.

However, the Paris Convention is silent on a number of key aspects of trademark protection. Accordingly, the trademark section of the TRIPS Agreement contains a comprehensive definition of trademarks and a description of the rights conferred by registered trademarks, as well as provisions on limitations and on the term of protection. The TRIPS Agreement also adds some significant substantive provisions regarding service marks and the protection of well-known marks. These provisions codify and concretize to some extent the jurisprudence and general practice that had already been developed under the Paris Convention and relevant national laws.

B   TRIPS provisions on trademarks

The obligations of Members with respect to the availability, scope and permissible limitations of trademark protection are contained in Articles 15 to 21 of Part II of the TRIPS Agreement, and also include the substantive provisions of the Paris Convention incorporated into the Agreement by the reference in Article 2.1. These provisions also have to be read in the context of provisions in other parts of the TRIPS Agreement.

1   *What is the subject matter to be protected and what are the conditions for registration?*

(a)   Subject matter of trademark protection

(i) **Distinctive signs**   According to Article 15.1 of the TRIPS Agreement, any sign, or any combination of signs, capable of distinguishing the goods and services of one 'undertaking' from those of other undertakings must be eligible for trademark protection. These signs could be words including personal names, letters, numerals, figurative elements and combinations of colours, as well as any combination of signs. This means that in principle there is no limitation on the type of signs that can constitute trademarks under the TRIPS Agreement. Rather, the emphasis is on *distinctiveness* – i.e. the ability of these signs to distinguish products of one enterprise from those of others. Members can require that signs be visually perceptible to be registered as trademarks, leaving them free to determine whether or not to allow the registration as trademarks of signs such as smells and sounds. The latter are often referred to as 'non-traditional' trademarks.

Signs are considered distinctive in relation to a certain class or classes of product (e.g. automobiles) if consumers associate these signs with products from a particular enterprise (e.g. 'Mazda'), rather than a type of product (e.g. 'Hatchback' or 'Pick-Up'). It follows therefore that the more descriptive a term is for the product, the less distinctive it will be in relation to such products. Conversely, the more peculiar or fanciful a term is in relation to the product it is used for, the more likely it is to be distinctive for these products. Fantasy words or completely unrelated words like 'Yahoo', 'Kodak' or 'Exxon' are therefore more likely to be distinctive (with regard to any product) than descriptive words like 'four-wheel drive' for cars or 'lightweight' for bicycles.

Where signs are not inherently (i.e. 'by the nature of the sign itself') capable of distinguishing the relevant products, Members can allow their registration as trademarks on the basis of distinctiveness that has been acquired through use. Distinctiveness is acquired if an otherwise descriptive term (e.g. 'Raisin-Bran' for bran cereal with raisins or 'Federal Express' for express mail service at the Federal level), through extensive advertising or use for a product by a particular enterprise, has ceased to be understood as a general term and has come to be associated with the product of that specific supplier. It then serves to distinguish those products from the products of other suppliers, which makes it capable of constituting a trademark.[4]

While most trademarks are word marks, graphic symbols, labels, or logos, there have also been registrations of shapes of products themselves (e.g. the triangular shape of 'Toblerone' chocolate, or the particular shape of the 'Coca-Cola' bottle) and colours (the magenta colour of 'Deutsche Telekom') and some countries have allowed the registration of

---

[4] This process also works in the opposite direction. A sign can lose its distinctiveness if the consumer no longer understands it as identifying the product of one specific enterprise, but rather sees it as denoting a type of product in general, regardless of the originating enterprise. This may happen if the trademark owner does not take sufficient action against unauthorized use and consumers start using the term more widely, so that the term becomes generic. (e.g. zipper and escalator). The term can also have different significance in different countries, depending on use and legal status – so that 'Thermos' is a registered mark in some countries for insulated vessels, but is mentioned in dictionaries as a generic term elsewhere.

sounds ('Nokia' ringtone; 'MGM' lion roar) and, more recently, smells (the smell of fresh cut grass for tennis balls).

(ii) Trade names The notion of a trade name is interpreted in different ways in existing legislations – the term 'business name' is sometimes used. It can generally be defined as being the name or designation identifying the enterprise of a natural or legal person – for instance, Maria Luisa might call her bakery 'Marisa's Cakeshop'. The protection of trade names has been held by the Appellate Body to also fall within the scope of the TRIPS Agreement by virtue of the incorporation of Article 8 of the Paris Convention into the TRIPS Agreement by its Article 2.1 (Appellate Body in the dispute settlement case *US – Section 211 Omnibus Appropriations Act* (DS176)). Neither the Paris Convention nor the TRIPS Agreement specify in detail the level of protection that must be applied, so national practice can differ considerably, but it is clear that no formalities are required, and that essentially the same protection must be available to foreign nationals' business names as for those of domestic nationals.

(iii) Collective marks and certification marks According to Article 7*bis* of the Paris Convention, Members must also accept the registration of signs as collective marks. This means that signs can be registered not only with respect to products from one enterprise, but also with respect to those of a group of enterprises or an association. These enterprises can then own, use and defend the trademark collectively. The collective mark may be used to show that an individual producer or trader is a member of a trade or industry association, and to distinguish their products from those of other undertakings. Such marks are often used to distinguish the geographical origin or other common characteristics of products of different enterprises which use the collective mark under the control of its owner, or to certify that the product bearing the mark has certain characteristics such as a particular mode of production, regional or other origin, or fulfils certain standards of quality. Such marks are similar to certification marks or guarantee marks – marks that certify or guarantee certain properties or origin of a product – but are technically different under some national laws. For example, a certification mark could be owned by a separate certifying authority, rather than an association of traders. But these kinds of marks are often grouped together as having a similar character and function.

Examples of terms that have been registered as collective marks in the European Union are 'Bayerisches Bier', 'Royal Thai Silk' (figurative), 'Darjeeling' and 'Madeira' (Community Trademark CTM Register, November 2010).

(b) Conditions for registration as a trademark

As registration of a trademark is the principal way of obtaining trademark protection, a number of rules concern the conditions under which trademark registrations can be obtained, and mechanisms for facilitating the obtaining of registrations in other Members. While, according to Article 6(1) of the Paris Convention and Article 15.2 of the TRIPS Agreement, the conditions for the filing and registering of a trademark are in principle determined by the domestic legislation of each Member country, there are a number of common rules that have to be observed by all Members.

(i) **Priority** The right of priority ensures that on the basis of a regular first trademark application filed in a Member, the applicant (or the successor in title) may, within a specified period of time, apply for registration of his or her trademark in another Member using the same priority date as the first application. According to Article 4 of the Paris Convention, the priority period for trademarks is six months from the date of the first filing of that trademark in a Member. During the six-month priority period, applications of the owner for the same trademark in all other Members will be regarded as if they had been filed on the same day as the first application and therefore enjoy priority status with respect to any actions (such as use) or applications for similar trademarks that occurred since the date of the first application.

(ii) **Publishing requirement** According to Article 15.5 of the TRIPS Agreement, Members must publish a trademark either before, or promptly after, it is registered. They must further provide for a reasonable opportunity to request the cancellation of the trademark, so that interested parties can challenge a registration. In addition, Members may, but are not obliged to, allow for trademark opposition, a procedure practised in many Members where a trademark can be challenged after it is accepted by the trademark office, but before it is registered.

This provision ensures transparency in the trademark registration process, which is a prerequisite of an effective challenge procedure. It also illustrates the TRIPS Agreement's flexibility in accommodating different registration procedures already in existence in different Members. These differ typically with regard to how the owner of a mark is determined. Some systems give ownership to whoever is the first to use a mark ('first to use'), others to those who are the first to file a trademark application ('first to file').

(iii) Reasons which *may not* constitute grounds for refusal of trademark registrations According to the rules laid down in the Paris Convention and the TRIPS Agreement, a number of reasons may not constitute grounds for the refusal of a trademark registration in a Member:

'*Failure to register in the country of origin*'

A registration of a sign as a trademark may not be refused by a Member on the grounds that the trademark is not registered in its country of origin (i.e. country of commercial establishment, domicile or nationality of the applicant). This principle, provided for in Article 6.2 of the Paris Convention, is called 'independence of protection' and asserts that for a trademark to enjoy protection in a Member, the owner is not obliged to first seek registration in his home country.

'*Form of the mark, if already registered in other Member countries*'

Although registration in the country of origin is not obligatory for enjoying trademark protection elsewhere, Article 6*quinquies* of the Paris Convention provides that once a trademark has been registered in its country of origin that is a Member, other Members have to accept the registration of the mark in that form 'as is' (i.e. *telle quelle*, in the original French version of the Paris Convention). This means that other Members cannot refuse protection of such a trademark for the reason that the mark, with regard to the signs of which it is composed, does not comply with the requirements of their domestic legislation. This provision reflects the interest of both owners of trademarks and the public in having the same trademark apply to the same products in various countries.

However, Article 6*quinquies* makes clear that such trademarks can still be denied registration in cases where they infringe third-party rights in the country where protection is claimed, if they are essentially devoid of distinctive character, or if they are contrary to morality or public order. For the details of these exceptions, see the text of Article 6 *quinquies* itself.

In the dispute settlement case *US – Section 211 Omnibus Appropriations Act* (DS176) the Panel and Appellate Body confirmed that this provision only applies to *the form* of the trademark. This means that Members remain free to apply their domestic rules as regards other aspects of trademark registration such as the definition of a trademark or any requirement of previous use of the trademark.

'Nature of the goods or services identified by the trademark'

As was already provided for in Article 7 of the Paris Convention in respect of goods, and has been confirmed and extended by Article 15.4 of the TRIPS Agreement, Members may not refuse the registration of a trademark because of the nature of the goods or services the mark is applied to. Thus, a trademark registration may not be refused merely because the mark identifies products that could be considered immoral, dangerous or otherwise undesirable.

This does not, of course, mean that governments cannot regulate the sale of the goods bearing trademarks. Rather, this rule reflects the nature of IPRs as essentially negative rights – i.e. rights to prevent the use of a trademark by other parties – and not as positive rights to sell or market products. The sale, marketing or use of socially sensitive products such as alcohol, firearms, pharmaceuticals and hazardous chemicals is usually regulated by specific areas of law other than IP, such as regulations on medicines, weapons and chemicals, and in some cases criminal law or general civil law. Enterprises must comply with these laws before they can legitimately sell or use such products. Trademark protection only protects the enterprise's signs against confusing use by its competitors on similar products – it does not amount to a licence to sell the product – and therefore a mark may not be refused registration on grounds of the nature of the goods or services to which the mark is to be applied.

'Actual use of the trademark at the time of registration'

According to Article 15.3 of the TRIPS Agreement, where countries make trademark registrations dependent on the use of a mark, *actual* use of a trademark may not be a condition for filing an application to register that trademark. Although Members may make registration dependent on the use of the trademark, a registration may not be refused solely on the ground that the intended use has not taken place within three years of the application date. This means that, while in principle a Member may require that the applicant at least intends to actually use the trademark, he or she must be given at least three years from the filing of the trademark application before actual use must have taken place. A Member may cancel a registration if the trademark is still not used after three years, unless the trademark owner has valid reasons for the non-use, such as import restrictions or other government regulations covering the goods or services protected by the trademark.

In practice, enterprises often register trademarks before they launch the corresponding product, because the design of a new product and the planned advertisement campaign are usually developed on the basis of the trademark for the product. Such investments would be lost if the trademark was no longer available at the time of the actual product launch – for instance, if a competitor applies for a similar mark in the meantime.

(iv)   Reasons which *may* constitute grounds for refusal of trademark registrations   The TRIPS Agreement recognizes in Article 15.2 that Members may also refuse the registration of a trademark in their territory on grounds other than those addressed in Article 15.1 (e.g. lack of distinctiveness or visual perceptibility), provided they do not derogate from the provisions of the Paris Convention.

The Panel and Appellate Body in the dispute settlement case *US – Section 211 Omnibus Appropriations Act* (DS176) established that the grounds Members may use to refuse registration are not limited to those expressly mentioned in TRIPS or the Paris Convention, such as those listed in Article 6*quinquies* of the Paris Convention (Box III.1) (see above under B1(b)(iii)).

(v)   Reasons which *must* constitute grounds for refusal or invalidation of trademark registration in Members   Finally, the regime of trademark protection under the TRIPS Agreement provides for a number of situations in which Members must refuse or invalidate the registration of a trademark.

'Well-known marks'

According to Article 6*bis* of the Paris Convention as incorporated in the TRIPS Agreement, well-known trademarks – i.e. those that, without necessarily being registered in that country, are well known there – enjoy stronger protection than ordinary trademarks, and registrations of signs

---

BOX III.1 US — SECTION 211 OMNIBUS APPROPRIATIONS ACT[5] (DS176)

PARTIES		AGREEMENTS	TIMELINE OF THE DISPUTE	
Complainants	EC	TRIPS Articles 2, 3, 4, 15, 16 and 42	Establishment of Panel	26 September 2000
		Paris Convention	Circulation of Panel report	6 August 2001
Respondent	United States		Circulation of Appellate Body report	2 January 2002
			Adoption	1 February 2002

1. Measure and intellectual property at issue
   • Measure at issue: Section 211 of the US Omnibus Appropriations Act of 1988, prohibiting those having an interest in trademarks/trade names related to certain goods confiscated by the Cuban government from registering/renewing such trademarks/names without the original owner's consent.
   • IP at issue: Trademarks or trade names related to such confiscated goods.
2. Summary of key Panel/Appellate Body findings[6]

Section 211(a)(1)

• TRIPS Article 15 and Article 2.1 (Paris Convention Art. 6 *quinquies* A(1)): As Article 15.1 embodies a definition of a trademark and sets forth only the eligibility criteria for registration as trademarks (but not an obligation to register 'all' eligible trademarks), the Appellate Body found that Section 211 (a)(1) was not inconsistent with Article 15.1, as the regulation concerned 'ownership' of a trademark. The Appellate Body also agreed with the Panel that Section 211(a)(1) was not inconsistent with Paris Convention Article 6 *quinquies* A(1), which addresses only the 'form' of a trademark, not ownership.

Sections 211(a)(2) and (b)

• TRIPS Articles 16.1 and 42: As there are no rules determining the 'owner' of a trademark (i.e. discretion left to individual countries), the Appellate Body

---

[5] *United States — Section 211 Omnibus Appropriations Act of 1998.*
[6] Other issues addressed in this case: TRIPS, Article 15.2; Paris Convention, Article 8; scope of appellate review (question of fact or law, DSU, Article 17.6); characterization of the measure ('ownership'); information from WIPO.

BOX III.1 *(cont.)*

found that Section 211(a)(2) and (b) were not inconsistent with Article 16.1. The Appellate Body, reversing the Panel, found that Section 211(a)(2) on its face was not inconsistent with Article 42, as it gave right holders access to civil judicial procedures, as required under Article 42, which is a provision on procedural obligations, while Section 211 affects substantive rights.

- Paris Convention Article 2(1) (TRIPS, Article 3.1): As to the effect on 'successors-in-interest', the Appellate Body found that Section 211(a)(2) violated the national treatment obligation, because it imposed an extra procedural hurdle on Cuban nationals. As for the effect on original owners, the Appellate Body reversed the Panel and found that Section 211(a)(2) and (b) violated the national treatment obligations as they applied to 'original owners' who were Cuban nationals but not to 'original owners' who were US nationals.
- TRIPS Article 4: Reversing the Panel, the Appellate Body found that Section 211(a)(2) and (b) violated the most-favoured-nation obligation, because only an 'original owner' who was a Cuban national was subject to the measure at issue, whereas a non-Cuban 'original owner' was not.

Trade names

- Scope of the TRIPS Agreement: Reversing the Panel, the Appellate Body concluded that trade names are covered under the TRIPS Agreement, because, *inter alia*, Paris Convention, Article 8 covering trade names is explicitly incorporated into Article 2.1 of the TRIPS Agreement.
- TRIPS Articles 3.1, 4 and 42 and Paris Convention: Completing the Panel's analysis on trade names, the Appellate Body reached the same conclusions as in the context of trademarks above, because Sections 211(a)(2) and (b) operated in the same manner for both trademarks and trade names.

as trademarks must be refused if they are liable to cause confusion with a well-known trademark. Well-known trademarks are explained in detail in section B2(c) below.

'*Geographical indications*'

According to Articles 22 and 23 of the TRIPS Agreement, Members must also refuse or invalidate the registration of a trademark which contains or consists of a GI, if use of such a trademark would mislead the public as to the true place of origin of the goods (in the case of all GIs), or if such a trademark is used on wines and spirits not having the indicated origin (in the case of GIs for wines or spirits). Certain exceptions to this obligation are provided for in Article 24 in

the Section on GIs of the TRIPS Agreement. The obligations of
Members under the provisions for GIs are explained in more detail
in Chapter IV.

'State emblems and official hallmarks'

Furthermore, according to Article 6*ter* of the Paris Convention, as incorporated in the TRIPS Agreement, Members must refuse or invalidate the
registration as trademarks, and prohibit by appropriate measures the use
without authorization, of state emblems, flags, official hallmarks,
emblems or abbreviations of intergovernmental organizations and other
official signs which have been communicated to the Members. A number
of exceptions to this obligation are provided for under that Article. The
purpose of Article 6*ter* is not to protect the official signs or hallmarks
mentioned above as subjects of industrial property but rather to exclude
them from becoming such subjects in certain circumstances.

WIPO maintains a database regarding Article 6*ter* of the Paris Convention. More detailed information on the interpretation of this Article
can be found at www.wipo.int/article6ter/en.

2   What are the rights to be conferred on trademark owners?

(a)   General

The TRIPS Agreement also stipulates which rights a trademark owner
must enjoy in a Member (Article 16) and what type of exceptions to
these rights are permissible (Article 17). As noted in Chapter I, the
TRIPS Agreement is a minimum standards agreement. This means that
the rights described here only constitute the minimum level of protection required by this international agreement, and that Members may –
and in many cases actually do – provide for higher or more stringent
protection in their national legislation. Therefore, in order to establish
what rights a trademark owner has in any individual Member, reference
should be made to the national laws of that country.

(b)   Trademark rights

According to Article 16.1 of the TRIPS Agreement, 'The owner of a
registered trademark shall have the exclusive right to prevent all third
parties not having the owner's consent from using in the course of trade
identical or similar signs for goods or services identical or similar to
those in respect of which the trademark is registered where such use

would result in a likelihood of confusion.' In short, this means that under a Member's national trademark regime the right holder must at least be able to stop the use of similar signs on similar products in the market, where such use would lead to confusion among consumers as to whether or not those products originate from or are endorsed by the right holder's undertaking. While the TRIPS Agreement only obliges Members to accord this right to the owners of registered trademarks, it explicitly recognizes in Article 16.1 the Members' ability to make trademark rights available without registration on the basis of use.

Each of the different elements of Article 16.1 of the TRIPS Agreement is set out below:

'exclusive right to prevent'

means that the owner of a registered trademark must have the exclusive right – i.e. he or she must be the only person or legal entity authorized – to authorize the use of his or her trademark or signs confusingly similar to it on similar or identical products. The next element

'from using in the course of trade'

means that the registered trademark must be protected against confusing use in the course of trade. Therefore trademarks only have to be protected in commercial dealings and there is no obligation to protect against use in a private context. Again

'where such use would result in the likelihood of confusion'

means that only the use:

(1) of a sign that is similar or identical to that registered as a trademark,
(2) on products similar or identical to those in respect of which the trademark is registered,
(3) that is likely to confuse the relevant group of consumers,

falls under the exclusive right of the trademark owner (for the more extensive protection of well-known trademarks see below under section B2(c)). Article 16.1 of the TRIPS Agreement requires that, in cases where an identical sign is used on identical products, it is presumed that a likelihood of confusion exists (e.g. even if the buyer is aware that he is buying a counterfeit product). When the signs and products are not identical but only similar to those registered, the question of likelihood of confusion has to be assessed case-by-case and on the basis of the individual market situation.

Typically, in assessing whether the use of a sign on particular products causes a likelihood of confusion with a registered trademark, the relevant authorities would consider both the similarity of the sign with the registered sign and the similarity of the products with those in respect of which the trademark is registered, and decide on the basis of the overall consumer impression whether there is a likelihood of confusion. Factors that may play a role in assessing the similarity of signs are the phonetic or linguistic similarity, as well as similarities in meaning. As regards the similarity of products, courts have taken into account factors such as whether the products in question compete with each other in the marketplace, whether they share the same distribution channels, the likely degree of vigilance of the targeted customers (e.g. children or business owners) and the degree of recognition a trademark has in the market. The fact that the likelihood of confusion is established on the basis of the overall impression of the use of a sign on a product means that a strong similarity of signs might be balanced out by a strong dissimilarity of the products on which the sign is used and vice versa.

To illustrate this point consider the following examples. The trademark 'Euron' is registered for 'surgical, medical apparatus and instruments'. An application requests the registration of the trademark 'Curon' for a variety of goods including also 'surgical, medical, dental and veterinary apparatus, instruments and devices ...'. In assessing whether the use of the 'Curon' trademark might result in a likelihood of confusion with the earlier 'Euron' trademark, it would be taken into account that although the goods on which the marks are used may be identical (namely surgical medical apparatus and instruments), the signs that are used are rather dissimilar. On that basis, an overall assessment in a certain territory could come to the conclusion that hardly any relevant consumer would have the impression that medical instruments marked with the 'Curon' trademark could possibly come from the owner of the earlier mark 'Euron', and that there is therefore no likelihood of confusion.[7]

Inversely, use of virtually identical signs may not cause a likelihood of confusion among consumers if the products on which the different signs are used are sufficiently different. In assessing, for example, whether the use of the trademark 'Tosca' registered for 'perfume products' and the trademark 'Tosca Blu' registered for 'leatherwear' and 'clothing' would

---

[7] Case so decided by the European Court of First Instance on 13 February 2007 – (T-353/04).

cause confusion among consumers, the difference in the goods for which the two marks are registered may well be seen to outweigh the similarity (or, in fact, partial identity) of the signs used. An overall assessment for a certain territory may therefore come to the conclusion that no likelihood of confusion exists between these two trademarks, as consumers may not be confused between a perfume producer and a producer of leatherwear.[8]

In a similar vein, the trademark 'Waterford' registered for 'articles of glassware, earthenware, chinaware and porcelain' might not cause a likelihood of confusion with the trademark 'Waterford Stellenbosch' which is registered for 'alcoholic beverages, namely wines produced in the Stellenbosch district, South Africa' because consumers may perceive the goods glass- and porcelainware on the one hand and wine from Stellenbosch, South Africa on the other hand to be sufficiently different so as not to be confused by the use of these partially identical signs.[9]

A further consequence of the fact that the assessment of whether there is a likelihood of confusion is an overall assessment of the two levels of comparison (i.e. similarity at the level of the signs used and at the level of products, on which the signs are used) is that there may be identical trademarks registered for different products. As an illustration, in the European trademark register for Community trademarks (CTMs) there are, for example, numerous registrations for the trademark 'Speedy' by different enterprises for different groups of products (Box III.2).

As mentioned above, the assessment of whether there is a likelihood of confusion is to be made on a case-by-case basis taking into account the situation in the territory in question.

(c)   Rights with respect to well-known trademarks

As explained above, well-known trademarks are those that, without necessarily being registered in a country, are well known as belonging to a particular trademark owner. Such marks enjoy stronger protection than normal trademarks. According to Article 6*bis* of the Paris Convention, as incorporated into the TRIPS Agreement, the registration of a sign as a trademark must be refused or cancelled, and its use prohibited in a Member, if that trademark is liable to cause confusion with a mark that is considered well known in that Member and used for identical or similar goods – whether or not the well-known trademark is registered

---

[8] Case so decided by the German Federal Supreme Court on 30 March 2006 – (I ZR 96/03).
[9] Case so decided by the Court of the European Communities on 7 May 2009 – (C-398/07 P).

BOX III.2 COMMUNITY TRADEMARKS

Trademark (word)	List of goods and services for which the mark is registered	Trademark Registration Number[10]
Speedy	Metal fittings for doors and windows as far as contained in Class 06	CTM 00711648
Speedy	Electric and electronic equipment for operating lamps, small transformers, throttles and electronic apparatus for light control installations	CTM 001318054
Speedy	Chocolate products and confectionery, in particular bars, including filled bars, including with caramel and/or nuts and/or chopped nuts	CTM 001998939
Speedy	Mobile and modular aluminium scaffolding; Mobile and modular scaffolding, not of metal	CTM 005654744
Speedy	Clothing, footwear, headgear	CTM 006835433

---

in that country. Such refusal, cancellation or prohibition of use should be effected *ex officio* by the competent authority of a Member if its legislation permits its authorities to act on their own initiative. Otherwise such action must be available at the request of an interested party (such as the owner of the well-known mark).

Whether a trademark is liable to create confusion with a well-known mark will be determined by the competent authority of the Member concerned, and in so doing the said authority will have to consider the question from the viewpoint of the consumers of the products to which the marks are applied. Article 6*bis* specifies that such confusion may occur in cases of reproduction, imitation or translation of the well-known mark, or even if only an essential part of a mark constitutes a reproduction or confusing imitation of the well-known mark.

---

[10] Community Trademark Registrations checked at http://oami.europa.eu on 26 November 2010.

Article 16.2 of the TRIPS Agreement extends the protection afforded in Article 6*bis* of the Paris Convention to well-known service marks. Article 16.3 also extends protection under Article 6*bis* of the Paris Convention to protection against use of the mark on non-similar goods or services, provided the well-known mark is registered and that such use would indicate a connection between those products and the owner of the well-known mark and that his interests are likely to be damaged by such use.

Article 16.2 of the TRIPS Agreement provides that, in determining whether a trademark is well known in its territory, a Member must take account of the knowledge of the trademark in the relevant sector of the public (e.g. for trademarks on skis among skiers) and must include knowledge obtained through the promotion of the trademark. This means that knowledge based on advertising efforts as well as on use of the trademark on the products shall be taken into account.

(d)   Licensing and assignment of rights

The TRIPS Agreement provides in Article 21 that, while it is up to each Member to prescribe conditions on the licensing and assignment of trademark rights, an owner of a registered trademark must always be able to assign the trademark with or without the transfer of the business to which the trademark belongs. Before the introduction of the TRIPS Agreement, quite a number of countries allowed the transfer or assignment of trademark only with the transfer of the corresponding business or goodwill located in the relevant territory, which effectively barred trademark rights from being traded as independent assets. While countries are free to regulate this aspect in their national legislation under the Paris Convention (Article 6*quater*), it has become an obligation under the TRIPS Agreement to allow the assignment of trademarks independently from the corresponding business operation.

(e)   Other requirements

According to Article 20 of the TRIPS Agreement, use of the trademark in the course of trade must not be unjustifiably encumbered by special requirements, such as use with another trademark (so-called 'twinning' requirements), use in a special form, or use in a manner detrimental to the trademark's ability to distinguish the goods or services of one undertaking from those of other undertakings.

3   What are the permissible exceptions to trademark rights?

With regard to the exceptions to trademark rights that Members may
provide, Article 17 of the TRIPS Agreement provides a general exception
clause laying down the criteria that permitted exceptions must meet.

(a)   Permissible exceptions

Article 17 of the TRIPS Agreement, entitled 'Exceptions', stipulates that
Members may provide for exceptions to the rights conferred by a
trademark, provided that such exceptions are (1) limited, (2) take
account of the legitimate interests of the owner of the trademark and
of those of (3) third parties. Article 17 cites 'fair use of descriptive terms'
as an illustrative example of a limited exception.

Article 17 was interpreted by the Panel in *EC – Trademarks and
Geographical Indications* (DS174). In its decision, the Panel considered
that the limitation should be assessed as a legal rather than an economic matter. It interpreted the phrase 'limited exceptions' to refer to a
narrow exception to the rights conferred by a trademark, rather than to
an exception that affected only a few trademarks or a few trademark
owners. In other words, the number of trademark owners affected by
such an exception or the number of third parties benefiting from an
exception was irrelevant, but what counted was whether the exception
affected only a limited portion of the spectrum of rights conferred by the
trademark. With regard to the legitimate interests of the trademark
owner and third parties to be taken into account, it held that these
interests must be something different from merely the full enjoyment of
the legal rights conferred by a trademark, but would rather include the
'owner's interest in the economic value of the mark arising from the
reputation that it enjoys and the quality it denotes'.[11]

The Panel also noted that the formulation in Article 17 to 'take
account' instead of 'do not unreasonably prejudice' legitimate interests,
which is used in Articles 13 and 30, suggested that a lesser standard of
regard for the legitimate interests of the owner of a trademark was
required in the context of trademark exceptions than in the context of
patents or copyright (Box III.3).[12]

---

[11] Panel reports on *EC – Trademarks and Geographical Indications (US)*, para. 7.664, and
(Australia), para. 7.664.

[12] Panel reports on *EC – Trademarks and Geographical Indications (US)*, paras. 7.670–7.671,
and *(Australia)*, paras. 7.670–7.671.

(b) No compulsory licensing permitted

Article 21 of the TRIPS Agreement makes it clear that Members' legislation shall not permit any compulsory licensing of trademarks. This reflects the view that, unlike in the patent area (see Chapter V on Patents), there is no public policy rationale for allowing compulsory licensing in the area of trademark rights and governments may not, therefore, permit the use of a trademark without the authorization of the right holder (Box III.3).

BOX III.3 EC – TRADEMARKS AND GEOGRAPHICAL INDICATIONS[13]
(DS174, DS290)

PARTIES		AGREEMENTS	*TIMELINE OF THE DISPUTE*	
Complainants	United States Australia	TRIPS Articles 3, 4, 16 and 24 GATT Article III:4	Establishment of Panel Circulation of Panel report	2 October 2003 15 March 2005
Respondent	EC		Circulation of Appellate Body report	NA
			Adoption	20 April 2005

1. Measure and product at issue
   - Measure at issue: EC Regulation related to the protection of geographical indications and designations of origin ('GIs').
   - Products at issue: Agricultural products and foodstuffs affected by the EC Regulation.
2. Summary of key Panel findings[14]

---

[13] *European Communities – Protection of Trademarks and Geographical Indications for Agricultural Products and Foodstuffs.*

[14] Other issues addressed in this case: TRIPS Article 1, 2, 4; Paris Convention Article 2, 10; extension of submission deadline; separate Panel Reports; request for information from WIPO; preliminary ruling; Panel request (DSU Article 6.2); terms of reference; evidence; specific suggestions for implementation (DSU 19); order of analysis (GATT and TRIPS).

BOX III.3 *(cont.)*

National treatment *(TRIPS Art. 3.1)*

- Availability of protection: The Panel found that the equivalence and reciprocity conditions in respect of GI protection under the EC Regulation[15] violated the national treatment obligation under TRIPS Art. 3 by according less favourable treatment to non-EC nationals than to EC nationals. By providing 'formally identical', but in fact different procedures based on the location of a GI, the EC modified the 'effective equality of opportunities' between different nationals to the detriment of non-EC nationals. The Regulation was also found to accord less favourable treatment to imported products inconsistently with GATT Art. III:4.
- Application procedures: The Panel found that the application procedures under the Regulation requiring non-EC nationals to file an application in the European Communities through their own government (but not directly with EC Member States) for a GI registration located in their own countries, provided less favourable treatment to other nationals in violation of Art. 3.1. The Regulation was also found to accord less favourable treatment to imported products inconsistently with GATT Art. III:4.
- Objection procedures (verification and transmission): The Panel found that the objection procedures under the Regulation violated Art. 3.1 to the extent that they did not provide persons resident or established in non-EC countries with a right to directly object to applications for a GI registration in the European Communities.
- Inspection structures: The Panel found that the 'government participation' requirement under the inspection structures violated TRIPS Art. 3.1 by providing an 'extra hurdle' to third-country applicants: for a third-country GI to be registered in the European Community, third-country governments were required to provide a declaration that the inspection structures were established on their territories. The Regulation was also found inconsistent with GATT Art. III:4 in respect of these third-country products.

Relationship between GIs and *(prior)* trademarks

- TRIPS Arts. 16.1 and 17 (trademarks): Having found that Art. 16.1 obligates Members to make available to trademark owners a right against certain uses, including uses as a GI, the Panel initially concluded that the EC Regulation was inconsistent with Art. 16.1 as it limited the availability of such a right for the owners of trademarks. However, the Panel ultimately found that the

---

[15] For registration in the European Communities of third-country GIs, third countries were required to adopt a GI protection system equivalent to that in the European Communities and provide reciprocal protection to products from the European Communities.

BOX III.3 (*cont.*)

Regulation was justified under Art. 17, which permits Members to provide limited exceptions to the rights conferred by trademarks, including Art. 16.1 rights, provided that such exceptions take account of the legitimate interests of the owner of the trademark and of third parties.

4 Term of protection

According to Article 18 of the TRIPS Agreement, the initial registration and each renewal of registration shall be for a term of no less than seven years. It also stipulates that the registration of a trademark must be renewable indefinitely. This means that trademark rights, in contrast to copyright or patent rights, can last for an indefinite period of time, provided the right owner renews the registration at the expiry of each term and pays the required renewal fees.

If Members require the actual use of a trademark in order to maintain registration, Article 19 of the TRIPS Agreement provides that cancellation of a trademark may only occur after an uninterrupted period of three years of non-use. This means that even if a country wants to require use of a trademark as a condition for renewal, it must allow for a period of at least three years of uninterrupted non-use before the trademark can be cancelled for that reason.

IV

Geographical indications

A   Introduction

1   General

This chapter explains the provisions of Section 3 of Part II of the TRIPS Agreement entitled 'Geographical Indications'. A geographical indication (GI) is defined in the TRIPS Agreement as an indication which identifies a good as originating in the territory of a Member, or a regional locality in that territory, where a given quality, reputation or other characteristic of the good is essentially attributable to its geographical origin. Typical examples would be 'Cognac' for a brandy coming from that region of France and 'Darjeeling' for tea coming from that region of India.

Like other sections in Part II of the TRIPS Agreement that cover standards of IPRs, Section 3 has to be read together with the relevant provisions of the pre-existing treaties in the area of international intellectual property law which are incorporated by reference into the TRIPS Agreement. In the case of GIs, the relevant treaty is the Paris Convention. Explanations of the provisions of the Paris Convention relevant to GIs are integrated along with explanations of the TRIPS provisions in this chapter.

This chapter also has to be read with other relevant provisions of the TRIPS Agreement that are explained in other chapters, notably those on basic principles, on trademarks, on procedures for the acquisition and maintenance of rights (Article 62) and on enforcement. For example, in respect of GIs, Members have to respect the requirements of national and MFN treatment, in the same way as for other categories of IPRs. A WTO Panel has confirmed that those obligations apply in respect of the availability of GI protection, including application and opposition procedures (see Chapter III).

2   Background

The TRIPS Section on GIs represents a delicate balance that was found in the Uruguay Round between different interests. While the negotiations on some TRIPS issues could, to a large extent, be characterized as a North–South debate, the negotiations on GIs, particularly on wines and spirits, were characterized by what was then described as an 'Old World–New World' debate; that is to say between the 'Old World' countries of Europe and the 'New World' countries of the United States, Australia, Canada, New Zealand, Argentina and Chile and some others. These differences also, to a significant extent, paralleled those between agricultural importers and exporters and links were made with the Uruguay Round negotiations on agriculture.

An additional consideration in the Uruguay Round negotiations, and one that continues to apply today, is the diversity of national systems for the protection of GIs, where there is a considerably lower level of harmonization than, for example, in the areas of patents or trademarks. The rules of the TRIPS Agreement on GIs reflect this diversity and complexity of systems, as seen in the language used in certain provisions of the GI Section. This is illustrated in the WTO Secretariat's summary of Members' responses to a checklist of questions regarding the way they apply the TRIPS provisions on GIs.[1] That document shows how Members' national and regional systems for the protection of GIs include a mixture of laws of general application relating to business practices, in particular against consumer deception and unfair competition, certification or collective mark protection (see Chapter III) under trademark law, and a range of *sui generis* systems (i.e. systems created specifically for a category of IP) dedicated to the protection of GIs.

3 What is the relationship with the pre-existing provisions of the Paris Convention?

As mentioned in the other chapters dealing with industrial property, TRIPS Article 2 incorporates by reference the substantive provisions of the Paris Convention, i.e. Articles 1 to 12 and 19. Article 10 of the Paris Convention deals with seizure or prohibition of importation of goods bearing 'false' indications of source and defines the 'interested parties' entitled, under certain conditions, to request seizure on importation, namely producers, manufacturers, or merchants. Article 10*ter* further extends, under certain conditions, the

---

[1] See WTO document IP/C/W/253/Rev.1.

possibility to take action to federations and associations representing interested producers or traders.

Article 22.2 of the TRIPS Agreement specifically refers to Article 10*bis* of the Paris Convention, which deals with unfair competition. This provision obliges Members to assure effective protection against acts of competition that are contrary to honest practices in industrial or commercial matters.

B   TRIPS provisions on GIs

Section 3 of Part II of the TRIPS Agreement consists of three provisions. Article 22 deals with the definition of GIs and sets out the minimum level of protection to be available for GIs identifying any type of good. Article 22 further deals with the question of trademarks bearing GIs. Article 23 provides for a higher level of protection for GIs identifying wines and spirits. It further sets out additional rules regarding the use of such GIs in or as trademarks and provides for a built-in agenda for the negotiation of a multilateral system of notification and registration of GIs for wines. Article 24 provides, in particular, for certain exceptions allowing continued use of GIs for goods not coming from the place indicated, e.g. when a term has become generic.

1   *What is the subject matter to be protected?*

(a)   TRIPS definition of geographical indications

Article 22.1 of the TRIPS Agreement defines GIs as follows:

> Geographical indications are, for the purposes of this Agreement, indications which identify a good as originating in the territory of a Member, or a region or locality in that territory, where a given quality, reputation or other characteristic of the good is essentially attributable to its geographical origin.

(b)   Elements of the Article 22.1 definition

According to that definition in Article 22.1, a GI:

- is a sign
- used to identify
- a good

- coming from a specific location, which could be:
  - the territory of that country,
  - a region in that territory, or
  - a locality in that territory,
- having:
  - a given quality,
  - reputation, or
  - other characteristics
- that are essentially due to that geographical origin.

(i) **It is a sign** Article 22.1 does not specify which kind of sign should be considered as a GI. Should it be a word or combination of words or could it be another kind of sign, such as an image or a map? In general, geographical names are words or combinations of words. For example, 'Roquefort' for ewe's milk cheese is the name of a place located in a region of France. In certain countries, graphical representations of places, symbols and emblems are accepted as GIs: for example, the image of a famous mountain in Switzerland, the Matterhorn, is, under Swiss law, an 'indirect geographical indication', which identifies that a product comes from Switzerland.

(ii) **Function of identification** Like trademarks, GIs have an identification function. Unlike trademarks, which distinguish the goods of one enterprise from those of another, GIs identify the location from where the good originates. For example, while there are many countries producing tea, 'Darjeeling' identifies tea coming from that region in India and 'Ceylon' (the old name for Sri Lanka), tea coming from Sri Lanka.

(iii) **Subject matter of identification** Article 22.1 is limited to goods. However, it is not limited to any particular kind of goods. Thus all categories could be covered, whether agricultural produce, foodstuffs, handicrafts or industrial products. It is open to each Member to decide which products should benefit from GI protection. As the TRIPS Agreement prescribes a minimum level of protection, Members may go beyond the scope of protection limited to goods and extend protection to GIs for services, e.g. financial services or tourism.

(iv)   The geographical origin identified by the geographical indication
The geographical origin identified by a GI could be the name of the
country ('territory'). It could be the designation as a noun or in its
adjective form. For example, 'Colombia' in Café de Colombia, 'Swiss' in
Swiss Made for watches, identify the country associated with the GI.
The GI could be the name of a region: 'Beaujolais' (for red wine
produced in a region in the eastern part of France), 'Napa Valley' for
wine coming from a region in the US State of California, 'Pinggu
peaches' (for peaches coming from a region in China), or 'Idaho' for
potatoes produced in the US State of Idaho. It could be a more limited
area like a locality, for example a town or a village. Names that are not
geographical names are, in several Members, considered as GIs if they
evoke a geographical location, for example, 'Cava' for sparkling wines
from a region of Spain, 'Vinho Verde' for a Portuguese white wine,
'Fendant' for a white wine from the Canton of Valais in Switzerland, or
'Feta' for a Greek cheese in brine. These examples are not necessarily
considered to be eligible for GI protection in other countries.

**(v)   Quality, reputation, or other characteristics essentially due to the
geographical origin**   An important requirement under the Article 22.1
definition is that the good identified by the GI has a given quality,
reputation or other characteristic that is essentially due to the geographical origin. In other words, there must be a direct linkage between the
place identified by the geographical indication and these features. For
example, olive oil in one part of a country may possess a particularly
high concentration of certain organoleptic elements. It may also be
reputed for being extracted from olives that are carefully pruned and
collected in a net, which helps avoid the fruits being mixed with dust or
dirt, and pressed after a careful sorting of the olive fruits according to
defined practices. Note that, in principle, meeting only one of the three
requirements – quality, reputation or other characteristics – can suffice
for eligibility as a GI (Box IV.1).

**(c)   Geographical indications, indications of source, rules of
origin, appellations of origin and trademarks**

The packaging of a single product may contain a number of designations. To illustrate this, consider two bottles of brandy in a wine store:
one with a label bearing in big characters the word 'Cognac' and, under
that word, 'Maria®'; the other with a label bearing the words 'Cognac'

BOX IV.1 SOME EXAMPLES OF GIS AND LOGOS OR SYMBOLS

In the European Union, the *sui generis* GI system of protection available for agricultural products and foodstuffs provides for two categories of GIs: the 'Protected Designation of Origin' (PDO) and the 'Protected Geographical Indication' (PGI).
Left: PDO symbol (red and yellow).
Right: PGI symbol (blue and yellow)

Swiss 'appellation d'origine contrôlée' (AOC) 'L'Etivaz' with the logo of Swiss AOC.

Mexican geographical indication ('denominación de origen') 'Tequila'; also registered under N° 666 under the WIPO Lisbon Agreement.

French cheese 'Roquefort': French collective mark and AOC symbol; European Union's AOP symbol; and certification mark in the US

Right: French collective mark of ewe's milk producers and of 'Roquefort' producers

BOX IV.1 (*cont.*)

Left: French AOC symbol
AOC (French Institut National de
l'Origine et de la Qualité (INAO));
Right: European
Union's AOP* symbol

Right: 'Roquefort' registered as
certification mark in the United
States (US Reg. No. 571798)

US geographical indication registered
as certification mark in the United
States: 'Idaho' (for potatoes).

'Café de Colombia': 'Denominación
de origen' and certification mark
in Colombia; PGI in the European
Union; certification mark in the
United States and several other
countries (picture on the
right: see symbol ®).

*AOP = The French term for PDO (Protected Designation of Origin) in the EU.

and 'Henry®'. Both labels bear in small characters the words 'Produce of France'. Cognac is a French appellation of origin identifying the geographical region from which the product originates, 'Henry®' and 'Maria®' are individual trademarks identifying the enterprise producing the product, and 'Produce of France' is an indication of source identifying the country or place of origin. The following paragraphs will briefly address the relationship between GIs and other terms.

(i) **Geographical indications and indications of source** 'Made in Switzerland' or 'Produce of Switzerland' are indications of source. Under Swiss law, they are different from 'Swiss Made' for watches, which is defined in a special piece of legislation as a GI as defined by Article 22.1. Indications of source give the consumer the basic information that the good comes from a particular country. Indications of source are not GIs as defined under Article 22.1, unless the good they identify possesses a certain quality, reputation or other characteristics essentially due to the origin indicated. Thus, while 'Swiss Made' is a GI under Swiss national law, 'Made in Switzerland' is an indication of source.

(ii) **Geographical indications and rules of origin** There is often some confusion between GIs and rules of origin. Rules of origin are used for various trade policy purposes, including the application of marking requirements or to implement measures such as tariff preferences or anti-dumping duties. They are not designed to be used for the purpose of assessing eligibility for GI protection.

(iii) **Geographical indications and appellations of origin** Appellations of origin are a special type of GI. The WIPO Lisbon Agreement – which does not form part of the TRIPS Agreement – gives, in Article 2, the following definition:

> (1) 'appellation of origin' means the geographical name of a country, region, or locality, which serves to designate a product originating therein, the quality and characteristics of which are due exclusively or essentially to the geographical environment, including natural and human factors.

> (2) The country of origin is the country whose name, or the country in which is situated the region or locality whose name, constitutes the appellation of origin which has given the product its reputation.

It should be noted that the requirements under Article 2(1) of the Lisbon Agreement appear in many respects similar to those in Article 22.1 of the TRIPS Agreement but in other respects appear stricter.[2] 'Roquefort', 'Tequila' and 'Cognac' are appellations of origin, registered under the Lisbon Agreement.

(iv) **Geographical indications, trademarks and certification marks** While both trademarks and GIs convey information about the source and reputation of goods, they are normally very different in that

---

[2] For additional information, see www.wipo.int/geo_indications/en.

trademarks convey information about the company or undertaking that is responsible for the goods whereas GIs identify their geographical origin (and carry information about the quality, reputation or other characteristics linked to that origin). However certain types of trademarks, known as certification (or guarantee) and collective marks, can be and are used to protect GIs. The above two examples of GIs protected under trademark laws show that 'Roquefort' is also protected in France as a collective mark, and in the United States as a certification mark. To put it simply, both types of marks are different from individual trademarks that identify individual companies in that they can be used by a multiplicity of producers who fulfil the requirements for the use of the mark in question agreed to by those producers. While the right holder of the collective mark can also use it, the right holder of a certification mark, under many laws, cannot do so, and is usually a certification agency whose function is to certify the eligible products.

(d)   Right holders and eligible users

The definition in Article 22.1 does not address the question of who may own the GI or the question of who may use it. This is, in principle, dealt with in domestic laws. In general, producers that are in the region identified by the GI would be the eligible users of that GI. Depending on the system adopted in a Member, the GI may be collectively owned by the producers organized as an entity (e.g. cooperative or association) representing them and ensuring that the product fulfils certain requirements they have agreed upon or adhered to. Under some systems, the GI belongs to the state or the public authority administering the area identified by a GI, and producers in the area are entitled to use the GI provided that, when producing the product in question, they abide by any applicable rules or regulations governing the use of the GI.

2   What are the conditions for getting protection?

Under Article 62.1 of the TRIPS Agreement Members can require compliance with reasonable procedures and formalities as a condition of the acquisition and maintenance of rights in GIs. In practice, as mentioned earlier, Members use a variety of different legal means to protect GIs. Some, such as most laws of general application focusing on deceptive or unfair business practices, are typically available without the need to comply with prior procedures and formalities; whereas others, such as protection under trademark law and under most forms of *sui generis* GI protection, generally require compliance with the formalities and procedures necessary to secure prior recognition of the GI as eligible for protection. In the case of collective or certification marks under trademark law, the rules on the registration and renewal of trademarks apply. In this connection it might be noted that, for nationals of countries participating in WIPO's Madrid Agreement and Madrid Protocol on the international registration of marks,[3] it is possible to obtain an international registration for collective and certification marks providing for protection in a number of countries through a single application. In regard to *sui generis* forms of protection, procedures vary, from the 'automatic' to more or less sophisticated systems of registration with regulations or specifications regarding the production of the products. For example, in Mexico 'Tequila' is a registered 'denominación de origen' with strict rules regarding the production of the spirit and the use of the GI.

3   Protection and rights conferred

(a)   For geographical indications for all goods (Article 22)

(i)   Protection against use by others (Article 22.2)   Under Article 22.2, Members must provide the 'legal means for interested parties' to prevent two types of use of GIs:

- the use of any means in the designation or presentation of a good that indicates or suggests that the good in question originates in a geographical area other than the true place of origin in a manner which misleads the public as to the geographical origin of the good; and
- any use which constitutes an act of unfair competition within the meaning of Article 10*bis* of the Paris Convention:

'Use which misleads the public'

The provision refers to 'any means in the designation or presentation of a good that indicates or suggests' the origin in a way which may mislead the public. This could include, in addition to the use of the word name of the GI for a product that does not come from the area indicated, the presentation of the product using features that may remind the consumer of an origin protected by a GI. Such features could include the colours of the flag or emblem of the country of origin of the GI, or a photograph or drawing of a landscape or statue well known to the public

---

[3] See www.wipo.int/madrid/en/legal_texts/trtdocs_wo015.html for the Madrid Agreement.
  See www.wipo.int/madrid/en/legal_texts/trtdocs_wo016.html for the Madrid Protocol.

as representative of that country of origin. In general, the test in respect of whether such use would mislead the public would be the overall perception that the consumer would have of the product. The assessment of whether a given use would be misleading or not may well vary from one country to another, and from one product to another. For example, the average consumer in India could be expected to be more discerning when looking at labels that relate to rice than the average consumer in Switzerland, and vice versa for cheese.

'Unfair competition'

Article 22.2(b) does not define acts of unfair competition but refers to Article 10*bis* of the Paris Convention. Article 10*bis* of the Paris Convention gives a non-exhaustive list of acts of competition contrary to honest practices in industrial or commercial matters that constitute an act of unfair competition. These are:

- all acts of such a nature as to create confusion by any means whatever with the establishment, the goods, or the industrial or commercial activities, of a competitor;
- false allegations in the course of trade of such a nature as to discredit the establishment, the goods, or the industrial or commercial activities, of a competitor;
- indications or allegations the use of which in the course of trade is liable to mislead the public as to the nature, the manufacturing process, the characteristics, the suitability for their purposes, or the quality, of the goods.

Depending on national law, the use of a GI for goods coming from another geographical area with a view to benefiting from the reputation of that GI, sometimes referred to as 'free riding' on that reputation, may be considered an act of unfair competition.

'Legal means'

It should be noted that Article 22.2 does not specify any particular legal means by which the protection is to be provided, but rather leaves this to each Member. As mentioned earlier there is a considerable diversity in the legal means found in Members.

'Interested parties'

It should also be noted that the TRIPS Agreement states that it is 'interested parties' that are to have the right to invoke these legal means.

The TRIPS Agreement itself does not specify who should be these 'interested parties'. However, as indicated earlier, Articles 10 and 10*ter* of the Paris Convention give a list of persons entitled to take action in respect of false indications of source and acts of unfair competition.

(ii)   **Protection against use as a trademark (Article 22.3)**   This provision relates to a situation different from the one where the GI itself is protected as a certification or collective mark and is used on goods from the area indicated by the GI. This provision deals with the question of the extent to which a person can obtain and maintain a trademark registration incorporating a GI for goods not originating in the area indicated by the GI. For example, to what extent could the French GI 'Roquefort' be employed in a trademark for goods not coming from that area of France?

What the TRIPS Agreement requires is that, if the use of a GI in a trademark with respect to goods not originating in the territory indicated by the GI would be of such a nature as to mislead the public as to the true place of origin of the good, there must be legal means to refuse or invalidate the registration of such a trademark. This means that, if the trademark is still at the application stage, the consequence will be the refusal of the application (this is, in general, done by the trademark office which has received the application). If the trademark has already been registered, the consequence will be invalidation of the registered mark (depending on the system of the Member concerned, invalidation can be pronounced by the trademark office or by a court).

This action is to be taken *ex officio*, i.e. by the competent public authority on its own initiative, if so provided in the law of the country concerned, or upon request by any interested party, for example the importer of the product protected by the GI or, if so provided in the law of the country concerned, an association of consumers.

(iii)   **Factually true but misleading use (Article 22.4)**   This provision addresses the situation where there are geographical names that are identical in respect of spelling or pronunciation (that is, 'homonyms'), but designate different geographical areas, within a country or in different countries. For example, it could be the case that the true place name is correctly identified on a product, but could mislead the consumer into thinking that the product comes from a much better-known place bearing the same name.

For example, the name 'Moillesulaz' exists both in France and in Switzerland. In the latter, there is a commune called 'Moillesulaz' in the Canton of Geneva; there are also many places bearing the same name in France. Supposing that one of the French places has developed a famous sausage protected by a GI 'Moillesulaz', the question would be to what extent could producers of processed meat located in the Geneva commune of 'Moillesulaz' use that name as a GI for marketing their products. What the rule in Article 22.4 says is that, even if the use of such a GI is literally true as to the origin of the goods, the rights under Articles 22.2 and 22.3 to prevent such use by producers in Moillesulaz, Geneva must be applicable if that use would falsely represent to the public that the sausage originates in the reputed French place 'Moillesulaz'.

(b)   Additional protection for geographical indications for wines and spirits (Article 23)

In the Uruguay Round, another issue at stake was whether or not the protection afforded under the future Article 22 would be sufficient. At that time, a higher level of protection of GIs – termed 'additional' or 'absolute' – protection was available in certain countries, either by virtue of domestic laws and systems, or under bilateral or plurilateral agreements. In those countries, the protection granted to GIs for all products or to a specific category of products was higher in the sense that only producers coming from the geographical area identified by a GI could use that GI and enjoy protection against any other producer that did not come from that geographical area and used the GI with, for example, an indication that it came from the locality where that other producer was situated. This 'higher' level of protection existed, for example, in the United States under a labelling – and classification – system of names for wines, administered by the US Bureau of Alcohol, Tobacco and Firearms (BATF), and in the European Communities under a set of regulations dealing with wine production requirements and GIs. This convergence of factors facilitated the agreement between these two major players in the Uruguay Round on a special provision on GIs for wines and spirits.

Article 23 requires Members to make available additional protection, compared to Article 22, for GIs for wines and spirits. The main difference between these two levels of protection is that, under Article 23, an interested party must have the legal means to prevent the use of a GI for a wine on a wine which does not come from the geographical area indicated irrespective of whether or not such use misleads the public or constitutes unfair competition. The same goes for spirits. Thus, Article 23 is often referred to as an 'absolute' form of protection since no such tests have to be satisfied in order to exercise it. However, it should be noted that the 'absoluteness' of the protection is significantly tempered by the important exceptions contained in Article 24, which are addressed below.

(i) **Protection against use by others (Article 23.1)** Under Article 23.1, Members have to provide interested parties with the legal means to prevent use of a GI identifying wines for wines not originating from the place indicated by the GI or identifying spirits for spirits not originating from the place indicated by the GI. It is made clear that this has to be possible even where:

- the true origin of the goods is indicated (i.e. there is not necessarily any confusion on this point);
- the GI is used in translation; or
- the use of the GI is accompanied by expressions such as: 'type', 'kind', 'style', 'imitation', or the like.

It should be noted that Article 23.1 uses the same wording as Article 22.2 in stating that the obligation is to provide the 'legal means for interested parties to prevent...'. The observations made under Article 22.2 regarding this language are thus equally relevant here. Some delegations to the WTO have recently referred to the test of 'correctness' or 'correct use' when referring to an Article 23 level of protection, i.e. a term used is exactly the one identifying the true place of origin, as opposed to the misleading test under Article 22.

It should also be noted that a footnote to Article 23 stipulates that, notwithstanding the first sentence of Article 42, Members may, with respect to these obligations, instead provide for enforcement by administrative action. As an exception to the normal requirement in the enforcement chapter of the TRIPS Agreement that civil judicial procedures must be available for the enforcement of any IPR, Members may instead provide for enforcement by administrative action in this particular case. Thus countries which have administrative systems for the enforcement of the protection of GIs which otherwise meet the requirements of the TRIPS enforcement rules – for example, through labelling laws – are not obliged to introduce judicial enforcement mechanisms.

(ii)   **Protection against use as a trademark (Article 23.2)**   Article 23.2 deals with the rights that have to be available to an interested party in a GI for a wine or a spirit to prevent the registration of a trademark containing or consisting of that GI with respect to goods not originating in the territory indicated. These rights are similar to those that have to be available under Article 22.3 in respect of all GIs, except that they apply irrespective of whether or not the use of the indication in the trademark would be of such a nature as to mislead the public as to the true place of origin.

For example, suppose that an application for the registration as a trademark is made for a spirit called 'Tequila Paradise Delight', which does not come from Mexico. The trademark office has, as a general rule, to reject the application, either if the law so permits or upon request of an interested party. There is no need for the owner of the GI 'Tequila' to demonstrate that the use in the trademark is misleading.

(iii)   **Homonymous geographical indications for wines (Article 23.3)**   Homonymous GIs, i.e. where two wine producing regions have the same name or the same-sounding name (termed 'homonyms'), are not unknown. One prominent example, which was much referred to in the negotiation of this provision, is 'Rioja', a name identifying wines coming from important wine producing regions in both Spain and Argentina. In this kind of situation, Article 23.3 provides for coexistence of the homonymous GIs, subject to Article 22.4 (i.e. provided there is no false representation to the public that a wine from a place identified by one of the GIs comes from the place identified by the other GI). In providing for such coexistence each Member is required to determine the practical conditions to differentiate the GIs from each other, e.g. by way of labelling or the representation of a map showing the country where the region is. Differentiation should be done in a manner that ensures equitable treatment of the producers concerned and that consumers are not misled.

(iv)   **Negotiation of a multilateral register of geographical indications for wines (Article 23.4)**   Article 23.4 calls upon the Council for TRIPS to negotiate a multilateral system of notification and registration of GIs for wines, eligible for protection in those Members participating in the system, with a view to facilitating the protection of GIs for wines. This built-in mandate is limited to wines. It was extended by the Doha

Ministerial Declaration in 2001 to also cover spirits, confirming a decision taken at the 1996 Singapore Ministerial Conference. Currently, the negotiation of the system is taking place in a negotiating group of the Doha Round, which takes the form of Special Sessions of the Council for TRIPS. For further information on these negotiations, please see Chapter X.

4   Exceptions and international negotiations

The obligations to protect GIs in the TRIPS Agreement, especially the additional protection for GIs for wines and spirits, were only acceptable to many Members under the condition that some important exceptions be provided for, notably to cover pre-existing uses in their countries of the GIs of other countries that would be brought under protection. However the main *demandeurs* in the negotiations on GIs were not prepared to provide such exceptions, to 'grandfather' pre-existing uses, without any possibility of obtaining full rights over their GIs at some stage in the future. Thus Article 24 deals both with exceptions and with the possibility for negotiations about the continued use of those exceptions.

(a)   Exceptions

(i)   Generic terms (Article 24.6)   This provision indicates that the TRIPS rules on GIs do not require a Member to protect a GI of another Member if that indication is 'identical with the term customary in common language as the common name' for the goods or services in question in that Member, i.e. has become the generic term for describing the goods or services in the local language. An example would be 'cheddar' for cheese. This type of cheese is named after a village in south-west England, but has lost its association with that place and become, in England and many other countries, the name for a type of cheese.

The provision contains a special exception concerning GIs of other Members with respect to products of the vine where the indication in question is identical with the customary name of a grape variety. In such cases Members are not required to apply the TRIPS rules on GIs if the indication was already used in this way prior to the beginning of 1995 when the TRIPS and WTO Agreements came into force. Examples of grape varieties that might be covered include 'Chardonnay', 'Merlot', 'Syrah', 'Cabernet', 'Cabernet Sauvignon', and 'Gamay'. It may be noted that this provision refers to 'products of the vine' and not 'wines'. The scope is therefore wider; it can cover, for example, spirits obtained from products of the vine.

(ii)   Prior trademark rights (Article 24.5)   This exception concerns trademarks that have been applied for or registered in good faith or where rights to a trademark have been acquired through use in good faith. For the exception to apply, this has to have been done either before the date of application of the TRIPS Agreement in the Member concerned (i.e. at the end of any relevant transition period) or before the date that the GI became protected in its country of origin. In these circumstances Members are under an obligation to ensure that, in implementing the TRIPS rules on GIs, they do not prejudice the prior trademark rights in question on the basis that the trademark is identical with or similar to a GI. In other words, the eligibility for, or the validity of, the registration of the trademark or the right to use the trademark must not be impaired. It should be noted that, unlike most of the other exceptions provided for in Article 24, this one puts an obligation on Members to provide the exception and is not merely permissive. With respect to the issue of the relationship between prior trademarks and GIs, see also the *EC – Trademarks and Geographical Indications* cases (DS174, DS290) discussed in Chapter III.

(iii)   Prior use of the geographical indication (Article 24.4)   This provision relates to the prior use of a GI, and is mainly relevant to situations where there has been prior use of a GI that is not covered by the exceptions in relation to generic terms and prior trademark rights. Its scope is limited to GIs for wines and spirits. It is optional in the sense that it allows, but does not oblige, a Member to permit the continuation of the forms of prior use covered by the provision.

For prior use of a GI in that Member to be covered by the exception, it must be:

- continued and similar use
- of a particular GI (of another Member) identifying a wine or a spirit
- in connection with goods or services
- by nationals or domiciliaries of that Member
- who have used that GI in a continuous manner
- with regard to the same or related goods or services
- in the territory of that Member,

- either for at least ten years preceding 15 April 1994 (the date of signature of the TRIPS and WTO Agreements), or
- for any period before that date, provided the use has been in good faith.

The 'similar' use that can be continued is understood by at least some Members to require that the use be similar in respect of both scale and nature.

(iv)   Time limit to challenge trademarks under Article 22.3 and Article 23.2 (Article 24.7)   As indicated in the previous paragraphs on Articles 22.3 and 23.2, these provisions provide that a trademark consisting of, or containing, a GI may be challenged. Article 24.7 allows a Member to provide a time limit of five years for such actions, counting from:

- the time the adverse use of the protected GI became generally known in that Member or
- the date of registration of the trademark in that Member if the trademark has been published by that date, if that date is earlier than the date on which the adverse use became generally known in that Member,
- provided that the GI is not used or registered in bad faith.

(v)   Use by a person of his name (Article 24.8)   This paragraph covers the situation where a person has been using 'in the course of trade' his or her personal name (or predecessor's name) that is the same as a GI. This provision, which is mandatory for Members, requires such persons to be able to continue this use provided it would not mislead the public.

(vi)   GIs not protected in their country of origin or which have fallen into disuse in their country (Article 24.9)   No Member is required to protect on its territory another Member's GI:

- if that geographical name is not protected as a GI in that other Member (called in the provision the 'country of origin');
- if the geographical name, which was protected as a GI, ceases to be protected as a GI in the country of origin; or
- if the GI has fallen into disuse in the country of origin.

It should be noted that the possibility for a Member not to protect such GIs is optional. It does not prevent a country from protecting such GIs if it so wishes.

(b)   International negotiations, review and standstill

(i)   **International negotiations (Article 24.1)**   In Article 24.1 Members have agreed in advance to their readiness to enter into negotiations aimed at increasing the protection of individual GIs under Article 23, which concerns wines and spirits. They have further agreed that they will not use the exceptions provisions in paragraphs 4–8 of Article 24 to refuse to conduct such negotiations or to conclude bilateral or multilateral agreements. They have also agreed that in such negotiations they will be willing to consider the continued applicability of these exceptions to individual GIs whose use is the subject of such negotiations. In other words, Member A, which has a certain term protected as a GI in its territory may, in the context of bilateral negotiations with Member B, request the latter to cease permitting the use of that term as a generic and, hence protect it as a GI in its territory ('roll-back' or 'claw-back'). Member B may, of course, counter such a request if it desires to permit the generic use to continue in its territory.

Article 24.2 provides for the Council for TRIPS to keep under review the application of the TRIPS rules on GIs. Extensive work has been done in the Council for TRIPS pursuant to this requirement, including responses by many Members to a questionnaire about their national systems for the protection of GIs and a summary of these responses prepared by the Secretariat. Further information on this review can be found in Chapter X and Appendix 1.

The second and third sentences of Article 24.2 relate to interventions of the Council for TRIPS regarding any issues about compliance with the TRIPS provisions on GIs: at the request of a Member, the Council shall consult the Member or Members concerned if it has not been possible to find a satisfactory solution through bilateral or plurilateral consultations. So far, there has not been any action of this kind by the TRIPS Council.

(ii)   **Standstill (Article 24.3)**   This provision requires each Member, in implementing the TRIPS provisions, not to diminish the level of protection of GIs that existed in that Member immediately prior to the date of entry into force of the WTO Agreement, i.e. 1 January 1995.

V

Patents

A Introduction

This chapter explains the provisions of Section 5 of Part II of the TRIPS Agreement entitled 'Patents'. Section 5, which contains eight articles, from Article 27 to Article 34, sets out the obligations of Members with respect to standards concerning the availability, scope and use of patents. Starting with a general explanation of terms, this chapter goes on to explain each specific provision in this Section of the TRIPS Agreement.

1 What are patents?

The term 'patent' is not specifically defined in the TRIPS Agreement. A patent is the title given to the IPR that is granted to protect new inventions. A patent, which is granted by the authorities in a specified jurisdiction, gives its owner an exclusive right to prevent others from exploiting the patented invention in that jurisdiction for a limited period of time without his or her authorization, subject to a number of exceptions.

The term 'invention' is not defined in the TRIPS Agreement. One informal definition (used, for example, in some WIPO capacity building materials) characterizes an invention as a new solution to a technical problem. Other approaches to defining 'invention' can also be found in national laws. Many national laws exclude such material as scientific theories, aesthetic creations, schemes, and rules and methods for performing mental acts. These activities do not aim at any direct technical result but are rather of an abstract and intellectual character.

Unlike copyright, where protection does not require meeting with prior formalities, a patent is not automatically available for eligible inventions. In order to get a patent, an inventor or other eligible person has to file an application for each jurisdiction in which he or she wants protection and meet certain substantive and formal requirements. Patents in each jurisdiction are independent of each other i.e. the application, grant or cancellation of a patent in one jurisdiction does not have an automatic effect for the same invention in any other jurisdiction (Article 4*bis* of the Paris Convention).

The social purpose of patent protection is to aim to provide an incentive for technological change, and in particular for further investment into research and development ('R&D') in order to make new inventions. As a condition of obtaining protection, patent applicants must disclose certain details of the invention covered in the application for protection. This would, for example, help others to study the invention and thus build on the technology contained in it. The patent system thus aims to contribute to the promotion of technological innovation and to the transfer and dissemination of technology (as set out in Article 7 of the TRIPS Agreement). However, as mentioned above, the patent system also enables the patent owner to limit the extent to which others can use the patented invention during its term of protection. Thus, it is vital to find in the patent system a proper balance between these considerations. Such a balance can be found, *inter alia*, through appropriate ways of defining and structuring commercial relationships and other mechanisms for the development, transfer and dissemination of technology, including various approaches to licensing and R&D contracts.

2   What is the relationship with the pre-existing provisions of the Paris Convention?

As seen in Chapter I, the main provisions of the Paris Convention (Articles 1 to 12 and 19), which is the relevant pre-existing treaty in the case of patents, are incorporated into the TRIPS Agreement by reference.

The Paris Convention refers to patents as an object of the protection of industrial property (Article 1.2). It contains a number of other important provisions, details of which are provided below. However, the Paris Convention is silent on some important issues relating to what subject matter has to be patentable, the scope of patent rights and their duration.

B TRIPS provisions on patents

The patent provisions of the TRIPS Agreement have to be read along with other parts of the Agreement, including the transitional arrangements given in Part VI of the TRIPS Agreement, which are explained in Chapter I. This Section attempts to strike the aforementioned balance between the long-term objective of providing incentives for future inventions, and the short-term cost of restricting access to existing inventions.

Also of importance are the provisions in Article 70 which cover the extent to which Members are required to apply the new rules of IP to protect subject matter existing at the time they come under an obligation to apply the TRIPS Agreement. See the discussion on Article 70 in Chapter I.

1 What is the subject matter to be protected by patents?

Each IPR covered by the TRIPS Agreement relates to a different kind of subject matter. As explained in the introductory section above, in the case of patents the subject matter of protection is an invention. In order to answer the question posed above, the TRIPS Agreement has provisions on:

(1) the areas in which inventions must be eligible for protection;
(2) the substantive conditions and formal requirements to be met in order for these inventions to be protected; and
(3) the inventions which may be excluded from patent grant, even when they meet the general conditions of eligibility.

These issues will be dealt with below in turn.

(a) In which areas must inventions be eligible for protection?

TRIPS Article 27.1 obliges Members to make patents available[1] for inventions:

- whether products or processes
- in all fields of technology without discrimination (subject to optional exclusions set out in paragraphs 2 and 3 of Article 27 as explained further below).

---

[1] Since, as explained earlier, patent protection is not automatically granted but accorded to applicants that meet some substantive and formal conditions, the TRIPS provisions that are set out below are couched in terms of the patent protection that is to be made 'available'.

This means that those interested in obtaining a patent for their invention must have the legal means to do so in every Member's jurisdiction irrespective of whether the invention is a product or a process (for example, whether it is a toothpaste with a new formulation or a new process for making the toothpaste) and irrespective of the field of technology (for example, whether it pertains to chemistry or mechanical engineering). Thus, Members cannot exclude from patenting classes of inventions, for example those pertaining to the field of medical technologies, unless there is a specific exclusion allowed under the TRIPS Agreement (see below).

(b) What conditions must inventions meet to be eligible for patent protection?

There are two types of conditions on patent applicants under the TRIPS Agreement:

- substantive conditions linked with the nature of the invention to be protected; and
- formal conditions linked with the fulfilment of certain formalities in the patent grant process.

Article 27.1 of the TRIPS Agreement states, *inter alia*, that 'patents shall be available for any inventions, . . . provided that they are new, involve an inventive step and are capable of industrial application'. These three substantive conditions are recognized as the basic tests of patentability, namely novelty, inventive step and industrial applicability, which were already present in some form in many countries' laws prior to the TRIPS Agreement. In addition to these three tests of patentability, there is one other condition that is considered to be substantive, namely that of disclosure of the invention.

(i) Novelty, inventive step and industrial applicability
Novelty   To be eligible for patent protection, the invention must be 'new'. The term 'new' is not defined in the TRIPS Agreement but the concept is understood in many jurisdictions to mean that the claimed invention shows a new characteristic which has not already been disclosed to the public before the relevant date in the body of existing knowledge in its technical field (called 'prior art' or 'state of the art'). In other words, the invention must not have been disclosed to the public through having been made, carried out or used before. The ingredients of an invention may not all be new, but the way of applying them must

not have been made public before: for example, a new type of electrical battery that uses materials not previously used for this purpose may be considered as a novel invention. This criterion of 'novelty' is generally understood to safeguard against patenting of technologies that are already available to the public, to ensure that a patented invention is a genuine contribution to existing knowledge.

Inventive step   To be eligible for patent protection, in addition to being new, the invention must involve an inventive step. There is no definition of this term in the TRIPS Agreement except that the TRIPS Agreement says in footnote 5 that 'inventive step' may be deemed by a Member to be synonymous with the term 'non-obvious'. This requirement is understood in many jurisdictions to mean that the invention must represent a sufficient advance in relation to the state of the art, i.e. an advance from what has been used or described before, such that it could not be obvious to a person working in the technical field related to the invention with 'ordinary skill' or average knowledge. Sometimes, this is also described as an 'unexpected' or 'surprising' effect that is not evident to the average person familiar with that area of technology.

For example, a new type of washing machine is invented that includes a particular type of motor coupled to a particular type of pump. For the inventive step to be denied, it is necessary that not only the combination, but also the choice of the combined elements, is obvious. It is the sum of the differences that have been discovered which must be compared with the prior art and judged as to obviousness, and not each of the new elements taken individually, except where there is no technical link between them. (Taken from www.wipo.int/export/sites/www/about-ip/en/iprm/pdf/ch2.pdf.)

This criterion of 'inventive step' or 'non-obviousness' is generally understood to safeguard against patents being granted for inventions which – while strictly new in the sense of not having been disclosed before – only represent a trivial or routine advance on existing knowledge, reserving patents for inventions that represent a clear and non-obvious advance on the state of the art.

Industrial applicability   To be eligible for protection, the invention must also be capable of industrial application. There is no further definition of this term except that the TRIPS Agreement says that 'capable of industrial application' may be deemed by a Member to be synonymous with the term 'useful'. In some countries this is also termed 'utility'. This requirement is interpreted in many jurisdictions to mean that the invention has to be susceptible of practical use in some way in any kind of industry, including agriculture.

Activities that do not aim at any direct technical result but are rather of an abstract and intellectual character are generally excluded from patent grant. This criterion of 'industrial applicability' or 'utility' is generally viewed as reserving patents for technologies that actually achieve a practical purpose, and do not represent a mere abstract theory or speculative notion. For more details, see www.wipo.int/export/sites/www/about-ip/en/iprm/pdf/ch2.pdf.

Priority   A patent is often assessed as to whether the claimed invention is new and involves an inventive step, including whether it has been anticipated by an earlier patent application, long after the original patent application was filed. Generally, the novelty or inventive step of the claims is assessed against the existing technology not at the time of this examination, but rather as of the date of filing of the original patent. In this regard, Article 4 of the Paris Convention, as incorporated in the TRIPS Agreement, provides for a right of priority to benefit applicants from Members who file patent applications abroad after an initial original filing. This right ensures that on the basis of a regular first application filed in any Member, the applicant may, within a period of twelve months, apply for protection in any of the other Members. These later applications will be regarded, including for purposes of determining whether the inventions are patentable, as if they had been filed on the same day as the first application. That is to say that that priority date will be used for the purpose of determining the relevant body of prior art. For further information, see www.wipo.int/export/sites/www/about-ip/en/iprm/pdf/ch2.pdf.

(ii)   **Disclosure**   Article 29 of the TRIPS Agreement requires Members to oblige patent applicants to disclose the invention in a manner sufficiently clear and complete for the invention to be carried out by a person skilled in the art. This is held to mean in many national legislations that a person of ordinary knowledge or skills in the technical field to which the invention pertains must be able, from the information disclosed, to understand how to carry out the invention, for example how to make the product or use the process. Sometimes this is called the 'teaching' or 'enabling' function of the patent document. Patent authorities may additionally require the applicant to indicate the best mode for carrying out the invention known to the inventor at the filing date or, where priority is claimed, at the priority date of the application (Article 29.1). Thus, if there are several ways in which the invention may be put into practice, the applicant can be required to disclose that which is most practicable. The 'best mode' requirement is optional, i.e. Members have the choice of deciding whether or not to impose it on patent applicants.

The disclosure requirement is generally viewed as forming part of a contract between the patent holder and society at large where a period of exclusive rights is granted to a patent holder on the basis of a transfer of the knowledge about the invention to the public. This has long been the policy function of the patent system and indeed lies behind the very word 'patent', which means 'laid open'.

Formal conditions   As seen in Chapter I, Part IV of the TRIPS Agreement contains some general rules concerning acquisition and maintenance of IPRs. Article 62 permits Members to impose reasonable procedures and formalities as a condition for granting a patent, such as requiring application forms to be filled and fees to be paid before a patent is granted. Thus, as mentioned before, patent protection is not automatic but made available to applications that meet the applicable formal and substantive requirements.

It might also be noted that under Article 12 of the Paris Convention, as incorporated into the TRIPS Agreement, each Member must maintain a special industrial property service and a central office for the communication to the public of, *inter alia*, patents.

Non-discrimination   Article 27.1 of the TRIPS Agreement also lays down certain rules of non-discrimination with respect to the availability and enjoyment of patent rights. Article 27.1 requires that patents be available and patent rights enjoyable without discrimination as to (a) the place of invention, (b) the field of technology and (c) whether products are imported or locally produced.[2]

Here are three examples to illustrate the three types of non-discrimination required with respect to the grant of patents:

---

[2] The principal obligations on non-discrimination with respect to all IPRs, namely national treatment and MFN treatment are found in Articles 3 and 4, as was discussed in Chapter I. These provisions relate to the nationalities of the persons involved unlike the non-discrimination clause in Article 27.1 which prevents discrimination on other bases.

(a) The place of invention A Member cannot impose a different practice with respect to the relevant date for determining prior art based on whether the invention was made in that or another country.

(b) The field of technology Members cannot grant less favourable treatment according to class of technology.

(c) Whether products are imported or locally produced Members cannot exclude an invention from patent grant on the ground that the patented product is produced in another Member country and imported.

(iii) What are the permissible exclusions from patentable subject matter? The TRIPS Agreement permits Members to exclude inventions from being granted a patent even where they would meet the substantive and formal conditions outlined above. This can be done on three grounds, explained below.

Ordre public or morality Article 27.2 permits Members the option of excluding from patent availability inventions that are considered to be contrary to *ordre public* or morality. '*Ordre public*' is a French term. It is literally translated into English as 'public order' but the French term was preferred because it was felt by some to have a more precise meaning; even so this term is not defined in the TRIPS Agreement. However, it has been understood to represent ideas such as the general security and core values of society.

Article 27.2 specifically mentions inventions contrary to human, animal or plant life or health or seriously prejudicial to the environment. The use of the exception is subject to the condition that the commercial exploitation of the invention must be prevented and this prevention must be necessary for the protection of *ordre public* or morality. This provision prohibits Members from excluding from patentability product or process inventions merely because their exploitation is prohibited by law. This makes it clear that inventions cannot be excluded from patentability merely because, for example, they have not yet received marketing approval from health regulatory authorities under the law. Article 4*quater* of the Paris Convention, as incorporated into the TRIPS Agreement, also prevents a Member from refusing the grant of a patent or invalidating a patent on the ground that the sale of the patented product or of a product obtained by means of a patented process is subject to restrictions or limitations resulting from domestic law.

An example of inventions contrary to *ordre public* could be an invention which meets the conditions for patent grant, and is a device whose explicit and only use is to ensure that radars that control speed limits on highways are de-activated. A Member may be able to justify its exclusion on the grounds that this invention is intended to disrupt *ordre public*. However, a Member cannot exclude the invention from patentability on this ground and then allow the sale or other commercial exploitation of this device. An example on inventions contrary to morality could be processes for the cloning of human beings or for modifying the germ line identity of humans.

Methods of treatment   Under Article 27.3(a) of the TRIPS Agreement a second optional exclusion to a patent grant allows Members to exclude from patentability (1) diagnostic, (2) therapeutic and (3) surgical methods for the treatment of humans or animals. In some Members' jurisdictions that follow the patentability criterion of industrial applicability, these methods are, in any event, considered to be not susceptible of industrial application.

In their legislation, Members have generally understood that this permissible exclusion from patentability applies to methods for the treatment of humans or animals, not to medical or veterinary products, including devices, substances and compositions, for use in any of these methods. Under this approach, while a new and inventive way of removing a cataract from the eye may be excluded from patent protection, an instrument invented to perform this new surgical method would not be so excluded.

Plants and animals   The third optional exclusion from patentability allowed under the TRIPS Agreement is given under Article 27.3(b). Members are not required to provide patent protection for inventions of (1) plants and animals and (2) essentially biological processes for their production. They are, however, required to provide patent protection for (1) micro-organisms and (2) non-biological and microbiological processes for the production of plants and animals. Where Members do not provide patent protection for new plant varieties, they are required to protect plant varieties through an effective *sui generis* system (i.e. a system created specially for this purpose). Members also have the option of using a combination of both systems of protection, namely patents and a *sui generis* system. There is no further explicit guidance in the TRIPS Agreement as to what is to be considered an effective *sui generis* system.

The main *sui generis* system for the protection of plant varieties at the international level is that contained in the convention establishing the International Union for the Protection of New Plant Varieties (the UPOV Convention). UPOV has been specifically adapted for the process of plant breeding and has been developed with the aim of encouraging breeders to develop new varieties of plants. The UPOV system of plant variety protection came into being in 1961. For more details see www.upov. int. Many WTO Members have chosen to meet their TRIPS obligations in this area by joining UPOV upon adopting systems based on it. However, it is generally understood that there are other ways in which the TRIPS option of 'effective *sui generis* system' can be met and there is no presumption that Members must join UPOV to comply with this provision.

(iv)   **Review of Article 27.3(b)**   Article 27.3(b) provides for the provision to be reviewed four years after the entry into force of the WTO Agreement.

The TRIPS Council accordingly began a review of Article 27.3(b) in 1999. The Council initiated the review through an information gathering exercise. It invited Members that were already under an obligation to apply Article 27.3(b) to respond to questions prepared by the WTO Secretariat and several Members in order to provide information on how the matters addressed in this provision were treated in their national laws. Up to the end of 2002, the Council had received information from twenty-four Members, and compiled all the information in the form of a structured summary in document IP/C/W/273/Rev.1. This document contains tables that illustrate how these Members had implemented the obligations in Article 27.3(b).

In the review, Members have discussed two general issues relating to the provisions of Article 27.3(b): (1) the extent to which patent protection should be available for plant and animal inventions and (2) what is the nature of an effective *sui generis* system for plant varieties. The WTO Secretariat has prepared a summary of the points made and issues discussed under the review of Article 27.3(b) which is available in IP/C/W/369/Rev.1.

(v)   **Relationship between the TRIPS Agreement and the Convention on Biological Diversity (CBD) and the protection of traditional knowledge and folklore**   The work on these matters was formalized in the 2001 Doha Declaration which mandated the TRIPS Council to work on them.

Work in the WTO on these issues, especially on the relationship between the TRIPS Agreement and the CBD, has also been undertaken pursuant to the provisions of the Doha Ministerial Declaration on the so-called 'outstanding implementation issues' identified by developing countries.

The WTO Secretariat has prepared two summary notes of the points made and issues discussed: (1) on the relationship between the TRIPS Agreement and the CBD available in IP/C/W/368/Rev.1 and (2) on the protection of traditional knowledge and folklore in IP/C/W/370/Rev.1. The subject is further discussed in Chapter X.

2   What are the rights to be conferred on patent owners?

The TRIPS Agreement recognizes two types of patents: product patents and process patents.

(a)   What are the rights to be conferred on owners of product patents?

Article 28.1(a) says that, where the subject matter of a patent is a product, the patent owner shall have the right to prevent others from the acts of: making, using, offering for sale, selling, or importing[3] for these purposes that product. It should be noted that a patent holder's rights are essentially rights to exclude others from doing certain acts. A patent, by itself, does not give its owner the right to make, use, sell, or import the patented invention, as such acts could be governed by other laws. For example, the patent owner of an invention that is a pesticide has the right to exclude others from exploiting his invention without his authorization in a territory where he has a patent, but may still not be able to make or sell his invention in that jurisdiction without marketing approval from the relevant regulatory authority.

(b)   What are the rights to be conferred on owners of process patents?

(i)   Rights of process patent owners   Article 28.1(b) states that where the subject matter of a patent is a process, the patent owner must be conferred the exclusive rights to prevent others from the act of using the

---

[3]   The word 'importing' in Article 28.1(a) has a footnote cross-referencing Article 6 of the TRIPS Agreement on exhaustion, making it clear that the extent to which this right can be exercised against parallel imports is subject to Article 6. (See the discussion in Chapter 1, section B2.)

process, and from the acts of: using, offering for sale, selling, or importing for these purposes at least the product obtained directly[4] by that process. For example, a patented process is being used outside Member A's jurisdiction where the patent has been obtained and the resulting product is being imported into this territory. The patent owner has the right to prevent the importation from Member B's jurisdiction and the sale of the product in Member A if it has been directly obtained by using the patented process.

(ii) Burden of proof There is a specific provision in the TRIPS Section 5 on patents that deals with civil proceedings in respect of infringement of process patent rights, such as when a patent holder takes a court action against a competitor with the claim that their patent is being infringed. Generally, it is up to the patent holder to show that the defending party is infringing their patent. However, Article 34 states that, if the subject matter of a patent is a process for obtaining a product, courts shall have the authority, in at least one of the circumstances (given below), to reverse the burden of proof, i.e. to order the defendant to prove that he did not use the patented process. That is, in these circumstances, the court must be able to find that the patent was infringed unless the defendant proves that the product was obtained by some other process and not by the patented process.

Members must provide in their legislation that this reversal of the burden of proof applies in at least one of the following circumstances:

- Option (a): The product obtained by the patented process is new; or
- Option (b): If there is substantial likelihood that the identical product was made by the patented process and the patent owner has been unable to determine what process is in fact being used.

For example, suppose a patent has been granted in a Member for an invention of a more efficient process for producing a chemical that is already on the market. If that Member follows option (a) in Article 34.1 and its courts have the authority to reverse the burden of proof only if the product obtained by the patented process is new, then those courts dealing with a complaint of infringement of the process

---

[4] 'Directly' in this context has been generally understood to mean 'immediately' or 'without further transformation or modification'. The term 'at least' is used to denote that this is a minimum standard and Members are free to go beyond this.

patent would not have the authority to do so in this case, since the product obtained by that process is not new.

If, however, the legislation gives courts the authority to reverse the burden of proof in the circumstance identified in option (b) of Article 34.1, then the court would still have the authority to put the burden on the alleged infringer to prove that a different process was used if the court considers that there is a substantial likelihood that the product was made by the patented process and also considers that the patent owner has been unable through reasonable efforts to determine the process actually used.

(c)   Non-discrimination with respect to enjoyment of patent rights

Under Article 27.1, Members are not to discriminate with respect to the enjoyment of patent rights on the basis of (a) the place of invention, (b) field of technology and (c) whether products are imported or locally produced. Here are some examples to illustrate what this may mean:

(i)   **The place of invention**   For example, Members are not to discriminate by circumscribing the rights conferred for inventions made outside their jurisdiction.

(ii)   **The field of technology**   For example, Members are not to discriminate by providing special rights only for inventions in certain technological classes.

(iii)   **Whether products are imported or locally produced**   This last provision was a compromise outcome in the TRIPS negotiations to a debate on whether exploitation of a patent through importing the patented product rather than through local production should be admissible as a ground for compulsory licences. The interpretation of the provision has not been addressed in any written opinion delivered in WTO dispute settlements. It was, however, at issue in one dispute settlement case. The United States lodged a complaint against, *inter alia*, a provision in Brazil's patent law stating that a patent shall be subject to compulsory licensing if the patented product is not fully manufactured or the patented process not fully used in Brazil. A mutually agreed settlement was reached between Brazil and the United States (WT/DS/199/4) but this did not settle the substance of their differences on this point.

We have some guidance from the *Canada – Pharmaceutical Patents* case (DS114), explained below, as to how to determine whether or not there has, in fact, been discrimination with respect to field of technology.

(d)   What other rights do patent owners have?

Under Article 28.2, both product and process patent owners shall also have the right to assign, or transfer by succession, the patent and to conclude licensing contracts.

Thus, the owner of a patented invention can assign, i.e. transfer his ownership of the patent (for example through a sale) or transfer it by succession (for example, by inheritance) or license the right to use the patented invention to any other person. Such other person may then, depending on the terms of the assignment, transfer or licence, have the same rights as the original patent owner.

3   What are the permissible exceptions to patent rights?

Other than the question of exhaustion of IPRs dealt with in Chapter I, there are two types of permissible exceptions to the exclusive rights conferred on patent owners: (1) limited exceptions and (2) compulsory licences. These are explained in detail below.

(a)   Limited exceptions

Article 30 recognizes that Members may allow limited exceptions to the exclusive rights conferred by a patent, provided that such exceptions do not unreasonably conflict with a normal exploitation of the patent and do not unreasonably prejudice the legitimate interests of the patent owner, taking account of the legitimate interests of third parties. The exception is thus subject to three conditions, usually called the three-step test as seen in Chapter II, namely that the exception:

- be limited;
- not unreasonably conflict with a normal exploitation of the patent; and
- not unreasonably prejudice the legitimate interests of the patent owner, taking account of the legitimate interests of third parties.

These apply cumulatively, each being a separate and independent requirement that must be satisfied.

TRIPS negotiators adopted the approach of establishing general principles rather than an exhaustive list. Many countries use this provision to provide that certain uses shall not infringe the patent rights. Often, limited exceptions to patent rights cover the use of the patented invention by third parties for:

- private, non-commercial purposes;
- research or experimental purposes (to varying degrees according to national legislation and jurisprudence);
- 'early working' of patented pharmaceuticals for the purposes of obtaining marketing approval or the so-called 'Bolar' provision;[5]
- prior use, i.e. continuing use of the invention initiated secretly prior to the priority date/filing date;
- temporary use on vessels, aircraft or land vehicles temporarily or accidentally entering the waters, airspace or land. This exception is expressed as an explicit obligation in Article 5ter of the Paris Convention.

Such uses, while taking into account the interests of the society and third parties, have not been considered to be unreasonably prejudicial to the interests of patent owners (Box V.1).

(b)   Compulsory licences

The TRIPS Agreement does not use the term 'compulsory licences' but rather 'use without authorization of the right holder'. Article 31 covers both compulsory licences granted to third parties for their own use and use by or on behalf of governments without the authorization of the right holder. A compulsory licence can be said to be a licence given by a government authority to a person other than the patent owner that authorizes the production, importation, sale or use of the patent-protected product without the consent of the patent owner.

---

[5] The early working exemption allows manufacturers of generic drugs to use the patented invention without the patent owner's permission and before the patent protection expires for the purposes of obtaining marketing approval from health regulatory authorities. The generic producers can then be in a position to market their versions as soon as the patent expires. This exception has been upheld as conforming to the TRIPS Agreement in a WTO dispute ruling (*Canada – Pharmaceutical Patents* (DS114)).

Box V.1 *Canada – Pharmaceutical Patents*[6] (DS114)

PARTIES		AGREEMENTS	TIMELINE OF THE DISPUTE	
Complainants	EC	TRIPS Articles 27, 28 and 30	Establishment of Panel	1 February 1999
			Circulation of Panel report	17 March 2000
Respondent	Canada		Circulation of Appellate Body report	NA
			Adoption	7 April 2000

---

1. Measure and intellectual property at issue

   - Measure at issue: Certain provisions under Canada's Patent Act: (i) 'regulatory review provision (Sec. 55.2(1))'; and (ii) 'stockpiling provision (Sec. 55.2(2))' that allowed general drug manufacturers to override, in certain situations, the rights conferred on a patent owner. The regulatory review provision permitted the general manufacturers of pharmaceuticals to produce samples of the patented product for use during the regulatory review process. The stockpiling provision allowed producers of generic drugs to make the drugs and begin stockpiling them six months prior to the expiration of the patent.
   - Product at issue: Patented pharmaceuticals from the European Communities.

2. Summary of key Panel findings

Stockpiling provision

- TRIPS Arts. 28.1 (patent owner rights) and 30 (exceptions): (Canada practically conceded that the stockpiling provision violated Art. 28.1, which sets out exclusive rights granted to patent owners.) Concerning Canada's defence under Art. 30, the Panel found that the measure was not justified under Art. 30 because there were no limitations on the quantity of production for stockpiling which resulted in a substantial curtailment of extended market exclusivity, and, thus, was not 'limited' as required by Art. 30. Accordingly, the Panel concluded that the stockpiling provision was inconsistent with Art. 28.1 as it constituted a 'substantial curtailment of the exclusionary rights' granted to patent holders.

---

[6] *Canada – Patent Protection of Pharmaceutical Products.*

Box V.1 (*cont.*)

Regulatory review provision

- TRIPS Arts. 28.1 and 30: (Canada also practically conceded on the inconsistency of the provision with Art. 28.1) The Panel found that Canada's regulatory review provision was justified under Art. 30 by meeting all three cumulative criteria: the exceptional measure (i) must be limited; (ii) must not 'unreasonably conflict with normal exploitation of the patent'; and (iii) must not 'unreasonably prejudice the legitimate interests of the patent owner', taking account of the legitimate interests of third parties. These three cumulative criteria are necessary for a measure to be justified as an exception under Art. 30.
- TRIPS Art. 27.1 (non-discrimination): The Panel found that the European Communities failed to prove that the regulatory review provision discriminated based on the field of technology (i.e. against pharmaceutical products in this case), either de jure or de facto, under Art. 27.1. The Panel's view was that Members may treat different fields of patent protection differently if they do so for a legitimate purpose. The Panel said that the 'ordinary meaning of the word "discriminate" ... certainly extends beyond the concept of differential treatment. It is a normative term, pejorative in connotation, referring to results of the unjustified imposition of differentially disadvantageous treatment. Discrimination may arise from explicitly different treatment, sometimes called "*de jure* discrimination", but it may also arise from ostensibly identical treatment which, due to differences in circumstances, produces differentially disadvantageous effects, sometimes called "*de facto* discrimination".'

The TRIPS Agreement builds upon the provision in Article 5A of the Paris Convention[7] and recognizes the right of Members to authorize compulsory licences subject to conditions aimed at protecting the legitimate interests of the right holder that are detailed in Article 31. This was reaffirmed in the Doha Declaration on the TRIPS Agreement and Public Health (see details in Chapter IX).

---

[7] Article 5A recognizes the right of Members to take legislative measures providing for the grant of compulsory licences to prevent the abuses which might result from the exercise of the exclusive rights conferred by the patent, for example failure to work. A compulsory licence may not be applied for on the ground of failure to work or insufficient working before four years from the date of filing of the patent application or three years from the date of grant of the patent, whichever period expires last. It must be refused if the patentee justifies his inaction by legitimate reasons. Such a compulsory licence must be non-exclusive and not transferable, even in the form of the grant of a sub-licence, except with that part of the enterprise or goodwill which exploits such licence.

While setting out certain conditions, the TRIPS Agreement does not limit the grounds or underlying reasons that might be used to justify the grant of compulsory licences (except in the case of semi-conductor technology[8]). Article 31 does mention (1) national emergencies, (2) other circumstances of extreme urgency and (3) anti-competitive practices – but only as grounds when some of the normal requirements for compulsory licensing do not apply, such as the need to try for a voluntary licence first.

The main conditions to be respected in the grant of compulsory licences given in Article 31 are listed below:

- Applications to be considered on their individual merits (TRIPS Article 31(a))

  Governments must not decide to automatically compulsorily license a 'class' of patents, for example steel making processes, without considering the application on its individual merits.

- First, an unsuccessful attempt ... (TRIPS Article 31(b))

  As a general rule, an unsuccessful attempt must have been made first to obtain a voluntary licence on reasonable commercial terms and conditions within a reasonable period of time before a compulsory licence is granted. There are three circumstances in which this rule need not be applied: (1) in case of a national emergency or other circumstances of extreme urgency; (2) in cases of public non-commercial use and (3) when a compulsory licence is granted as a remedy in an adjudicated case of anti-competitive practices. The Doha Declaration on the TRIPS Agreement and Public Health clarified that Members have the right to determine what constitutes a national emergency or other circumstances of extreme urgency, it being understood that public health crises, including those relating to HIV/AIDS, tuberculosis, malaria and other epidemics, can represent a national emergency or other circumstances of extreme urgency (see Chapter IX).

- Scope and duration to be limited to purposes for which granted (TRIPS Article 31(c))

---

[8] In the case of semi-conductor technology the grounds for compulsory licences are limited (1) to public non-commercial use or (2) to remedy a practice determined after judicial or administrative process to be anti-competitive (TRIPS Article 31(c)).

The scope and duration of compulsory licences must be limited to the purpose for which they were authorized. For example, if a compulsory licence has been granted on a patented invention for the purpose of meeting a particular need, the scope and duration of the licence must be limited to what is necessary to achieve this purpose. Compulsory licences should be liable to termination when the circumstances that justified their creation no longer apply. However, in doing so the legitimate interests of the licensee may be protected – for example, any investment that the licensee has made to produce the product under the compulsory licence.

- Licences to be non-exclusive (TRIPS Article 31(d))

Compulsory licences must be non-exclusive, i.e. the licensee must not have the right to prevent the grant of other licences or the use of the invention by the patent owner.

- Predominantly for supply of domestic market (TRIPS Article 31(f))

Compulsory licences shall be authorized predominantly for the supply of the domestic market of the Member authorizing such use. This condition may be relaxed when the government grants a compulsory licence to remedy anti-competitive practices. Due to subsequent WTO decisions, this condition is also relaxed to permit compulsory licensing for export to countries lacking sufficient domestic manufacturing capacities and wanting to import generic pharmaceuticals to meet a public health problem (see Chapter IX).

- Right holder: adequate remuneration (TRIPS Article 31(h))

The right holder must be paid adequate remuneration in the circumstances of each case, taking into account the economic value of the licence. When the grant of a compulsory licence is to remedy anti-competitive practices, the need for such a remedy may be taken into account in determining the amount of remuneration (Article 31(k)). This condition has been waived under certain conditions by subsequent WTO decisions related to public health (see Chapter IX for more details).

- Decisions on grant and remuneration to be subject to judicial or other independent review (TRIPS Article 31(i))

The legal validity of any decision relating to the grant of compulsory licences, and any decision relating to the remuneration provided in respect of such use, must be subject to judicial review or other independent review by a distinct higher authority in that Member.

- Certain conditions to be met in the case of dependent patents (TRIPS Article 31(l))

  Where a later patented invention cannot be exploited without infringing an earlier patent (i.e. the case of dependent patents), a compulsory licence may only be granted on the earlier patent if the invention in the later patent involves an important technical advance and the owner of the earlier patent has a right to obtain a cross-licence for the later patent.

4   What is the minimum period of protection to be accorded?

The last principal issue in this chapter is the duration of patent rights and the circumstances under which these can be terminated.

(a)   Term of protection

The minimum term of protection available for patents shall be a period of twenty years from the filing date (Article 33). The filing date is the date of the application.[9]

Members may make the patent term subject to the payment of renewal or maintenance fees. Procedures for this are governed by Article 62 on the acquisition and maintenance of IPRs. If these fees are not paid, the patent lapses; many patents lapse before the available full term of twenty years where there is no economic interest in maintaining them. There are some relevant provisions in the Paris Convention which provide for grace periods for fee payment and clarify the term of patents that rely on a right of priority from a patent application filed elsewhere.[10]

---

[9]   The TRIPS Agreement states that Members who do not have a system of original grant may provide that the term of protection shall be calculated from the date of filing the original patent application (footnote 8). This was intended to take account of the situation of Members which did not have a system of original grant but had a system for re-registering patents granted elsewhere.

[10]   Article 5*bis* of the Paris Convention obliges Members to grant a period of grace for the payment of the fees prescribed for the maintenance of a patent application. With respect to the duration of a patent right, Article 4*bis* of the Paris Convention, as incorporated into the TRIPS Agreement, says that patents applied for during the period of priority are independent as regards their normal duration and that those obtained with the benefit of

In some jurisdictions an extension of the patent term is given to certain classes of product to compensate for delays in obtaining the regulatory approvals that are needed before products can be marketed. The TRIPS Agreement does not require the grant of patent term extension, and thus as a minimum obligatory standard the available term need only run to twenty years from the filing date.

(b)   Revocation

Can Members terminate a patent even before its expiry date? If 'yes', on what grounds? What does the Paris Convention say in this regard?

With respect to the duration of a patent right, Articles 4*bis* and 5A of the Paris Convention recognize that patents for the same invention in different countries are independent of each other and also that forfeiture of the patent shall not be provided for in a Member to prevent the abuse of exclusive rights except in cases where the grant of compulsory licences would not have been sufficient to prevent such abuses. No proceedings for the forfeiture or revocation of a patent may be instituted before the end of two years from the grant of the first compulsory licence. In addition, importation by the patentee into the Member where the patent has been granted of an article manufactured in any of the Members shall not entail forfeiture of the patent.

Article 32 of the TRIPS Agreement adds to the relevant provisions in the Paris Convention and provides for the availability of an opportunity for judicial review of any decision to revoke or forfeit a patent.

There has been a discussion on the interpretation of Article 32 in the TRIPS Council recorded in IP/C/M/8 and IP/C/M/9. Some Members considered that the subject of revocation of patents was dealt with in Articles 27, 29 and 33 of the TRIPS Agreement, meaning that patents could not be revoked by Members except on grounds that would have justified denial of the grant of a patent on the underlying application. According to this view, the TRIPS Agreement precluded a Member from revoking a patent in order to serve other general societal goals, such as promoting technology transfer for environmentally sound technologies. Some others took the view that revocation was dealt with in Article 32 only and that this provision did not restrict the rights of Members to decide on the grounds of revocation subject to the limitations prescribed under Article 5 of the Paris Convention.

---

priority must have a duration equal to that which they would have had, had they been applied for or granted without the benefit of priority.

VI

Industrial designs, layout-designs of integrated circuits, undisclosed information, anti-competitive practices

A Introduction

This chapter deals with the provisions of several sections of the TRIPS Agreement, namely Sections 4, 6, 7 and 8 of Part II of the TRIPS Agreement entitled 'Industrial Designs' (Articles 25, 26), 'Layout-Designs (Topographies) of Integrated Circuits' (Articles 35 to 38), 'Protection of Undisclosed Information' (Article 39) and 'Control of Anti-Competitive Practices in Contractual Licences' (Article 40), respectively. Thus this chapter covers eight articles as noted above and deals with a variety of topics.

Each section covered in this chapter has to be read, like other sections in Part II of the TRIPS Agreement that cover standards of IPRs, together with the relevant provisions of pre-existing treaties in the area of international IP law which are incorporated by reference into the TRIPS Agreement. Reference will be made to these treaties in the sections below.

This chapter will also have to be read in conjunction with other relevant provisions of the TRIPS Agreement that are explained in other chapters. Wherever appropriate, cross-references are made to other chapters.

B Industrial designs

WTO Members' obligations with respect to the protection of industrial designs are set out in Articles 25 and 26, which make up Section 4 of Part II of the TRIPS Agreement. Under these provisions, at least ten years of protection must be available for industrial designs, during which owners of protected designs must be able to prevent the manufacture, sale or importation for commercial purposes of articles bearing or embodying a design which is a copy, or essentially a copy, of the protected design. Members must also comply with the relevant provisions of the Paris Convention on industrial designs.

1 What is an industrial design?

The term 'industrial design' is not defined in the TRIPS Agreement, but is generally understood to refer to the ornamental or aesthetic aspect of an article rather than its technical features. Designs can consist of three-dimensional features, such as the shape of an article, or of two-dimensional features, such as patterns, lines or colours. Industrial designs are present in a wide variety of industrial products including medical instruments, watches, jewellery, electrical appliances and vehicles.

2 What has to be eligible for protection as an industrial design?

According to Article 25.1 of the TRIPS Agreement, industrial design protection must be available for designs that are:

- new or original; and
- independently created.

Members may provide that designs are not new or original if they do not significantly differ from known designs or combinations of known design features (Article 25.1). The additional requirement of independent creation allows Members to provide for a cumulative application of novelty and originality, as is the case under certain Members' laws. Members may provide that design protection shall not extend to designs dictated essentially by technical or functional considerations. This means that Members can exclude from design protection features that are necessary for the technical functioning of the product.

Many products to which designs are applied are not themselves novel and are produced by a large number of manufacturers, such as belts, shoes or screws. If a design for one such article, for example, screws, is dictated purely by the function which the screw is intended to perform, it would not generally be eligible to be protected as an industrial design.[1]

---

[1] The WIPO *Intellectual Property Handbook* provides further explanation of this legal issue, WIPO Publication No.489, or see www.wipo.int/export/sites/www/about-ip/en/iprm/pdf/ch2.pdf, pages 114–15.

This provision leaves considerable scope for Members to tailor their system for the protection of industrial designs more towards a copyright-type system (based on protection against copying of original works) or more towards a patent type system (creating an exclusive right over technological innovation), or by combining the elements identified in the provision in different ways.

(a)   General formalities for the protection of industrial designs

(i)   **Formalities**   The TRIPS Section 4 on industrial designs does not prescribe any formalities to be fulfilled before protection can be accorded to the right owner. However, Article 62.1 of the TRIPS Agreement explicitly recognizes that Members may require compliance with reasonable procedures and formalities. Members are therefore free to prescribe formalities in their laws and regulations, e.g. with respect to the filing of applications, the fees to be paid, the examination and publication of such applications and their eventual registration. Members that choose to prescribe such formalities must, however, respect the provisions of Article 62 which provide that any such procedures must permit a reasonably speedy grant or registration so as to avoid unwarranted curtailment of the period of protection.

(ii)   **Priority**   As with patents and trademarks, the right of priority deriving from Article 4 of the Paris Convention, as incorporated into the TRIPS Agreement by Article 2.1, applies equally to the area of industrial designs. As already mentioned, this means that on the basis of a regular application for an industrial design filed by a given applicant in one of the Member countries, the same applicant (or the successor in title) may, within six months, apply for protection in the territories of all the other Members. Within this six-month period, such later applications will be regarded as if they had been filed on the same day as the earliest application and therefore enjoy a priority status with respect to all applications relating to the same design filed after the date of the first application.

(b)   Provisions regarding formalities for industrial designs in the textile sector

Textile designs typically have a short product cycle, are numerous and are particularly liable to copying. They are therefore given special attention under Article 25.2 of the TRIPS Agreement. According to this provision, requirements for obtaining protection of textile designs, in particular as regards their cost, examination or publication, must not unreasonably impair the opportunity to seek and obtain such protection.

The provision recognizes three areas in particular where problems could arise, namely costs, examination and publication. High fee levels could deter applicants in the textile sector where numerous applications may be necessary to secure effective protection; this would especially present difficulties for small enterprises and firms in developing countries. Examination of applications should not unreasonably delay the granting of protection or curtail its duration in such a way as to render the protection ineffective. Finally, publication, which is generally considered one of the basic principles of registration systems could, in the case of textile designs, produce the adverse effect of facilitating the counterfeiting of the published design before the original articles can be put on the market.

The provision explicitly recognizes that Members are free to meet this obligation through industrial design law or through copyright law, where protection is accorded without formalities (see Chapter II).

'Textile designs' could cover two-dimensional designs (e.g. the pattern on a tie or on a clothing material or embroidery) as well as three-dimensional designs (e.g. the model for a dress).

3   What are the rights to be conferred on an owner of a protected industrial design?

According to Article 26.1 of the TRIPS Agreement, the owner of a protected industrial design must have the right to prevent third parties not having the owner's consent from making, selling or importing articles bearing or embodying a design which is a copy, or substantially a copy, of the protected design, when such acts are undertaken for commercial purposes.

It is important to note the difference between the protection for industrial designs and that for trademarks. While TRIPS requires that trademark owners must be able to also prevent the use of similar signs where their use may cause confusion among consumers, owners of industrial designs only have to be protected against the making, selling or importing of goods that carry or include a design that is a copy, or substantially a copy, of the protected design. In other words, the test for infringement essentially concerns the act of copying, rather than deception or confusion of consumers.

Article 5B of the Paris Convention provides that the protection of industrial designs may not, under any circumstances, be subject to any measure of forfeiture as a sanction in cases of failure to work or where articles corresponding to those protected are imported. 'Forfeiture' in this provision includes equivalent measures, such as cancellation, invalidation or revocation. This means that Members cannot provide for the revocation or cancellation of design protection where a design is not produced in, or is only imported into, a country.

4   What are the permissible exceptions to the rights conferred?

According to Article 26.2 of the TRIPS Agreement exceptions to the rights conferred on the owner of industrial designs are allowed if these:

- are limited;
- do not unreasonably conflict with the normal exploitation of protected industrial designs; and
- do not unreasonably prejudice the legitimate interests of the owner of the protected design, taking account of the legitimate interests of third parties.

This provision uses language similar to that found in Article 13, Article 17 and Article 30 of the TRIPS Agreement. Article 26.2 itself has never been considered in a WTO dispute settlement ruling, and so there is no direct guidance as to how this provision would be interpreted. However, dispute settlement rulings have addressed each of these three similar provisions, considering these concepts in ways which may have a bearing on the interpretation of Article 26.2, even though disputes are decided independently based on the facts of each case and the legal and policy context of exceptions to design rights is distinct from these other areas of IP law. See the explanations of Article 30 in Chapter V, of Article 13 in Chapter II and of Article 17 in Chapter III for more details. Some Members' laws provide for exceptions such as private use, use for experimental or teaching purposes or prior use of a protected design.

5   How long does the protection of an industrial design have to last?

According to Article 26.3 of the TRIPS Agreement the duration of protection available shall amount to at least ten years.

The wording 'amount to' allows Members to maintain systems where the term is divided into, for example, shorter successive periods of protection that can be renewed upon request of the right holder. As the TRIPS regime on industrial designs does not oblige Members to require registration of designs the provision is not specific on the starting point of the period of protection. This could therefore be the date of creation, as is the case under copyright law, or the date of application or the date of grant under specific industrial design laws.

C Layout-designs (topographies) of integrated circuits

The provisions on the protection of layout-designs of integrated circuits are found in Articles 35 to 38, which make up Section 6 of Part II of the TRIPS Agreement. According to Article 35 of the TRIPS Agreement, Members are required to protect the layout-designs ('topographies') of integrated circuits in accordance with provisions of the Treaty on Intellectual Property in Respect of Integrated Circuits ('IPIC Treaty') and the additional provisions of Articles 36 to 38 of the TRIPS Agreement. The latter provisions relate to the term of protection, the treatment of innocent infringers, the application of the protection to articles containing infringing integrated circuits, and compulsory licensing.

The IPIC Treaty was negotiated under the auspices of WIPO and signed in Washington in 1989 but has never entered into force as an insufficient number of countries have ratified it. It is therefore only through their incorporation into the TRIPS Agreement that a number of provisions from the IPIC Treaty have become binding on WTO Members.

1 What is a layout-design (topography) of an integrated circuit?

An integrated circuit (or 'chip') is an electronic device that incorporates individual electronic components within a single 'integrated' platform of semi-conductor material, typically silicon, configured so as to perform a complex electronic function. Typically, an integrated circuit comprises active elements such as electronic switches and gates (like transistors or diodes) and passive electronic components (such as resistors and capacitors). Broadly, integrated circuits are classified into microprocessors and memories. A microprocessor typically performs information-processing functions because it has logic circuits capable of electronically performing information processing. Memories enable storing and retrieval of data.

An integrated circuit is thus formed when a miniaturized electrical circuit is embodied within a chip. All the active and passive components are created in the semi-conductor wafer during the fabrication process itself and are therefore inseparable once the chip has been produced.

A layout-design, also known as an integrated circuit topography, is defined in Article 2(i) of the IPIC Treaty, as incorporated into the TRIPS Agreement, as the three-dimensional disposition, however expressed, of the elements at least one of which is an active element, and of some or all of the interconnections of an integrated circuit, or such a three-dimensional disposition prepared for an integrated circuit intended for manufacture. In other words, a layout-design is the three-dimensional layout of an integrated circuit, i.e. the arrangement in a chip (usually made of semi-conductor crystal) of active and passive electronic components.

Such layout-designs do not fall easily under the pre-existing categories of IP law. They may be too functional for copyright or design protection but not inventive enough to merit patent protection. Thus the TRIPS Agreement contains rules specifically addressing their protection. However, these rules are flexible enough to allow countries to use more patent-like approaches with formalities or more copyright-like approaches without formalities as they see fit.

Article 4 of the IPIC Treaty, as incorporated in the TRIPS Agreement, recognizes that Members are free in the manner in which they implement this protection of layout-designs in their national law and explicitly mentions the possibility to achieve such protection through copyright, patent, utility model, industrial design or unfair competition law, or any other law or combinations thereof. Members, therefore, are not obliged to create a separate law for layout-designs of integrated circuits, but can meet their obligation to protect layout-designs by providing for it in existing categories of IP or in other laws.

2   What has to be eligible for protection as a layout-design of an integrated circuit?

According to Article 3(2) of the IPIC Treaty, as incorporated into the TRIPS Agreement, protection extends to such layout-designs that are:

- original in the sense that they are the result of their creators' own intellectual effort; and

- not commonplace among creators of layout-designs and manufacturers of integrated circuits at the time of their creation.

While the originality requirement is similar to the concept of originality in copyright, the requirement of the layout-design not being commonplace is closer to the more objective test of novelty in industrial property law. It is explicitly recognized in Article 3(2)(b) of the IPIC Treaty that a layout-design using elements that are commonplace can still meet these criteria if the combination of these elements is original and not commonplace.

Neither the TRIPS Agreement nor the incorporated provisions of the IPIC Treaty stipulate formality requirements for obtaining protection of a layout-design of integrated circuits. However, Article 7 of the IPIC Treaty explicitly states that Members are free to require, as a condition of protection:

- that the layout-design has been ordinarily commercially exploited somewhere in the world (Article 7(1));
- the application for registration of the layout-design with the competent public authority, including the disclosure of information on its electronic function. This may include specifying that filing has to be effected within a certain time period from the date of the first commercial exploitation and the payment of a fee for the registration of the layout-design (Article 7(2)).

Members are therefore free to prescribe such formalities or not in their law. However, Members that choose to prescribe such formalities must respect the provisions of Article 62 of the TRIPS Agreement which provide that any such procedures must permit a reasonably speedy grant or registration so as to avoid unwarranted curtailment of the period of protection.

3 What are the rights to be conferred on the owner of a protected layout-design?

According to Article 36 of the TRIPS Agreement and Article 6 of the IPIC Treaty, Members are to consider unlawful:

- the reproduction; and
- the importation, sale or other distribution for commercial purposes

of a protected layout-design, if it was not authorized by the right holder. These prohibitions also extend to integrated circuits incorporating such a design, and to articles that contain such integrated circuits.

This means that the owner of the layout-design has the exclusive right to authorize the reproduction and the commercial distribution of the protected layout-design itself, as well as of products incorporating such a design (e.g. mobile phones or other consumer electronics).

4   What are the permissible limitations and exceptions to the rights conferred?

The TRIPS Agreement and the IPIC Treaty provide for a number of limitations to the owner's exclusive rights.

(a)   Reproduction for private or research purposes

Article 6(2)(a) of the IPIC Treaty, as incorporated in the TRIPS Agreement, provides that it shall not be considered unlawful if a third party, without the authorization of the right holder, engages in the reproduction of a protected layout-design:

• for private purposes; or
• for the sole purpose of evaluation, analysis, research or teaching.

This means that private (i.e. non-commercial) reproduction and reproduction for the purposes indicated above cannot be prevented by the right holder.

(b)   Parallel creation

Article 6(2)(c) of the IPIC Treaty, as incorporated in the TRIPS Agreement, provides that the right owner of a protected layout-design may not exercise his rights in respect of an identical layout-design that was independently created by a third party.

(c)   Innocent infringement

The rights of the owner of a protected layout-design are also limited with regard to so-called 'innocent infringement'. According to Article 37.1 of the TRIPS Agreement, it shall not be considered unlawful to import, sell or otherwise commercially distribute an integrated circuit incorporating an unlawfully reproduced layout-design (or a product incorporating such a chip), where the person performing or ordering such acts did not know or had no reasonable grounds to know that that such was the case at the time of acquiring the integrated circuit or product. This means that the commercial distribution of an unlawfully copied layout-design (either in a chip or a product incorporating such a chip) cannot be prevented, if the person was legitimately unaware that the chip was unlawful.

Even after such an 'innocent infringer' has been sufficiently notified of the offending chip, he must be allowed to continue distributing his existing or pre-ordered stock of such chips or products in return for compensation to the right holder equivalent to a reasonable commercial royalty rate. So even after the innocent infringer has learned about the infringing chip in the products he is distributing for commercial purposes, he must be allowed to sell off the remaining stock of the product or chip in question, as long as he pays royalties at the going commercial rate to the right owner. It is worth noting, however, that this privilege of the 'innocent infringer' exists only with respect to acts of commercial distribution of unlawfully reproduced layout-designs, and not with respect to the reproduction itself.

(d) Exhaustion

The issue of exhaustion and the fact that Members are not obliged to adopt a particular exhaustion regime under the TRIPS Agreement has already been discussed in Chapter I. Article 6(5) of the IPIC Treaty, as incorporated in the TRIPS Agreement, specifically states that Members may provide for the exhaustion of distribution rights with regard to layout-designs of integrated circuits that have been put on the market by, or with the consent of, the holder of the right.

(e) Compulsory licensing

With regard to compulsory licensing regarding layout-designs of integrated circuits, Article 37.2 of the TRIPS Agreement provides that the same conditions apply as in the patent area under Article 31(a) to (k) of the TRIPS Agreement. For more details on Article 31, see Chapter V. While the TRIPS Agreement does not generally make provisions regarding the grounds on which compulsory licences can be granted by Members, Article 31(c) of the TRIPS Agreement stipulates that, in the case of semi-conductor technology, compulsory licences may only be granted for non-commercial use or to remedy a practice that has been determined to be anti-competitive.

5 *How long does the protection of a layout-design have to last?*

According to Article 38 of the TRIPS Agreement protection is to last for a minimum of ten years counted from either the date of filing an application for registration or from the first commercial exploitation wherever it occurs in the world. As the TRIPS regime on the protection of layout-designs contains no obligation for Members to require, as a condition for protection, the registration or the commercial exploitation of a layout-design, Article 38 provides thus alternative starting points for the required ten-year period of protection. As a further possibility, Article 38.3 of the TRIPS Agreement suggests that Members may also provide for protection of a layout-design to lapse fifteen years after the creation of the layout-design.

D   Undisclosed information

The protection of undisclosed information, which covers both trade secrets and test data submitted to government agencies, is not explicitly covered by pre-existing international IP law, such as the Paris Convention. However, the protection for this subject matter under Article 39 of the TRIPS Agreement is framed in terms of the more general concept of ensuring effective protection against unfair competition pursuant to Article 10*bis* of the Paris Convention.

Article 10*bis* of the Paris Convention, as incorporated into the TRIPS Agreement, obliges Members to ensure effective protection against acts of competition that are contrary to honest practices in industrial or commercial matters. It contains a non-exhaustive list of some acts of unfair competition which must be prohibited by Members, including all acts of such a nature as to create confusion by any means whatever with the establishment, the goods, or the industrial or commercial activities, of a competitor; false allegations in the course of trade of such a nature as to discredit the establishment, the goods, or the industrial or commercial activities, of a competitor; and indications or allegations the use of which in the course of trade is liable to mislead the public as to the nature, the manufacturing process, the characteristics, the suitability for their purpose, or the quantity, of the goods.

1   Undisclosed information (trade secrets)

The TRIPS Agreement builds on the Paris Convention to introduce specific obligations to protect undisclosed information. Accordingly, its Article 39.2 obliges Members to protect information that:

- is secret in the sense that it is not, as a body or in the precise configuration and assembly of its components, generally known among or readily accessible to persons within the circles that normally deal with the kind of information in question;

> It is not necessarily the case that trade secrets should be only known to one or two persons to be entitled to protection, but they should not be generally known to the public or other persons in the same trade or business. The information as a whole can be secret, such as the formula for 'Coca-Cola', or the information may be composed of individual pieces of information that may be in the public domain, but the compilation of which is not, such as a law firm's client list.

- has commercial value because it is secret;

> The information should be of commercial value to its holder or the holder's competitors and this value would be lost or impaired if the information ceased to be secret. For example, the formula for 'Coca-Cola' would be of less value to that company if all competitors also had access to it.

- has been subject to reasonable steps under the circumstances by the person lawfully in control of the information, to keep it secret.

> What constitutes 'reasonable steps' to keep information secret may vary from case to case, mostly depending on the nature and value of the information to be protected. For example, in one case, an issue before a court was whether a chemical company should be required, as a reasonable step, to put a roof over the machinery in its plant in order to protect its secret process of making methanol from aerial photography. The court held that, as such a requirement would be too costly to the company, it was not reasonable.

The TRIPS Agreement requires that a natural or legal person lawfully in control of such undisclosed information must have the possibility of preventing it from being disclosed to, acquired by, or used by others without his or her consent in a 'manner contrary to honest commercial practices'. According to a footnote to the provision, a manner contrary to honest commercial practices means at least the following practices:

- breach of contract,
- breach of confidence,
- inducement to breach of contract or confidence,
- acquisition of undisclosed information by third parties who knew, or were grossly negligent in failing to know, that the above-mentioned practices were involved in the acquisition.

Unlike other IPRs, such as patents and copyright, for which the term of protection is finite, the protection of undisclosed information continues unlimited in time as long as the conditions for its protection continue to be met, i.e. it meets those conditions mentioned above. However, unlike patent protection, there is no protection against a competitor that develops the information independently.

2   Undisclosed test and other data

Most countries require pharmaceutical or agricultural chemical producers to submit test and other data as a condition of approving the marketing of their products, especially when they utilize new chemical entities. Pharmaceutical test data are generated through extensive preclinical trials on animals and clinical trials on humans and submitted to governmental agencies in order to provide evidence with respect to the safety, quality and efficacy of these products. Data on the efficacy and environmental effect of agricultural chemicals, such as pesticides or herbicides, are collected through field trials and similar tests. Considerable efforts by the originator company may be required to obtain such test data, both in terms of time and costs. The TRIPS Agreement is the first international instrument in the field of IP that contains obligations specifically with respect to the protection of undisclosed test and other data required to be submitted in order to get marketing approval for pharmaceutical or for agricultural chemical products. This issue is dealt with in Article 39.3, which tries to achieve a balance between competing interests. Protection under Article 39.3 is available independently of other IPRs, including patents. Members have to provide for test data protection irrespective of whether or not the products are covered by patents. The test data may have been generated by a firm or entity that is entirely different from the holder or holders of one or more patents that cover the use of the product in question, and if a patent has been filed on the product, this usually takes place years before the bulk of the trials or tests that produce data on safety, efficacy and environmental effect.

Article 39.3 of the TRIPS Agreement requires Members to protect such test or other data when:

- the data have not been disclosed;
- their submission is required as a condition of approving the marketing of pharmaceutical or agricultural chemical products;

- the products utilize new chemical entities; and
- the origination of the test or other data has required a considerable effort.

There are two forms of protection to be accorded to such test and other data. First, the TRIPS Agreement requires Members to protect them against unfair commercial use. In addition, Members are required to protect such data against disclosure. An exception to this obligation is available where disclosure is necessary to protect the public or where steps are taken to ensure that the data are protected against unfair commercial use.

An issue that has been much debated is whether a pharmaceutical regulatory authority can rely on test data supplied by the originator of a drug in its application for marketing approval to show its safety and efficacy when granting marketing approval for generic versions; in other words, whether it can limit itself to requiring only data necessary to demonstrate the bio-equivalency, or the same uptake in the body, of the generic version.

Members have differing perspectives on the obligation to protect test data against unfair commercial use under Article 39.3 of the TRIPS Agreement. Some are of the view that the most effective method of implementing Article 39.3 is to give the originator of the data a reasonable period of exclusivity during which the regulatory authorities must not rely on the data when approving other versions. Some others believe that there are other ways in which such data can be protected against 'unfair commercial use' other than through periods of data exclusivity.

There is no WTO jurisprudence on the question. The matter was at issue in a dispute settlement proceeding between the United States and Argentina. While on other issues the parties reached a mutually satisfactory solution, they only agreed on this issue that differences should be resolved under the rules of the WTO dispute settlement system (document WT/DS196/4). However, the issue has not been addressed under the DSU since the resolution of that specific dispute.

E   Control of anti-competitive practices in contractual licences

1   Introduction

An important element of the overall balance embodied in the TRIPS Agreement is a recognition of the legitimate role of competition law and policy vis-à-vis IPRs and licensing practices. The term 'competition law and policy' refers to laws and related policies that address anti-competitive practices of enterprises (sometimes they are also referred to as 'anti-trust' or 'anti-monopoly' laws and/or policies). The set of practices that can be addressed by such laws typically includes anti-competitive and/or collusive agreements (cartels), mergers that lessen competition and abuses of a dominant position or 'monopolization'.[2] In addition, the competition laws of some countries contain specific provisions relating to the abuse of IPRs.

The TRIPS Agreement provisions on competition law and policy, to be discussed in this section, reflect concerns regarding potential anti-competitive effects of IPRs protected under the Agreement that were expressed particularly by developing countries during the negotiation of the Agreement in the course of the Uruguay Round of multilateral trade negotiations. They are intended to enable governments to implement appropriate remedies in relation to harmful anti-competitive practices, so long as they act in ways that are consistent with the relevant provisions of the Agreement.

It is important to note that, properly understood, the goals and modalities of IPRs systems, and of the TRIPS Agreement, are *not* intrinsically in conflict with competition law and policy. Indeed, in general, both competition policy and IP serve the same overall objectives – i.e. those of promoting a dynamic and innovative economy, while also facilitating appropriate diffusion of new technologies, and thereby promoting the welfare of citizens. For example, competition law and policy can serve to prevent/deter practices such as collusive pricing or the use of abusive clauses in licensing agreements that unreasonably restrict access to new technologies or the uses to which such technologies can be put.

A related point worth emphasizing is that IPRs normally do not confer 'monopolies' to right holders in the sense that they are recognized under competition law. The reason is that in most (though not all) cases, substitutes are available for products and technologies that are protected by IPRs. For this reason, under the competition laws of most countries, the mere existence or exercise of IPRs is not, by itself, treated as being in violation of competition law (just as the mere existence/exercise of other forms of property rights, for example over real property, is not viewed as a violation of such law). Rather, competition law is likely to come into

---

[2] See, for general background, World Trade Organization, 'Special study on trade and competition policy', in *Annual Report of the World Trade Organization for 1997*, Geneva: WTO, 1997, Chapter IV.

play only in a minority of circumstances where there are few, or no, close substitutes for IP-protected technology or products and/or where rights are deliberately employed in an abusive manner.

Apart from the enforcement of competition law, many countries attach importance to the advocacy of competition principles in relation to other government policies, including IP. An important example of this is a 2003 report by the US Federal Trade Commission which argued in favour of greater attention to the preservation of competition in aspects of US patent policy.[3]

2   Overview of the relevant provisions of the TRIPS Agreement

The main provisions of the TRIPS Agreement having a bearing on the application of competition policy are Article 8.2 dealing with the abuse of IPRs generally, Article 40 dealing with anti-competitive licensing practices, and elements of Article 31, particularly Article 31(k), relating to the use of a patent without the authorization of the right holder. At a broad level, Article 8.2 of the Agreement stipulates that:

> Appropriate measures, provided that they are consistent with the provisions of this Agreement, may be needed to prevent the abuse of intellectual property rights by right holders or the resort to practices which unreasonably restrain trade or adversely affect the international transfer of technology.

It is noted that Article 8.2 is not necessarily concerned only with competition law violations but with the arguably more general concept of 'abuse' of IPRs.

In a related vein, but focusing on the specific issue of licensing practices that restrain competition, Article 40.1 of the Agreement notes that:

> Members agree that some licensing practices or conditions pertaining to intellectual property rights which restrain competition may have adverse effects on trade and may impede the transfer and dissemination of new technology.

To address this concern, Article 40.2 recognizes the right of WTO Member governments to take measures to prevent anti-competitive

---

[3] US Federal Trade Commission, *To Promote Innovation: The Proper Balance of Competition and Patent Law and Policy*, 2003, available at www.ftc.gov/os/2003/10/innovationrpt.pdf.

abuses of IPRs, provided that such measures are consistent with relevant provisions of the Agreement. Article 40.2 also contains a short illustrative list of practices that may be treated as abuses. These are exclusive grant-back conditions, conditions preventing challenges to validity and coercive package licensing.[4]

A further important aspect of Article 40 is the authority that it provides for WTO Members to ask for consultations with other Members in cases of possible anti-competitive abuses. Specifically, Article 40.3 of the Agreement provides that a Member considering action against an IP owner that is a national or domiciliary of another Member can seek consultations with that Member. The latter Member is required to cooperate through the supply of publicly available non-confidential information of relevance, and of other information available to that Member, subject to domestic law and to the conclusion of mutually satisfactory agreements concerning the safeguarding of its confidentiality. In addition, Article 40.4 provides that a Member whose nationals are subject to proceedings in another Member concerning alleged violation of that other Member's laws shall, upon request, be granted an opportunity for consultation by the other Member.

Article 31 of the TRIPS Agreement, relating to the use of a patent without the authorization of the right holder, sets out detailed conditions that must be respected in the granting of compulsory licences by Member States. However, subparagraph (k) of Article 31 makes clear that Members are not obliged to apply certain of these conditions in circumstances where the compulsory licence is granted 'to remedy a practice determined after judicial or administrative process to be anti-competitive'. In particular, requirements to show that a proposed user has made efforts to obtain voluntary authorization from the right holder on reasonable terms and conditions and that such efforts have not been successful within a reasonable period of time (see Article 31(b)) are not applicable in these circumstances. In addition, the requirement in Article 31(f) that authorization for use of a patent under a compulsory licence be predominantly for the supply of the domestic market of the

---

[4] 'Exclusive grant-back conditions' refer to any obligation on a licensee to grant an exclusive licence to the licensor in respect of its own improvements to or its own new applications of the licensed technology. 'Conditions preventing challenges to validity' are those that impose an obligation on a licensee not to challenge the validity of IPRs held by the licensor. 'Coercive package licensing' refers to an obligation on a licensee to accept a licence on several different technologies when the licensee's interest is limited to only part of these technologies.

Member authorizing such use can be rendered inapplicable by such a finding. Moreover, the authorities may consider the need to correct anti-competitive practices while determining the amount of remuneration due under Article 31(h).

It is important to note that the provisions described above leave important issues to be resolved at the national level. For example, neither Article 8.2 nor Article 40.2 indicates that specific practices *must* be treated as abuses or specifies remedial measures that must be taken. In this sense, the competition provisions of the Agreement are permissive rather than mandatory. In addition, with respect to Article 31(k), this provision does not define the basis on which practices may be deemed to be anti-competitive – i.e. the evaluative standards to be employed. Further, the full set of practices that may be deemed anti-competitive (beyond the three examples mentioned) is left undefined. The Agreement also provides relatively little in the way of guidance regarding the remedies that may be adopted in particular cases, beyond making clear that any measures adopted must be consistent with other provisions of the Agreement. In this context, it is of interest that, in a number of jurisdictions, national governments have found it useful to put in place guidelines that address some or all of these matters. Typically, these guidelines draw on past case decisions and economic learning in addition to the relevant agencies' experience on related issues.[5]

There is a range of current issues of interest that fall within the interaction of competition and IP policy. Some of these are as follows:

- The application of competition law to the acquisition of IPRs, particularly when IPRs are acquired by one firm from another, for example, under competition law provisions relating to mergers and acquisitions.

---

[5] See, for example, US Department of Justice and Federal Trade Commission, *Antitrust Guidelines on Intellectual Property Licensing* (US Government Printing Office: 1995; available at www.usdoj.gov/atr/public/guidelines/0558.htm); European Commission, *Guidelines on the Application of Article 81 of the EC Treaty to Technology Transfer Agreements* (2004; available at http://eur-lex.europa.eu/LexUriServ/LexUriServ.do?uri= CELEX:52004XC0427(01):EN:NOT); Canada, Competition Bureau, *Intellectual Property Enforcement Guidelines* (Ottawa: 2000; available at www.competitionbureau.gc.ca/eic/site/ cb-bc.nsf/vwapj/ipege.pdf/$FILE/ipege.pdf); and Japan, Fair Trade Commission, *Guidelines for the Use of Intellectual Property under the Antimonopoly Act* (2007; available at www.jftc.go.jp/en/legislation_guidelines/ama/pdf/070928_IP_Guideline.pdf), *Guidelines on Standardization and Patent Pool Arrangements* (2005; available at www.jftc.go.jp/en/ legislation_guidelines/ama/pdf/Patent_Pool.pdf), *Guidelines Concerning Joint Research and Development under the Antimonopoly Act* (1993; available at www.jftc.go.jp/en/legislation_ guidelines/ama/pdf/jointresearch.pdf).

- The treatment of licensing and related practices, such as grant-backs, exclusive dealing requirements, tie-ins, territorial market limitations, field-of-use restrictions and price maintenance clauses. National approaches have been reported as varying, with different approaches on whether such practices should be assessed case-by-case for their impact on competition.
- Issues concerning 'patent thickets': for example, the scenario in which a single semi-conductor product can be potentially subject to hundreds or thousands of patents owned by diverse firms. In some cases, the challenges posed by patent thickets have been addressed, or partially addressed, through the establishment of patent pools or cross-licensing arrangements that permit enterprises the use of technologies held by multiple right holders. However, some of these arrangements can raise attention because of the potential anti-competitive impact and measures may be necessary to ensure they are pro-competitive.
- The treatment of settlements in patent infringement cases: one scenario in which competition issues may arise is when they potentially impede the public policy interest in facilitating market entry by generic competitors of an original pharmaceutical.
- Refusals to licence: there are differing views in diverse jurisdictions about whether, and in what particular circumstances, such behaviour may be treated as a competition law violation, or whether, and in what circumstances, patent holders can be presumed to have an entitlement to refuse to licence their inventions.

VII

Enforcement

A   Introduction

The purpose of this chapter is to introduce the key features of the provisions of Part III, Sections 1 to 5, of the TRIPS Agreement entitled 'Enforcement of Intellectual Property Rights'. This part of the Agreement elaborates in twenty-one articles the enforcement procedures that Members have to make available to permit prompt and effective action against infringements of IPRs covered by the TRIPS Agreement. It is divided into five sections:

- general obligations (Article 41);
- civil and administrative procedures and remedies (Articles 42 to 49);
- provisional measures (Article 50);
- special requirements related to border measures (Articles 51 to 60); and
- criminal procedures (Article 61).

Unlike the substantive standards for the protection of IPRs in Part II of the TRIPS Agreement, which draws extensively on the existing body of international IP law, Part III incorporates only a few relevant provisions from earlier treaties; these are mentioned briefly below.

1   Background

Concerns in the multilateral trading system about counterfeiting and piracy and the perception that the international IPR system lacked effective rules on enforcement pre-dated the negotiations on the TRIPS Agreement. As seen in Chapter I, a proposal on trade in counterfeit goods was developed in the GATT, in 1978, as part of the Tokyo Round of trade negotiations, but no agreement was reached at that time. Subsequent work led to the inclusion of a specific mandate on IPRs in the Uruguay Round negotiations, which included a call for the development of a multilateral framework of principles, rules and disciplines dealing with international trade in counterfeit goods. When adopted, the TRIPS Agreement was the first multilateral treaty with detailed rules on the enforcement of IPRs, although earlier IP treaties, notably the Paris and Berne Conventions, do have some provisions specifically on enforcement.

2   What is IPR enforcement?

As seen in Chapter I, an IPR gives the owner an 'exclusive right' or a right to exclude. This means that an owner of an IPR is entitled to prevent others from undertaking certain acts without his or her authorization. Those rights may be infringed in several ways – either accidentally or deliberately. Infringement occurs when an act is undertaken which is covered by the rights of the owner of the IPR and which is not subject to an exception in the domestic law. Typical examples are:

- unauthorized reproduction of copyright-protected material for commercial gain;
- unauthorized reproduction of trademarks with the intention of passing off the good as a genuine product of the trademark owner; or
- unauthorized manufacture, use or sale of a patent-protected invention.

Industry and product areas concerned by IPR infringements range widely across international commerce. They include textiles and clothing, foodstuffs, automobile and aviation spare parts, pharmaceuticals, music and software. Potential repercussions go far beyond the mere protection of IPR assets, given that infringing acts often affect one or more of the following aspects: consumer safety and health, employment, tax and excise losses, fair competition, combating organized crime and the conditions for FDI.

The two main legal traditions – common law and civil law – differ considerably on some key points, for example with respect to the value of precedents in judgments. The enforcement provisions of the TRIPS Agreement have been designed so as to be compatible with both systems. As indicated in the Preamble, it was one of the ground rules for the negotiation of this part of the TRIPS Agreement that 'differences in national legal systems' would be taken into account.

There is little value in developing substantive standards of IP protection if the right holder cannot enforce them effectively through fair and expeditious procedures, including in an environment in which modern technologies have significantly facilitated the infringement of IPRs. It must be possible for the owners of IPRs to stop infringement and prevent further infringement, as well as to recover the losses incurred from an infringement. This is why the Preamble to the TRIPS Agreement recognizes the need to make available effective and appropriate means for the enforcement of such rights. In line with the Uruguay Round negotiating mandate, it also reiterates the need for a multilateral framework of principles, rules and disciplines dealing with international trade in counterfeit goods.

TRIPS provisions specify the civil and administrative procedures and remedies, including provisional measures, which must be available in respect of acts of infringement of any covered IPR. The enforcement requirements are stronger for trademark counterfeiting and copyright piracy. Members have to make border measures available to allow action against importation of counterfeit trademark goods and pirated copyright goods. Criminal procedures also have to be applied in cases of wilful trademark counterfeiting and copyright piracy on a commercial scale. The term 'making available' and similar terms for many enforcement remedies signal that the TRIPS rules leave the onus generally on the right holder to initiate enforcement procedures, with the government having the onus to put in place effective procedures and deterrent remedies. This general approach is consistent with the fact that IPRs are private rights, as stated in the TRIPS Preamble. Many of the provisions take the form of requiring Members to empower judicial or other competent authorities to take certain actions (see Articles 43.1; 44.1; 45; 46; 47; 48.1; 50.1, 2, 3 and 7; 53; 56; 59). In these cases, the authorities retain discretion in the application of the rules in specific cases.

Part III identifies a number of optional forms of enforcement, such as the extension of border measures, for instance to cover exports of infringing goods, or applying criminal procedures to the infringement of IPRs other than trademark counterfeiting and copyright piracy.

3 Application of basic principles

The basic principles of the TRIPS Agreement apply to the provisions on enforcement of IPRs along with other aspects of IP protection. This means, *inter alia*, that Members are free, but not obliged, to implement stricter enforcement procedures and remedies, provided that they are TRIPS-consistent (Article 1.1), for example that the safeguards against abuse are respected. Members are also free to determine the appropriate method of implementing Part III of the TRIPS Agreement within their own legal system and practice. Taking into account the existing differences in national laws in regard to enforcement rules, the TRIPS Agreement does not attempt to harmonize enforcement rules, but sets certain minimum standards (Article 1.1). In addition, Members are obliged to grant non-discriminatory treatment to the nationals of all other Members, i.e. national treatment and MFN treatment (Articles 3 and 4), in regard to enforcement procedures and remedies. Finally, like the substantive standards of protection for the IPR categories covered by the TRIPS Agreement, Part III on enforcement is subject to the WTO dispute settlement system (Article 64.1).

4   What is the relationship of the TRIPS Agreement with pre-existing provisions in other conventions and treaties?

The provisions of the Paris Convention and of the Berne Convention are incorporated by reference into the TRIPS Agreement (see Articles 2.1 and 9.1) and thus form part of the obligations to be respected by all Members under the latter agreement. Several provisions in those conventions relate to enforcement, for instance:

- the provisions on seizure on importation of goods unlawfully bearing a trademark or trade name (Article 9 of the Paris Convention). Those provisions also apply to seizure on importation of goods unlawfully bearing a false indication of source or the identity of the producer (Article 10 of the Paris Convention);
- liability to seizure of infringing copies of a work enjoying copyright protection, including when they are imported (Article 16 of the Berne Convention).

B   General obligations

The general obligations of Members concerning enforcement are found in Article 41. They apply to all judicial and administrative enforcement procedures specified in Part III. The objective is to permit effective action against any infringement of IPRs while ensuring that basic principles of due process are met, avoiding the creation of barriers to legitimate trade, and providing safeguards against the abuse of the procedures.[1]

---

[1] India and Brazil invoked, *inter alia*, Article 41 in their respective requests for consultations with the European Union and the Netherlands in *European Union and a Member State – Seizure of Generic Drugs in Transit* (DS408 and DS409). At the time of writing, the consultations were pending.

Members must make enforcement procedures available in their national law to enable right holders to take effective action against infringement of the IPRs covered by the TRIPS Agreement. This obligation typically implies granting the competent authorities, judicial or other, the authority to order certain legal measures. Enforcement procedures must include expeditious remedies to prevent infringements, and remedies to deter further infringements (Article 41.1).[2]

Article 41.1 requires the application of enforcement procedures in such a manner so as to:

- avoid the creation of barriers to legitimate trade; and
- provide for safeguards against the abuse of such procedures. This requirement is further elaborated by specific provisions in subsequent sections, for example regarding the indemnification of the defendant (Article 48) and the requirement to provide a security or equivalent assurance where border measures are applied (Article 53.1), as well as by other detailed procedural safeguards in the areas of provisional and border measures. The general principles of fair and equitable treatment also secure this objective, as this involves a balance of interests between the right holder and the alleged infringing party.

Basic principles of due process include the following requirements:

- **procedures must be fair and equitable** for all parties involved, without being unnecessarily complicated or costly, or entailing unreasonable time limits or unwarranted delays (Article 41.2);
- **decisions on the merits of a case** shall be made available at least to the parties to the proceeding without undue delay, ensuring thus the necessary transparency of the procedures. They shall be preferably in writing and reasoned, and based only on evidence in respect of which parties were offered an opportunity to be heard (Article 41.3); and

---

[2] In *European Communities/Greece – Enforcement of Intellectual Property Rights for Motion Pictures and Television Programs* (WT/DS124 and 125), the US claimed that a significant number of television stations in Greece had regularly broadcast copyright-protected movies and television programmes without authorization of copyright owners, and that effective remedies against such infringements, as well as sufficient deterrents to further infringements, were lacking. Subsequently, Greece passed legislation that provided for the immediate closure of television stations infringing IPRs. The estimated level of piracy fell significantly, and criminal convictions for television piracy were issued. Based on those developments, the parties to the dispute agreed to terminate consultations and to notify a mutually agreed solution to the WTO.

- parties to enforcement proceedings must have an **opportunity for review** by a judicial authority of final administrative decisions. Subject to jurisdictional provisions in a Member's law, the same applies to, at least, the legal aspects of initial judicial decisions on the merits of the case. However, Members have no obligation to provide for review of acquittals in criminal cases (Article 41.4).

In addition, Article 41.5 addresses some general understandings about resource constraints and the relation with other areas of law enforcement. The principles which guide Part III on enforcement include the understanding that:

- Members are not obliged to put in place a judicial system for the enforcement of IPRs which is distinct from that for the enforcement of law in general;
- TRIPS enforcement rules are not to affect the capacity of Members to enforce their laws in general; and
- Members are not required to redistribute resources between enforcement of IPRs and the enforcement of law in general.

C   Civil and administrative procedures and remedies

The obligations of Members with respect to civil and administrative procedures on the merits of a case as well as any resulting remedies are addressed in Section 2 of Part III of the TRIPS Agreement (Articles 42 to 49). They provide that a right holder must be able to initiate civil judicial procedures against an infringer of IPRs covered by the Agreement. Administrative procedures are not an obligation, but Article 49 requires the same principles to be applicable to them to the extent that civil remedies can be ordered as a result of administrative procedures on the merits of a case.

1   Fair and equitable procedures

Civil and administrative procedures must be fair and equitable (Article 42). This means that:

- defendants are entitled to written notice that is timely and contains sufficient details of the claims, including their basis;
- all parties, including defendants and the alleged infringer, must be allowed to be represented by independent legal counsel;

- procedures may not impose overly burdensome requirements concerning mandatory personal appearances;
- all parties are entitled to substantiate their claims and to present all relevant evidence; and
- the procedure must provide a means to identify and protect confidential information, unless this would be inconsistent with existing constitutional requirements. This could, for example, be relevant where an expert opinion is sought to determine damages.

2   Evidence

Article 43 describes how the rules on evidence should be applied in civil and administrative procedures. Where evidence that is likely to be important for one party is in the possession of the opposing party, the judicial authorities must be empowered to order that the evidence be produced. Any such order is, however, subject to conditions ensuring the protection of confidential information; this could, for example, be relevant where the production of evidence risks revealing trade secrets. This obligation only applies where the party has presented reasonably available evidence sufficient to support its claims of infringement and specified the evidence relevant to substantiation of its claims which lies in the control of the opposing party that it wishes disclosed.

If a party refuses without good reason to provide access to evidence in its possession, fails to provide the information within a reasonable period, or significantly impedes a procedure relating to an enforcement action, courts may be authorized to make their decisions on the basis of information presented to them. The parties must, in any event, be provided an opportunity to be heard.

3   Remedies

Judicial authorities must have the authority to award three types of remedies: injunctions, damages, and other remedies.

(a)   Injunctions

An injunction is a court order that either prohibits a party from doing a specified act or commands a party to undo some wrong or injury. The party that fails to adhere to the injunction faces civil or criminal contempt of court and may have to pay damages or face other sanctions for failing to follow the court's order.

Article 44.1 says that the judicial authorities must be empowered to order injunctions, i.e. to order a party to stop any action that infringes IPRs. Among other things, the objective is to prevent the distribution on the domestic market of imported infringing goods, immediately after their customs clearance.

There are two qualifications:

- Members are not obliged to make injunctions applicable to products acquired or ordered in good faith (innocent infringement) (Article 44.1);
- regarding use by governments, or by third parties authorized by governments, without the authorization of the right holder that is consistent with the TRIPS rules allowing such use (Article 31 and Article 37.2), Members may limit the remedies available in such cases to payment of remuneration in accordance with Article 31(h). In other cases, where TRIPS remedies are not consistent with domestic law, declaratory judgments and adequate compensation shall be available.

(b)   Damages

Available remedies must include damages, depending on the knowledge of the infringement or on negligence. Article 45.1 says that where the infringer acted in bad faith, e.g. engaged in infringing activity knowingly, or with reasonable grounds to know of the infringement, the judicial authorities must be empowered to order an infringer to pay the right holder:

- adequate damages to compensate for the injury that the right holder suffered due to the infringement of his or her IPRs; and
- expenses, which may include appropriate attorney fees.

In appropriate cases, the courts may also be authorized to order recovery of profits and/or payment of pre-established damages even where the infringer acted in good faith (Article 45.2). While courts will often experience difficulty in quantifying the damages and determining adequate compensation, the problem also occurs in other fields of law and is therefore not unique to IPR infringement.

(c)   Other remedies

In addition to injunction and damages, and with a view to creating an effective deterrent to infringement, the judicial authorities must also have the authority to order, without compensation:

- removal of the infringing goods from the channels of commerce; or
- their destruction (unless not permitted under a country's constitution).

This authority must also extend to ordering the non-commercial disposal of the materials and instruments predominantly used in the production of the infringing goods. In considering such requests to destroy or take goods out of commercial circulation, the courts must take into account the proportionality between the seriousness of the infringement and the remedies ordered, as well as the interests of third parties (Article 46). In the case of counterfeit trademark goods, the simple removal of the trademark unlawfully affixed shall normally not be sufficient for the goods to be released into the channels of commerce.

4   Right of information

With a view to assisting the right holder to find the source of infringing goods and to take appropriate action against other persons in the distribution channels, judicial authorities may be authorized to order the infringer to inform the right holder of:

- the identity of third persons involved in the production and distribution of the infringing goods or services; and
- their channels of distribution (Article 47).

This provision is again subject to the basic principle of proportionality since this authority must be applied in a way that is in proportion to the seriousness of the infringement.

5   Indemnification of the defendant

As one of the safeguards built into the enforcement section, Article 48.1 requires courts to have the authority to order an applicant who has abused enforcement procedures to pay adequate compensation to the defendant who has been wrongfully enjoined or restrained. Compensation may cover both the injury suffered by the defendant and his or her expenses, which may include appropriate attorney's fees.

Article 48.2 applies to the actions of public authorities and officials in the administration of any law pertaining to the protection or enforcement of IPRs. Members may only exempt them from liability where they have acted or are intending to act in good faith.

D　Provisional measures

Article 50 of the TRIPS Agreement requires Members to provide provisional enforcement measures to permit effective and expeditious action against alleged infringements. Such temporary or interim injunctions constitute an important tool pending the resolution of a dispute at a trial. They are different from the injunctions provided for in Article 44.1 insofar as the alleged IPR infringement has not yet been fully established. As for the other civil and administrative measures required by the TRIPS Agreement, provisional measures must be available in respect of all IPRs covered by the Agreement.

1　Why and what type of provisional measures?

Given that full judicial procedures on the merits of a case may take time to complete, it is sometimes necessary for the judicial authorities to have the authority to act promptly and effectively to stop an alleged infringement immediately, either on notice or, in cases of urgency, without prior notice to the alleged infringer. With this in mind, Article 50.1 obliges Members to authorize the courts to order provisional measures in two situations:

- to prevent an IPR infringement from occurring, in particular to prevent goods from entering the distribution channels, including imported goods immediately after customs clearance.
- to preserve relevant evidence concerning an alleged infringement.

In cases of deliberate infringement, such as trademark counterfeiting or copyright piracy, the defendant is likely to attempt to remove or destroy evidence if he or she is given advance notice of an investigation. Therefore, the TRIPS Agreement requires Members to give judicial authorities the authority to adopt provisional measures without prior hearing of the alleged infringer (or '*inaudita altera parte*'), in particular where any delay could cause irreparable harm to the right holder, or where there is a demonstrable risk of evidence being destroyed (Article 50.2).

2　Procedural requirements and safeguards against abuse

The courts may require the applicant to provide evidence of being the right holder and that the right concerned is being infringed or that such infringement is imminent (Article 50.3). The applicant may also be required to supply information necessary for the identification of the goods (Article 50.5).

Where provisional measures are taken without prior notice, the parties affected must, however, be given notice without delay, after the execution of the measures at the latest. The defendant has a right to review with a view to deciding within a reasonable period after the notification of the measures, whether provisional measures shall be modified, revoked or confirmed (Article 50.4).

Article 50 provides for certain additional safeguards against abuse of provisional measures, such as the authority of courts:

- to order the applicant to provide a security or equivalent assurance that is sufficient to protect the defendant and to prevent abuse (Article 50.3);
- upon request by the defendant, to revoke or nullify provisional measures if the applicant fails to initiate proceedings leading to a decision on the merits of the case within a reasonable period fixed by the judicial authority, or, if such a period has not been determined, within twenty working days or thirty-one calendar days, whichever is longer (Article 50.6); and
- upon request by the defendant, to order the applicant to pay compensation to the defendant for any injury caused by provisional measures, where:
  - they are revoked;
  - they lapse because the applicant has not acted or omitted to take appropriate action; or
  - it is subsequently found that there has been no infringement or threat of infringement of an IPR (Article 50.7).

As for civil and administrative procedures (Article 49), Article 50.8 clarifies that these principles also apply to administrative procedures to the extent that any provisional measure can be ordered as a result of such procedures.[3]

---

[3] A number of settled dispute settlement cases have addressed the availability of provisional measures. *Denmark – Measures Affecting the Enforcement of Intellectual Property Rights* (WT/DS83) and *Sweden – Measures Affecting the Enforcement of Intellectual Property Rights* (WT/DS86) concerned the obligation to make available prompt and effective provisional measures *inaudita altera parte* (see Article 50.2) in civil proceedings involving IPRs. Following amendments to the Danish and Swedish laws, parties to the cases notified mutually agreed solutions. In its request for consultation in (*Argentina – Certain Measures on the Protection of Patents and Test Data* (DS196)), the United States claimed, *inter alia*, that Argentina had failed to provide prompt and effective provisional measures, such as

E   Border measures

The most efficient enforcement action is generally at the point of production of infringing goods. The TRIPS Agreement takes into account that enforcement at that point may not be possible where imported goods are involved and therefore incorporates special proced-ures regarding enforcement of IPRs at the border. These special require-ments are contained in Articles 51 to 60 of the TRIPS Agreement. They enable IPR holders to obtain the cooperation of customs administrations to intercept infringing goods at the border and to prevent the release of these goods into circulation. This is termed 'suspension of release' of the goods by the customs authorities; it is not the same as a full infringement action, and to be ultimately effective must be followed by legal proceed-ings leading to a decision on the merits of the case. As a general rule, the right holder must request the customs authorities to take action; there is no obligation on customs authorities to act *ex officio*, although Members may provide for this.

1   Scope and coverage

(a)   Mandatory coverage of pirated copyright goods and counterfeit trademark goods

The goods subject to border enforcement procedures must include at least counterfeit trademark and pirated copyright goods (Article 51).

Footnote 14(a) defines counterfeited trademark goods as 'any goods, including packaging, bearing without authorization a trademark which is identical to the trademark validly registered in respect of such goods, or which cannot be distinguished in its essential aspects from such a trademark, and which thereby infringes the rights of the owner of the trademark in question under the law of the country of importation'. The term 'counterfeit' is therefore used in the TRIPS Agreement only in the trademark area. Counterfeit trademark goods are goods involving

---

preliminary injunctions, for purposes of preventing infringements of patent rights from occurring. The case was settled through a mutually agreed solution, as part of which Argentina undertook to submit a bill to its National Congress containing precise language with respect to the authority of judicial authorities to order provisional measures in relation to patents.

slavish copying of trademarks. A counterfeit good gives the impression of being the genuine product (for instance a 'Louis Vuitton' bag, 'Rolex' watch, 'Puma' shoes) originating from the genuine manufacturer or trader. It can therefore be usually characterized as fraud since confusion between the genuine product and the substantially identical copy is intended. This is distinct from 'ordinary' trademark infringement: in such cases, the issue may be whether an alleged infringer's mark is sufficiently close to a registered mark for there to be a likelihood of confusion between the marks.

Footnote 14(b) defines pirated copyright goods as 'any goods which are copies made without the consent of the right holder or person duly authorized by the right holder in the country of production and which are made directly or indirectly from an article where the making of that copy would have constituted an infringement of a copyright or a related right under the law of the country of importation'. The term 'pirated' thus relates to infringement of copyright and related rights. Piracy is not a recent phenomenon. However, it has increased with advances in the means by which works may be communicated (print, media, audio and visual recordings), as well as the advances in technology (computer and digital technology) which facilitate reproduction and communication of copyright works.

(b)   Optional coverage

Members may, but are not required to, make border measures available for:

- infringement of other IPRs: the extension of border measures to goods which involve other infringements of IPRs, such as patents, GIs, industrial designs, or layout-designs, is optional, as long as the other requirements of Section 4 are met;
- infringing goods destined for exportation;
- goods in transit: footnote 13 of the TRIPS Agreement clarifies that Members are not obliged to make border measures available for such goods;
- *de minimis* imports, that is the importation of small quantities of goods of a non-commercial nature, typically contained in travellers' personal luggage or sent in small consignments. This reflects the fact that customs authorities will often find it difficult to control such imports, and that the right holder may be less disposed to bear the

costs of enforcement. However, some Members have opted for a 'no tolerance' policy, where even imports of this nature are considered to be infringing and the importer (such as a traveller) may be held to be guilty of an offence in such cases; and

- parallel imports: Members are not obliged to apply border measures to imports of goods put on the market in another country by or with the consent of the right holder. This is because parallel or grey-market imports are not imports of counterfeit products produced without any authorization of the right holder, and may not be considered infringing goods in the importing country. As explained in Chapter I, these products are marketed by the right holder or with his permission in one country and subsequently imported into another country without his or her approval.

2   *Procedural requirements and safeguards against abuse*

Like other enforcement procedures, border measures are also subject to certain procedural requirements and safeguards against abuse. Some of those are similar to the requirements applying to provisional measures under Article 50.

(a)   Application, including evidence and description of goods

Each Member must designate a 'competent authority' to which applications by right holders for customs action shall be lodged (Article 51). This can be a judicial authority, such as a judge or a court, or an administrative authority, such as a special service within the customs administration.

Right holders applying for border measures must provide adequate evidence satisfying the competent authorities that there is prima facie an IPR infringement under the importing country's laws. This task is facilitated where rights are subject to registration, but may prove more difficult in regard to those rights which are not based on registration, such as copyright-protected works, and which therefore may require customs to develop some IPR expertise. The right holder is also due to supply a sufficiently detailed description of the goods concerned so as to facilitate their identification by customs authorities. The competent authorities shall then inform the applicant within a reasonable period about the acceptance of the application and for how long they will take the requested action, where the latter has been determined by the authority (Article 52).

(b) Notice of suspension

Where customs release of particular goods has been suspended, the importer and the applicant must be promptly notified of the detention of the goods (Article 54).

(c) Duration of suspension

A time limit applies to the suspension of customs release of the goods: if the applicant fails to initiate proceedings leading to a decision on the merits of a case within ten working days from the notice of suspension, and the duly empowered authority has not provisionally prolonged the suspension, the goods shall normally be released. It is possible to extend this delay by an additional ten days (Article 55).

Once judicial proceedings on the merits of a case have been initiated, the defendant may request a review of the suspension in order to decide whether the measure is to be modified or revoked, or whether it is to be confirmed.

Special rules apply where the suspension of the allegedly infringing goods takes place based on a decision other than by a court or other independent authority and where such goods involve industrial designs, patents, layout-designs or undisclosed information. In such cases, the importer must be entitled to obtain their release on the posting of a security sufficient to protect the right holder from any infringement, if the period for the initiation of proceedings has expired without the granting of provisional measures by the duly empowered authority (Article 53.2).

(d) Posting of security/payment of compensation

As in the case of provisional measures, the Section on border measures provides for certain additional safeguards against abuse, under which the competent authority may require the applicant:

- to provide a security or equivalent assurance sufficient to protect the defendant and the competent authorities and to prevent abuse. However, such security may not be such as to unreasonably deter the applicant from having recourse to these procedures (Article 53.1); and
- to pay appropriate compensation to persons whose interests have been adversely affected by the wrongful detention of goods or through detention of goods released pursuant to the failure of the applicant to initiate in time proceedings leading to a decision on the merits of the case (Article 56).

3   Right of inspection and information

In most cases, the right holder is obviously best placed to assist in the identification of infringing goods. The competent authorities may therefore give the right holder, and also the importer, sufficient opportunity to inspect any goods detained by the customs authorities. This is meant to allow the right holder to substantiate his or her claims, and the importer to prepare the defence. Where goods have been found infringing as a result of a decision on the merits, the TRIPS Agreement leaves it to Members to decide whether the right holder should be enabled to be informed of other persons in the distribution channel so that appropriate action could also be taken against them (Article 57). Both the right of inspection and information are subject to the protection of confidential information.

4   Remedies

Under Article 59, the competent authorities must have the power to order the destruction or disposal outside the channels of commerce of infringing goods in such a manner as to avoid any harm to the right holder. Unlike in Article 46 (which deals with general civil remedies), remedies regarding the material used to produce the infringing goods are not available, because this section addresses imported goods, for which the production material is usually located in a third country. Otherwise, the same principles as in Article 46 on civil remedies apply to border measures:

- need to ensure proportionality of the measure;
- no compensation is paid to the defendant;
- the measure is ordered to avoid any harm caused to the right holder; and
- the measure is not contrary to constitutional requirements.

The remedies are without prejudice to other rights of action open to the right holder, such as to obtain damages through civil litigation, and are subject to the right of the defendant to seek review by a judicial authority.

As regards counterfeit trademark goods, it is clarified that the authorities may not allow the re-exportation of the infringing goods in an unaltered state or subject them to a different customs procedure (e.g. transit), other than in exceptional circumstances.

5 Special rules for ex officio action

Providing for *ex officio* action by the competent authorities (i.e. without a request from the right holder) is not mandatory under the TRIPS Agreement. However, where Members provide for the competent authorities to act upon their own initiative and to suspend the release of goods on the basis of prima facie evidence of IPR infringement, certain additional rules apply (Article 58):

- right holders may be asked at any time to provide information assisting the competent authorities to act upon their own initiative; and
- the importer and the right holder are to be promptly notified of the suspension. Where the importer has appealed against the suspension, the conditions regarding the duration of the suspension (Article 55) apply *mutatis mutandis.*

Like under Article 48.2, actions of public authorities must be taken or intended in good faith if they are not to give rise to liability to appropriate remedial measures.

The application of the provisions on border measures was considered by the panel in *China – Intellectual Property Rights* (DS362). This case is summarized in Box VII.1.

F   Criminal procedures

1   Scope and coverage

Section V, the fifth and final section in the enforcement part of the TRIPS Agreement covers criminal procedures. Article 61 stipulates that criminal procedures and penalties are only mandatory in cases of:

- wilful acts;
- of trademark counterfeiting or copyright piracy;
- carried out on a commercial scale.

Article 61 explicitly recognizes that Members may provide for criminal procedures to be applied in other cases of infringement of intellectual property rights, in particular where those are committed wilfully and on a commercial scale.

2   Remedies

Criminal sanctions must include imprisonment and/or monetary fines sufficient to provide a deterrent, consistent with the level of penalties applied for crimes of a corresponding gravity. In appropriate cases, remedies must also include seizure, forfeiture and destruction of the infringing goods and of materials and equipment used to produce them (Box VII.1).

BOX VII.1 CHINA – INTELLECTUAL PROPERTY RIGHTS[4] (DS362)

PARTIES		AGREEMENT	TIMELINE OF THE DISPUTE	
Complainant	*United States*	*TRIPS Articles 9, 41, 46, 59, 61*	Establishment of Panel	25 September 2007
			Circulation of Panel report	13 November 2008
Respondent	*China*	*Berne Convention*	Circulation of Appellate Body report	NA
			Adoption	20 March 2009

(a) Measures and intellectual property rights at issue

- *Measures at issue*:

  (i) China's Criminal Law and related Supreme People's Court Interpretations that establish thresholds for criminal procedures and penalties for infringements of IPRs;

  (ii) China's Regulations for Customs Protection of Intellectual Property Rights and related Implementing Measures that govern the disposal of infringing goods confiscated by customs authorities; and

  (iii) Article 4 of China's Copyright Law that denies protection and enforcement to works that have not been authorized for publication or distribution within China.

- *IP at issue*: Copyright and trademarks.

(b) Summary of key Panel findings[5]

Criminal Thresholds

- *TRIPS Article 61:* The Panel found that while China's criminal measures exclude some copyright and trademark infringements from criminal liability where the

---

[4] *China – Measures Affecting the Protection and Enforcement of Intellectual Property Rights* (DS362).

[5] Other issues addressed in this case: prima facie case; Panel's terms of reference; exhaustiveness of TRIPS Article 59; information from WIPO.

BOX VII.1 (*cont.*)

infringement falls below numerical thresholds fixed in terms of the amount of turnover, profit, sales or copies of infringing goods, this fact alone was not enough to find a violation because Article 61 does not require Members to criminalize all copyright and trademark infringement. The Panel found that the term 'commercial scale' in Article 61 meant 'the magnitude or extent of typical or usual commercial activity with respect to a given product in a given market'. The Panel did not endorse China's thresholds but concluded that the factual evidence presented by the United States was inadequate to show whether or not the cases excluded from criminal liability met the TRIPS standard of 'commercial scale' when that standard is applied to China's marketplace.

Customs Measures

- *TRIPS Article 59:* The Panel found that the customs measures were not subject to Articles 51 to 60 of the TRIPS Agreement to the extent that they apply to exports. With respect to imports, although auctioning of goods is not prohibited by Article 59, the Panel concluded that the way in which China's customs auctions these goods was inconsistent with Article 59, because it permits the sale of goods after the simple removal of the trademark in more than just exceptional cases.

Copyright Law

- *TRIPS Article 9.1 (Berne Convention Article 5(1) and Article 17), Article 41.1:* The Panel found that while China has the right to prohibit the circulation and exhibition of works, as acknowledged in Article 17 of the Berne Convention, this does not justify the denial of all copyright protection in any work. China's failure to protect copyright in prohibited works (i.e. that are banned because of their illegal content) is therefore inconsistent with Article 5(1) of the Berne Convention as incorporated in Article 9.1, as well as with Article 41.1.

G   Cooperation and contact points

1   *Cooperation between Members*

Although Article 69 on international cooperation is incorporated in Part VII of the TRIPS Agreement on institutional arrangements, it is directly related to Part III on enforcement of IPRs. It provides that Members agree to cooperate with a view to eliminating international trade in IPR-infringing goods.

2   Contact points

As a concrete measure to promote this goal, Members are required to establish contact points in their administrations and be ready to exchange information on trade in infringing goods. There is a particular obligation to promote the exchange of information and cooperation between customs authorities with respect to two categories of IPR infringement: trade in counterfeit trademark goods and pirated copyright goods.

The TRIPS Council receives notifications and updates of these contact points from its Members. For more information, see Appendix 1, B2.

VIII

Dispute prevention and settlement

A   Introduction

Chapters I to VII have dealt with Members' commitments as regards the substantive standards for protection of IPRs under domestic laws, as well as their enforcement through their domestic legal systems. An important feature of the TRIPS Agreement is that disputes between governments about compliance by Member governments with these TRIPS obligations are subject to the dispute settlement system of the WTO. The TRIPS provisions on dispute settlement are contained in Part V of the TRIPS Agreement entitled 'Dispute Prevention and Settlement'.

Dispute settlement is a major feature of the WTO legal system, and this chapter outlines how it applies to disputes between Members concerning compliance with TRIPS obligations. First, however, it reviews the main TRIPS provisions and working methods relating to transparency, whose main goal is to contribute to preventing disputes from arising between governments in the first place. This chapter then reviews the main principles governing dispute settlement, including the jurisdiction of the WTO, and briefly describes the WTO dispute settlement procedures. A particular matter, still unresolved, concerns the applicability of the so-called non-violation and situation complaints to the settlement of disputes under the TRIPS Agreement. This chapter then reviews the experience to date with disputes about TRIPS compliance. A complete list of disputes in the area of TRIPS is provided at the end of this chapter, together with information about how to access the key documents.

This chapter provides a general overview of how the WTO dispute settlement system relates to the TRIPS Agreement. A guide to resources is provided at the end of this chapter.

B   Dispute prevention and the review of national implementing legislation

Chapter I described how the Council for TRIPS is the body, open to all Members of the WTO, that has responsibility for the administration of the TRIPS Agreement, in particular for monitoring the operation of the Agreement. The Council also constitutes a forum for consultations on any problems relating to TRIPS arising between Members as well as for clarifying and interpreting provisions of the TRIPS Agreement. The aim is, whenever possible, to resolve differences between Members without the need for formal recourse to dispute settlement.

The TRIPS Agreement promotes transparency by requiring Members to publish laws and regulations and final judicial decisions and administrative rulings of general application made effective by a Member pertaining to the subject matter of the Agreement. Relevant bilateral and other agreements must also be published (Article 63.1).

Article 63.2 requires Members to notify relevant laws and regulations to the Council for TRIPS in order to assist the Council in its review of the operation of the Agreement. This is also designed to promote transparency. Chapter I discussed these procedures in detail.

One of the characteristics of the former GATT and now of the WTO is the detailed and continuous follow-up of the implementation of obligations and the monitoring of compliance with them. The underlying belief is that unless there is a monitoring of compliance with international commitments, those commitments will be worthless. Monitoring of compliance in the TRIPS Council is done in two main ways.

First, the TRIPS Council is a body in which any Member can raise any issue relating to compliance with the TRIPS Agreement by other parties. This has happened on a number of occasions, either in relation to the practices of a specific country, or concerning the application of a specific provision of the TRIPS Agreement.

The second approach to monitoring compliance is a systematic examination of each Member's national implementing legislation by the other Members, involving the notification and a review of the legislation of Members. The initial notification of implementing laws and regulations made by each Member pursuant to Article 63.2 at the end of its transition period forms the basis for the review of the implementing legislation of that Member carried out by the Council. Reviews were held for developed country Members starting in 1996, and for developing countries in 2000. For newly acceded Members they are held after the entry into force of their membership. For the discussion of the procedures for these reviews and resulting documentation, see Chapter I, section E2(b).

By providing an opportunity to identify deficiencies in notified laws and regulations, as well as differences in interpretation, the review mechanism is an important vehicle for resolving issues that might otherwise become the subject of formal dispute settlement proceedings.

Another provision promoting transparency and aimed at preventing disputes is found in Article 63.3. It requires each Member to be prepared to supply, in response to a written request from another Member, information on its relevant laws and regulations, decisions of general application, and bilateral agreements. A Member, having reason to believe that a specific judicial decision, administrative ruling or bilateral agreement affects its rights under the TRIPS Agreement, may also request in writing to be given access to or be informed in sufficient detail of such material.

C   Dispute settlement

1   General

An important feature of the TRIPS Agreement is that it provides an operational system for the settlement of disputes between governments of Members about compliance with their respective obligations relating to IPRs. Pre-existing international law in this area did not provide any practical means of recourse, at the multilateral level, to a government that believed that another government was not respecting its treaty obligations. Now, Member governments who wish to take action against an alleged violation of a TRIPS obligation have recourse to the multilateral WTO dispute settlement procedures in order to obtain a satisfactory settlement of the matter. These procedures also apply to alleged violations of the provisions of the Berne and Paris Conventions, and other treaties, where incorporated in the TRIPS Agreement.

Article 64.1 of the TRIPS Agreement provides that Articles XXII and XXIII of the General Agreement on Tariffs and Trade 1994 ('GATT 1994'), as elaborated and applied by the Dispute Settlement Understanding ('DSU'), shall apply to consultations and the settlement of disputes under the TRIPS Agreement. The full name of the DSU is

'Understanding on Rules and Procedures Governing the Settlement of Disputes'. As noted in Chapter I, like the TRIPS Agreement, it is an annex to the to the Marrakesh Agreement Establishing the World Trade Organization (the 'WTO Agreement'). The DSU provides rules and procedures for consultations and the settlement of disputes between Members concerning their rights and obligations under WTO Agreements. It applies to the WTO Agreement and its Annexes, except Annex 3 on the Trade Policy Review Mechanism.

In general, the procedures are based on previous experience in the GATT, which was the forerunner of the WTO. This is why Article 64.1 of the TRIPS Agreement refers to the provisions of Articles XXII and XXIII of GATT 1994 as elaborated and applied by the DSU.

Only Member governments can initiate and participate in the dispute settlement procedure in the WTO and such complaints can only be directed at other Member governments, due to the intergovernmental nature of the WTO. Member governments decide which disputes to bring to the WTO. Neither the WTO as an organization, nor its Secretariat, nor any private party can make that decision. Before bringing a case, a Member must exercise its judgment as to whether action under the dispute settlement procedures would be fruitful but, once it has engaged the dispute settlement mechanism, the WTO must follow its procedures to their conclusion or until the parties agree otherwise. Parties to the dispute can agree to settle the case at any stage of the process. A solution mutually agreed by the parties and consistent with the WTO Agreements is clearly to be preferred.

Private parties whose rights and interests are affected by implementation of the WTO Agreements have no standing in WTO procedures, but must rely on their government to bring or defend an action, or to intervene as a so-called third party. A 'third party' is a Member not party to a dispute. It can request to take part in consultations if it has a substantial trade interest in the matter at dispute (Article 4.1 of the DSU). Such third party also has an opportunity to be heard by the panel and make written submissions to it (Article 10.2 of the DSU). It may also participate in the appellate review (Article 17.4 of the DSU).

Article XXIII.1 of GATT 1994 provides for three grounds for complaints: (1) the failure of another Member to carry out its obligations under WTO Agreements; (2) the application by another Member of any measure, whether or not it conflicts with the provisions under those agreements; or (3) the existence of any other situation.

In practice, most complaints brought to the WTO dispute settlement system are of the first type: concerning an alleged failure by another Member to carry out its obligations under WTO Agreements, including the TRIPS Agreement. These are commonly known as 'violation complaints'.

The second and third grounds for complaint allow a government to initiate the dispute settlement proceedings even when an agreement has not been violated, so-called 'non-violation complaints' or 'situation complaints'. While these complaints can be raised about other WTO Agreements, Members have agreed on a moratorium on the use of non-violation and situation complaints in the area of TRIPS (see section C2 below).

The Member addressed in the complaint must engage in the procedures in good faith in an effort to resolve the dispute and must comply with the final rulings, pending which compensation should be accorded or retaliation can be authorized.

Members have agreed to have recourse to the WTO procedures when they seek to take action against a violation of an obligation, and not to make unilateral determinations of violation or on retaliatory action. A Member must first go through the dispute settlement procedure before it makes a determination that a violation has occurred, which requires it to prove its claims before an impartial ad hoc panel, and on appeal if this avenue is chosen. Where its claims are upheld, a committee of all Members known as the Dispute Settlement Body ('DSB') will request the Member concerned to bring its measures into conformity with its obligations under the TRIPS Agreement.

The WTO dispute settlement system is designed to ensure the rule of law in international trade relations through the impartial and effective resolution of disputes between governments.

Section D below contains a brief description of the dispute settlement procedures.

2   Non-violation and situation complaints

As noted above, most complaints brought to the dispute settlement system concern an alleged failure by another Member to carry out its obligations under WTO Agreements. These are commonly known as 'violation complaints'. 'Non-violation' deals with a government's ability to bring a dispute to the WTO, based on loss of an expected benefit caused by another Member's actions – even if no WTO Agreement or

---

BOX VIII.1 PARAGRAPH 1 OF ARTICLE XXIII OF GATT 1994 ON THE
THREE GROUNDS FOR COMPLAINTS

If any contracting party should consider that any benefit accruing to it directly or indirectly under this Agreement is being nullified or impaired or that the attainment of any objective of the Agreement is being impeded as the result of

(a) the failure of another contracting party to carry out its obligations under this Agreement, or
(b) the application by another contracting party of any measure, whether or not it conflicts with the provisions of this Agreement, or
(c) the existence of any other situation,

the contracting party may, with a view to the satisfactory adjustment of the matter, make written representations or proposals to the other contracting party or parties which it considers to be concerned. Any contracting party thus approached shall give sympathetic consideration to the representations or proposals made to it.

---

commitment has actually been violated. An example of this could be where a government has agreed to lower tariffs on certain goods, but then introduces national measures that nullify the effect of tariff reduction, for example by providing an equivalent production subsidy to its domestic producers.

In general, the aim of non-violation complaints is to help preserve the balance of benefits struck during multilateral negotiations, recognizing that it is not possible or desirable to seek to regulate all government measures that may affect the value of such benefits.

A 'situation' complaint is understood to cover any situation that results in nullification or impairment of benefits, not necessarily through a specific government measure, but this concept has never been analysed in WTO and GATT dispute settlement.

Initially, Article 64.2 of the TRIPS Agreement prevented the application of non-violation and situation complaints to disputes under the TRIPS Agreement within the first five years of the entry into force of the Agreement. Article 64.3 of the TRIPS Agreement instructed the TRIPS Council to examine the extent and way ('scope and modalities') in which complaints of this type could be made and make recommendations to the General Council by the end of 1999.

This 'moratorium' on the use of non-violation and situation complaints has been extended a number of times, namely by Ministers at the

Doha Ministerial Conference in 2001,[1] by the WTO General Council in 2004 as part of the so-called 'July 2004 package',[2] by the Ministerial Conference in Hong Kong, China in 2005[3], and by the Ministerial Conferences in Geneva in 2009 and 2011.[4] At the same time, the TRIPS Council has been instructed to continue its examination of the scope and modalities for this type of complaints and make recommendations.[5]

D   Description of the dispute settlement procedures

This section reviews what happens when one WTO Member chooses to bring a formal complaint against another Member concerning compliance with TRIPS standards. The procedures are the same as for any other WTO dispute, there being no special procedures for TRIPS (apart from the restriction to 'violation' disputes, discussed above). The dispute settlement process has three main phases: (i) consultations between the parties; (ii) adjudication by Panels and, if either party appeals a Panel ruling, by the Appellate Body; and (iii) adoption of Panel/Appellate reports(s) and implementation of the ruling, which includes the possibility of countermeasures in the event of failure by the losing party to implement the ruling. Figure VIII.1 illustrates the procedural steps in a typical WTO dispute settlement case, which are discussed below.

1   Consultations between the parties

The procedures begin with a mandatory consultation period in an effort to find a mutually satisfactory solution. Members must enter into consultations in good faith within thirty days of a formal request for consultations, and the consultations must last at least sixty days from the

---

[1] Paragraph 11.1 of the Decision of 14 November 2001 on Implementation-Related Issues and Concerns in document WT/MIN(01)/17.

[2] Paragraph 1.h of the Decision of 1 August 2004 in document WT/L/579.

[3] Paragraph 45 of the Ministerial Declaration of 18 December 2005 in document WT/MIN (05)/DEC.

[4] Decisions of 2 December 2009 and 17 December 2011 on TRIPS Non-Violation and Situation Complaints in documents WT/L/783 and WT/L/842, respectively.

[5] Further information can be found in a Secretariat summary note on delegations' positions on non-violation complaints at the TRIPS Council in document IP/C/W/349/ Rev.1, and in a factual background note on experience with non-violation complaints under the GATT/WTO in document IP/C/W/124.

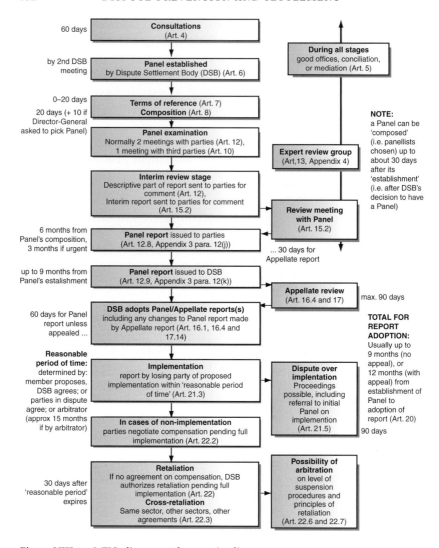

Figure VIII.1 WTO dispute settlement timeline

date of receipt of the request, unless the parties agree otherwise or the Member addressed by the request refuses to consult. During this time, the issues in dispute can be clarified and this may help the parties settle the dispute then, without further procedures, as indeed happens in a number of cases. Other Member governments with a substantial trade interest can also request to join the consultations. All requests for consultations are circulated to all Members and made available to the public on the WTO website; they outline the substance of the complaint and identify the provisions that are at issue.

2 Panel examination

If the consultations fail to settle a dispute, the complaining Member may request the DSB to establish a 'Panel' to examine the matter and make such findings as will assist the DSB in making recommendations to secure a positive solution to the dispute. A Panel must be established at the latest by the second request to the DSB. Other Member governments with a substantial interest in the matter can join the dispute as third parties.

Panels normally comprise three persons of appropriate background and experience, who are not citizens of Members party to the dispute or third parties, unless the parties to the dispute agree otherwise. They serve in their individual capacity and not as government representatives. They are never serving WTO Secretariat officials. The parties to the dispute attempt to agree on the composition of the Panel on the basis of names proposed by the Secretariat, failing which the Director-General can, upon request, determine its composition in consultation with the parties to the dispute. The names of the panellists are made public on the WTO website.

The parties to the dispute make written submissions and oral statements at meetings with the Panel. Third parties also have an opportunity to be heard by the Panel and make written submissions to it. A Panel will normally complete its work within six months, by publishing a report containing findings of fact and law, with its conclusions. The report is circulated to all Members and made available to the public on the WTO website. If there is no appeal, it can be proposed for adoption by the DSB.

3 Appellate review

A party to the dispute may appeal the Panel's findings to the Appellate Body, which is a standing body of seven individuals, three of whom serve on any one case. Member governments appoint Appellate Body Members in the DSB for four-year terms.

Appeals are limited to issues of law covered in the Panel report and legal interpretations developed by the Panel. The parties make written submissions and oral statements at a meeting with the Appellate Body and third parties may also participate. The Appellate Body completes its work within ninety days, by publishing a report containing its findings on the issues raised in the appeal, which may uphold, modify or reverse the legal findings and conclusions of the Panel. The report is circulated to all Members and made available to the public on the WTO website.

4   Adoption of the Panel/Appellate report(s) and implementation

The effectiveness of the WTO dispute settlement procedures flows partly from the way in which the reports on particular disputes are 'adopted', or acquire legal force. The DSB considers the Panel report, together with any modifications to it determined by the Appellate Body in cases of appeal, after it has been circulated to Members, and adopts it unless there is consensus not to do so. This negative consensus rule effectively requires the consent of the Member which prevailed in the report to prevent its adoption. As a result, Panel and Appellate Body reports are adopted almost automatically.

Where a Panel or the Appellate Body has concluded that a measure was inconsistent with the TRIPS Agreement, or any other WTO Agreement covered by the DSU, its report will recommend that the Member concerned bring the measure into conformity with that Agreement. The Member is given a reasonable period of time in which to do so. The reasonable period of time is agreed by the parties, failing which it can be determined by arbitration. In TRIPS cases this has generally ranged from six months, where a regulation had to be repealed, to twelve months, where a statute had to be amended by the legislature.

In the great majority of cases, Members comply with the recommendations contained in a report as adopted by the DSB. However, if there is disagreement as to whether a Member has indeed complied, the disagreement can be decided through another proceeding before a Panel, wherever possible the same three persons who formed the original Panel. This has only occurred in a small number of cases so far, sometimes because there was a disagreement as to whether amendments made to the law to comply with the recommendations were themselves consistent with the WTO Agreements. The Panel normally completes its work within ninety days, by publishing another report, which can also be appealed to the Appellate Body, which normally completes its work within a further ninety days.

The DSB monitors implementation of its recommendations. The Member concerned must provide regular status reports on implementation from at least six months after the date on which the reasonable period of time is established until the issue is resolved.

Full implementation of a recommendation to bring a measure into conformity with the WTO Agreements is the aim of this part of the procedures. However, pending implementation there is a possibility for the party which prevailed in the dispute to obtain voluntary compensation from the Member concerned, or authorization from the DSB to suspend obligations or withdraw concessions *vis-à-vis* that Member (in other words to 'retaliate'). This possibility is intended to give credibility to the system and ensure prompt compliance within the reasonable period of time. Although findings are normally implemented within this period, in a relatively small number of cases retaliation has been authorized.

Retaliation can be authorized, as a general principle, in the same WTO agreement where WTO inconsistencies have been found. So, for example, import duties can be increased above the bound rates on goods from a Member that has been found in breach of the GATT rules on trade in goods. Where this general principle is not practicable or effective, retaliation can be authorized under another WTO Agreement from the one in which the WTO inconsistencies have been found, which is known as 'cross-retaliation'.

The DSB has authorized countermeasures in seventeen cases. Three of them involved 'cross-retaliation', namely *EC – Bananas III*, *US – Gambling* and *US – Upland Cotton*. In each of them, countermeasures were authorized *inter alia* in the area of TRIPS concerning violation in the area of GATT or the General Agreement on Trade in Services (GATS).[6] For example, the first of them concerned the failure of the European Communities to bring its banana regime into compliance with a Panel ruling. In 2000, Ecuador got the authorization to cross-retaliate against the European Communities by denying them protection of related rights, GIs and industrial designs. This and other related disputes were finally settled by the Geneva Agreement on Trade in Bananas in December 2009.[7]

---

[6] The complaining parties in these three cases were Ecuador, Antigua and Barbuda, and Brazil, respectively. The authorizations by the DSB were based on reports by Arbitrators that acted pursuant to Article 22.6 to examine whether the level of suspension of concessions or other obligations proposed by the complaining party was equivalent to the level of nullification or impairment, and to determine if the proposed suspension was allowed under the covered agreement. The decisions of the arbitrators can be found in documents WT/DS27/ARB/ECU, WT/DS285/ARB, and WT/DS267/ARB/1 and 2, respectively.

[7] See document WT/L/784.

E   Experience in the area of TRIPS

It would appear that most cases relating to matters of compliance with the requirements of the TRIPS Agreement are resolved in bilateral consultations between the Members concerned, either in Geneva or in capitals, without invoking the dispute settlement procedures in the DSB. Many issues have also come up in the review of the national TRIPS implementing legislation carried out by the TRIPS Council, but only very rarely do these issues get a follow-up in dispute settlement proceedings. And even after the invocation of formal dispute settlement procedures, developing a mutually acceptable solution consistent with the WTO provisions to a problem between Members is encouraged throughout the dispute settlement process. In fact, the settlement rate has so far been quite high in the area of TRIPS.

As of July 2011, twenty-nine dispute settlement complaints had been initiated in the WTO in the area of TRIPS in relation to twenty-three distinct matters or specific cases. This represents about 7 per cent of cases filed under all WTO Agreements. Panel reports and, when they have been appealed, Appellate Body reports, have been adopted in ten cases. Fourteen of the other cases have been settled bilaterally between the parties to the dispute; the terms of these settlements are made public and can be important in influencing the way others implement the Agreement. As regards the rest, consultations are still pending or the case has become inactive.

Table VIII.1 at the end of this chapter contains a listing of all the TRIPS cases, their status as of July 2011 and selected documents relating to them, with guidance on accessing these documents.

Some of the early TRIPS cases only concerned transitional arrangements. For example, the first TRIPS complaint concerned the extent to which sound recordings that had been made before the TRIPS Agreement became applicable had to be protected (*Japan – Measures Concerning Sound Recordings* (DS28 and 42), two cases that were both settled). The first two Panel and/or Appellate reports were issued on two complaints concerning the so-called 'mail-box' and exclusive marketing rights provisions in paragraphs 8 and 9 of Article 70 (*India – Patents I and II* (DS50 and 79)). Another case on the same issue was settled (*Pakistan – Patent Protection for Pharmaceutical and Agricultural Chemical Products* (DS36)). Panel and Appellate reports in a further case concerned the extent to which patents issued prior to the entry into force of the Agreement benefited from the protection under it (*Canada – Term of Patent Protection* (DS170)).

Table VIII.1 *Dispute settlement cases in the area of TRIPS (as of January 2012)*

Document Series	Defendant and full title of dispute settlement case (*short titles provided for cases in respect of which the DSB has adopted a report*)	Complainant	Request for consultations	Status	List of selected documents
IP/D/29 WT/DS409	EUROPEAN UNION – Seizure of Generic Drugs in Transit	BRAZIL	12 May 2010	Consultations pending	
IP/D/28 WT/DS408	EUROPEAN UNION – Seizure of Generic Drugs in Transit	INDIA	11 May 2010	Consultations pending	
IP/D/27 WT/DS372 (also S/L/319)	CHINA – Measures Affecting Financial Information Services and Foreign Financial Information Suppliers	EC	3 March 2008	Mutually agreed solution notified on 4 December 2008	Mutually agreed solution WT/DS372/4
IP/D/26 WT/DS362 (also G/L/819)	CHINA – Measures Affecting the Protection and	UNITED STATES	10 April 2007	Panel report adopted on 20 March 2009	Panel report WT/DS362/R

Table VIII.1 (*cont.*)

Document Series	Defendant and full title of dispute settlement case (*short titles provided for cases in respect of which the DSB has adopted a report*)	Complainant	Request for consultations	Status	List of selected documents
	Enforcement of Intellectual Property Rights (*China – Intellectual Property Rights*)				
IP/D/25 WT/DS290 (also G/L/623 G/TBT/D/27)	EUROPEAN COMMUNITIES – Protection of Trademarks and Geographical Indications for Agricultural Products and Foodstuffs (*EC –*	AUSTRALIA	17 April 2003	Panel report adopted on 20 April 2005	Panel report WT/DS290/R

Trademarks and Geographical Indications)

IP/D/24 WT/DS224	UNITED STATES – US Patent Code	BRAZIL	31 January 2001	Consultations pending	
IP/D/23 WT/DS199	BRAZIL – Measures Affecting Patent Protection	UNITED STATES	30 May 2000	Mutually agreed solution notified on 5 July 2001	Mutually agreed solution WT/DS199/4
IP/D/22 WT/DS196	ARGENTINA – Certain Measures on the Protection of Patents and Test Data	UNITED STATES	30 May 2000	Mutually agreed solution notified on 31 May 2002	Mutually agreed solution WT/DS196/4
IP/D/21 WT/DS186	UNITED STATES – Section 337 of the Tariff Act of 1930 and Amendments thereto	EC	12 January 2000	Consultations pending	
IP/D/20 WT/DS176	UNITED STATES – Section 211 Omnibus Appropriations Act of 1998 (US – Section 211 Appropriations Act)	EC	8 July 1999	Appellate Body and Panel reports adopted on 1 February 2002	Panel report WT/DS176/R Appellate Body report WT/DS176/AB/R

Table VIII.1 (*cont.*)

Document Series	Defendant and full title of dispute settlement case (*short titles provided for cases in respect of which the DSB has adopted a report*)	Complainant	Request for consultations	Status	List of selected documents
IP/D/19 WT/DS174 IP/D/19/Add.1 WT/DS174/Add.1 (also G/L/619)	EUROPEAN COMMUNITIES – Protection of Trademarks and Geographical Indications for Agricultural Products and Foodstuffs (*EC – Trademarks and Geographical Indications*)	UNITED STATES	1 June 1999 4 April 2003 (additional consultations)	Panel report adopted on 20 April 2005	Panel report WT/DS174/R
IP/D/18 WT/DS171	ARGENTINA – Patent Protection for Pharmaceutical and Agricultural Chemical Products	UNITED STATES	6 May 1999	Mutually agreed solution notified on 31 May 2002	Mutually agreed solution WT/DS171/3

IP/D/17 WT/DS170	CANADA – Term of Patent Protection (*Canada – Patent Term*)	UNITED STATES	6 May 1999	Appellate Body and Panel reports adopted on 12 October 2000	Panel report WT/DS170/R Appellate Body report WT/DS170/AB/R
IP/D/16 WT/DS160	UNITED STATES – Section 110(5) of the US Copyright Act (*US – Copyright Act*)	EC	26 January 1999	Panel report adopted on 27 July 2000 Recourse to Arbitration under Article 25 of the DSU on 23 July 2001 Referral to Arbitration under Article 22.6 of the DSU on 18 January 2002 Notification of a Mutually Satisfactory Temporary Arrangement notified on 23 June 2003 (effective until 21 December 2004)	Panel report WT/DS160/R Award of the Arbitrators WT/DS160/ARB25/1 Mutually Satisfactory Temporary Arrangement WT/DS160/23

Table VIII.1 (*cont.*)

Document Series	Defendant and full title of dispute settlement case (*short titles provided for cases in respect of which the DSB has adopted a report*)	Complainant	Request for consultations	Status	List of selected documents
IP/D/15 WT/DS153	EUROPEAN COMMUNITIES – Patent Protection for Pharmaceutical and Agricultural Chemical Products	CANADA	2 December 1998	Consultations pending	
IP/D/14 WT/DS125 (Concerns same measures as DS124)	GREECE – Enforcement of Intellectual Property Rights for Motion Pictures and Television Programs	UNITED STATES	30 April 1998	Mutually agreed solution notified on 20 March 2001	Mutually agreed solution WT/DS125/2
IP/D/13 WT/DS124 (Concerns same measures as DS125)	EUROPEAN COMMUNITIES – Enforcement of Intellectual Property Rights for Motion Pictures and Television Programs	UNITED STATES	30 April 1998	Mutually agreed solution notified on 20 March 2001	Mutually agreed solution WT/DS124/2

Number	Title	Complainant	Date	Status	Result
IP/D/12 WT/DS115 (Concerns same measures as DS82)	EUROPEAN COMMUNITIES – Measures Affecting the Grant of Copyright and Neighbouring Rights	UNITED STATES	6 January 1998	Mutually agreed solution notified on 6 November 2000	Mutually agreed solution WT/DS82/3
IP/D/11 WT/DS114	CANADA – Patent Protection of Pharmaceutical Products (*Canada – Pharmaceutical Patents*)	EC	19 December 1997	Panel report adopted on 7 April 2000	Panel report WT/DS114/R
IP/D/10 WT/DS86	SWEDEN – Measures Affecting the Enforcement of Intellectual Property Rights	UNITED STATES	28 May 1997	Mutually agreed solution notified on 2 December 1998	Mutually agreed solution WT/DS86/2
IP/D/9 WT/DS83	DENMARK – Measures Affecting the Enforcement of Intellectual Property Rights	UNITED STATES	21 May 1997	Mutually agreed solution notified on 7 June 2001	Mutually agreed solution WT/DS83/2
IP/D/8 WT/DS82 (Concerns same measures as DS115)	IRELAND – Measures Affecting the Grant of Copyright and Neighbouring Rights	UNITED STATES	14 May 1997	Mutually agreed solution notified on 6 November 2000	Mutually agreed solution WT/DS82/3

Table VIII.1 (*cont.*)

Document Series	Defendant and full title of dispute settlement case (*short titles provided for cases in respect of which the DSB has adopted a report*)	Complainant	Request for consultations	Status	List of selected documents
IP/D/7 WT/DS79	INDIA – Patent Protection for Pharmaceutical and Agricultural Chemical Products (*India – Patents II*)	EC	28 April 1997	Panel report adopted on 22 September 1998	Panel report WT/DS79/R
IP/D/6 WT/DS59 (*See* related complaints by the EC DS54 and Japan DS55 and 64)	INDONESIA – Certain Measures Affecting the Automobile Industry (*Indonesia – Autos*)	UNITED STATES	8 October 1996	Panel report adopted on 23 July 1998	Panel report WT/DS59/R
IP/D/5 WT/DS50	INDIA – Patent Protection for Pharmaceutical and Agricultural Chemical Products (*India – Patents I*)	UNITED STATES	2 June 1996	Appellate Body and Panel reports adopted on 16 January 1998	Panel report WT/DS50/R Appellate Body report WT/DS50/AB/R

IP/D/4 WT/DS42	JAPAN – Measures Concerning Sound Recordings	EC	24 May 1996	Mutually agreed solution notified on 7 November 1997	Mutually agreed solution WT/DS42/4
IP/D/3 WT/DS37	PORTUGAL – Patent Protection under the Industrial Property Act	UNITED STATES	30 April 1996	Mutually agreed solution notified on 3 October 1996	Mutually agreed solution WT/DS37/2 and Corr.1
IP/D/2 WT/DS36	PAKISTAN – Patent Protection for Pharmaceutical and Agricultural Chemical Products	UNITED STATES	30 April 1996	Mutually agreed solution notified on 28 February 1997	Mutually agreed solution WT/DS36/4
IP/D/1 WT/DS28	JAPAN – Measures Concerning Sound Recordings	UNITED STATES	9 February 1996	Mutually agreed solution notified on 24 January 1997	Mutually agreed solution WT/DS28/4

A number of the adopted reports relate in substantial part to the scope of allowable exceptions under the Agreement. *Canada – Pharmaceutical Patents* (DS114) focused on the three-step test under Article 30,[8] *US – Copyright Act* on the three-step test under Article 13 (DS160),[9] and *EC – Trademarks and Geographical Indications* (DS174, 290) on Article 17.[10]

The reports on *US – Section 211 Omnibus Appropriations Act* (DS176)[11] and *EC – Trademarks and Geographical Indications* (DS174, 290) focused on the central principle of non-discrimination. Some bilaterally settled cases have focused on enforcement (*Denmark and Sweden – Measures Affecting the Enforcement of Intellectual Property Rights* (DS83 and 86)), and *European Communities and Portugal – Enforcement of Intellectual Property Rights in Motion Pictures and Television Programs* (DS124 and 125)).

The reports on *US – Copyright Act* (DS160), *US – Section 211 Omnibus Appropriations Act* (DS176), *EC – Trademarks and Geographical Indications* (DS174 and 290) and *China – IPRs* (DS372) have had to interpret provisions of the Berne and Paris Conventions as incorporated into the TRIPS Agreement. Panels and the Appellate Body have sought to take care to interpret the provisions of the TRIPS Agreement and these WIPO conventions in ways which reconcile them and avoid conflicts between them, taking into account the drafting history of the Berne and Paris Conventions and the subsequent practice relating to them. Panels have invariably sought and obtained factual information from the International Bureau of the WIPO about drafting history and subsequent practice in regard to WIPO provisions that they have been called upon to interpret.

1   A guide to resources

All the documents referred to above are available on the WTO website at docsonline.wto.org. A special document portal – accessed through the Dispute Settlement Gateway on the WTO website – provides easy access to documents on specific TRIPS disputes. Appendix 2 to this *Handbook* provides more information on how to access WTO documents.

---

[8] For a brief summary of the case, see Chapter V.
[9] For a brief summary of the case, see Chapter II.
[10] For a brief summary of the cases, see Chapter III.
[11] For a brief summary of the cases, see Chapter III.

WORLD TRADE ORGANIZATION

| Home | About WTO | News and events | Trade topics | WTO membership | Documents and resources | WTO and you |

home > trade topics > dispute settlement > chronological list

DISPUTE SETTLEMENT: THE DISPUTES

Chronological list of disputes cases

The cases listed below are in reverse chronological order (the newest appear first).

Type in a dispute number then click "Go" or click on the case ("DS") number below to go to the page for that dispute.

Dispute number: DS [   ] (Go)

This summary has been prepared by the Secretariat under its own responsibility. The summary is for general information only and is not intended to affect the rights and obligations of Members.

See also:
› Find disputes cases
› Find disputes documents
› Disputes by agreement
› Disputes by country/territory
› Disputes by current status
› Disputes by short title
› Disputes by subject
› Map of disputes
› GATT disputes (pre-WTO)

› Problems viewing this page?
Please contact
webmaster@wto.org giving
details of the operating system
and web browser you are using.

DS428	Turkey — Safeguard measures on imports of cotton yarn (other than sewing thread) (Complainant: India)	13 February 2012
DS427	China — Anti-Dumping and Countervailing Duty Measures on Broiler Products from the United States (Complainant: United States)	20 September 2011
DS426	Canada — Measures Relating to the Feed-in Tariff Program (Complainant: European Union)	11 August 2011
DS425	China — Definitive Anti-Dumping Duties on X-Ray Security Inspection Equipment from the European Union (Complainant: European Union)	25 July 2011
DS424	United States — Anti-Dumping Measures on Imports of Stainless Steel Sheet and Strip in Coils from Italy (Complainant: European Union)	1 April 2011
DS423	Ukraine — Taxes on Distilled spirits (Complainant: Moldova, Republic of)	3 March 2011
DS422	United States — Anti-Dumping Measures on Shrimp and Diamond Sawblades from China (Complainant: China)	28 February 2011
DS421	Moldova, Republic of — Measures Affecting the Importation and Internal Sale of Goods (Environmental Charge) (Complainant: Ukraine)	17 February 2011
DS420	United States — Anti-dumping measures on corrosion-resistant carbon steel flat products from Korea (Complainant: Korea, Republic of)	31 January 2011
DS419	China — Measures concerning wind power equipment (Complainant: United States)	22 December 2010
DS418	Dominican Republic — Safeguard Measures on Imports of Polypropylene Bags and Tubular Fabric (Complainant: El Salvador)	19 October 2010
DS417	Dominican Republic — Safeguard Measures on Imports of Polypropylene Bags and Tubular Fabric (Complainant: Honduras)	18 October 2010
DS416	Dominican Republic — Safeguard Measures on Imports of Polypropylene Bags and Tubular Fabric (Complainant: Guatemala)	15 October 2010
DS415	Dominican Republic — Safeguard Measures on Imports of Polypropylene Bags and Tubular Fabric (Complainant: Costa Rica)	15 October 2010
DS414	China — Countervailing and Anti-Dumping Duties on Grain Oriented Flat-rolled Electrical Steel from the United States (Complainant: United States)	15 September 2010

Figure VIII.2   Accessing dispute settlement documents

A more detailed description of the dispute settlement system can be found in a WTO Secretariat *Handbook on the WTO Dispute Settlement System*. The *WTO Analytical Index* is a guide to the legal interpretation and application of the WTO Agreements by the WTO Appellate Body, WTO dispute settlement panels and other WTO bodies. It provides information on jurisprudence or decisions relating to each provision of the WTO Agreements. An online version is available on the WTO website, and a printed form is available in two volumes. The provisions of GATT 1994 referred to in the TRIPS Agreement and the DSU are not included in this volume. They can be found, for example, in the *Handbook on the WTO Dispute Settlement System*, or on the WTO website.

IX

TRIPS and Public Health

A   Introduction

This chapter provides an overview of work done in the WTO on IP and public health. Chapter X briefly covers important work done in this area outside the WTO, notably in the WHO.

The TRIPS Agreement represents an attempt at the multilateral level to achieve the difficult task of balancing the interest of providing incentives for research and development of new drugs with the interest of making these drugs as widely accessible as possible to patients needing them. Consequently, in setting minimum standards for the protection and enforcement of IPRs, the TRIPS Agreement recognizes the right of countries to take various kinds of measures to qualify or limit IPRs, including for public health purposes. If a Member wants to avail itself of these flexibilities under the Agreement, it may need to implement them into its domestic law in order to be in a position to make use of them. That is, the mere recognition of these flexibilities as legal options under the international TRIPS Agreement does not necessarily mean that Members' national laws already provide sufficient flexibility. Further, the TRIPS Agreement – and the IP system more generally – is only one element of the bigger challenge of access to medicines, which also includes such important factors as the public health system in general, drug regulatory authorities, financing, health insurance, infrastructure, procurement regimes and import tariffs applied to pharmaceutical products.

The importance of creating a positive, mutually reinforcing link between the IP system and access to medicines was explicitly recognized at the WTO's Fourth Ministerial Conference in Doha, Qatar, in November 2001, when Ministers adopted a Declaration on the TRIPS Agreement and Public Health ('the Declaration'). The Declaration responded to concerns that had been expressed about the possible implications of the TRIPS

Agreement for public health, in particular access to patented medicines. The text of the Declaration is provided in Annex 6.

The TRIPS provisions pertinent to public health, especially those relating to patents and undisclosed information, have already been set out in preceding chapters. This section discusses the flexibilities within the TRIPS Agreement that are most relevant to public health, and the way in which they were clarified and further developed by the Declaration and the so-called Paragraph 6 System.

B   Doha Declaration on the TRIPS Agreement and Public Health

1   Concerns that triggered the discussions

The TRIPS Agreement was negotiated to ensure that countries could take various kinds of measures to qualify or limit IPRs, including for public health purposes. However, some uncertainty arose as to whether the flexibilities in the TRIPS Agreement and the interpretation given to them were sufficient to ensure that it is supportive of public health, especially in promoting affordable access to existing medicines while also promoting research and development of new ones:

- first, different views were expressed about the nature and scope of the flexibilities in the TRIPS Agreement, for example in regard to compulsory licensing and parallel imports;
- second, questions were raised as to whether these flexibilities would be interpreted by the WTO and its Members in a broad, pro-public health way; and
- third, there was concern about the extent to which governments would feel free to use to the full these flexibilities without the fear of coming under pressure from their trading partners.

With a view to effectively addressing these concerns, the Declaration contains some general statements on the relationship between the TRIPS Agreement and the protection of public health, clarifies some of the flexibilities incorporated into the TRIPS Agreement, and also provides some instructions for further work.

2   Scope

Paragraph 1 of the Declaration is generally considered as defining the scope of its application. In this paragraph, Ministers recognized the gravity of the public health problems afflicting many developing countries and LDCs, especially those resulting from HIV/AIDS, tuberculosis, malaria and other epidemics. This language, which was heavily negotiated, makes it clear that the Declaration is not limited to the diseases that are explicitly mentioned there, but is broader in its application.

3 General statements

The general statements provide important guidance to both individual Members and, in the event of disputes, WTO dispute settlement bodies. As part of those statements, the Declaration emphasizes that the TRIPS Agreement does not and should not prevent Members from taking measures to protect public health and reaffirms the right of Members to fully use the flexibilities available in the TRIPS Agreement for this purpose.

In addition, the Declaration makes it clear that the TRIPS Agreement should be interpreted and implemented in a manner supportive of Members' right to protect public health and, in particular, to promote access to medicines for all. These important declarations signal an acceptance by all Members that they will not seek to prevent other Members from using TRIPS flexibilities.

Furthermore, it highlights the importance of the objectives and principles of the TRIPS Agreement for the interpretation of its provisions. Although the Declaration does not refer specifically to Articles 7 and 8 of the TRIPS Agreement, it refers to 'objectives' and 'principles', words that are the titles of these two articles, respectively. See also the explanation in Chapter I, section B1.

Finally, as another expression of the continual search for the right balance between incentivizing R&D into new medicines and providing access to them, the Declaration recognizes the importance of IP protection for the development of new medicines, while also noting the concerns about the effects of IP protection on prices.

4 Clarification of flexibilities

The Declaration contains a number of important clarifications of certain TRIPS flexibilities, while reiterating the commitment of Members to the TRIPS Agreement.

With respect to compulsory licences and emergency situations, it clarifies that each Member has the right to grant compulsory licences and the freedom to determine the grounds upon which such licences are granted. This, for example, is a useful corrective to the views that have sometimes been heard implying that some form of emergency is a pre-condition for compulsory licensing. The TRIPS Agreement does indeed refer to national emergencies or other circumstances of extreme urgency in connection with compulsory licensing (Article 31(b)). However, this reference is only to indicate that, in these circumstances, the usual condition that efforts must be first made to seek a voluntary licence does not apply. In any event, the Declaration confirms that each Member has the right to determine what constitutes a national emergency or other circumstances of extreme urgency and that public health crises, including those relating to HIV/AIDS, tuberculosis, malaria and other epidemics, can represent such circumstances.

In regard to the exhaustion of IPRs, which impinges on a Member's right to permit parallel imports, Article 6 of the TRIPS Agreement states that a Member's practices in this area cannot be challenged under the WTO dispute settlement system. The Declaration clarifies that the effect of this and other relevant provisions in the TRIPS Agreement is to leave each Member free to establish its own regime without challenge – subject to the general TRIPS provisions prohibiting discrimination on the basis of the nationality of right holders. Accordingly, Members can choose, for example, between national, regional or international exhaustion. Under national exhaustion, a right holder can prevent importation of IP-protected products from other countries even if they have been put on the market there by the right holder or with the right holder's consent. Under international exhaustion, the right holder would not be able to do this since all IPRs would be held to have been exhausted by his earlier sale of the product. See also the discussion on exhaustion in Chapter I, section B5 and Box IX.1.

5   Transfer of technology

The Declaration also reaffirmed the commitment of developed countries regarding the provision of incentives to their enterprises and institutions to promote and encourage technology transfer to LDCs under Article 66.2. See Chapter I, section D3.

**BOX IX.1 TRIPS FLEXIBILITIES AS RECOGNIZED BY THE DOHA
DECLARATION**

While the concept of TRIPS flexibilities is broader, the Doha Declaration explicitly
recognizes certain specific measures:

- The right to grant compulsory licences and the freedom to determine the
  grounds.
- The right to determine what constitutes a national emergency or other circumstances of extreme urgency (with the understanding that this concept can
  include public health crises, such as those relating to HIV/AIDS, tuberculosis,
  malaria and other epidemics).
- The freedom for each Member to establish its own regime for exhaustion
  without challenge, subject to the principle of non-discrimination.

---

6   Follow-up

There were two specific instructions given by Ministers in the Declaration with respect to further work to be undertaken in the TRIPS
Council, which were implemented as follows:

- Based on the Declaration, a TRIPS Council Decision (IP/C/25)
  extended the transition period for LDC Members of the WTO until
  1 January 2016 in regard to the protection and enforcement of
  patents and rights in undisclosed information with respect to
  pharmaceutical products. To complete this measure, a decision by
  the General Council (WT/L/478) waived the otherwise applicable
  provision on exclusive marketing rights in Article 70.9 for the same
  period. This specific extension of the transition period applying to
  pharmaceutical products is in addition to the general extension of
  the transition period given to LDCs for the implementation of the
  TRIPS Agreement by July 2013 (IP/C/40). These two decisions are
  provided in Annexes 9 and 10.
- Following the instruction given by the Declaration to seek an
  expeditious solution to the potential problems of countries with
  limited or no manufacturing capacities in making effective use of
  compulsory licensing, Members agreed to establish the so-called
  Paragraph 6 System, waiving certain obligations under the TRIPS
  Agreement. The Paragraph 6 System is explained in the next
  section.

C   Paragraph 6 System

1   The issue

The Declaration recognized the problem of countries with insufficient or no manufacturing capacities in the pharmaceutical sector in making effective use of compulsory licensing, and instructed the Council for TRIPS to find an expeditious solution. Such countries would have to import under a compulsory licence if the needed medicine is patent-protected. This, in itself, is possible under the TRIPS Agreement as Members can issue compulsory licences for importation as well as for domestic production. However, the potential problem identified was whether supply of generic medicines from patent-protected sources would be adequate. In other words, whether generic producers in countries with manufacturing capacity would be able to export sufficient quantities if the needed medicine was patent-protected in those countries. This is because the TRIPS Agreement limits the amount such countries can export under a compulsory licence; Article 31(f) requires that the production under a compulsory licence be 'predominantly for the supply of the domestic market'. This constraint was expected to become more important in 2005 as some developing countries with significant generic industries and export capacities became obligated to provide patent protection for pharmaceutical products pursuant to the special transition arrangements in Article 65.4.

2   The solution: establishment of the Paragraph 6 System

This problem was recognized in Paragraph 6 of the Declaration (hence the reference to the 'Paragraph 6 System'). Subsequent work in the TRIPS Council prepared the ground for the adoption of two important General Council decisions establishing the Paragraph 6 System, which were both adopted in the light of a Chairman's statement setting out several key shared understandings of Members on how the Paragraph 6 System would be interpreted and implemented. These two decisions are provided in Annexes 7 and 8.

The General Council Decision of 30 August 2003 on the Implementation of Paragraph 6 of the Doha Declaration on the TRIPS Agreement and Public Health (WT/L/540 and Corr.1) waives under certain circumstances (i) the obligation on exporting Members to ensure that compulsory licences are only granted for the purpose of predominantly supplying the domestic market (Article 31(f)) and (ii) the obligation on importing

Members to pay adequate remuneration to the right holder if a compulsory licence is granted (Article 31(h)).

Given that the waivers contained in the 2003 Decision are of a temporary nature, Paragraph 11 of that Decision called for the TRIPS Council to prepare a permanent amendment to the TRIPS Agreement based, where appropriate, on the 2003 Decision. Agreement on such an amendment was reached on 6 December 2005 when the General Council adopted a Protocol Amending the TRIPS Agreement (WT/L/641) in the light of a Chairman's statement along the lines accepted in August 2003.

The 2005 Protocol is the first amendment of any WTO agreement to be agreed to by WTO Members since the WTO Agreement came into force in 1995. It closely tracks the text of the 2003 Decision. No substantive changes were made to the original Paragraph 6 System implemented by the waiver Decision of 2003. It was submitted to Members for acceptance and requires acceptance by two-thirds of the Members to enter into force, which had not yet occurred as of the time of writing.[1]

Accepting the Protocol is clearly distinct from implementing the Paragraph 6 System in a Member's domestic legal framework. In other words, the Protocol can be accepted independently from adopting domestic implementing legislation, and vice versa. Accepting the Protocol is a legal act whereby a Member expresses its consent to be bound by the Protocol at the international level or, in other words, its consent that all WTO Members are *entitled* – that is permitted but not required – to use the Paragraph 6 System, which is incorporated in the TRIPS Agreement through the agreed amendment. This process of acceptance needs to follow the relevant Member's own constitutional requirements.[2] Should a WTO Member wish to make use of the additional flexibilities provided in the Protocol, it may need to implement laws or regulations following its normal domestic legislative and regulatory processes.

The waiver provisions of the 2003 Decision came into effect on 30 August 2003 and remain applicable until the date on which the TRIPS amendment takes effect for a Member. Given that the content of the August 2003 Decision and the proposed amendment of the TRIPS

---

[1] A list of Members which have notified their acceptance to the WTO is available at www.wto.org/english/tratop_e/trips_e/amendment_e.htm.

[2] More information on how to accept the Protocol Amending the TRIPS Agreement, including a model instrument of acceptance, is available at www.wto.org/english/tratop_e/trips_e/accept_e.htm.

Agreement is the same, the substance of the legal regime applying to Members will remain the same, whether they have accepted the Protocol or not.

3   Description of the System

The Paragraph 6 System established under the 2003 Decision and the 2005 Protocol provides for three distinct derogations from the obligations set out in Article 31 with respect to pharmaceutical products, subject to certain conditions. These derogations are meant to address a public health problem in the importing country, and a legal problem in the exporting country. Two of those modifications relate to Article 31(f), whereas the third refers to Article 31(h):

- first, the obligation of the exporting Member under Article 31(f) to issue compulsory licences predominantly for the domestic market does not apply to the extent necessary to enable that Member to authorize production and export of the needed pharmaceutical products under a compulsory licence to those countries that do not have sufficient capacity to manufacture them. This derogation is subject to certain conditions to ensure transparency in the operation of the Paragraph 6 System and to ensure that only countries with insufficient domestic capacity import under it. It also provides for safeguards against the diversion of products to markets for which they are not intended;
- second, the requirement under Article 31(h) to pay adequate remuneration for compulsory licences is modified to avoid double remuneration of the right holder. If a compulsory licence has to be granted in both the exporting and the importing countries, remuneration need only be paid in the exporting country;
- third, a further derogation to Article 31(f) enables a WTO Member to export products manufactured or imported under a compulsory licence more easily amongst members of a regional trade agreement (RTA) at least half the membership of which consists of LDCs.

(a)   Scope and coverage

The Paragraph 6 System covers any patented products, or products manufactured through a patented process, of the pharmaceutical sector needed to address the public health problems as recognized in Paragraph 1 of the Declaration, including active ingredients necessary for their manufacture and diagnostic kits needed for their use.

(b)   Eligible importing Members

The following Members qualify as eligible importing countries:

- LDCs, which are automatically eligible to import under the Paragraph 6 System;
- any other Member that notifies the TRIPS Council of its intention to use the Paragraph 6 System. This is a one-time notification that can be made at any time, including together with the first detailed notification regarding specific needs addressed below. Note, however, that:
  - certain Members have agreed to opt out of using the Paragraph 6 System as importers (full opt-out countries): Australia; Austria; Belgium; Canada; the Czech Republic; Cyprus; Denmark; Estonia; Finland; France; Germany; Greece; Hungary; Iceland; Ireland; Italy; Japan; Latvia; Lithuania; Luxemburg; Malta; the Netherlands; New Zealand; Norway; Poland; Portugal; the Slovak Republic; Slovenia; Spain; Sweden; Switzerland; the United Kingdom and the United States;
  - certain other Members have agreed to only use the Paragraph 6 System as importers in situations of national emergency or other circumstances of extreme urgency (partial opt-out countries): Hong Kong, China; Israel; Korea; Kuwait; Macao, China; Mexico; Qatar; Singapore; Chinese Taipei; Turkey; and the United Arab Emirates.

(c)   Exporting Members

No restriction applies to the eligibility of Members as exporting countries. But like compulsory licensing in general, the additional flexibility under the Paragraph 6 System is optional, and therefore no Member is obliged to implement the Paragraph 6 System in its domestic legislation.

(d)   Notifications

Certain notifications to the TRIPS Council by both importing and exporting Members are required as a prerequisite for the use of the Paragraph 6 System.[3] These notifications are for information purposes and do not require approval by any WTO body before the Paragraph 6 System can be used. They can be accessed in the three official WTO languages (English, French and Spanish) on a dedicated webpage.[4]

---

[3] A set of model notifications is available at www.wto.org/english/tratop_e/trips_e/trips_e.htm.
[4] Available at www.wto.org/english/tratop_e/trips_e/public_health_e.htm.

Apart from the one-time notification by eligible importing Members mentioned in (b) above, they are to notify certain information each time they want to use the Paragraph 6 System. These details are:

- the names and expected quantities of the product(s) needed;
- confirmation that the eligible importing Member in question has established, in one of the ways set out in the Annex to the Decision, that it has insufficient or no manufacturing capacity in the pharmaceutical sector for the product(s) in question. The Chairman's statement calls for the notification to include information on how this assessment has been established. LDCs are deemed to have insufficient or no manufacturing capacities and are therefore automatically exempted from this requirement; and
- where a pharmaceutical product is patented in the territory of the Member concerned, confirmation that it has granted or intends to grant a compulsory licence in accordance with Article 31 and the provisions of the Paragraph 6 System.

In response to the notification of the specific needs made by the importing Member, the exporting Member is to notify the TRIPS Council of the grant of the exporting country's compulsory licence and the conditions attached to it (see (e) below), the details of the licence (the name and address of the licensee; the product(s) involved; the quantity or quantities to be produced under the licence; the designated importing country or countries; and the duration of the licence), and the website address where the licensee is required to post the information, before shipment takes place, of the quantities being supplied to each destination and the distinguishing features of the product(s).

(e)   Safeguards against diversion

During the preparatory work leading to the establishment of the Paragraph 6 System, concerns were expressed about the potential risk of diversion of pharmaceutical products to be manufactured under the System. With a view to ensuring that such products are used for the public health purposes underlying their importation into the eligible importing Member, it was agreed that specific safeguards against diversion would be required in addition to the above provisions ensuring transparency of the operation of the Paragraph 6 System and establishing certain notification requirements.

For this purpose, exporting Members must attach the following conditions to the compulsory licence:

- only the amount necessary to meet the needs of the eligible importing Member can be manufactured under the licence;
- the entirety of the production must be exported to the Member which has notified its needs to the TRIPS Council; and
- products manufactured under the Paragraph 6 System must be clearly identified as such through specific labelling or marking. Suppliers should distinguish the products through special packaging and/or special colouring or shaping of the products – provided that these distinguishing characteristics are feasible and do not have a significant impact on price.

Importing Members must take measures to prevent the re-exportation of the products concerned. Several qualifiers apply to this requirement, namely that the measures must be reasonable, within the means of the Member concerned and proportionate to its administrative capacities and to the risk of trade diversion.

In addition, in order to counter the risk of the importation and sale of any diverted products produced under the Paragraph 6 System in their territories, all Members are required to make available the legal means which have to be put at the disposal of the right holder in any event under the TRIPS Agreement; in other words the normal enforcement procedures and remedies in the event that the product is patent-protected in that jurisdiction.

(f)   Avoidance of double remuneration

Where patents on the needed medicines exist in both the importing and the exporting country and two compulsory licences are granted, the basic rule in Article 31(h) would require that adequate remuneration be paid in both countries to the right holder.

However, with a view to avoiding double remuneration of the patent owner for the same product consignment, the Paragraph 6 System derogates from the obligation of the importing country under Article 31(h) with respect to products for which remuneration has already been paid in the exporting Member. The derogation also specifies that the remuneration in the exporting Member is to be calculated taking into account the economic value of the use in the importing Member.

(g)   The special case of regional trade agreements

A developing country or LDC may export pharmaceutical products manufactured or imported under a compulsory licence, notwithstanding the obligation under Article 31(f) to the extent that it is a party to an RTA and the following conditions are met:

- the RTA complies with GATT Article XXIV and the Decision of 28 November 1979 on Differential and More Favourable Treatment Reciprocity and Fuller Participation of Developing Countries (L/4903) (also called the Enabling Clause);
- at least half of the RTA members are LDCs listed as such by the United Nations; and
- the exporting country and the country needing the product manufactured or imported under a compulsory licence share the public health problem in question.

The purpose of this derogation is to respond to concerns expressed by some developing countries, in particular those with smaller markets, about not being in a position to effectively attract generic suppliers to produce medicines for their populations and to enable such countries to better harness economies of scale for the purposes of enhancing purchasing power for, and facilitating the local production of, pharmaceutical products.

While the derogation facilitates export from one RTA member to another, it does not remove any need to grant a compulsory licence to cover the import of a medicine into other RTA members, if the medicine in question is patent-protected in those members. This is the logical consequence of the territorial application of national patents in the absence of regional patents. This aspect is also recognized by the Paragraph 6 System that calls for the promotion of regional patent systems.

4   Chairman's statement

As mentioned above, the 2003 Decision and the 2005 Protocol were both adopted in the light of similar General Council Chairman's statements read prior to their adoption. The statement was designed to respond to the concerns that the Decision was too open-ended and might be abused in a way that would undermine the benefits of the patent system. For this purpose, the statement:

- recognizes that the Paragraph 6 System should be used in good faith to protect public health and should not be an instrument to pursue industrial or commercial policy objectives;

- addresses the concerns expressed relating to the risk of diversion by establishing that all reasonable measures should be taken to avoid diversion of the medicines from the markets for which they were produced; and
- sets out ways in which any differences arising from the implementation of the system can be settled expeditiously and adequately.

The statement also notes that thirty-three developed countries have agreed to opt out of using the Paragraph 6 System as importers. In addition, the statement records that eleven other Members agreed to use the Paragraph 6 System, as importers, only in situations of national emergency or other circumstances of extreme urgency.

The Chairman's statement read out prior to the adoption of the 2005 Protocol further set out that the fact that non-violation complaints are considered non-applicable in this context would be without prejudice to the overall question of the applicability of such complaints to the TRIPS Agreement.

5 Domestic implementing legislation

The additional flexibilities made available under the Paragraph 6 System are optional, not mandatory. To take advantage of them, a number of WTO Members have adopted domestic implementing laws or regulations that incorporate the Paragraph 6 System into their respective legal frameworks. Among the WTO Members with implementing laws or regulations, three categories can be observed, i.e. (i) those Members that have implemented the Paragraph 6 System to act exclusively as exporters (ii) those Members that have implemented the Paragraph 6 System to act exclusively as importers, and (iii) those Members that have put in place laws or regulations allowing them to act both as exporters or importers under the Paragraph 6 System.[5] As explained in section C2 above, the adoption of such legislation follows the normal domestic legislative and regulatory processes and is distinct from the acceptance of the Protocol Amending the TRIPS Agreement.

---

[5] An overview of national implementing legislation notified to the TRIPS Council is available at www.wto.org/english/tratop_e/trips_e/par6laws_e.htm. Additional information on certain Members' implementing legislation can also be found in Section 2 of the Annex to the TRIPS Council's 2010 Report to the General Council on the Annual Review of the Paragraph 6 System (IP/C/57).

BOX IX.2 THE PARAGRAPH 6 SYSTEM IN A NUTSHELL

The scenario

The Paragraph 6 System is not intended to be a panacea for procuring medicines, but addresses a particular problem that was identified in the Doha Declaration. The System provides a specific legal avenue for an eligible WTO Member to procure medicines in the following circumstances:

- a Member wants to import a pharmaceutical product, which it cannot produce locally, from a generic producer in another WTO Member (exporting Member);
- the product is covered by a patent/patents in the exporting Member; and
- there is a need in the exporting Member for a compulsory licence to enable the generic production of the needed pharmaceutical product exclusively for export, including where the supply of the non-predominant part of the production under an existing compulsory licence to service the exporting Member's domestic market cannot meet the needs of the importing Member.

The requirements

The essential steps that need to be taken to exercise this flexibility are:

- the importing Member informs the TRIPS Council of its intention to use the Paragraph 6 System (other than an LDC). This is a one-time notification. It also informs about the name of the product and the quantities it wants to import for each use;
- where the needed pharmaceutical product is patented in the importing Member, that Member confirms that it has granted or intends to grant a compulsory licence or, in the case of an LDC, states alternatively that it is availing itself of the additional transition period;
- the exporting Member issues a compulsory licence that permits production and exportation and notifies the TRIPS Council of the grant of the compulsory licence and the conditions attached to it;
- the product is identified as having been produced under this System, such as through labelling or marking; and prior to shipment,
- details of the shipment(s) are posted on a website by the licensee, the address of which is notified to the TRIPS Council by the exporting Member.

The Paragraph 6 System only deals with the freedom of third parties not having the right holder's permission to produce and fully export the desired pharmaceutical product patented – it does not deal with questions such as procurement policies or regulatory questions, which are dealt with by national systems in whatever manner Members choose. For instance, the importing Member may require regulatory

BOX IX.2 (*cont.*)

approval before the product is imported for distribution to the public in its territory, especially if it is a new formulation that hasn't been distributed there before.

The Paragraph 6 System also recognizes the need to harness economies of scale for the purposes of enhancing purchasing power for, and facilitating the local production of, pharmaceutical products, as well as the desirability of promoting the transfer of technology and capacity building in the pharmaceutical sector in order to overcome the problem identified in paragraph 6 of the Doha Declaration.

6 Use of the Paragraph 6 System

As regards the experience on the Paragraph 6 System's operation so far, one case of use has been reported to the TRIPS Council. In July 2007, Rwanda notified the TRIPS Council of its intention to import a pharmaceutical product from Canada under the Paragraph 6 System pursuant to paragraph 2(a) of the Decision.[6] In response, Canada issued a compulsory licence, under its Access to Medicines Regime, to a domestic pharmaceutical manufacturer in October 2007, authorizing the manufacture of a fixed-dose combination medicine for the treatment of HIV/AIDS infection for export to Rwanda under the Paragraph 6 System. This was notified to the TRIPS Council in accordance with paragraph 2(c) of the Decision. Shipments of the medicine in question took place in September 2008 and 2009.[7]

7 Review of the Paragraph 6 System's functioning

According to Paragraph 8 of the 2003 Decision, the TRIPS Council is to review annually the functioning of the Paragraph 6 System with a view to ensuring its effective operation. Since 2004, a report to the General Council has been prepared every year.[8] While earlier reviews were fairly short, more thorough debates have taken place in the TRIPS Council since October 2009. Beyond the question of the operation of the Paragraph 6 System itself, broader issues, in particular as regards any alternatives to

---

[6] IP/N/9/RWA/1.   [7] IP/N/10/CAN/1 and IP/C/W/526.
[8] The annual reports can be accessed at www.wto.org/english/tratop_e/trips_e/pharmpatent_e.htm. For the latest reports, see WTO Documents IP/C/57 and Corr.1 (2010) and IP/C/61 (2011).

the use of the Paragraph 6 System to achieve the objective of access to medicines, procurement policies, and other related aspects affecting access to medicines, have also been raised.

In the discussions, some Members raised concerns about the Paragraph 6 System's functioning and considered it to be too complex and bureaucratic. In their view, the Paragraph 6 System did not represent the expected effective and expeditious solution to public health problems encountered by developing countries. According to these countries, the Paragraph 6 System's inadequacy is evidenced by its limited use, as well as by the still relatively small number of acceptances of the Protocol. Some other Members have argued that the shipments of medicines from Canada to Rwanda had demonstrated that the Paragraph 6 System could operate effectively. They further argue that the success of the Paragraph 6 System should not be measured in terms of the number of compulsory licences granted, but whether it had contributed towards better access to affordable medicines. In their view, there may have been less need to use the System due to other measures taken to enhance access to medicines, including through improved international procurement, increased donations of free medicines and lower prices often provided by right holders.

D   Access to medicines: the broader picture

While emphasizing the scope in the TRIPS Agreement available for Members to tailor their domestic implementation with a view to promoting access to medicines, the Doha Declaration stresses the need for the Agreement to be 'part of the wider national and international action to address these problems'. It is generally accepted that there is a need for a broad-based approach to access to medicines, which should include dimensions such as innovation, access and funding. Other policies affecting access to medicines that have regularly been referred to in recent discussions include (i) transparent, competitive and non-discriminatory procurement procedures and practices; (ii) effective competition policies; (iii) the need to ensure the safety, quality and efficacy of medicines; (iv) the elimination of tariffs and taxes; and (v) the need to have a sound health care infrastructure in place. It has also been emphasized that alternative funding mechanisms, donations, partnership programmes and licensing agreements, as well as the increased application of tiered-pricing schemes by pharmaceutical companies have contributed to a positive change regarding access to medicines.

The issue of access to medicines is influenced by a number of key players intervening at different levels ranging from discussions, norm-setting and jurisprudence at the international level to action taken by civil society and concrete decisions adopted by the pharmaceutical industry. Coherence, cooperation and dialogue are indispensable at all levels in order to find effective responses to public health challenges, and to ensure that the IP regime is balanced, fair and responsive.

The broader issues have fostered cooperation between the three inter-governmental organizations with key responsibilities in this area, namely the WHO, WIPO and the WTO. This cooperation was initially framed by the Doha Declaration and has now led to an intensified process of trilateral cooperation, which also includes the implementation of the WHO's Global Strategy and Plan of Action. This partnership between the three organizations builds on the complementary roles of each organization and takes into account the different nature of their respective mandates and priorities. As a concrete result, the three organizations have initiated a series of joint technical symposia addressing issues at the intersection of public health, trade and IP. The symposia are designed to provide a platform for the discussion of current issues and the exchange of information and experiences. They are expected to enhance the dialogue between the relevant organizations and other key stakeholders, and foster the mutual understanding of public health and IP policy. In July 2010, the first symposium addressed 'Access to Medicines: Pricing and Procurement Practices' and, in February 2011, the second symposium provided an opportunity to review issues related to 'Access to Medicines, Patent Information and Freedom to Operate'.[9]

---

[9] Presentations and background information from the symposia are available at www.wto.org/english/news_e/news10_e/trip_16jul10_e.htm and www.wto.org/english/news_e/news11_e/trip_18feb11_e.htm. A joint study on 'Promoting Access and Medical Innovation: Intersections between Public Health, Intellectual Property and Trade' will be published in 2012. More information on the trilateral cooperation is available at www.wto.org/english/tratop_e/trips_e/who_wipo_wto_e.htm.

X

Current TRIPS issues[*]

A Introduction

1 *Current issues*

The TRIPS Agreement was not envisaged as an entirely static legal instrument: TRIPS negotiators included several provisions within the Agreement that set out a work programme for the future – the so-called 'built-in agenda'. And since the TRIPS Agreement entered into force, WTO Members have decided to elaborate and enhance these review processes. The most significant addition to these processes is the work on public health and access to medicines issues in line with the Doha Declaration on the TRIPS Agreement and Public Health, which is covered in Chapter IX. This chapter provides a general overview of the ongoing work in the TRIPS Council and other WTO bodies on other aspects of TRIPS and public policy as of the time of writing, focusing on the following issues, which have been the most prominent:

- GIs – the Article 23.4 negotiations on a system of notification and registration, a review of GI protection under Article 24.2, and work on the question of possibly extending to other products the protection provided to wine and spirits under Article 23 (so-called 'GI extension').
- Biodiversity and traditional knowledge – the review of the provisions on what can broadly be called 'biotechnology patenting' established under Article 27.3(b) of the TRIPS Agreement, and a wider slate of

---

[*] Since this chapter describes continuing processes and negotiations that were actively under way, but still unresolved at the time of writing, some of the information given in this chapter is likely to be superseded by subsequent developments. The current status of these issues can be checked on the WTO website, under 'trade topics'. In this chapter only, the symbol [*] is used to identify points that may well have changed since the time of writing.

related issues, especially the work on the relationship between the TRIPS Agreement and the CBD, and the protection of TK and folklore.

- Non-violation complaints – the examination by the TRIPS Council of the scope and modalities of such disputes which is required under Article 64.3, and which has been considered by several Ministerial Conferences as mentioned in Chapter VIII, section C2.
- LDCs and TRIPS: specific recognition of the distinct context and interests of LDCs.
- Transfer of technology – the review mechanism set up by the TRIPS Council to monitor the implementation of the obligation, under Article 66.2, on developed country Members to provide incentives for technology transfer to LDCs.
- Electronic commerce and its implications for the TRIPS Agreement.

A number of other issues have been considered in the TRIPS Council, and are of ongoing interest, but are not covered in this publication for reasons of space – these include the policy dimensions of the enforcement of IPRs, and the provision of technical assistance, in particular the review by the TRIPS Council of the reports made by developed country Members on the technical cooperation provided in accordance with Article 67. However, some of these issues have been covered in previous chapters, notably Chapter I and Chapter VII.

The interplay between IP and such policy concerns as biodiversity, the environment, access to technologies, and social and economic development touches on complex and multifaceted issues that involve diverse stake holders. These questions are actively debated outside the WTO in many international policy forums, international and regional organizations, and national legislatures and policy processes. This *Handbook* focuses only on the TRIPS Agreement as such and the related work of the WTO. However, to assist in understanding this broader context, the last section of this chapter briefly outlines some of the work undertaken in certain multilateral organizations on these issues. No attempt is made to analyse the substance of the issues, nor to provide an account of the full range of debates and institutions that have addressed the TRIPS Agreement and public policy issues. The literature on each of these issues is vast, including a number of important resolutions, studies and reports prepared by organizations beyond the WTO; a brief guide to some of this work is provided, but this should not be taken as comprehensive or authoritative.

2   The mandates for work on TRIPS issues

To understand the continuing substantive work of the WTO on the current issues identified above, it is useful also to have some familiarity with the mandate of each policy discussion or set of negotiations – in other words, what is the procedural context and the agreed basis for each element of work, and how this differs between issues. Specific TRIPS and IP issues have been taken up in the WTO as a result of decisions taken collectively by Members to work on them. There are several bases for ongoing work:

- some of the issues are already part of the built-in agenda, agreed to during the Uruguay Round negotiations and are part of the TRIPS Agreement itself;
- in some cases, such a built-in agenda process has been elaborated further with the agreement of all Members; and
- further, distinct, issues have been taken up as a result of decisions taken by the various WTO Ministerial Conferences.

Take, for example, the ongoing negotiations on the establishment of a notification and registration system for GIs for wines and spirits. The TRIPS Agreement itself in Article 23.4 mandates negotiations on a register for GIs for wines (hereinafter called the Register). The Singapore Ministerial Conference in 1996 broadened this mandate to cover spirits as well, and preliminary work proceeded in the TRIPS Council. Then the Doha Ministerial Conference, in 2001, incorporated this existing mandate into the overall structure of the Doha Development Agenda, and the negotiations on the register were then undertaken in a so-called 'Special Session' of the TRIPS Council (see Chapter I, section A3).

The Doha Ministerial Conference also agreed that the WTO should work on other issues relating to TRIPS implementation – the question of extension of higher-level GI protection to products other than wines and spirits, and the matter of the relationship between TRIPS and the CBD and the protection of traditional knowledge and folklore. These issues were not part of the original built-in agenda under the TRIPS Agreement, but were subsequently identified by some Members as in need of specific attention along with other implementation issues from the Uruguay Round package that are yet to be resolved. This led to agreement to include them in the Doha Work Programme as 'outstanding implementation issues'. Yet against a background of disagreement as to how they should be handled by Members, a debate continued about the exact negotiating status of these issues and therefore how work on them should proceed in the WTO. The Doha Ministerial Declaration stipulated that 'negotiations on outstanding implementation issues shall be an integral part' of the Doha work programme, and that implementation issues 'shall be addressed as a matter of priority by the relevant WTO bodies'. It provided that 'issues related to the extension of the protection of geographical indications provided for in Article 23 to products other than wines and spirits will be addressed in the Council for TRIPS'. Further, the ministers instructed the Council for TRIPS 'in pursuing its work programme including under the review of Article 27.3(b), the review of the implementation of the TRIPS Agreement under Article 71.1 and the work foreseen pursuant to paragraph 12 of this declaration, to examine, *inter alia*, the relationship between the TRIPS Agreement and the Convention on Biological Diversity, the protection of traditional knowledge and folklore, and other relevant new developments raised by Members pursuant to Article 71.1'.

The substance of these two issues is discussed below. When considering the nature of the mandate on these issues, it has been a significant factor in the work of the WTO that delegations have interpreted the Doha Declaration differently – especially on the question of whether or not there is or should be a mandate to renegotiate the TRIPS text to deal with these issues. Many developing and European countries have taken the position that the outstanding implementation issues should be part of the Doha Round negotiations and should be an integral part of its package of results (the 'single undertaking'). A number of other countries have maintained the view that these issues can only become negotiating subjects if the Trade Negotiations Committee decides by consensus to include them in the talks – and so far it has not done so; they have said that, under the circumstances, the work on these issues cannot be part of the results of the Doha Round.

*   This difference of opinion over the nature of the mandates to work on these issues means that the discussions have had to be organized carefully. These issues were taken up in the TRIPS Council until the end of 2002. Since then, they have been the subject of informal consultations chaired by the WTO Deputy Director-General and since March 2009 undertaken by the WTO Director-General himself. In 2005, the Hong Kong Ministerial Declaration took note of the work undertaken by the Director-General in his consultative process, including on issues related to the extension of the protection of geographical indications provided for in Article 23 of the TRIPS Agreement to products other than wines

and spirits and those related to the relationship between the TRIPS Agreement and the CBD. It requested him to intensify his consultative process, which has continued up to the time of writing without any specific outcome.

The debate over these issues, and over the nature of the mandate to work on them, has generally been pursued by groups or coalitions of Members who share particular interests and priorities. One point of disagreement has been whether the issues should be linked together within a negotiating package or handled separately. For instance, in July 2008, a group of Members tabled a proposal (TN/C/W/52 and Add. 1 to 3) to the Trade Negotiations Committee, which linked the Register negotiations both to the GI extension issue and to the question of the relationship between the CBD and the TRIPS Agreement. Other Members maintained that there should be no linkages drawn between these issues – for instance, that progress on the Register mandate should not be dependent on progress on the other questions – and that they should be handled separately; these same countries have generally also argued that the mandate to work on the two 'implementation issues' did not extend to a mandate to initiate negotiations on these issues. These divergent perspectives had not been resolved at the time of writing, and different groups of Members continued to differ on how to handle the implementation issues; for instance, in April 2011, just as the Trade Negotiations Committee were reviewing the overall state of play of Doha Round negotiations, two groups of Members with particular interests tabled new proposals (TN/C/W/59 on TRIPS/CBD and TN/C/W/60 on GI extension) to renegotiate TRIPS in these two areas.

B   Current issues

1   Geographical indications

(a)   Background

The ongoing work of the WTO on GIs has concentrated on two specific issues, relating in different ways to the higher level of protection afforded to GIs for wines and spirits under Article 23 of the TRIPS Agreement – first, negotiations on a multilateral system of notification and registration of GIs for wines and spirits; and, second, the possible extension of this higher level of protection to GIs for other products.

As seen already in Chapter IV, the TRIPS Agreement established two specific processes on GIs, which form part of its 'built-in agenda':

- under Article 23.4, the negotiations on a multilateral system of notification and registration of GIs for wines;
- under Article 24.2, a review by the Council for TRIPS of the application of the GI provisions of the Agreement.

In 1998, to progress the Article 24.2 review, the Council took note of a Checklist of Questions and invited those Members already bound by TRIPS provisions on GIs to provide responses, with other Members free to furnish replies on a voluntary basis. The Secretariat has prepared and updated a summary of these responses (document IP/C/W/253/Rev.1). This review has produced a considerable body of information on the protection of GIs in the national systems of Members, and has illustrated how they have employed a wide variety of legal means, including specific laws on GIs, trademark law, consumer protection and unfair competition law, and common law remedies. The review process has been less active since the last updated compilation in 2003, but more recently has briefly addressed bilateral agreements on GI protection that several Members have entered into.

Since the Agreement came into force in 1995, decisions by the Ministerial Conference have elaborated or augmented the built-in TRIPS agenda on GIs:

- the 1996 Singapore Ministerial Conference agreed to extend the scope of the Register negotiations to spirits, and the 2001 Doha and 2005 Hong Kong Ministerial Conferences updated the mandate for these negotiations in the context of the overall negotiations in the Doha Round.
- the Doha Declaration also took up the question of possible extension of GI protection, stating that 'issues related to the extension of the protection of geographical indications provided for in Article 23 to products other than wines and spirits will be addressed in the Council for TRIPS pursuant to paragraph 12 of this Declaration' which, in turn, concerned 'implementation-related issues and concerns raised by Members'. This mandate was renewed at the Hong Kong Ministerial Conference.

These decisions therefore determined that two issues on GIs would be considered under the Doha mandate: the Register (in line with a pre-Doha mandate with its roots in the TRIPS Agreement itself); and extending the higher (Article 23) level of protection beyond wines and spirits, identified as an implementation issue at Doha. The different categorization of these issues, however, meant that they were dealt with in separate ways, as the following sections outline – although, as noted above, some Members have proposed that the Register negotiations be linked with the two implementation issues.

(b)   The multilateral register for wines and spirits

Work on a multilateral system of notification and registration began in 1997 in line with the original mandate under Article 23.4 of the TRIPS Agreement. The Register negotiations were subsequently covered by the 2001 Doha Declaration and have since been conducted by the Special Session of the TRIPS Council, as mentioned above.

In 2011, the work had evolved to a point where delegations were negotiating directly on a draft text to establish the Register (although numerous differences continued to be unresolved in these negotiations at the time of publication). Until then, the work had been characterized by debate over three sets of proposals that had been submitted earlier, expressing positions that continue to reflect the key issues under consideration:

- The European Communities (now the EU) circulated a detailed proposal (TN/IP/W/11) in June 2005. Under this system, when a GI was registered, the TRIPS Agreement would be amended to establish, *inter alia*, a 'rebuttable presumption' in all Members that the term is eligible for protection and not generic in other WTO Members – except in a country that has lodged a reservation within a specified period (for example, eighteen months). A reservation would have to be on permitted grounds such as that a term has become generic or does not fit the definition of a GI. If it does not make a reservation, a country would not be able to refuse protection on these grounds after the term has been registered. In a subsequent negotiating proposal (TN/C/W/52 and Add. 1–3, noted in Section A2 above) in which a group of Members including the European Union and Switzerland put forward combined negotiating positions on the Register and the two outstanding implementation issues, the position on the GI Register was substantially modified. It now proposed that registration of a GI in the system would serve as *prima facie* evidence that the term met the definition of a GI in all other WTO Members, while permitting that this evidence be challenged in individual Members under national procedures without prescribing a time limit for such challenges. It further proposed that domestic authorities should permit assertions of genericness under Article 24.6 only if these are substantiated.

- A 'joint proposal' (TN/IP/W/10/Rev.4) was first submitted in 2005 and revised in 2008 and 2011 by another group of Members. This group does not want to amend the TRIPS Agreement. Instead, it proposes a decision by the TRIPS Council to set up a voluntary system where a notified GI would be registered in a database. Members choosing to participate in the system would commit to ensure that its procedures include the provision to consult the database when taking decisions on protection in their own countries. Non-participating Members would be 'encouraged' but not 'obliged' to consult the database.
- Hong Kong, China proposed a compromise (TN/IP/W/8), under which a registered GI term would enjoy a more limited 'presumption' than under the previous EC proposal, and only in those countries choosing to participate in the system.

The WTO Secretariat prepared two working papers to assist the negotiations, one a side-by-side comparison of the three proposals (TN/IP/W/12), and the other a compilation of the issues raised and points made in these negotiations (TN/IP/W/12/Add.1 and Corr.1).

At the heart of the negotiations lie several key issues, on which groups of Members have continued to differ:

- 'legal effect' – when a GI is registered in the system, what consequences, if any, would its registration have for WTO Members?
- 'participation' – could Members choose not to participate in the system, or would it be mandatory for all Members to recognize the Register in their domestic systems?
- questions concerning the kind of information that would be required for a notification and how the Register would be administered, including how its costs would be covered; and
- considerations such as 'special and differential treatment', i.e. the kind of provisions that would assist and support developing countries and LDCs in particular.

* When the negotiations moved to a single composite text in early 2011, this working draft incorporated a range of provisions proposed and supported by different delegations, thus representing these diverse options and issues within one document. One version of this draft, including many unresolved textual elements, was circulated to the Trade Negotiations Committee in April 2011 as part of a general review of the state of play of the Doha negotiations (TN/IP/21).

(c)   Extending the 'higher level of protection' beyond
wines and spirits

Chapter IV explains the difference between Article 22 protection for GIs, and the 'higher' protection prescribed for wine and spirit GIs under Article 23. The question of extending this higher protection to other products was identified as an implementation issue in the Doha Declaration. A number of countries – including the EU and Switzerland and several developing countries – have called to renegotiate TRIPS to broaden the coverage of goods covered by Article 23 to other products. They have argued for the higher level of protection as a way to better defend the marketing terms for their locally based products and to counter more effectively the 'usurpation' of geographical terms by countries adopting them as generic descriptions for similar products. The EC circulated a formal proposal (document TN/IP/W/11) on this extension issue in 2005. The TN/C/W/52 proposal in 2008 called for extension of Article 23 protection 'for all products, including the extension of the Register'. It proposed negotiations to amend the TRIPS Agreement to apply Article 23 to GIs for all products as well as to apply to these the exceptions provided in Article 24 of the TRIPS Agreement *mutatis mutandis.* As seen above, a further formal proposal to renegotiate the TRIPS Agreement to extend GI protection was circulated by a number of active proponents in April 2011 (TN/C/W/60).

The Members opposing extension essentially comprise those countries that have opposed a stronger version of the Register. They have argued that the existing (Article 22) level of protection is adequate, and cautioned that providing enhanced protection would be a burden and would disrupt existing legitimate marketing practices. They have also rejected the claim of 'usurpation', arguing that in some cases migrants have taken the methods of making the products and the names with them to their new homes and have been using them there in good faith. (See also Chapter IV, section A2.) Further, they have maintained that there is no agreement on a mandate to undertake negotiations on the TRIPS Agreement text on this issue, and that the only negotiating mandate concerns the register for wine and spirit GIs.

The Secretariat has compiled the issues raised and the views expressed in this debate, in document WT/GC/W/546-TN/C/W/25. More recently, the issue has been considered in the consultative process convened by the WTO Director-General since March 2009. While these consultations are informal, their proceedings have been reported periodically by the Director-General to the General Council and TNC as well as published

on the WTO website, including a report by the Director-General in April 2011 as part of a general stocktaking process at that time (WT/GC/W/ 633-TN/C/W/61). Reports from the consultations have noted the con-
* tinuing differences between Members, with emphasis in the discussions lying on the analysis and clarification of the technical and legal aspects of the question of extension of GI protection and the existing character of national systems of protection.

2 The 'triplets': biotechnology, traditional knowledge, biodiversity

In establishing the forward work programme for the WTO on TRIPS issues, the Doha Declaration referred to three distinct but closely inter-related issues, which have become known informally as the 'triplets'. Paragraph 19 of the Doha Declaration referred to the Article 27.3(b) review that was already required in the text of the TRIPS Agreement itself, and instructed the TRIPS Council

> in pursuing its work programme including under the review of Article 27.3(b), the review of the implementation of the TRIPS Agreement under Article 71.1 and the work foreseen pursuant to paragraph 12 of this Declaration, to examine, *inter alia*, the relationship between the TRIPS Agreement and the Convention on Biological Diversity, the protection of traditional knowledge and folklore, and other relevant new developments raised by Members pursuant to Article 71.1.

The Doha Declaration directed the TRIPS Council to be guided in this work by the objectives and principles set out in Articles 7 and 8 of the TRIPS Agreement and to take fully into account the development dimension.

This section looks at these three issues in turn – the Article 27.3(b) review, traditional knowledge and folklore, and the TRIPS–CBD relationship.

(a)   Article 27.3(b) review

Article 27.3(b) concerns the scope of permissible exceptions to patentable subject matter in biotechnology patenting, and leaves open an option for Members to rule out patents on certain biological inventions within their national IP systems. In particular, it provides for optional exclusions from the scope of patentable subject matter for plants and animals other than micro-organisms, and essentially biological processes for the production of plants or animals other than non-biological and microbiological processes. However, it does require 'protection of plant varieties either by patents or by an effective *sui generis* system or by any combination thereof'. As part of the built-in TRIPS agenda, this subparagraph became due for review in 1999, four years after the Agreement came into force. When this review commenced, it was clear that WTO Members had a wide range of perspectives and concerns in the general field of biotechnology patenting. The 2001 Doha Declaration broadened the discussion, in setting the mandate for future work of the Organization, linking this review to the TRIPS–CBD and traditional knowledge issues, as outlined in section A2 above.

The TRIPS Council prepared for the Article 27.3(b) review in 1998 through an information gathering exercise, and invited Members that were already under an obligation to apply the provision to provide information on how the matters addressed in this provision were presently treated in their national law. While it was up to each Member to decide how to provide this information, the Secretariat was asked to prepare an illustrative list of questions to assist Members to prepare their contributions (see IP/C/W/122). These questions covered a range of legal and technical matters concerning, first, the patent protection of plant and animal inventions and, second, the protection of plant varieties. Following two rounds of contributions by Members, a revised compilation of the answers received was prepared by the Secretariat in 2003 (IP/C/W/273/Rev.1), including a synoptic table to illustrate the choices made by individual Members in this area of IP law.

* The TRIPS Council maintains this review on its agenda. Discussions, which have been inconclusive, have included debate on:

- patentability of certain life forms and whether there should be exclusions for any such invention
- how to strike a balance, in the protection of plant varieties, between private and community interests and other issues such as farmers' rights and maintaining biodiversity.

(b)   Traditional knowledge and folklore

In line with the instructions given in the Doha Declaration, the TRIPS Council has continued to work on the protection of traditional knowledge (TK) and folklore since 2002. The Secretariat was instructed to prepare summaries of the wide range of issues and perspectives that have been covered in this debate. The most recent update, document IP/C/W/370/Rev.1, issued in 2006, covered general issues relating to the protection of TK, the grant of patents relating to traditional knowledge, and consent and benefit sharing, including use of the existing IP system, protecting TK under a *sui generis* system (a distinct form of protection created specifically for TK), and information on Members' national legislation, practices and experiences.

The general issues covered, for instance, the question of why there is need for international action on the protection of TK and folklore; and the international forum/forums most appropriate to pursue such a work. Proponents of international action to protect TK and folklore were reported as voicing

- concern about the granting of patents or other IPRs covering TK to persons other than those indigenous peoples or communities who have originated and legitimately control the TK;
- concern that TK is being used without the authorization of the indigenous peoples or communities who have originated and legitimately control it and without proper sharing of the benefits that accrue from such use.

* The issue remains on the agenda of the TRIPS Council but discussion has been relatively limited more recently, in contrast to the discussion in other processes, such as the work of the WIPO Intergovernmental Committee on IP and Genetic Resources, Traditional Knowledge and Folklore, which has been undertaking negotiations on legal instruments in this field.

(c) Relationship between the TRIPS Agreement and
the Convention on Biological Diversity

The third of the 'triplets' issues concerns the relationship between the TRIPS Agreement and the CBD; like the other two issues, this has remained on the agenda of the TRIPS Council as a distinct item since 2002, although it deals with issues that had earlier been raised under the Article 27.3(b) review. A comprehensive summary of issues raised and points made has been prepared by the Secretariat, and was issued in revised form in 2006 as document IP/C/W/368/Rev.1. This summary identified two general issues raised concerning the overall relationship between the TRIPS Agreement and the CBD:

- whether or not there is conflict between the TRIPS Agreement and the CBD;
- whether something needs to be done, at least on the TRIPS side, to ensure that the two instruments are applied in a non-conflicting and mutually supportive way and, if so, what should be done.

The views expressed on these two questions were grouped into four broad categories:

- that there is no conflict between the two Agreements and governments can implement the two in a mutually supportive way through national measures;
- that there is no conflict between the two Agreements and, while governments can implement the two in a mutually supportive way through national measures, further study is required to determine whether any international action in relation to the patent system is called for;
- that there is no inherent conflict between the two Agreements but there is a case for international action in relation to the patent system in order to ensure or enhance, in their implementation, the mutual supportiveness of both Agreements. There are differences of view on the exact nature of the international action needed, including on whether or not an amendment is needed to the TRIPS Agreement, to promote the objectives of the CBD;
- that there is inherent conflict between the two instruments, and the TRIPS Agreement needs to be amended to remove such conflict.

A number of proposals have been put forward and extensively debated. It is argued that these proposals reinforce the relationship between the CBD and the TRIPS Agreement, preclude possible conflicts in the practical implementation of the two treaties, or deal with claimed areas of conflict or tension between them. Proposals include amending the TRIPS Agreement to introduce a mandatory requirement for patent applicants to disclose the source and country providing genetic resources or traditional knowledge used in inventions, and to demonstrate that they had obtained prior informed consent from the competent authority in the country of origin and entered into fair and equitable benefit sharing arrangements or that they followed national legal requirements.

Extensive substantive debate has ensued on these issues, including through a series of submissions by Members to the TRIPS Council, concentrating in particular on:

- how to deal with instances of erroneous patenting of genetic resources and associated traditional knowledge; and
- the principles of prior informed consent and equitable benefit sharing under the CBD, and whether, and if so how, they should be recognized explicitly or directly applied in the TRIPS Agreement or through its implementation at the national level.

More recent discussions on these questions have focused especially on:

- use of national solutions, including legislation on genetic resources access and benefit sharing and contracts to enforce the principles of prior informed consent and equitable sharing of benefits;
- the use of databases on traditional knowledge (TK) and genetic resources to preclude erroneous patents on this subject matter;
- proposals to amend the TRIPS Agreement to oblige Members to require that a patent applicant for an invention relating to genetic or biological materials or to traditional knowledge provide information on source and origin, prior informed consent and equitable benefit sharing.

As already noted above, a negotiating proposal, tabled in the TNC in 2008 by a number of Members (TN/C/W/52), linked this issue to the two current GI issues. It proposed negotiations to amend the TRIPS Agreement to introduce a mandatory disclosure requirement concerning the country providing/source of genetic resources, and/or associated TK, and also referred to prior informed consent and access and benefit sharing. Other Members disagreed that there was, or should be, a mandate to negotiate a TRIPS amendment on this issue, and disagreed that such a disclosure mechanism was the best way to ensure compliance with prior informed consent and equitable benefit sharing obligations. More recently, as part of the April 2011 stocktaking exercise, a group of active proponents of the disclosure approach tabled in the Trade Negotiations Committee a new formal proposal to revise the TRIPS Agreement to introduce a mandatory disclosure mechanism, linking this issue also with the Nagoya Protocol on Access to Genetic Resources and the Fair and Equitable Sharing of Benefits Arising from their Utilization which was concluded in October 2010 under the aegis of the CBD (TN/C/W/59).

* Along with the issue of GI extension, the TRIPS–CBD relationship has also been considered in the consultative process convened by the Director-General. As noted above, while these consultations are informal, their proceedings have been reported periodically, including a report by the Director-General as part of the general stocktaking of Doha-related work in April 2011. Reports from the consultations have noted the continuing differences between Members on the choice between these options, although general consensus has been reported concerning the principle of equitable benefit sharing and the need to avoid erroneous patenting. Reports have described how the consultations have focused on the analysis and clarification of the technical

and legal aspects of the questions of erroneous patenting and misappropriation, and the different approaches that have been put forward in the general debate – the tailored disclosure mechanism, greater use of databases to preclude erroneous patents on genetic resources and traditional knowledge subject matter, and the national contract-based approach to enforcing access and benefit sharing obligations.

3   Non-violation complaints

Chapter VIII, section C2 discussed the issue of non-violation and situation complaints relating to the TRIPS Agreement. As noted in that chapter, Article 64.2 of the TRIPS Agreement gave a moratorium on the application of such complaints to the TRIPS Agreement for a period of five years and Article 64.3 instructed the TRIPS Council to examine the extent and manner ('scope and modalities') in which complaints of this type could be made; it required the TRIPS Council to make recommendations to the General Council by the end of 1999. The 'moratorium' on the use of non-violation and situation complaints has been extended a number of times, namely by the Doha Ministerial Conference in 2001, by the WTO General Council in 2004 as part of the so-called 'July 2004 package', by the Hong Kong Ministerial Conference in 2005 and, most recently, by the Ministerial Conferences in Geneva in 2009 and 2011. At the same time, the TRIPS Council has been instructed to continue its examination of the scope and modalities for this type of complaint, and to make recommendations. Despite extensive analysis and debate on this issue (see in particular the Summary Note by the Secretariat, document IP/C/W/349/Rev.1), WTO Members remain divided on whether non-violation or situation complaints should apply to the TRIPS Agreement.
* Debate therefore addresses not merely the scope and modalities of such disputes, but whether they should be admissible at all within the WTO dispute settlement system.

4   Least-developed countries and TRIPS

The negotiators of the TRIPS Agreement recognized the particular concerns and needs of LDCs concerning the IP system. The preamble of the TRIPS Agreement already acknowledges LDCs' particular need for maximum flexibility in implementing laws and regulations domestically. The objective was to enable them to create a sound and viable technological base.

Consequently, the TRIPS Agreement obliged developed countries to provide incentives for technology transfer to LDCs (Article 66.2). It also allowed LDCs ten years from 1995 to apply the bulk of TRIPS obligations, with the possibility that this transition period might be extended in response to a specific request. With this transition period due to expire in January 2006, the TRIPS Council decided in 2005 to extend this period until July 2013 for all LDCs, following a request by the LDC Members. The 2011 Ministerial Conference invited the TRIPS Council to give 'full consideration' to a request for a further extension. Separately, pursuant to the directions given to it in the 2001 Doha Declaration on TRIPS and Public Health, the TRIPS Council had already, in 2002, extended the period to January 2016 for LDCs to implement and enforce TRIPS provisions relating to patents and test data with respect to pharmaceutical products.

When the TRIPS Council agreed to the general extension for LDCs until July 2013, it also set up a process to help LDC Members implement TRIPS within their national IP regimes, on the basis of their individual priority needs, and to enhance the necessary technical cooperation to address those needs. The TRIPS Council's decision (document IP/C/40) recognized the special needs and requirements of LDC Members, the economic, financial and administrative constraints that they continue to face, and their need for flexibility to create a viable technological base, as well as their continuing needs for technical and financial cooperation so as to enable them to realize the cultural, social, technological and other developmental objectives of IP protection. The decision laid out three operational elements:

- LDCs were asked to provide the TRIPS Council with as much information as possible on their individual priority needs for technical and financial cooperation in order to assist them taking steps necessary to implement the TRIPS Agreement. Between 2007 and mid-2011, six LDCs provided this information to the TRIPS Council in the form of comprehensive needs assessments.
- Developed countries were asked to provide technical and financial help in order to 'effectively address the needs identified' by LDC Members. Article 67 of the TRIPS Agreement already created a general obligation on developed country Members to provide technical and financial cooperation for developing country and LDC Members, 'on request and on mutually agreed terms and conditions'. This additional decision focused especially on the specific needs identified by LDC

Members, and recognized that technical cooperation should be demand-driven, centred on actual requirements each LDC identifies, in line with a general WTO policy by which assistance is provided upon request.

- The WTO was asked to enhance its cooperation with the World Intellectual Property Organization (WIPO) and other relevant international organizations, with a view to making technical assistance and capacity building as effective and operational as possible. WIPO and the WTO have cooperated extensively on technical assistance, in response to the request and based on a Cooperation Agreement adopted in 1995, as well as a Joint Initiative on Technical Cooperation for Least-Developed Countries, launched in June 2001. Other important international partners in technical cooperation also include the United Nations Conference on Trade and Development (UNCTAD) and the WHO, the latter on TRIPS and public health issues.

5   The TRIPS Agreement and transfer of technology

Developing countries, in particular, see technology transfer as part of the bargain in which they have agreed to protect IPRs. The TRIPS Agreement includes a number of provisions on this. The preamble recognizes the underlying public policy objectives of national systems for the protection of IP, including developmental and technological objectives. Article 7 ('Objectives') states that the protection and enforcement of IPRs should contribute to the promotion of technological innovation and to the transfer and dissemination of technology, to the mutual advantage of producers and users of technological knowledge and in a manner conducive to social and economic welfare, and to a balance of rights and obligations.

As seen in Chapter I, section D3, Article 66.2 of the TRIPS Agreement defines an obligation specifically for developed country Members of the WTO to provide 'incentives to enterprises and institutions in their territories for the purpose of promoting and encouraging technology transfer' to LDC Members, to enable those countries 'to create a sound and viable technological base'. Reflecting continuing interest in the implementation of this provision, ministers agreed at the 2001 Doha Ministerial Conference that the TRIPS Council would 'put in place a mechanism for ensuring the monitoring and full implementation of the obligations' under Article 66.2. The Council duly adopted a decision setting up this mechanism in February 2003. It details the information developed countries are to supply for the review by the Council at its annual end-of-year meeting. More details on this monitoring mechanism and where the resulting documentation can be found are provided in Appendix 1, section 5(a).

At the same time, various other WTO decisions have raised the question of technology transfer and TRIPS, reaffirming the commitment to implement Article 66.2, such as the Doha Declaration on TRIPS and Public Health, and the ensuing 2003 and 2005 decisions on TRIPS and public health.

6   Electronic commerce

The Ministerial Conference adopted a 'Declaration on Global Electronic Commerce' in 1998. Ministers recognized that global electronic commerce was growing and creating new opportunities for trade, and urged the General Council to establish a comprehensive work programme to examine all trade-related issues relating to global electronic commerce, taking into account the economic, financial and development needs of developing countries. They also declared that Members would continue their current practice of not imposing customs duties on electronic transmissions. The WTO General Council subsequently established a Work Programme on Electronic Commerce (WT/L/274) for the relevant WTO bodies, including the TRIPS Council. It provided that 'the Council for TRIPS shall examine and report on the intellectual property issues arising in connection with electronic commerce. The issues to be examined shall include:

– protection and enforcement of copyright and related rights;
– protection and enforcement of trademarks;
– new technologies and access to technology.'

The issue of electronic commerce was addressed by the TRIPS Council as a standing item on its agenda from 1998 to 2003, and the Council provided a series of reports to the General Council. The reports reflected a view of Members that the novelty and complexity of the IP issues arising in connection with electronic commerce were such that continued further study was required by the international community to better understand the issues involved, and noted the related work of WIPO. Some specific issues discussed included transfer of technology, the potential application of the TRIPS Agreement's provisions relating to anti-competitive practices in the context of electronic commerce and the Internet, the WIPO Copyright Treaty ('WCT') and the WIPO Perform-ances and Phonograms Treaty ('WPPT'), the use of trademarks on the Internet, domain names, and the liability of Internet service providers. Details of these issues, and the extensive documentation circulated within the TRIPS Council, are provided in documents IP/C/W/128 and IP/C/W/128/Add.1. No specific conclusions or follow-up actions emerged from the TRIPS Council discussions.

C   The TRIPS Agreement in other multilateral policy processes

This *Handbook* focuses on the TRIPS Agreement as one of the legal agreements within the WTO system, and – for reasons of space and design – it does not provide details of the wider debates, negotiations and policy discussions that touch on the provisions of the TRIPS Agreement and their implementation in national law. However, even when looking at the Agreement in isolation, it is important to understand that the TRIPS Agreement has been considered by a range of international and regional organizations beyond the WTO. Without attempting to be comprehensive or authoritative, this section provides a brief overview of some of these discussions outside the WTO that have considered the TRIPS Agreement, usually in relation to some wider public policy issues, such as health, the environment or human rights. This section only provides a general and illustrative set of examples of the way TRIPS has been considered in other policy processes – it is neither complete nor fully representative.

This section provides an informal guide only, to help understand the wider context of the TRIPS Agreement and to provide general orientation. It should not be relied on as a source of information about the legal or policy issues, or about the activities of other international organizations. Detailed information is available directly from the organizations concerned.

---

1   The TRIPS Agreement and public health beyond the World Trade Organization

The TRIPS Agreement itself and the Doha Declaration on TRIPS and Public Health have been extensively analysed and debated in forums beyond the WTO. Foremost amongst these is the WHO, which has considered the TRIPS Agreement extensively in its work on innovation, access to medicines, and public health. The TRIPS provisions on patenting of pharmaceuticals, exceptions and limitations to patent rights, and the protection of clinical trial data have been central in the work of the WHO on public health and IP issues. Particular processes include:

- The Commission on Intellectual Property Rights, Innovation and Public Health, which was established by the World Health Assembly (WHA) in 2003. (The WHA is the decision-making body of the WHO, analogous to the WTO Ministerial Conference.) Many of the working papers of the Commission dealt with TRIPS-related issues, and its final report, delivered in 2006, extensively discussed the TRIPS Agreement and the Doha Declaration on TRIPS and Public Health throughout.
- The Global Strategy and Plan of Action on Public Health, Innovation and Intellectual Property (GSPOA) was established by the WHA in 2008. This strategy notes, as part of its context, that:

> The Doha Ministerial Declaration on the TRIPS Agreement and Public Health confirms that the agreement does not and should not prevent Members from taking measures to protect public health. The declaration, while reiterating commitment to the Agreement on Trade-Related Aspects of Intellectual Property Rights (TRIPS), affirms that the Agreement can and should be interpreted and implemented in a manner supportive of the rights of WTO Members to protect public health and, in particular, to promote access to medicines for all. Article 7 of the TRIPS Agreement states that 'the protection and enforcement of intellectual property rights should contribute to the promotion of technological innovation and to the transfer and dissemination of technology, to the mutual advantage of producers and users of technological knowledge and in a manner conducive to social and economic welfare, and to a balance of rights and obligations'.

- This strategy refers to the TRIPS Agreement in several areas, including on the transfer of health-related technology, the application and management of IP to contribute to innovation and promote public health, and improving delivery and access for health products. Furthermore, the plan of action to give effect to the strategy notes the role of the TRIPS Agreement, its provisions and flexibilities, in a number of the specific actions that constitute the overall plan.

The WHO Secretariat is charged with the practical implementation of the GSPOA, which it undertakes in part through cooperation with other international organizations, including the WTO.

2   TRIPS and human rights

The principal mechanism within the UN system dealing with human rights is the Human Rights Council, an intergovernmental body responsible for strengthening the promotion and protection of human rights. It was created by the UN General Assembly in 2006, to replace the former Human Rights Commission. Both human rights bodies have considered the TRIPS Agreement, from the perspective of several areas of human rights. Those that have been most discussed include:

- The right to benefit from moral and material interests resulting from creative work
- The right of everyone to the enjoyment of the highest attainable standard of physical and mental health (the 'right to health')
- The right to adequate food
- Rights of Indigenous Peoples.

In 2001, the High Commissioner for Human Rights issued a report on the impact of the Agreement on Trade-Related Aspects of Intellectual Property Rights on Human Rights (UN document E/CN.4/Sub.2/2001/13). This report discussed several aspects of the TRIPS Agreement relating to human rights, with a particular emphasis on the right to health.

The Council (and formerly the Commission) appoints 'Special Rapporteurs' to look into specific human right issues. Special Rapporteurs on the Right to Food, the Right to Health, and the Rights of Indigenous Peoples have discussed various aspects of the TRIPS Agreement.

The United Nations Committee on Economic, Social and Cultural Rights (CESCR) adopted in 2005 a General Comment on Article 15.1(c) of the International Covenant on Economic, Social and Cultural Rights (ICESCR) that concerns an author's right to benefit from the protection of moral and material interests resulting from his or her creative work (UN document E/C.12/GC/17). The purpose of the General Comment is to assist states that are parties to the Covenant to implement its provisions. It explores, *inter alia,* the scope of protection of the moral and material interests in relation to IPRs under national legislation or international agreements, including the TRIPS Agreement.

Other organizations dealing with human rights issues have also considered the TRIPS Agreement: for instance, the United Nations Educational, Scientific and Cultural Organization (UNESCO) Universal Declaration on

Human Rights and Bioethics cites both the TRIPS Agreement and the Doha Declaration on TRIPS and Public Health in its preamble.

3 TRIPS and development issues

The relationship between IP systems and economic, social and cultural development has been a cross-cutting question, analysed and debated throughout the UN system, and other intergovernmental and regional organizations. These discussions frequently consider the provisions, role and implications of the TRIPS Agreement, with specific focus on the situation of developing countries and LDCs in particular. The development implications of the TRIPS Agreement have been considered extensively in many forums within WIPO, since the Agreement came into force in 1995, and especially since the cooperation agreement between the WTO and WIPO on TRIPS, which came into force the following year. For example, when, in 2007, the General Assembly of WIPO adopted forty-five recommendations relating to the WIPO Development Agenda, these recommendations included the following:

- Within the framework of the agreement between WIPO and the WTO, WIPO shall make available advice to developing countries and LDCs, on the implementation and operation of the rights and obligations contained in the TRIPS Agreement, as well as on the understanding and use of flexibilities.
- To approach IP enforcement in the context of broader societal interests and especially development-oriented concerns, with a view that 'the protection and enforcement of intellectual property rights should contribute to the promotion of technological innovation and to the transfer and dissemination of technology, to the mutual advantage of producers and users of technological knowledge and in a manner conducive to social and economic welfare, and to a balance of rights and obligations', in accordance with Article 7 of the TRIPS Agreement.

UNCTAD has also undertaken a wide range of policy analysis and technical cooperation in relation to the TRIPS Agreement and development issues. Its programme on technical cooperation aims at improving understanding of the development implications of the TRIPS Agreement, and strengthening the analytical and negotiating capacity of developing countries so that they are better able to participate in IPRs-related negotiations in an informed fashion in furtherance of their sustainable development objectives.

Other elements of the UN system have worked extensively on the TRIPS Agreement – these include the United Nations Development Programme (UNDP) and the United Nations Department of Economic and Social Affairs (UNDESA).

4   Intellectual property and competition policy

There are several forums where the application of competition policy provisions in the area of IP is discussed – these include WIPO, UNCTAD and the WTO; the interplay between competition policy and the IP system is one element of the WIPO Development Agenda. At the level of individual WTO Members, the application of competition law *vis-à-vis* IP has, in many cases, been the subject of relevant guidelines in addition to enforcement proceedings and/or policy discussion and debate. It should, nonetheless, be emphasized that approaches to these issues vary across WTO Members and, indeed, are by no means settled in all jurisdictions. Within the WTO, a number of Members have reported on their national experiences in relation to the Working Group on the Interaction between Trade and Competition Policy (WGTCP).

5   TRIPS and environmental agreements

The provisions of the TRIPS Agreement, especially those concerning patents and plant variety rights, have been considered in a number of multilateral environmental forums, and by the United Nations Environment Programme (UNEP), as the UN system's designated entity for addressing environmental issues at the global and regional level. Two specific clusters of issues concerning TRIPS and environmental agreements have received particular attention:

- Policy discussions concerning the Convention on Biological Diversity (CBD) have considered the TRIPS Agreement in the context of two sets of issues in particular – first, the IP issues relating to the CBD's principles of prior informed consent and equitable sharing of benefits from the use of genetic resources and associated traditional knowledge, within its work programme on access and benefit sharing (a work programme which also led, in October 2010, to the conclusion of the Nagoya Protocol) and, secondly, the role of incentives and other technology transfer mechanisms in relation to provisions of the CBD dealing with access to and transfer of technologies that are relevant to the conservation and sustainable use of biological diversity or that make use of genetic resources and do not cause significant damage to the environment, as part of a CBD cross-cutting programme on technology transfer and cooperation.

- The development, diffusion and transfer of technology relating to climate change mitigation and adaptation has been a key issue in multilateral work on climate change since the conclusion of the United Nations Framework Convention on Climate Change (UNFCCC) in 1992. More recent negotiations under the UNFCCC have paid attention to the role of and impact of IP, and the patent system especially, in relation to innovation and diffusion of technology relevant to climate change mitigation and adaptation. Policy discussions concerning climate change have therefore included consideration of the TRIPS provisions on the scope of patentable subject matter, flexibilities such as compulsory licensing, and mechanisms for technology transfer.

Appendix 1

Guide to TRIPS notifications

A General

The TRIPS Agreement gives effect to a principle of transparency, founded on a system of notifications about how countries choose to implement TRIPS provisions. These notifications, built up since 1996, now amount to a useful collection of factual information about national IP systems, as well as specific details on key issues such as incentives for transfer of technology, and contact points within national systems. These notifications help the Council for TRIPS to monitor the operation of the Agreement and to promote understanding of Members' IP policies.

These transparency provisions oblige WTO Members to

- notify to the Council for TRIPS their IP laws and regulations;
- establish and notify contact points in their administrations for the purposes of cooperation with each other aimed at the elimination of trade in infringing goods;
- notify the Council in the event that they wish to avail themselves of certain possibilities provided for in the Agreement that relate to the substantive obligations. These concern, for example, modifications of the criteria of eligibility for protection, exceptions to the MFN treatment, and protection of state emblems.

In order to implement these notification obligations, the Council has adopted procedures and guidelines relating thereto. Appendix 2 contains a list of the IP/N/- series of documents in which such notifications are circulated.

Developed country Members have also agreed to provide certain information and make notifications which are not specifically provided for in the Agreement: these include technical cooperation and transfer of technology. Members also often share information on their legislation and practices as part of the Council's work. This has been done in a structured way when the Council has undertaken reviews of national implementing legislation, the review of the application of the provisions of the Section on geographical indications under Article 24.2 (see Chapter IV), and the review of the provisions of Article 27.3(b) (see Chapter V).

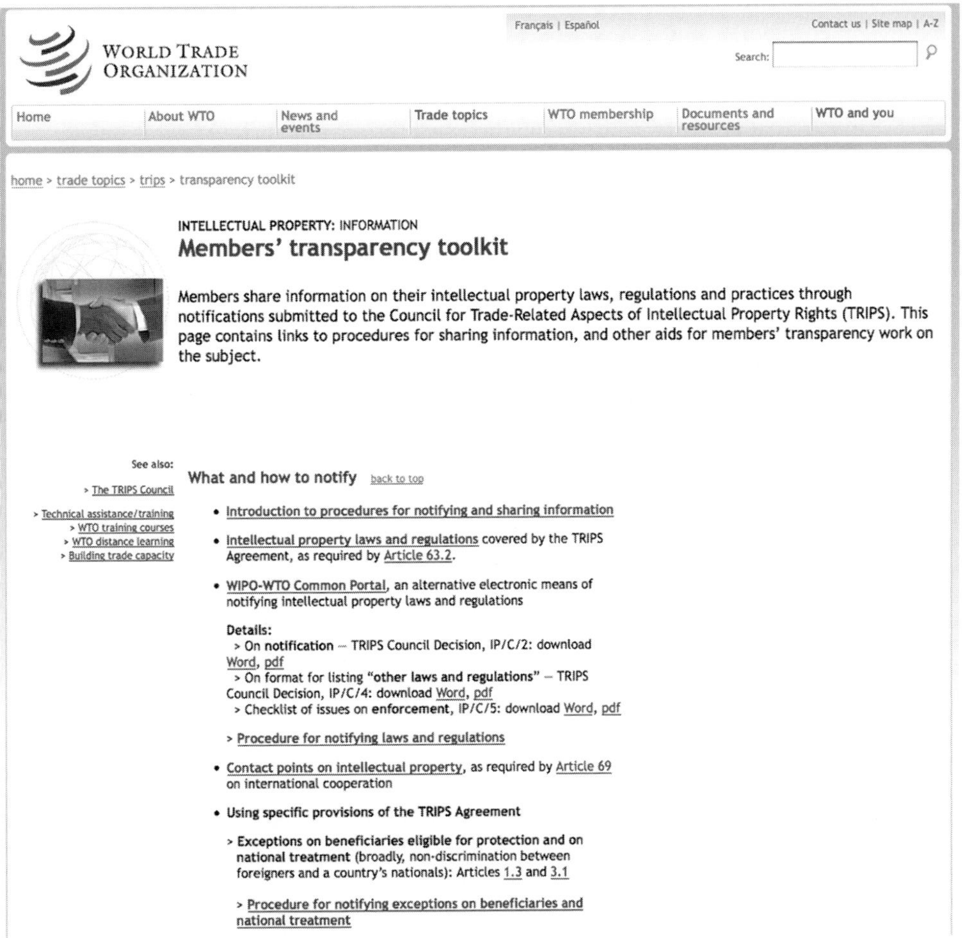

Français | Español

Contact us | Site map | A-Z

WORLD TRADE ORGANIZATION

Search:

Home | About WTO | News and events | Trade topics | WTO membership | Documents and resources | WTO and you

home > trade topics > trips > transparency toolkit

INTELLECTUAL PROPERTY: INFORMATION

Members' transparency toolkit

Members share information on their intellectual property laws, regulations and practices through notifications submitted to the Council for Trade-Related Aspects of Intellectual Property Rights (TRIPS). This page contains links to procedures for sharing information, and other aids for members' transparency work on the subject.

See also:

> The TRIPS Council

> Technical assistance/training
> WTO training courses
> WTO distance learning
> Building trade capacity

What and how to notify back to top

- Introduction to procedures for notifying and sharing information
- Intellectual property laws and regulations covered by the TRIPS Agreement, as required by Article 63.2.
- WIPO-WTO Common Portal, an alternative electronic means of notifying intellectual property laws and regulations

  Details:
  > On **notification** — TRIPS Council Decision, IP/C/2: download Word, pdf
  > On format for listing **"other laws and regulations"** — TRIPS Council Decision, IP/C/4: download Word, pdf
  > Checklist of issues on **enforcement**, IP/C/5: download Word, pdf

  > Procedure for notifying laws and regulations
- Contact points on intellectual property, as required by Article 69 on international cooperation
- **Using specific provisions of the TRIPS Agreement**

  > **Exceptions on beneficiaries eligible for protection** and on **national treatment** (broadly, non-discrimination between foreigners and a country's nationals): Articles 1.3 and 3.1

  > Procedure for notifying exceptions on beneficiaries and national treatment

Figure A1.1 Members' transparency toolkit

This Appendix summarizes these notification procedures and provides references to the relevant decisions as well as to background documents.

All of the WTO documents and notifications referred to in this Appendix are available on the WTO Documents Online database.[1] The easiest way to access this documentation is through the WTO TRIPS transparency toolkit webpage, which provides a single access point to various notifications and other reports from Members, as well to related formats, guidelines and background materials (Figure A1.1).[2] Notified laws and regulations are also available on the WIPO Lex search facility for national laws and treaties on intellectual property, which can be accessed through the WIPO GOLD online database.[3]

B   Relevant notification procedures

1   Notification of laws and regulations under Article 63.2

(a)   Procedures for the notification of laws and regulations

Article 63.2 of the TRIPS Agreement, in conjunction with Article 63.1, requires Members to notify the laws and regulations made effective pertaining to the subject matter of the Agreement (the availability, scope, acquisition, enforcement and prevention of the abuse of IPRs) to the Council in order to assist it in its review of the operation of the Agreement. The basic procedures for the notification of national laws and regulations under Article 63.2 are contained in document IP/C/2.[4] The Agreement between WIPO and the WTO is also relevant with regard to these procedures.

As regards the initial notification, the procedures provide that, as of the time that a Member is obliged to start applying a provision of the TRIPS Agreement, the corresponding laws and regulations shall be notified without delay (normally within thirty days, except where otherwise provided by the TRIPS Council). Accordingly, developed country Members were to make their initial notification of their TRIPS legislation at the end of their transition period in 1996, and developing country Members in 2000. Newly acceded Members are to notify their TRIPS implementing legislation as of the time they are to start to apply the provisions of the TRIPS Agreement in accordance with their accession protocol.

---

[1] From the WTO homepage at www.wto.org/, follow the links 'documents' and 'documents online'.

[2] From the WTO homepage, follow the links 'trade topics' and 'intellectual property'. From this TRIPS gateway page, follow the link 'Notifications – members' transparency toolkit'.

[3] WIPO GOLD can be accessed at www.wipo.int/wipogold/en/.

[4] Further procedures can be found in documents IP/C/4 and 5.

The general transition period for least-developed country Members has been extended until 1 July 2013.[5] As regards pharmaceutical products, the transition period has been extended until 1 January 2016.[6] LDC Members are not yet obliged to notify their TRIPS legislation implementing those provisions of the Agreement in respect of which they are availing themselves of the extended general transition period. However, as regards advance notifications, the procedures provide that a Member who has amended a law or regulation to bring it into conformity with the provisions of the Agreement in advance of its obligation under the Agreement to start applying those provisions will use its best endeavours to notify such law or regulation as soon as possible after its entry into force.

The procedures also provide that any subsequent amendments of a Member's laws and regulations shall be notified without delay after their entry into force (normally within thirty days where no translation is required and within sixty days where translation is necessary).

According to the procedures, notifications of laws and regulations need to comprise the following elements:

- the texts of all relevant laws and regulations in their *original language*;
- *translations* into one WTO language (i.e. English, French or Spanish) of the 'main dedicated intellectual property laws and regulations', if the original language is not a WTO language;
- a *listing* of 'other laws and regulations' in accordance with a specific format contained in document IP/C/4;
- responses to a *checklist* of questions on law and practice in the area of enforcement, in addition to the notification of the texts of enforcement laws and regulations; this 'Checklist of Issues on Enforcement' is contained in document IP/C/5.

These procedures for the notification of laws and regulations under Article 63.2 reflect a number of departures from traditional GATT/WTO practice regarding submission, translation and distribution of notifications. It was recognized that the volume of these notifications would be very large and procedures were adopted to attempt to reduce the burdens for Members in preparing them as well as for the Secretariat in processing them. At the same time, they nevertheless attempted to ensure that the purpose of the notification system as an instrument to monitor implementation would not be unduly impaired and could remain effective:

---

[5] Document IP/C/40.   [6] Document IP/C/25.

- Not all laws and regulations need to be notified in a WTO language. A distinction has been made between so-called '*main dedicated intellectual property laws and regulations*' and '*other laws and regulations*'. Document IP/C/2, paragraphs 6 and 9 and document IP/C/W/8 contain some guidelines for Members in order to help them make their assessment when dividing their laws and regulations into these two categories. Main laws and regulations have to be notified in English, French, or Spanish; other laws and regulations can be notified in a Member's national language. Translations of laws and regulations must be accompanied by the authentic texts of the laws and regulations in question in a national language.
- Under Article 2(5) of the Agreement between WIPO and the WTO, the assistance of WIPO will be available to developing country Members for translation of laws and regulations for the purposes of Article 63.2 of the TRIPS Agreement, whether or not they are Members of WIPO.
- Only the texts of main laws and regulations will be distributed in WTO documents and only in the WTO language in which they have been submitted.
- Other laws and regulations will not be distributed but only be available for consultation in the WTO Secretariat. However, in order to maximize transparency as to the contents of other laws and regulations, the notification of the texts of all 'other laws and regulations' must be accompanied by a listing of them according to the format contained in document IP/C/4. This listing must be submitted at the same time as the laws and regulations themselves. A model of such a listing can be found in document IP/C/W/8. According to the two-column format, the titles of the laws and regulations will be presented on the left-hand side and a brief description of them in English, French, or Spanish on the right-hand side.[7] In order to improve the user-friendliness of their notifications, recently some Members when updating their earlier notifications have provided such listings for both their 'main dedicated intellectual property laws and regulations' and 'other laws and regulations'.
- It has been recognized that adequate transparency of the contents of enforcement laws, in particular as to how TRIPS obligations have been implemented, may not necessarily be achieved by the notification of laws and regulations according to the above-mentioned procedures. For example, in countries with a common law tradition, this area of law is often not codified but governed by case law. Therefore, the Council has adopted a 'Checklist of Issues on Enforcement' (document IP/C/5),

---

[7] It should be noted that, unless an enforcement law is notified as a main law, enforcement laws must be taken up in this listing, including their brief description. In addition, a Member must provide responses to the Checklist of Issues on Enforcement.

responses to which Members have to submit in addition to any texts of laws and regulations including any brief description in the format referred to in the previous bullet. The responses to this checklist have to be submitted by each Member as soon as possible after the date on which it is obliged to start applying the TRIPS provisions on enforcement.

(b)   Availability of the information received

Notifications of laws and regulations under Article 63.2, including listings of 'other laws and regulations', are distributed in the IP/N/1/- series of documents. The actual texts of 'main dedicated intellectual property laws and regulations' are further categorized according to their substantive subject matter (see Appendix 2 for the detailed document codes).

Responses to the Checklist of Issues on Enforcement are circulated in the IP/N/6/- series of documents.

The notifications and the texts of the laws and regulations referred to in these documents are available on the WTO Documents Online database.[8] They can also be easily accessed through the TRIPS transparency toolkit webpage.

The procedures in document IP/C/2 provide that '[w]herever possible, notifications shall be made in machine-readable as well as hard copy form'. Earlier, the texts of most notified laws and regulations were received only in hard copy form. In these cases, the texts were attached to the WTO document containing the cover note as offset copies. Therefore, one could find only the cover note on the database, since these texts were not put into electronic form by the WTO Secretariat. However, all of the old offset documents have been scanned and prepared in .pdf format to be available in the database.[9] Some notifications continue to be received only in hard copy form or in such electronic formats that cannot be converted into a WTO document. In such cases, the texts are circulated and made available in the database as described above. Presently most texts are received in electronic form. These texts are generally included in an annex to the relevant document and also made available on the database.

Cooperation between WIPO and the WTO plays an important part in the management of notifications of laws and regulations. Article 2 of the WIPO–WTO cooperation agreement contains a number of provisions on notification procedures, translation of laws and regulations, and making them available.

---

[8] From the WTO homepage at www.wto.org/, follow the links 'documents' and 'documents online'.

[9] Search results on the WTO Document Online database indicate where such a second format for a document is available. The second format can be accessed by clicking on 'display second format'.

As provided in Article 2(4) of the cooperation agreement, the WTO Secretariat transmits to WIPO a copy of the laws and regulations notified to the WTO Secretariat by WTO Members under Article 63.2 of the TRIPS Agreement in the language or languages and in the form or forms in which they were received, and WIPO places such copies in its collection.[10] The main way WIPO makes this information available to the public is through its WIPO Lex search facility for national laws and treaties on IP. It can be accessed through the WIPO GOLD online database, which provides a one-stop gateway to WIPO's global collections of searchable IP data.

Article 63.2 of the TRIPS Agreement refers to the possibility of minimizing the burden on Members relating to notification obligations through the establishment of a common register in cooperation with WIPO. The provisions on close cooperation between the two organizations in the current notification procedures and in the WIPO–WTO cooperation agreement reflect this intention to streamline the administration of notifications. In 2010, the two organizations established a WIPO–WTO Common Portal that allows countries to simultaneously electronically submit texts of IP laws and regulations to the two organizations.

By the end of 2010, 127 Members had notified all or part of their implementing legislation and 99 Members had provided responses to the Checklist of Issues on Enforcement.

2 Notifications of contact points under Article 69

Article 69 of the Agreement provides that Members agree to cooperate with each other with a view to eliminating international trade in goods infringing IPRs and that, for this purpose, they shall establish and notify contact points

---

[10] As foreseen in Article 3(3) of the WIPO–WTO cooperation agreement, a WTO Member may choose to make its initial notification to the TRIPS Council by reference to WIPO's collection. The cooperation agreement provides that where, on the date of its initial notification of a law or regulation under Article 63.2, a WTO Member has already communicated that law or regulation, or a translation thereof, to the WIPO Secretariat and that WTO Member has sent to the WTO Secretariat a statement to that effect, and that law, regulation or translation actually exists in WIPO's collection, the WIPO Secretariat will transmit a copy of it to the WTO Secretariat.

At their meetings in December 1995, the Assemblies of the Berne and Paris Unions resolved that the receipt, by the International Bureau of WIPO from the WTO Secretariat, of a copy of any law or regulation that the WTO Secretariat received under Article 63.2 of the TRIPS Agreement shall have, for the purposes of, respectively, Article 24(2) of the Berne Convention and Article 15(2) of the Paris Convention, the same effect as if that law or regulation had been communicated to the International Bureau under the said Articles of the Berne or Paris Convention. See, respectively, paragraph 5 of WIPO document B/A/XVIII/2 and paragraph 5 of WIPO document P/A/XXIV/2.

in their administrations and be ready to exchange information on trade in infringing goods. They shall, in particular, promote the exchange of information and cooperation between customs authorities with regard to trade in counterfeit trademark goods and pirated copyright goods.

At its meeting in September 1995, the Council agreed that notifications should be made by 1 January 1996 and that any subsequent changes to the information should be notified promptly. The Council has agreed to invite each Member to notify the following information relating to the contact point, or each of the contact points, that it establishes for the purposes of Article 69: the name of the authority in question; its address; its telephone and telefax numbers and e-mail address and, where appropriate, to identify at each contact point a contact official.[11]

These contact points can be found in a database that can be accessed through the TRIPS transparency toolkit webpage.

By the end of 2010, 123 Members had notified their contact points under Article 69. The Council receives each year a number of updates to contact points notified earlier.

3   Notification requirements for Members availing themselves of certain possibilities under the TRIPS Agreement

Members wishing to avail themselves of certain possibilities in the Agreement that relate to the substantive rights and obligations or contain various flexibilities have to notify the Council. The following reviews these possibilities and summarizes the procedures and guidelines on such notifications that the Council has adopted.

(a)   Articles 1.3 and 3.1

Article 1.3 of the Agreement defines the persons that must be eligible for the protection to be made available by Members under the Agreement. The Article does so by referring to the criteria for eligibility as laid down in the Paris Convention, the Berne Convention, the Rome Convention and the Washington Treaty for the relevant areas of IP. Thus, the same criteria have to be applied among WTO Members as well, whether or not they are Member States to any of the Conventions or Treaty themselves. Certain of the exceptions allowed under these criteria, notably those of the Berne Convention or the Rome Convention, are allowed on condition that they are notified to the TRIPS Council, whether or not they have been notified to

---

[11]   See WTO/AIR/168.

the Secretary-General of the United Nations under the Berne Convention and the Rome Convention themselves.

Article 3.1 of the Agreement requires national treatment to be given to persons eligible for protection under Article 1.3, subject to the exceptions allowed under the Conventions and Treaty mentioned above. Equally as under Article 1.3, certain of these exceptions under Article 3.1 are allowed on condition that they are notified to the TRIPS Council.

Notification under Articles 1.3 and 3.1 is only required if a Member wishes to avail itself of one of the exceptions concerned. No special procedures have been adopted by the Council in respect of these notifications.[12]

These notifications are distributed in the IP/N/2/- series of documents. By the end of 2010, thirty-one Members had submitted such notifications.

(b)   Article 4(d)

Under the MFN treatment provisions of Article 4 of the Agreement, each Member has to ensure that any advantage, favour, privilege, or immunity that is available in its territory to certain foreign right holders is accorded to persons eligible under Article 1.3 for protection under the Agreement. Article 4 specifies the exemptions to MFN treatment allowed by the Agreement. One of these exceptions, that in subparagraph (d), requires a notification, namely where the advantage in question derives from an international agreement related to the protection of IP which entered into force prior to the entry into force of the WTO Agreement. The conditions for such exemptions are that the agreement in question is notified to the TRIPS Council and does not constitute an arbitrary or unjustifiable discrimination against persons eligible under Article 1.3 from other WTO Members.

Notification under Article 4(d) is only required if a Member wishes to avail itself of the exception concerned. No special procedures have been adopted by the Council in respect of these notifications.

These notifications are distributed in the IP/N/4/- series of documents. By the end of 2010, 28 Members or groups of Members had submitted such notifications.

(c)   Article 6*ter* of the Paris Convention

Article 6*ter* of the Paris Convention (1967) concerns the protection of state emblems, official hallmarks and the abbreviations and emblems of intergovernmental organizations against the registration or use as trademarks. Article 6*ter* applies in the TRIPS context by virtue of Article 2.1 of the TRIPS Agreement and lays down procedures for the communication by Members (and intergovernmental organizations) to other Members of such emblems

---

[12] Further details concerning these notification requirements can be found in a background note prepared by the Secretariat and circulated in document IP/C/W/5.

that they wish to prevent from being registered or used as trademarks and for the transmittal of objections to emblems communicated.

The application of the provisions of Article 6*ter* for the purposes of the TRIPS Agreement is addressed in Article 3 of the WIPO–WTO cooperation agreement and in the Decision of the TRIPS Council of 11 December 1995 (document IP/C/7). Accordingly, the International Bureau of WIPO administers the communication procedures under Article 6*ter* for the purposes of the TRIPS Agreement in accordance with the procedures applicable under Article 6*ter* of the Paris Convention (1967).

As regards the main features of these arrangements, following the entry into force of the TRIPS Agreement, notifications made under Article 6*ter* of the Paris Convention became effective under the TRIPS Agreement for all WTO Members (subject to the transition periods under the TRIPS Agreement) whether they were parties to the Paris Convention or not. This concerns all past as well as future notifications. The arrangements apply both to the communication of emblems and to objections to emblems communicated. The WIPO Secretariat communicated, in January 1996, all emblems communicated before that date under Article 6*ter* of the Paris Convention to those WTO Members which were not parties to the Paris Convention. Since January 1996, the practice has been that a newly acceded WTO Member that is not party to the Paris Convention receives a set of emblems as communicated through the WIPO Secretariat under the provisions of Article 6*ter* of the Paris Convention before the date on which the WTO Agreement entered into force for the new Member in question.

Signs for which protection was requested were earlier communicated individually and on paper. Since 2009, such communications have been replaced by a periodic (half-yearly) electronic communication that uses the WIPO '6*ter* Express' database.[13]

All state emblems of WTO Members and of parties to the Paris Convention, as well as emblems of international intergovernmental organizations, which benefit from the application of Article 6*ter* are available in the 6*ter* Express database. It contains some 2,500 individual records and is fully accessible and searchable online. Updated versions of the database are also being made available on CD-ROM, and can be ordered from WIPO.

(d) Other notification requirements under the Berne Convention and the Rome Convention incorporated by reference into the TRIPS Agreement

A number of notification provisions of the Berne and the Rome Conventions are incorporated by reference into the TRIPS Agreement but without being explicitly referred to in it. Such notifications are only required if a Member

---

[13] The database can be accessed at www.wipo.int/ipdl/en/search/6ter/search-struct.jsp.

wishes to avail itself of one of the possibilities concerned. No special procedures have been adopted by the Council in respect of these notifications. These
notifications are distributed in the IP/N/5/- series of documents. To date,
three Members have submitted such notifications. The following summarizes
the notification possibilities in question.[14]

Articles 14bis(2)(c) and 14bis(3) of the Berne Convention: Article 14*bis*(2)(b)
of the Berne Convention as incorporated into the TRIPS Agreement applies to
a WTO Member which in its legislation includes among the owners of
copyright in a cinematographic work authors who have brought contributions to the making of the work. In such a Member it must be presumed that
these authors have consented, in the absence of any contract to the contrary,
to certain ways in which the film may be exploited. If such a Member's
legislation requires that the consent of the authors must have been in writing,
Article 14*bis*(2)(c) requires that Member to inform other Members of this
requirement by means of a notification. Article 14*bis*(3) requires that a
Member the law of which does not make the presumption binding on the
principal director of the film must similarly make a notification. The purpose
of these notification requirements is to allow those concerned to know the
Members whose legislation applies the presumption in such a restricted way
and to make their arrangements accordingly.

Article 15(4) of the Berne Convention: Article 15(4) of the Berne Convention
as incorporated into the TRIPS Agreement is mainly directed at the protection of folklore. It deals with unpublished works where the identity of the
author is unknown, but where there is every ground to presume that he or she
is a national of a given WTO Member. In such a situation, the Member
concerned may designate a competent authority to protect the interests of
the author. Other Members should be informed about this authority by
means of a notification giving full information.

Appendix to the Berne Convention: Article 9.1 of the TRIPS Agreement
requires Members to comply with the Appendix to the Berne Convention
(1971), which contains special provisions for developing countries. The
Appendix contains a number of notification procedures which are discussed
below:

- *Article I of the Appendix:* Paragraph 1 requires a developing country
  Member wishing to avail itself of the possibilities provided in the Appendix
  to declare that it will avail itself of the faculty provided in Article II and/or

---

[14] Further details concerning these notification requirements can be found in a background
note prepared by the Secretariat and circulated in document IP/C/W/15. At its meeting
in February 1996, the Council invited each Member wishing to make such notifications
to make them to the TRIPS Council, even if the Member in question had already made a
notification under the Berne or the Rome Convention in regard to the same issue.

Article III of the Appendix (compulsory licences for, respectively, translations and reproductions) by means of a notification. According to paragraph 2 such declarations can be made for renewable periods of ten years. Such declarations may be renewed by means of a notification.[15] Paragraph 5 deals with the possibility for a country to make notifications in respect of territories for which it has international responsibility.

- *Article II(3)(b) of the Appendix*: This provision deals with the situation where a developing country Member secures the agreement of all developed country Members, in which the same language is in general use as in that developing country Member, to provide for a shorter period than the usual three years after publication for the application of compulsory licences to substitute for the exclusive right of translation. The provision requires that any such agreement shall be notified.

- *Article IV(2) of the Appendix*: This provision deals with the situation where an applicant for a compulsory licence of the types provided for in Articles II and III cannot find the owner of the right in question. In such a situation, he or she must send a copy of the application to any national or international information centre which may have been designated by the Member in which the publisher of the work concerned is believed to have his principal place of business. The paragraph provides that such information centres must have been designated in a notification by the Member concerned.

- *Article IV(4)(c)(iv) of the Appendix*: This provision allows developing country Members to export copies of translations made under compulsory licence, provided that a number of conditions are met: the language of the translation must not be English, French, or Spanish; the recipients are individuals who are nationals of the Member whose competent authority has granted the licence, or organizations grouping such individuals; the copies must be sent for teaching, scholarship, or research purposes; there must be no commercial purpose; and there must be an agreement between the Member granting the licence and that to which the copies are sent. The provision requires that such an agreement shall be notified by the Member in which the licence has been granted.

---

[15] At its meeting in July 1998, the TRIPS Council took note of a statement that its Chair made in the light of informal consultations with Members on the calculation of renewable periods of ten years under the provisions of the Appendix to the Berne Convention as incorporated by reference into the TRIPS Agreement, according to which the provisions of Article I(2) of the Appendix as incorporated into the TRIPS Agreement can be understood so that, for the purposes of the TRIPS Agreement, the relevant periods are calculated by reference to the same date, i.e. 10 October 1974, as for the purposes of the Berne Convention (see paragraphs 7–9 of the record of the meeting in IP/C/M/19).

- *Article V of the Appendix*: This Article provides that a developing country Member may choose, by way of a declaration made at the time of ratification or accession, the 'ten-year regime' which appeared in the 1896 Act of the Berne Convention for translations instead of the compulsory licensing system provided for in Article II of the Appendix.

Article 17 of the Rome Convention: Article 14.6 of the TRIPS Agreement allows a WTO Member to avail itself of exceptions permitted under the Rome Convention. Article 17 of the Rome Convention allows a state which, on 26 October 1961, granted protection to producers of phonograms solely on the basis of the criterion of fixation to continue to do so, provided it makes a notification to this effect at the time of ratification, acceptance or accession.

Article 18 of the Rome Convention: Articles 1.3, 3.1 and 14.6 of the TRIPS Agreement relate to certain exceptions under the Rome Convention, the invocation of which require notification. Article 18 of the Rome Convention provides th : any state which has invoked such an exception by means of notifications under Articles 5(3), 6(2), 16(1), or 17 of the Rome Convention may, by a further notification, reduce the scope of or withdraw the notification in question.

4   Notification requirements for Members making use of the additional flexibilities relating to TRIPS and public health

On 30 August 2003, the General Council adopted a decision on 'Implementation of Paragraph 6 of the Doha Declaration on the TRIPS Agreement and Public Health' (WT/L/540). The Decision grants three distinct waivers from the obligations set out in Article 31(f) and (h) of the Agreement with respect to pharmaceutical products, subject to certain conditions. These waivers are

- a waiver of the obligation of an exporting Member under Article 31(f) of the TRIPS Agreement to the extent necessary for the purposes of production and export of the needed pharmaceutical products to those countries that do not have sufficient capacity to manufacture them;
- a waiver of the obligation under Article 31(h) of the Agreement on the importing Member to provide adequate remuneration to the right holder in situations where remuneration in accordance with Article 31(h) is being paid in the exporting Member for the same products; and
- a waiver of the obligation under Article 31(f) of the Agreement on any developing country or LDC Member that is party to an RTA at least half of the current membership of which is made up of countries presently on the UN list of least-developed countries.

WTO Members wishing to make use of this 'Paragraph 6' system are required to make the following notifications:

- Paragraph 1(b): intention to use the system established by the Decision of 30 August 2003 as an importer. This notification needs to be made only once. It can be made at any time, either independently of any actual use of the system or together with the first notification under paragraph 2(a). This notification requirement does not apply to importing Members which are LDCs.
- Paragraph 2(a): specific imports under the system established by the Decision of 30 August 2003, for which an eligible importing Member is required to: (i) specify the names and expected quantities of the products needed; (ii) confirm that it has insufficient or no manufacturing capacities in the pharmaceutical sector for the products in question; and (iii) confirm that, where a pharmaceutical product is patented in its territory, it has granted or intends to grant a compulsory licence in accordance with Article 31 of the Agreement and the provisions of the Decision. No notification requirement applies to LDC Members as regards condition (ii), as they are deemed to have insufficient or no manufacturing capacities.
- Paragraph 2(c): grant of a compulsory licence under the system established by the Decision of 30 August 2003. The information provided shall include the name and address of the licensee, the product(s) for which the licence has been granted, the quantity(ies) for which it has been granted, the country(ies) to which the product(s) is (are) to be supplied and the duration of the licence. The notification shall also indicate the address of the website of the licensee that shall post on its website information on the quantities being supplied to each destination and the distinguishing features of the products in question.

To date, one notification has been received under each of paragraphs 2(a) and 2(c).

These three types of notifications are circulated in the IP/N/8–10 series of documents, respectively. The notifications discussed above can easily be accessed through the 'TRIPS and public health: dedicated webpage for notifications'.[16]

---

[16] The Decision of 30 August 2003 called for the establishment of such a dedicated page on the WTO website, in particular to make publicly available certain notifications made by Members in using the 'Paragraph 6' system established under the Decision. To access the page, follow from the WTO homepage the links 'trade topics', 'intellectual property' and 'Dedicated page: TRIPS and public health notifications'.

On 6 December 2005, the General Council adopted a Protocol Amending the TRIPS Agreement and submitted it to Members for acceptance (WT/L/ 641). The provisions of the waiver Decision will be replaced by identical provisions of Article 31*bis* of the TRIPS Agreement, once the amendment enters into force. The notification requirements will remain unchanged under the new Article 31*bis*.

5 Notification requirements for developed country Members agreed by the TRIPS Council in the context of Articles 66.2 and 67

(a) Reports under Article 66.2

Article 66.2 of the TRIPS Agreement requires developed country Members to provide incentives to enterprises and institutions in their territories for the purpose of promoting and encouraging technology transfer to LDC Members in order to enable them to create a sound and viable technological base. In its Decision on Implementation-Related Issues and Concerns, adopted on 14 November 2001, the Ministerial Conference reaffirmed that the provisions of Article 66.2 of the TRIPS Agreement are mandatory, and instructed the TRIPS Council to put in place a mechanism for ensuring the monitoring and full implementation of the obligations in question.

Having regard to the instructions of the Ministerial Conference, the TRIPS Council adopted a Decision on Implementation of Article 66.2 of the TRIPS Agreement on 20 February 2003 (IP/C/28). The Decision establishes a mechanism for ensuring the monitoring and full implementation of the obligations in Article 66.2. Paragraph 1 of the Decision provides that developed country Members shall submit annually reports on actions taken or planned in pursuance of their commitments under Article 66.2. To this end, they are to provide new detailed reports every third year and, in the intervening years, to provide updates to their most recent reports. These reports are to be submitted prior to the last Council meeting scheduled for the year in question. Moreover, paragraph 2 of the Decision provides that the submissions shall be reviewed by the Council at its end-of-year meeting each year.

The tri-annual new reports and the intervening updates are circulated in the IP/C/W- series of documents and made available on the WTO Documents Online database. They can be easily accessed through the TRIPS transparency toolkit webpage or a webpage on 'Technology transfer'[17] that contains a quick search documents online feature for reports under Article 66.2.

---

[17] From the WTO homepage, follow the links 'trade topics', 'intellectual property' and 'technology transfer'.

(b) Contact points for technical cooperation and reports under Article 67

(i) Contact points for technical cooperation on TRIPS At its meeting in July 1996, the Council for TRIPS agreed that each developed country Member should notify a contact point for technical cooperation on TRIPS, in particular for the exchange of information between donors and recipients of technical assistance. Information on the format for these notifications can be found in WTO/AIR/388.[18]

The information on such contact points can be found in a database that can be accessed through the TRIPS transparency toolkit webpage. In addition, the webpage on technical cooperation in the TRIPS area contains a link to this list of contact points.[19]

By the end of 2010, 29 developed country Members have notified their contact points for technical cooperation on TRIPS. The Council receives each year a number of updates to contact points notified earlier.

(ii) Reports under Article 67 Article 67 of the TRIPS Agreement requires developed country Members to provide, on request and on mutually agreed terms and conditions, technical and financial cooperation in favour of developing country and LDC Members. According to this provision, the objective of such cooperation is to facilitate the implementation of the Agreement. The Article specifies that such assistance shall include assistance in the preparation of laws and regulations on the protection and enforcement of IPRs as well as on the prevention of their abuse, and support regarding the establishment or reinforcement of domestic offices and agencies relevant to these matters, including the training of personnel.

In order to ensure that information on available assistance is readily accessible and to facilitate the monitoring of compliance with the obligation of Article 67, developed country Members have agreed to present descriptions of their relevant technical and financial cooperation programmes and to update them annually. For the sake of transparency, intergovernmental organizations have also presented, on the invitation of the Council, information on their activities. The Council normally holds its annual review of technical cooperation at its meeting in autumn.

---

[18] The document provides that developed country Members have been requested to notify, in particular, the following information concerning their contact point(s): (i) the name of the authority in question; (ii) its address; (iii) its telephone and telefax numbers and, where appropriate, e-mail reference; and (iv) where appropriate, to identify at each contact point a contact official.

[19] From the TRIPS gateway page, follow the link 'technical co-operation in the TRIPS area'.

The information from developed country Members, intergovernmental organizations and the WTO Secretariat on their technical cooperation activities in the area of TRIPS is circulated in the IP/C/W/- series of documents and made available on the WTO Documents Online database. The information can easily be accessed through the TRIPS transparency toolkit webpage, or a webpage on technical cooperation in the TRIPS area contains a quick search documents online feature for reports on technical cooperation activities in the area of TRIPS.[20]

6   Certain other information flows

(a)   Records of reviews of national implementing legislation

The initial notifications of laws and regulations made pursuant to Article 63.2 of the TRIPS Agreement form the basis for reviews of national implementing legislation carried out by the Council. Initially, the review exercise focused on those developed country Members whose transition period expired on 1 January 1996. Their legislation was reviewed in 1996 and 1997 in four week-long meetings according to the following subject areas: copyright and related rights; trademarks, GIs and industrial designs; patents, layout-designs of integrated circuits, undisclosed information and the control of anti-competitive practices in contractual licences; enforcement. The legislation of developing country Members whose transition period expired on 1 January 2000 was reviewed in 2000 and 2001. The totality of the legislation of each Member was reviewed at a single review meeting. The legislation of newly acceded Members is reviewed as of the time that they start to apply the provisions of the TRIPS Agreement in accordance with their accession protocol. By the end of 2010, the Council had completed 117 reviews, and three reviews already initiated remained on its agenda.

The procedures for these reviews provide for written questions and replies prior to the review meeting, with follow-up questions and replies during the course of the meeting. At subsequent meetings of the Council, an opportunity is given to follow up points emerging from the review session which delegations consider have not been adequately addressed.

After the completion of a review, the record of the introductory statement made by the delegation subject to review, the questions put to it and the responses given in the review are circulated in the IP/Q/- series of documents. The records of the reviews of developed country Members' legislation in the four subject areas referred to above were circulated, respectively, in the IP/Q/-, IP/Q2/-, IP/Q3/- and IP/Q4/- series of documents. Given that the totality of

---

[20] From the TRIPS gateway page, follow the link 'technical cooperation in the TRIPS area'.

the legislation of each developing country and newly acceded Member has been reviewed at a single review meeting, the records of these reviews have been circulated in single documents with four document symbols. These documents are available on the WTO Documents Online database. The webpage on 'review of implementing legislation' contains a quick search document online feature for these documents.[21]

(b)   Responses provided in the context of the review of the provisions of the Section on geographical indications under Article 24.2

In the context of the review of the application of the provisions of the Section on GIs under Article 24.2 of the TRIPS Agreement, the Council, at its meetings in May and July 1998, invited those Members already under an obligation to apply the provisions in question to provide their responses to a Checklist of Questions contained in document IP/C/13 and Add.1, it being understood that other Members could also furnish replies on a voluntary basis. By the end of 2010, forty-nine Members had provided responses thereto.

The responses from Members have been circulated in document IP/C/W/ 117, addenda, supplements and revisions. At the Council's request, the Secretariat has prepared a note summarizing these responses. An updated version of the summary, circulated in November 2003, can be found in document IP/ C/W/253/Rev.1. This documentation is available on the WTO Documents Online database.

(c)   Responses provided in the context of the review of the provisions of Article 27.3(b)

At its meeting in December 1998, the Council agreed to initiate the review of the provisions of Article 27.3(b) through an information gathering exercise. The Council invited Members that were already under an obligation to apply Article 27.3(b) to provide information on how the matters addressed in these provisions were presently treated in their national law. Other Members were invited to provide such information on a best-endeavours basis. While it was left to each Member to provide information as it saw fit, having regard to the specific provisions of Article 27.3(b), the Council requested the Secretariat to provide an illustrative list of questions relevant in this regard in order to assist Members to prepare their contributions. This list was circulated in document IP/C/W/122. A number of Members circulated an alternative format in document IP/C/W/126, and invited interested Members to be guided by it

---

[21] From the TRIPS gateway page, follow the link 'review of Members' implementing legislation'.

in completing their responses, if they so desired. By the end of 2010, twenty-five Members had provided such information.[22]

The responses from Members have been circulated in document IP/C/W/125, addenda, supplements and revisions.[23] At the Council's request, the Secretariat prepared a note summarizing these responses. An updated version of the summary, circulated in February 2003, can be found in document IP/C/W/253/Rev.1. This documentation is available on the WTO Documents Online database.

---

[22] Counting the European Communities and its member States as of February 1999, when the responses were provided, as one.

[23] A number of Members provided information by answering the questions listed in document IP/C/W/122, some others used the method in document IP/C/W/126, and some of them answered the questions in both documents. Finally, there were Members who provided information without referring to either of these documents.

Appendix 2

Guide to TRIPS documents

A   General

TRIPS includes a set of transparency mechanisms, which require Members to furnish extensive information about their IP laws and policies, and details about how IPRs are administered and enforced in their territories; these laws are also reviewed in detail in the TRIPS Council. The operation of these transparency mechanisms in the years since 1995 has yielded a uniquely comprehensive and systematic body of information that now covers some 130 jurisdictions (essentially all WTO Members other than LDCs, for whom these provisions do not yet apply).

The very purpose of these mechanisms is to enable understanding of national IP laws and policies; and in practice the TRIPS notifications and related TRIPS Council review materials are a useful and geographically broad resource for those – delegates, analysts, researchers, policy-makers – seeking detailed information on a wide range of questions of IP law, practice and policy. Other working documents and minutes of the Council's regular and special sessions also provide a wealth of information on Members' policy positions and international debate on these matters. Furthermore, dispute settlement panel and Appellate Body reports dealing with the TRIPS Agreement shed light on the interpretation of its provisions.

This Appendix provides a brief guide to WTO TRIPS documents and explains how these documents are organized. It is limited to those sets of documents that are circulated to the regular or special sessions of the TRIPS Council. It should be noted that other WTO documents may also include useful information on Members' IP policy. These include reports from the periodic reviews of individual countries' trade policies.

WTO documents are grouped into a number of collections that are usually identified by letters which appear as the first characters in document symbols. TRIPS documents are circulated in a document collection with a symbol IP/-. This and other collections are sub-divided into a number of document series. Each document is given a symbol that is made up of a combination of letters, numbers and suffixes.

Letters are used to identify collections, series, types and the status of documents. The following suffixes are used in the symbol to denote the status of a document:

- Add.   Addendum
- Corr.   Corrigendum
- Rev.   Revision
- Supp.   Supplement

Numbers are used to indicate sequential order. Three-letter ISO standard codes are also used to identify Members (e.g. POL for Poland, ZWE for Zimbabwe, etc.). All documents are numbered in chronological order of issue and some documents may have more than one symbol. Here are some examples:

- IP/N/1/SGP/1/Rev.1: first revision of this document containing a revised edition of Singapore's Copyright Act
- IP/C/M/61/Corr.1: first corrigendum to this document containing a correction to the minutes of a meeting of the TRIPS Council
- IP/C/W/117/Add.33: the thirty-third addendum to this document containing information provided by Members on their application of the TRIPS provisions on GIs.

The official working languages of the WTO Secretariat are English, French and Spanish. All formal documents (i.e. documents bearing a symbol) are produced and disseminated in the three official languages of the WTO. Most official documents are not generally circulated simultaneously by the WTO in the three languages. Most documents are first disseminated in English (or in their original language of submission when the English version is not available) and then distributed in the other official languages after the translation process is complete. Some document series, however, are always distributed simultaneously in the three official languages of the Organization. These include documents relating to dispute settlement circulated in the WT/DSnumber/- series of documents.

Official TRIPS documents are generally circulated as unrestricted documents, i.e. they are publicly available as soon as they have been circulated. However, minutes of meetings are initially circulated as restricted documents but become publicly available forty-five days after the date of circulation.[1]

Official WTO documents are available on the WTO Documents Online database.[2]

---

[1] The General Council's decision of 14 May 2002 on 'Procedures for the Circulation and Derestriction of WTO Documents' can be found in document WT/L/452.

[2] From the WTO homepage at www.wto.org/, follow the links 'documents' and 'documents online'.

The notifications under the TRIPS Agreement discussed in greater detail in Appendix 1 can serve as a useful source of information on the IP policy choices taken by a wide range of countries, as well as specific matters such as incentives for technology transfer. All of this material is now available on the WTO website (see details in Appendix 1). This section briefly describes several of the main sources of information from a user's point of view.

B   TRIPS notifications

Notifications under TRIPS Article 63.2 cover the substantive IP law of many countries in all of the areas covered by the TRIPS Agreement, as well as information on enforcement mechanisms which are often not dealt with in the substantive legislation. While there is no guarantee that this information is complete or up to date for any particular country, it is an invaluable resource for understanding the wide range of options that countries have chosen in implementing TRIPS-consistent legislation.

Contact points are established to provide a convenient means of getting in touch with national officials responsible for:

- Technical cooperation in the implementation of TRIPS provisions
- International cooperation with a view to eliminating international trade in goods infringing IPRs under TRIPS Article 69.

In addition, Members notify the Council in the event that they wish to avail themselves of certain possibilities provided for in the Agreement that related to the substantive obligations.

These notifications are described in detail in Appendix 1. Table A2.1 summarizes the documents or other sources where the notified information can be found.

C   Reviews of national legislation

As described in Appendix 1, each WTO Member undergoes a review of its national legislation after the main, substantive obligations of the TRIPS Agreement come into effect for it. This review, a peer-review process between governments within the TRIPS Council, has produced a unique record of information about national IP policies and explanations of legal and technical details, as well as some indications of why particular choices were taken. This material therefore supplements the legal texts, and provides accessible insights into the laws and regulations, as well as enforcement mechanisms.

After the completion of a review, the record of the introductory statement made by the delegation subject to review, the questions put to it and the responses given in the review, are circulated in the IP/Q/- series of documents.

Table A2.1 *WTO Document Series for the circulation of intellectual property notifications*

IP/N/1/-	Notification of laws and regulations under Article 63.2 of the Agreement
	The actual texts of 'main dedicated intellectual property laws and regulations' are available in the following sub-series of documents:
	IP/N/1/-/C/ Copyright and related rights
	IP/N/1/-/T/ Trademarks
	IP/N/1/-/G/ GIs
	IP/N/1/-/D/ Industrial designs
	IP/N/1/-/P/ Patents (including plant variety protection)
	IP/N/1/-/L/ Layout-designs (topographies) of integrated circuits
	IP/N/1/-/U/ Undisclosed information
	IP/N/1/-/I/ Industrial property (general)
	IP/N/1/-/E/ Enforcement
	IP/N/1/-/O/ Other
IP/N/2/-	Notification under Articles 1.3 and 3.1 of the Agreement
IP/N/4/-	Notification under Article 4(d) of the Agreement
IP/N/5/-	Notification under the provisions of the Berne Convention and the Rome Convention incorporated into the TRIPS Agreement but without being explicitly referred to therein
IP/N/6/-	Responses to the Checklist of Issues on Enforcement
IP/N/8/-	Notification under Paragraph 1(b) of the Decision of 30 August 2003 on the implementation of Paragraph 6 of the Doha Declaration on the TRIPS Agreement and Public Health
IP/N/9/-	Notification under Paragraph 2(a) of the Decision of 30 August 2003 on the implementation of paragraph 6 of the Doha Declaration on the TRIPS Agreement and Public Health
IP/N/10/-	Notification under Paragraph 2(c) of the Decision of 30 August 2003 on the implementation of Paragraph 6 of the Doha Declaration on the TRIPS Agreement and Public Health

Up-to-date information on contact points for technical cooperation on TRIPS and on international cooperation under Article 69 of the Agreement is available on the WTO website on the transparency toolkit webpage.

Notifications of state emblems made under Article 6*ter* of the Paris Convention, as incorporated into the TRIPS Agreement, are available, pursuant to the WIPO–WTO cooperation agreement, on the WIPO '6*ter* Express' database.[3]

---

[3] The database can be accessed at www.wipo.int/ipdl/en/search/6ter/search-struct.jsp.

The records of the reviews of developed country Members' legislation were circulated in the following document series:

- IP/Q/- copyright and related rights
- IP/Q2/- trademarks, GIs and industrial designs
- IP/Q3/- patents, layout-designs of integrated circuits, undisclosed information and the control of anti-competitive practices in contractual licences
- IP/Q4/- enforcement.

Given that the totality of the legislation of each developing country and newly acceded Member has been reviewed at a single review meeting, the records of these reviews have been circulated in single documents with four document symbols.

D   Dispute settlement

A request for consultations under the DSU that relate to the provisions of the TRIPS Agreement is circulated in the IP/D/- series of documents. The request is also given a WT/DSnumber- symbol. The notification of a mutually agreed solution or the adoption by the DSB of the panel or Appellate Body report, as well as certain other actions, are circulated in addenda to this document. All other documents relating to that particular dispute are circulated exclusively under the WT/DSnumber- series of documents.

A special document portal – accessed through the Dispute Settlement Gateway on the WTO website – provides easy access to all dispute settlement documents. They can be searched by agreement, including the TRIPS Agreement. The *WTO Analytical Index* is a guide to the legal interpretation and application of the WTO Agreements by the WTO Appellate Body, WTO dispute settlement panels and other WTO bodies. It provides information on jurisprudence or decisions relating to each provision of the WTO Agreements. An online version is available on the WTO website, and a printed form is available in two volumes.

E   Reports and decisions

Annual reports and certain other reports by the TRIPS Council are circulated in the IP/C- series of documents. The Council's decisions are also circulated in this series.

F   Minutes

The minutes of meetings of the TRIPS Council are circulated in the IP/C/M/- series of documents. They remain restricted for a period of forty-five days after their circulation.

G Working documents

The working documents of the TRIPS Council are circulated in IP/C/W-series of documents. Such working documents include submissions by WTO Members and Observers to the Council, and background notes prepared by the WTO Secretariat.

The specific reviews that the TRIPS Council has undertaken in line with the built-in agenda on GIs (Article 24.2) and biotech patenting and related issues (Article 27.3(b)), as well as reviews on issues such as incentives for technology transfer (Article 66.2) and technical cooperation (Article 67), have produced detailed reports and surveys of practical information on each of these issues. Examples of such documentation include:

- GIs (Article 24.2)
  - IP/C/W/117, addenda, supplements and revisions: information provided by Members on their application of the TRIPS provisions on GIs
  - IP/C/W/253/Rev.1: a Secretariat summary of the information provided by Members
- Biotech patenting and related issues (Article 27.3(b))
  - IP/C/W/125, addenda, supplements and revisions: information provided by Members on their application of the provisions of TRIPS Article 27.3(b)
  - IP/C/W/253/Rev.1: a Secretariat summary of the information provided by Members
- Incentives for technology transfer (Article 66.2)
  - The tri-annual new reports and the intervening updates by Members on the incentives they provide are circulated in the IP/C/W- series of documents. The document number is different each year. The reports can be easily accessed through the TRIPS transparency toolkit webpage, or a webpage on 'Technology transfer'[4] that contains a quick search documents online feature for reports under Article 66.2.
- Technical cooperation (Article 67)
  - The information from developed country Members, intergovernmental organizations and the WTO Secretariat on their technical cooperation activities in the area of TRIPS is circulated in the IP/C/W/- series of documents. The document numbers are different each year. The information can easily be accessed through the TRIPS transparency toolkit webpage or a webpage on technical cooperation in the TRIPS area contains a quick search documents online feature for reports on technical cooperation activities in the area of TRIPS.[5]

---

[4] From the WTO homepage, follow the links 'trade topics', 'intellectual property' and 'technology transfer'.

[5] From the TRIPS gateway page, follow the link 'technical cooperation in the TRIPS area'.

H   Documents of the Council for TRIPS in Special Session

TRIPS Article 23.4 calls upon the Council for TRIPS to negotiate a multilateral system of notification and registration of GIs for wines, eligible for protection in those Members participating in the system, with a view to facilitating the protection of GIs for wines. This built-in mandate was extended by the Doha Ministerial Declaration in 2001 to cover spirits also. Currently, the negotiation of the system is taking place in a negotiating group of the Doha Round, which takes the form of Special Sessions of the Council for TRIPS.

The documents of the Special Session are circulated in the TN/IP- series of documents as follows:

- TN/IP/M/- series: minutes of the regular meetings of the Special Session, which remain restricted for a period of forty-five days after their circulation
- TN/IP- series: reports by the Special Session
- TN/IP/W- series: working documents of the Special Session.

Annexes

TRIPS *Handbook*

Table of Contents

∽

Annex 1
Agreement on Trade-Related Aspects of Intellectual Property Rights (TRIPS Agreement) 1994

PART IV   ACQUISITION AND MAINTENANCE OF
           INTELLECTUAL PROPERTY RIGHTS AND
           RELATED *INTER PARTES* PROCEDURES

PART V   DISPUTE PREVENTION AND
           SETTLEMENT

PART VI   TRANSITIONAL ARRANGEMENTS

PART VII   INSTITUTIONAL ARRANGEMENTS; FINAL
           PROVISIONS

AGREEMENT ON TRADE-RELATED ASPECTS OF INTELLECTUAL PROPERTY RIGHTS

Members

Desiring to reduce distortions and impediments to international trade, and taking into account the need to promote effective and adequate protection of intellectual property rights, and to ensure that measures and procedures to enforce intellectual property rights do not themselves become barriers to legitimate trade;

Recognizing, to this end, the need for new rules and disciplines concerning:

(a) the applicability of the basic principles of GATT 1994 and of relevant international intellectual property agreements or conventions;
(b) the provision of adequate standards and principles concerning the availability, scope and use of trade-related intellectual property rights;
(c) the provision of effective and appropriate means for the enforcement of trade-related intellectual property rights, taking into account differences in national legal systems;
(d) the provision of effective and expeditious procedures for the multilateral prevention and settlement of disputes between governments; and
(e) transitional arrangements aiming at the fullest participation in the results of the negotiations;

Recognizing the need for a multilateral framework of principles, rules and disciplines dealing with international trade in counterfeit goods;

Recognizing that intellectual property rights are private rights;

Recognizing the underlying public policy objectives of national systems for the protection of intellectual property, including developmental and technological objectives;

Recognizing also the special needs of the least-developed country Members in respect of maximum flexibility in the domestic implementation of laws and regulations in order to enable them to create a sound and viable technological base;

Emphasizing the importance of reducing tensions by reaching strengthened commitments to resolve disputes on trade-related intellectual property issues through multilateral procedures;

Desiring to establish a mutually supportive relationship between the WTO and the World Intellectual Property Organization (referred to in this Agreement as 'WIPO') as well as other relevant international organizations;

Hereby agree as follows:

PART I   GENERAL PROVISIONS AND BASIC PRINCIPLES

Article 1

Nature and Scope of Obligations

1. Members shall give effect to the provisions of this Agreement. Members may, but shall not be obliged to, implement in their law more extensive protection than is required by this Agreement, provided that such protection does not contravene the provisions of this Agreement. Members shall be free to determine the appropriate method of implementing the provisions of this Agreement within their own legal system and practice.
2. For the purposes of this Agreement, the term 'intellectual property' refers to all categories of intellectual property that are the subject of Sections 1 through 7 of Part II.
3. Members shall accord the treatment provided for in this Agreement to the nationals of other Members.[1] In respect of the relevant

---

[1] When 'nationals' are referred to in this Agreement, they shall be deemed, in the case of a separate customs territory Member of the WTO, to mean persons, natural or legal, who are domiciled or who have a real and effective industrial or commercial establishment in that customs territory.

intellectual property right, the nationals of other Members shall be understood as those natural or legal persons that would meet the criteria for eligibility for protection provided for in the Paris Convention (1967), the Berne Convention (1971), the Rome Convention and the Treaty on Intellectual Property in Respect of Integrated Circuits, were all Members of the WTO members of those Conventions.[2] Any Member availing itself of the possibilities provided in paragraph 3 of Article 5 or paragraph 2 of Article 6 of the Rome Convention shall make a notification as foreseen in those provisions to the Council for Trade-Related Aspects of Intellectual Property Rights (the 'Council for TRIPS').

Article 2

Intellectual Property Conventions

1. In respect of Parts II, III and IV of this Agreement, Members shall comply with Articles 1 through 12, and Article 19, of the Paris Convention (1967).
2. Nothing in Parts I to IV of this Agreement shall derogate from existing obligations that Members may have to each other under the Paris Convention, the Berne Convention, the Rome Convention and the Treaty on Intellectual Property in Respect of Integrated Circuits.

Article 3

National Treatment

1. Each Member shall accord to the nationals of other Members treatment no less favourable than that it accords to its own nationals with regard to the protection[3] of intellectual property, subject to the

---

[2] In this Agreement, 'Paris Convention' refers to the Paris Convention for the Protection of Industrial Property; 'Paris Convention (1967)' refers to the Stockholm Act of this Convention of 14 July 1967. 'Berne Convention' refers to the Berne Convention for the Protection of Literary and Artistic Works; 'Berne Convention (1971)' refers to the Paris Act of this Convention of 24 July 1971. 'Rome Convention' refers to the International Convention for the Protection of Performers, Producers of Phonograms and Broadcasting Organizations, adopted at Rome on 26 October 1961. 'Treaty on Intellectual Property in Respect of Integrated Circuits' (IPIC Treaty) refers to the Treaty on Intellectual Property in Respect of Integrated Circuits, adopted at Washington on 26 May 1989. 'WTO Agreement' refers to the Agreement Establishing the WTO.

[3] For the purposes of Articles 3 and 4, 'protection' shall include matters affecting the availability, acquisition, scope, maintenance and enforcement of intellectual property

exceptions already provided in, respectively, the Paris Convention (1967), the Berne Convention (1971), the Rome Convention or the Treaty on Intellectual Property in Respect of Integrated Circuits. In respect of performers, producers of phonograms and broadcasting organizations, this obligation only applies in respect of the rights provided under this Agreement. Any Member availing itself of the possibilities provided in Article 6 of the Berne Convention (1971) or paragraph 1(b) of Article 16 of the Rome Convention shall make a notification as foreseen in those provisions to the Council for TRIPS.

2. Members may avail themselves of the exceptions permitted under paragraph 1 in relation to judicial and administrative procedures, including the designation of an address for service or the appointment of an agent within the jurisdiction of a Member, only where such exceptions are necessary to secure compliance with laws and regulations which are not inconsistent with the provisions of this Agreement and where such practices are not applied in a manner which would constitute a disguised restriction on trade.

Article 4

Most-Favoured-Nation Treatment

With regard to the protection of intellectual property, any advantage, favour, privilege or immunity granted by a Member to the nationals of any other country shall be accorded immediately and unconditionally to the nationals of all other Members. Exempted from this obligation are any advantage, favour, privilege or immunity accorded by a Member:

(a) deriving from international agreements on judicial assistance or law enforcement of a general nature and not particularly confined to the protection of intellectual property;

(b) granted in accordance with the provisions of the Berne Convention (1971) or the Rome Convention authorizing that the treatment accorded be a function not of national treatment but of the treatment accorded in another country;

(c) in respect of the rights of performers, producers of phonograms and broadcasting organizations not provided under this Agreement;

rights as well as those matters affecting the use of intellectual property rights specifically addressed in this Agreement.

(d) deriving from international agreements related to the protection of intellectual property which entered into force prior to the entry into force of the WTO Agreement, provided that such agreements are notified to the Council for TRIPS and do not constitute an arbitrary or unjustifiable discrimination against nationals of other Members.

Article 5

Multilateral Agreements on Acquisition or Maintenance of Protection

The obligations under Articles 3 and 4 do not apply to procedures provided in multilateral agreements concluded under the auspices of WIPO relating to the acquisition or maintenance of intellectual property rights.

Article 6

Exhaustion

For the purposes of dispute settlement under this Agreement, subject to the provisions of Articles 3 and 4 nothing in this Agreement shall be used to address the issue of the exhaustion of intellectual property rights.

Article 7

Objectives

The protection and enforcement of intellectual property rights should contribute to the promotion of technological innovation and to the transfer and dissemination of technology, to the mutual advantage of producers and users of technological knowledge and in a manner conducive to social and economic welfare, and to a balance of rights and obligations.

Article 8

Principles

1. Members may, in formulating or amending their laws and regulations, adopt measures necessary to protect public health and nutrition, and to promote the public interest in sectors of vital importance to their socio-economic and technological development, provided that such measures are consistent with the provisions of this Agreement.
2. Appropriate measures, provided that they are consistent with the provisions of this Agreement, may be needed to prevent the abuse

of intellectual property rights by right holders or the resort to practices which unreasonably restrain trade or adversely affect the international transfer of technology.

PART II STANDARDS CONCERNING THE AVAILABILITY, SCOPE AND USE OF INTELLECTUAL PROPERTY RIGHTS

SECTION 1 COPYRIGHT AND RELATED RIGHTS

Article 9

Relation to the Berne Convention

1. Members shall comply with Articles 1 through 21 of the Berne Convention (1971) and the Appendix thereto. However, Members shall not have rights or obligations under this Agreement in respect of the rights conferred under Article 6*bis* of that Convention or of the rights derived therefrom.
2. Copyright protection shall extend to expressions and not to ideas, procedures, methods of operation or mathematical concepts as such.

Article 10

Computer Programs and Compilations of Data

1. Computer programs, whether in source or object code, shall be protected as literary works under the Berne Convention (1971).
2. Compilations of data or other material, whether in machine readable or other form, which by reason of the selection or arrangement of their contents constitute intellectual creations shall be protected as such. Such protection, which shall not extend to the data or material itself, shall be without prejudice to any copyright subsisting in the data or material itself.

Article 11

Rental Rights

In respect of at least computer programs and cinematographic works, a Member shall provide authors and their successors in title the right to authorize or to prohibit the commercial rental to the public of originals or copies of their copyright works. A Member shall be excepted from this obligation in respect of cinematographic works unless such rental has led to widespread copying of such works which is materially impairing the exclusive right of reproduction conferred in that Member on authors and their successors in title. In respect of computer programs, this obligation does not apply to rentals where the program itself is not the essential object of the rental.

Article 12

Term of Protection

Whenever the term of protection of a work, other than a photographic work or a work of applied art, is calculated on a basis other than the life of a natural person, such term shall be no less than 50 years from the end of the calendar year of authorized publication, or, failing such authorized publication within 50 years from the making of the work, 50 years from the end of the calendar year of making.

Article 13

Limitations and Exceptions

Members shall confine limitations or exceptions to exclusive rights to certain special cases which do not conflict with a normal exploitation of the work and do not unreasonably prejudice the legitimate interests of the right holder.

Article 14

Protection of Performers, Producers of Phonograms (Sound Recordings) and Broadcasting Organizations

1. In respect of a fixation of their performance on a phonogram, performers shall have the possibility of preventing the following acts when undertaken without their authorization: the fixation of their unfixed performance and the reproduction of such fixation. Performers shall also have the possibility of preventing the following acts when undertaken without their authorization: the broadcasting by wireless means and the communication to the public of their live performance.
2. Producers of phonograms shall enjoy the right to authorize or prohibit the direct or indirect reproduction of their phonograms.

3. Broadcasting organizations shall have the right to prohibit the following acts when undertaken without their authorization: the fixation, the reproduction of fixations, and the rebroadcasting by wireless means of broadcasts, as well as the communication to the public of television broadcasts of the same. Where Members do not grant such rights to broadcasting organizations, they shall provide owners of copyright in the subject matter of broadcasts with the possibility of preventing the above acts, subject to the provisions of the Berne Convention (1971).

4. The provisions of Article 11 in respect of computer programs shall apply *mutatis mutandis* to producers of phonograms and any other right holders in phonograms as determined in a Member's law. If on 15 April 1994 a Member has in force a system of equitable remuneration of right holders in respect of the rental of phonograms, it may maintain such system provided that the commercial rental of phonograms is not giving rise to the material impairment of the exclusive rights of reproduction of right holders.

5. The term of the protection available under this Agreement to performers and producers of phonograms shall last at least until the end of a period of 50 years computed from the end of the calendar year in which the fixation was made or the performance took place. The term of protection granted pursuant to paragraph 3 shall last for at least 20 years from the end of the calendar year in which the broadcast took place.

6. Any Member may, in relation to the rights conferred under paragraphs 1, 2 and 3, provide for conditions, limitations, exceptions and reservations to the extent permitted by the Rome Convention. However, the provisions of Article 18 of the Berne Convention (1971) shall also apply, *mutatis mutandis*, to the rights of performers and producers of phonograms in phonograms.

SECTION 2   TRADEMARKS

Article 15

Protectable Subject Matter

1. Any sign, or any combination of signs, capable of distinguishing the goods or services of one undertaking from those of other undertakings, shall be capable of constituting a trademark. Such signs, in

particular words including personal names, letters, numerals, figurative elements and combinations of colours as well as any combination of such signs, shall be eligible for registration as trademarks. Where signs are not inherently capable of distinguishing the relevant goods or services, Members may make registrability depend on distinctiveness acquired through use. Members may require, as a condition of registration, that signs be visually perceptible.

2. Paragraph 1 shall not be understood to prevent a Member from denying registration of a trademark on other grounds, provided that they do not derogate from the provisions of the Paris Convention (1967).

3. Members may make registrability depend on use. However, actual use of a trademark shall not be a condition for filing an application for registration. An application shall not be refused solely on the ground that intended use has not taken place before the expiry of a period of three years from the date of application.

4. The nature of the goods or services to which a trademark is to be applied shall in no case form an obstacle to registration of the trademark.

5. Members shall publish each trademark either before it is registered or promptly after it is registered and shall afford a reasonable opportunity for petitions to cancel the registration. In addition, Members may afford an opportunity for the registration of a trademark to be opposed.

Article 16

Rights Conferred

1. The owner of a registered trademark shall have the exclusive right to prevent all third parties not having the owner's consent from using in the course of trade identical or similar signs for goods or services which are identical or similar to those in respect of which the trademark is registered where such use would result in a likelihood of confusion. In case of the use of an identical sign for identical goods or services, a likelihood of confusion shall be presumed. The rights described above shall not prejudice any existing prior rights, nor shall they affect the possibility of Members making rights available on the basis of use.

2. Article 6*bis* of the Paris Convention (1967) shall apply, *mutatis mutandis*, to services. In determining whether a trademark is well-known, Members shall take account of the knowledge of the trademark in the relevant sector of the public, including knowledge

in the Member concerned which has been obtained as a result of the promotion of the trademark.

3. Article 6*bis* of the Paris Convention (1967) shall apply, *mutatis mutandis*, to goods or services which are not similar to those in respect of which a trademark is registered, provided that use of that trademark in relation to those goods or services would indicate a connection between those goods or services and the owner of the registered trademark and provided that the interests of the owner of the registered trademark are likely to be damaged by such use.

Article 17

Exceptions

Members may provide limited exceptions to the rights conferred by a trademark, such as fair use of descriptive terms, provided that such exceptions take account of the legitimate interests of the owner of the trademark and of third parties.

Article 18

Term of Protection

Initial registration, and each renewal of registration, of a trademark shall be for a term of no less than seven years. The registration of a trademark shall be renewable indefinitely.

Article 19

Requirement of Use

1. If use is required to maintain a registration, the registration may be cancelled only after an uninterrupted period of at least three years of non-use, unless valid reasons based on the existence of obstacles to such use are shown by the trademark owner. Circumstances arising independently of the will of the owner of the trademark which constitute an obstacle to the use of the trademark, such as import restrictions on or other government requirements for goods or services protected by the trademark, shall be recognized as valid reasons for non-use.

2. When subject to the control of its owner, use of a trademark by another person shall be recognized as use of the trademark for the purpose of maintaining the registration.

Article 20

Other Requirements

The use of a trademark in the course of trade shall not be unjustifiably encumbered by special requirements, such as use with another trademark, use in a special form or use in a manner detrimental to its capability to distinguish the goods or services of one undertaking from those of other undertakings. This will not preclude a requirement prescribing the use of the trademark identifying the undertaking producing the goods or services along with, but without linking it to, the trademark distinguishing the specific goods or services in question of that undertaking.

Article 21

Licensing and Assignment

Members may determine conditions on the licensing and assignment of trademarks, it being understood that the compulsory licensing of trademarks shall not be permitted and that the owner of a registered trademark shall have the right to assign the trademark with or without the transfer of the business to which the trademark belongs.

SECTION 3   GEOGRAPHICAL INDICATIONS

Article 22

Protection of Geographical Indications

1. Geographical indications are, for the purposes of this Agreement, indications which identify a good as originating in the territory of a Member, or a region or locality in that territory, where a given quality, reputation or other characteristic of the good is essentially attributable to its geographical origin.
2. In respect of geographical indications, Members shall provide the legal means for interested parties to prevent:
    (a) the use of any means in the designation or presentation of a good that indicates or suggests that the good in question originates in a geographical area other than the true place of origin in a manner which misleads the public as to the geographical origin of the good;

(b) any use which constitutes an act of unfair competition within the meaning of Article 10*bis* of the Paris Convention (1967).

3. A Member shall, *ex officio* if its legislation so permits or at the request of an interested party, refuse or invalidate the registration of a trademark which contains or consists of a geographical indication with respect to goods not originating in the territory indicated, if use of the indication in the trademark for such goods in that Member is of such a nature as to mislead the public as to the true place of origin.

4. The protection under paragraphs 1, 2 and 3 shall be applicable against a geographical indication which, although literally true as to the territory, region or locality in which the goods originate, falsely represents to the public that the goods originate in another territory.

Article 23

Additional Protection for Geographical Indications for Wines and Spirits

1. Each Member shall provide the legal means for interested parties to prevent use of a geographical indication identifying wines for wines not originating in the place indicated by the geographical indication in question or identifying spirits for spirits not originating in the place indicated by the geographical indication in question, even where the true origin of the goods is indicated or the geographical indication is used in translation or accompanied by expressions such as 'kind', 'type', 'style', 'imitation' or the like.[4]

2. The registration of a trademark for wines which contains or consists of a geographical indication identifying wines or for spirits which contains or consists of a geographical indication identifying spirits shall be refused or invalidated, *ex officio* if a Member's legislation so permits or at the request of an interested party, with respect to such wines or spirits not having this origin.

3. In the case of homonymous geographical indications for wines, protection shall be accorded to each indication, subject to the provisions of paragraph 4 of Article 22. Each Member shall determine the practical conditions under which the homonymous indications in question will be differentiated from each other, taking into account

---

[4] Notwithstanding the first sentence of Article 42, Members may, with respect to these obligations, instead provide for enforcement by administrative action.

the need to ensure equitable treatment of the producers concerned and that consumers are not misled.

4. In order to facilitate the protection of geographical indications for wines, negotiations shall be undertaken in the Council for TRIPS concerning the establishment of a multilateral system of notification and registration of geographical indications for wines eligible for protection in those Members participating in the system.

Article 24

International Negotiations; Exceptions

1. Members agree to enter into negotiations aimed at increasing the protection of individual geographical indications under Article 23. The provisions of paragraphs 4 through 8 below shall not be used by a Member to refuse to conduct negotiations or to conclude bilateral or multilateral agreements. In the context of such negotiations, Members shall be willing to consider the continued applicability of these provisions to individual geographical indications whose use was the subject of such negotiations.

2. The Council for TRIPS shall keep under review the application of the provisions of this Section; the first such review shall take place within two years of the entry into force of the WTO Agreement. Any matter affecting the compliance with the obligations under these provisions may be drawn to the attention of the Council, which, at the request of a Member, shall consult with any Member or Members in respect of such matter in respect of which it has not been possible to find a satisfactory solution through bilateral or plurilateral consultations between the Members concerned. The Council shall take such action as may be agreed to facilitate the operation and further the objectives of this Section.

3. In implementing this Section, a Member shall not diminish the protection of geographical indications that existed in that Member immediately prior to the date of entry into force of the WTO Agreement.

4. Nothing in this Section shall require a Member to prevent continued and similar use of a particular geographical indication of another Member identifying wines or spirits in connection with goods or services by any of its nationals or domiciliaries who have used that geographical indication in a continuous manner with regard to the same or related goods or services in the territory of that

Member either (a) for at least 10 years preceding 15 April 1994 or (b) in good faith preceding that date.

5. Where a trademark has been applied for or registered in good faith, or where rights to a trademark have been acquired through use in good faith either:

   (a) before the date of application of these provisions in that Member as defined in Part VI; or

   (b) before the geographical indication is protected in its country of origin;

   measures adopted to implement this Section shall not prejudice eligibility for or the validity of the registration of a trademark, or the right to use a trademark, on the basis that such a trademark is identical with, or similar to, a geographical indication.

6. Nothing in this Section shall require a Member to apply its provisions in respect of a geographical indication of any other Member with respect to goods or services for which the relevant indication is identical with the term customary in common language as the common name for such goods or services in the territory of that Member. Nothing in this Section shall require a Member to apply its provisions in respect of a geographical indication of any other Member with respect to products of the vine for which the relevant indication is identical with the customary name of a grape variety existing in the territory of that Member as of the date of entry into force of the WTO Agreement.

7. A Member may provide that any request made under this Section in connection with the use or registration of a trademark must be presented within five years after the adverse use of the protected indication has become generally known in that Member or after the date of registration of the trademark in that Member provided that the trademark has been published by that date, if such date is earlier than the date on which the adverse use became generally known in that Member, provided that the geographical indication is not used or registered in bad faith.

8. The provisions of this Section shall in no way prejudice the right of any person to use, in the course of trade, that person's name or the name of that person's predecessor in business, except where such name is used in such a manner as to mislead the public.

9. There shall be no obligation under this Agreement to protect geographical indications which are not or cease to be protected in their country of origin, or which have fallen into disuse in that country.

SECTION 4   INDUSTRIAL DESIGNS

Article 25

Requirements for Protection

1. Members shall provide for the protection of independently created industrial designs that are new or original. Members may provide that designs are not new or original if they do not significantly differ from known designs or combinations of known design features. Members may provide that such protection shall not extend to designs dictated essentially by technical or functional considerations.
2. Each Member shall ensure that requirements for securing protection for textile designs, in particular in regard to any cost, examination or publication, do not unreasonably impair the opportunity to seek and obtain such protection. Members shall be free to meet this obligation through industrial design law or through copyright law.

Article 26

Protection

1. The owner of a protected industrial design shall have the right to prevent third parties not having the owner's consent from making, selling or importing articles bearing or embodying a design which is a copy, or substantially a copy, of the protected design, when such acts are undertaken for commercial purposes.
2. Members may provide limited exceptions to the protection of industrial designs, provided that such exceptions do not unreasonably conflict with the normal exploitation of protected industrial designs and do not unreasonably prejudice the legitimate interests of the owner of the protected design, taking account of the legitimate interests of third parties.
3. The duration of protection available shall amount to at least 10 years.

SECTION 5   PATENTS

Article 27

Patentable Subject Matter

1. Subject to the provisions of paragraphs 2 and 3, patents shall be available for any inventions, whether products or processes, in all

fields of technology, provided that they are new, involve an inventive step and are capable of industrial application.[5] Subject to paragraph 4 of Article 65, paragraph 8 of Article 70 and paragraph 3 of this Article, patents shall be available and patent rights enjoyable without discrimination as to the place of invention, the field of technology and whether products are imported or locally produced.

2. Members may exclude from patentability inventions, the prevention within their territory of the commercial exploitation of which is necessary to protect *ordre public* or morality, including to protect human, animal or plant life or health or to avoid serious prejudice to the environment, provided that such exclusion is not made merely because the exploitation is prohibited by their law.

3. Members may also exclude from patentability:
   (a) diagnostic, therapeutic and surgical methods for the treatment of humans or animals;
   (b) plants and animals other than micro-organisms, and essentially biological processes for the production of plants or animals other than non-biological and microbiological processes. However, Members shall provide for the protection of plant varieties either by patents or by an effective *sui generis* system or by any combination thereof. The provisions of this subparagraph shall be reviewed four years after the date of entry into force of the WTO Agreement.

Article 28

Rights Conferred

1. A patent shall confer on its owner the following exclusive rights:
   (a) where the subject matter of a patent is a product, to prevent third parties not having the owner's consent from the acts of: making, using, offering for sale, selling, or importing[6] for these purposes that product;

---

[5] For the purposes of this Article, the terms 'inventive step' and 'capable of industrial application' may be deemed by a Member to be synonymous with the terms 'non-obvious' and 'useful' respectively.

[6] This right, like all other rights conferred under this Agreement in respect of the use, sale, importation or other distribution of goods, is subject to the provisions of Article 6.

(b) where the subject matter of a patent is a process, to prevent third parties not having the owner's consent from the act of using the process, and from the acts of: using, offering for sale, selling, or importing for these purposes at least the product obtained directly by that process.

2. Patent owners shall also have the right to assign, or transfer by succession, the patent and to conclude licensing contracts.

Article 29

Conditions on Patent Applicants

1. Members shall require that an applicant for a patent shall disclose the invention in a manner sufficiently clear and complete for the invention to be carried out by a person skilled in the art and may require the applicant to indicate the best mode for carrying out the invention known to the inventor at the filing date or, where priority is claimed, at the priority date of the application.

2. Members may require an applicant for a patent to provide information concerning the applicant's corresponding foreign applications and grants.

Article 30

Exceptions to Rights Conferred

Members may provide limited exceptions to the exclusive rights conferred by a patent, provided that such exceptions do not unreasonably conflict with a normal exploitation of the patent and do not unreasonably prejudice the legitimate interests of the patent owner, taking account of the legitimate interests of third parties.

Article 31

Other Use Without Authorization of the Right Holder

Where the law of a Member allows for other use[7] of the subject matter of a patent without the authorization of the right holder, including use by the government or third parties authorized by the government, the following provisions shall be respected:

---

[7] 'Other use' refers to use other than that allowed under Article 30.

(a) authorization of such use shall be considered on its individual merits;

(b) such use may only be permitted if, prior to such use, the proposed user has made efforts to obtain authorization from the right holder on reasonable commercial terms and conditions and that such efforts have not been successful within a reasonable period of time. This requirement may be waived by a Member in the case of a national emergency or other circumstances of extreme urgency or in cases of public non-commercial use. In situations of national emergency or other circumstances of extreme urgency, the right holder shall, nevertheless, be notified as soon as reasonably practicable. In the case of public non-commercial use, where the government or contractor, without making a patent search, knows or has demonstrable grounds to know that a valid patent is or will be used by or for the government, the right holder shall be informed promptly;

(c) the scope and duration of such use shall be limited to the purpose for which it was authorized, and in the case of semi-conductor technology shall only be for public non-commercial use or to remedy a practice determined after judicial or administrative process to be anti-competitive;

(d) such use shall be non-exclusive;

(e) such use shall be non-assignable, except with that part of the enterprise or goodwill which enjoys such use;

(f) any such use shall be authorized predominantly for the supply of the domestic market of the Member authorizing such use;

(g) authorization for such use shall be liable, subject to adequate protection of the legitimate interests of the persons so authorized, to be terminated if and when the circumstances which led to it cease to exist and are unlikely to recur. The competent authority shall have the authority to review, upon motivated request, the continued existence of these circumstances;

(h) the right holder shall be paid adequate remuneration in the circumstances of each case, taking into account the economic value of the authorization;

(i) the legal validity of any decision relating to the authorization of such use shall be subject to judicial review or other independent review by a distinct higher authority in that Member;

(j) any decision relating to the remuneration provided in respect of such use shall be subject to judicial review or other independent review by a distinct higher authority in that Member;

(k) Members are not obliged to apply the conditions set forth in subparagraphs (b) and (f) where such use is permitted to remedy a practice determined after judicial or administrative process to be anti-competitive. The need to correct anti-competitive practices may be taken into account in determining the amount of remuneration in such cases. Competent authorities shall have the authority to refuse termination of authorization if and when the conditions which led to such authorization are likely to recur;

(l) where such use is authorized to permit the exploitation of a patent ('the second patent') which cannot be exploited without infringing another patent ('the first patent'), the following additional conditions shall apply:

    (i) the invention claimed in the second patent shall involve an important technical advance of considerable economic significance in relation to the invention claimed in the first patent;

    (ii) the owner of the first patent shall be entitled to a cross-licence on reasonable terms to use the invention claimed in the second patent; and

    (iii) the use authorized in respect of the first patent shall be non-assignable except with the assignment of the second patent.

Article 32

Revocation/Forfeiture

An opportunity for judicial review of any decision to revoke or forfeit a patent shall be available.

Article 33

Term of Protection

The term of protection available shall not end before the expiration of a period of twenty years counted from the filing date.[8]

Article 34

Process Patents: Burden of Proof

1. For the purposes of civil proceedings in respect of the infringement of the rights of the owner referred to in paragraph 1(b) of Article 28, if

---

[8] It is understood that those Members which do not have a system of original grant may provide that the term of protection shall be computed from the filing date in the system of original grant.

the subject matter of a patent is a process for obtaining a product, the judicial authorities shall have the authority to order the defendant to prove that the process to obtain an identical product is different from the patented process. Therefore, Members shall provide, in at least one of the following circumstances, that any identical product when produced without the consent of the patent owner shall, in the absence of proof to the contrary, be deemed to have been obtained by the patented process:

(a) if the product obtained by the patented process is new;

(b) if there is a substantial likelihood that the identical product was made by the process and the owner of the patent has been unable through reasonable efforts to determine the process actually used.

2. Any Member shall be free to provide that the burden of proof indicated in paragraph 1 shall be on the alleged infringer only if the condition referred to in subparagraph (a) is fulfilled or only if the condition referred to in subparagraph (b) is fulfilled.

3. In the adduction of proof to the contrary, the legitimate interests of defendants in protecting their manufacturing and business secrets shall be taken into account.

SECTION 6   LAYOUT-DESIGNS (TOPOGRAPHIES) OF INTEGRATED CIRCUITS

Article 35

Relation to the IPIC Treaty

Members agree to provide protection to the layout-designs (topographies) of integrated circuits (referred to in this Agreement as 'layout-designs') in accordance with Articles 2 through 7 (other than paragraph 3 of Article 6), Article 12 and paragraph 3 of Article 16 of the Treaty on Intellectual Property in Respect of Integrated Circuits and, in addition, to comply with the following provisions.

Article 36

Scope of the Protection

Subject to the provisions of paragraph 1 of Article 37, Members shall consider unlawful the following acts if performed without the authorization of the right holder:[9] importing, selling, or otherwise distributing for commercial purposes a protected layout-design, an integrated circuit in which a protected layout-design is incorporated, or an article incorporating such an integrated circuit only in so far as it continues to contain an unlawfully reproduced layout-design.

Article 37

Acts Not Requiring the Authorization of the Right Holder

1. Notwithstanding Article 36, no Member shall consider unlawful the performance of any of the acts referred to in that Article in respect of an integrated circuit incorporating an unlawfully reproduced layout-design or any article incorporating such an integrated circuit where the person performing or ordering such acts did not know and had no reasonable ground to know, when acquiring the integrated circuit or article incorporating such an integrated circuit, that it incorporated an unlawfully reproduced layout-design. Members shall provide that, after the time that such person has received sufficient notice that the layout-design was unlawfully reproduced, that person may perform any of the acts with respect to the stock on hand or ordered before such time, but shall be liable to pay to the right holder a sum equivalent to a reasonable royalty such as would be payable under a freely negotiated licence in respect of such a layout-design.

2. The conditions set out in subparagraphs (a) through (k) of Article 31 shall apply *mutatis mutandis* in the event of any non-voluntary licensing of a layout-design or of its use by or for the government without the authorization of the right holder.

Article 38

Term of Protection

1. In Members requiring registration as a condition of protection, the term of protection of layout-designs shall not end before the expiration of a period of 10 years counted from the date of filing an application for registration or from the first commercial exploitation wherever in the world it occurs.

---

[9] The term 'right holder' in this Section shall be understood as having the same meaning as the term 'holder of the right' in the IPIC Treaty.

2. In Members not requiring registration as a condition for protection, layout-designs shall be protected for a term of no less than 10 years from the date of the first commercial exploitation wherever in the world it occurs.

3. Notwithstanding paragraphs 1 and 2, a Member may provide that protection shall lapse 15 years after the creation of the layout-design.

SECTION 7   PROTECTION OF UNDISCLOSED INFORMATION

Article 39

1. In the course of ensuring effective protection against unfair competition as provided in Article 10*bis* of the Paris Convention (1967), Members shall protect undisclosed information in accordance with paragraph 2 and data submitted to governments or governmental agencies in accordance with paragraph 3.

2. Natural and legal persons shall have the possibility of preventing information lawfully within their control from being disclosed to, acquired by, or used by others without their consent in a manner contrary to honest commercial practices[10] so long as such information:

    (a) is secret in the sense that it is not, as a body or in the precise configuration and assembly of its components, generally known among or readily accessible to persons within the circles that normally deal with the kind of information in question;

    (b) has commercial value because it is secret; and

    (c) has been subject to reasonable steps under the circumstances, by the person lawfully in control of the information, to keep it secret.

3. Members, when requiring, as a condition of approving the marketing of pharmaceutical or of agricultural chemical products which utilize new chemical entities, the submission of undisclosed test or other data, the origination of which involves a considerable effort, shall protect such data against unfair commercial use. In addition, Members shall protect such data against disclosure, except where necessary to

---

[10] For the purpose of this provision, 'a manner contrary to honest commercial practices' shall mean at least practices such as breach of contract, breach of confidence and inducement to breach, and includes the acquisition of undisclosed information by third parties who knew, or were grossly negligent in failing to know, that such practices were involved in the acquisition.

protect the public, or unless steps are taken to ensure that the data are protected against unfair commercial use.

SECTION 8   CONTROL OF ANTI-COMPETITIVE PRACTICES IN CONTRACTUAL LICENCES

Article 40

1. Members agree that some licensing practices or conditions pertaining to intellectual property rights which restrain competition may have adverse effects on trade and may impede the transfer and dissemination of technology.

2. Nothing in this Agreement shall prevent Members from specifying in their legislation licensing practices or conditions that may in particular cases constitute an abuse of intellectual property rights having an adverse effect on competition in the relevant market. As provided above, a Member may adopt, consistently with the other provisions of this Agreement, appropriate measures to prevent or control such practices, which may include for example exclusive grant-back conditions, conditions preventing challenges to validity and coercive package licensing, in the light of the relevant laws and regulations of that Member.

3. Each Member shall enter, upon request, into consultations with any other Member which has cause to believe that an intellectual property right owner that is a national or domiciliary of the Member to which the request for consultations has been addressed is undertaking practices in violation of the requesting Member's laws and regulations on the subject matter of this Section, and which wishes to secure compliance with such legislation, without prejudice to any action under the law and to the full freedom of an ultimate decision of either Member. The Member addressed shall accord full and sympathetic consideration to, and shall afford adequate opportunity for, consultations with the requesting Member, and shall cooperate through supply of publicly available non-confidential information of relevance to the matter in question and of other information available to the Member, subject to domestic law and to the conclusion of mutually satisfactory agreements concerning the safeguarding of its confidentiality by the requesting Member.

4. A Member whose nationals or domiciliaries are subject to proceedings in another Member concerning alleged violation of that other

Member's laws and regulations on the subject matter of this Section shall, upon request, be granted an opportunity for consultations by the other Member under the same conditions as those foreseen in paragraph 3.

PART III ENFORCEMENT OF INTELLECTUAL PROPERTY RIGHTS

SECTION 1 GENERAL OBLIGATIONS

Article 41

1. Members shall ensure that enforcement procedures as specified in this Part are available under their law so as to permit effective action against any act of infringement of intellectual property rights covered by this Agreement, including expeditious remedies to prevent infringements and remedies which constitute a deterrent to further infringements. These procedures shall be applied in such a manner as to avoid the creation of barriers to legitimate trade and to provide for safeguards against their abuse.

2. Procedures concerning the enforcement of intellectual property rights shall be fair and equitable. They shall not be unnecessarily complicated or costly, or entail unreasonable time limits or unwarranted delays.

3. Decisions on the merits of a case shall preferably be in writing and reasoned. They shall be made available at least to the parties to the proceeding without undue delay. Decisions on the merits of a case shall be based only on evidence in respect of which parties were offered the opportunity to be heard.

4. Parties to a proceeding shall have an opportunity for review by a judicial authority of final administrative decisions and, subject to jurisdictional provisions in a Member's law concerning the importance of a case, of at least the legal aspects of initial judicial decisions on the merits of a case. However, there shall be no obligation to provide an opportunity for review of acquittals in criminal cases.

5. It is understood that this Part does not create any obligation to put in place a judicial system for the enforcement of intellectual property rights distinct from that for the enforcement of law in general, nor does it affect the capacity of Members to enforce their law in general. Nothing in this Part creates any obligation with respect to

the distribution of resources as between enforcement of intellectual property rights and the enforcement of law in general.

SECTION 2   CIVIL AND ADMINISTRATIVE PROCEDURES AND REMEDIES

Article 42

Fair and Equitable Procedures

Members shall make available to right holders[11] civil judicial procedures concerning the enforcement of any intellectual property right covered by this Agreement. Defendants shall have the right to written notice which is timely and contains sufficient detail, including the basis of the claims. Parties shall be allowed to be represented by independent legal counsel, and procedures shall not impose overly burdensome requirements concerning mandatory personal appearances. All parties to such procedures shall be duly entitled to substantiate their claims and to present all relevant evidence. The procedure shall provide a means to identify and protect confidential information, unless this would be contrary to existing constitutional requirements.

Article 43

Evidence

1. The judicial authorities shall have the authority, where a party has presented reasonably available evidence sufficient to support its claims and has specified evidence relevant to substantiation of its claims which lies in the control of the opposing party, to order that this evidence be produced by the opposing party, subject in appropriate cases to conditions which ensure the protection of confidential information.
2. In cases in which a party to a proceeding voluntarily and without good reason refuses access to, or otherwise does not provide necessary information within a reasonable period, or significantly impedes a procedure relating to an enforcement action, a Member may accord judicial authorities the authority to make preliminary and final

---

[11] For the purpose of this Part, the term 'right holder' includes federations and associations having legal standing to assert such rights.

determinations, affirmative or negative, on the basis of the information presented to them, including the complaint or the allegation presented by the party adversely affected by the denial of access to information, subject to providing the parties an opportunity to be heard on the allegations or evidence.

Article 44

Injunctions

1. The judicial authorities shall have the authority to order a party to desist from an infringement, *inter alia* to prevent the entry into the channels of commerce in their jurisdiction of imported goods that involve the infringement of an intellectual property right, immediately after customs clearance of such goods. Members are not obliged to accord such authority in respect of protected subject matter acquired or ordered by a person prior to knowing or having reasonable grounds to know that dealing in such subject matter would entail the infringement of an intellectual property right.
2. Notwithstanding the other provisions of this Part and provided that the provisions of Part II specifically addressing use by governments, or by third parties authorized by a government, without the authorization of the right holder are complied with, Members may limit the remedies available against such use to payment of remuneration in accordance with subparagraph (h) of Article 31. In other cases, the remedies under this Part shall apply or, where these remedies are inconsistent with a Member's law, declaratory judgments and adequate compensation shall be available.

Article 45

Damages

1. The judicial authorities shall have the authority to order the infringer to pay the right holder damages adequate to compensate for the injury the right holder has suffered because of an infringement of that person's intellectual property right by an infringer who knowingly, or with reasonable grounds to know, engaged in infringing activity.
2. The judicial authorities shall also have the authority to order the infringer to pay the right holder expenses, which may include appropriate attorney's fees. In appropriate cases, Members may authorize the judicial authorities to order recovery of profits and/or payment of

pre-established damages even where the infringer did not knowingly, or with reasonable grounds to know, engage in infringing activity.

Article 46

Other Remedies

In order to create an effective deterrent to infringement, the judicial authorities shall have the authority to order that goods that they have found to be infringing be, without compensation of any sort, disposed of outside the channels of commerce in such a manner as to avoid any harm caused to the right holder, or, unless this would be contrary to existing constitutional requirements, destroyed. The judicial authorities shall also have the authority to order that materials and implements the predominant use of which has been in the creation of the infringing goods be, without compensation of any sort, disposed of outside the channels of commerce in such a manner as to minimize the risks of further infringements. In considering such requests, the need for proportionality between the seriousness of the infringement and the remedies ordered as well as the interests of third parties shall be taken into account. In regard to counterfeit trademark goods, the simple removal of the trademark unlawfully affixed shall not be sufficient, other than in exceptional cases, to permit release of the goods into the channels of commerce.

Article 47

Right of Information

Members may provide that the judicial authorities shall have the authority, unless this would be out of proportion to the seriousness of the infringement, to order the infringer to inform the right holder of the identity of third persons involved in the production and distribution of the infringing goods or services and of their channels of distribution.

Article 48

Indemnification of the Defendant

1. The judicial authorities shall have the authority to order a party at whose request measures were taken and who has abused enforcement procedures to provide to a party wrongfully enjoined or restrained adequate compensation for the injury suffered because of such abuse.

The judicial authorities shall also have the authority to order the applicant to pay the defendant expenses, which may include appropriate attorney's fees.

2. In respect of the administration of any law pertaining to the protection or enforcement of intellectual property rights, Members shall only exempt both public authorities and officials from liability to appropriate remedial measures where actions are taken or intended in good faith in the course of the administration of that law.

Article 49

Administrative Procedures

To the extent that any civil remedy can be ordered as a result of administrative procedures on the merits of a case, such procedures shall conform to principles equivalent in substance to those set forth in this Section.

SECTION 3   PROVISIONAL MEASURES

Article 50

1. The judicial authorities shall have the authority to order prompt and effective provisional measures:
   (a) to prevent an infringement of any intellectual property right from occurring, and in particular to prevent the entry into the channels of commerce in their jurisdiction of goods, including imported goods immediately after customs clearance;
   (b) to preserve relevant evidence in regard to the alleged infringement.
2. The judicial authorities shall have the authority to adopt provisional measures *inaudita altera parte* where appropriate, in particular where any delay is likely to cause irreparable harm to the right holder, or where there is a demonstrable risk of evidence being destroyed.
3. The judicial authorities shall have the authority to require the applicant to provide any reasonably available evidence in order to satisfy themselves with a sufficient degree of certainty that the applicant is the right holder and that the applicant's right is being infringed or that such infringement is imminent, and to order the applicant to provide a security or equivalent assurance sufficient to protect the defendant and to prevent abuse.
4. Where provisional measures have been adopted *inaudita altera parte*, the parties affected shall be given notice, without delay after the

execution of the measures at the latest. A review, including a right to be heard, shall take place upon request of the defendant with a view to deciding, within a reasonable period after the notification of the measures, whether these measures shall be modified, revoked or confirmed.

5. The applicant may be required to supply other information necessary for the identification of the goods concerned by the authority that will execute the provisional measures.

6. Without prejudice to paragraph 4, provisional measures taken on the basis of paragraphs 1 and 2 shall, upon request by the defendant, be revoked or otherwise cease to have effect, if proceedings leading to a decision on the merits of the case are not initiated within a reasonable period, to be determined by the judicial authority ordering the measures where a Member's law so permits or, in the absence of such a determination, not to exceed 20 working days or 31 calendar days, whichever is the longer.

7. Where the provisional measures are revoked or where they lapse due to any act or omission by the applicant, or where it is subsequently found that there has been no infringement or threat of infringement of an intellectual property right, the judicial authorities shall have the authority to order the applicant, upon request of the defendant, to provide the defendant appropriate compensation for any injury caused by these measures.

8. To the extent that any provisional measure can be ordered as a result of administrative procedures, such procedures shall conform to principles equivalent in substance to those set forth in this Section.

SECTION 4   SPECIAL REQUIREMENTS RELATED TO BORDER MEASURES[12]

Article 51

Suspension of Release by Customs Authorities

Members shall, in conformity with the provisions set out below, adopt procedures[13] to enable a right holder, who has valid grounds for

---

[12] Where a Member has dismantled substantially all controls over movement of goods across its border with another Member with which it forms part of a customs union, it shall not be required to apply the provisions of this Section at that border.

[13] It is understood that there shall be no obligation to apply such procedures to imports of goods put on the market in another country by or with the consent of the right holder, or to goods in transit.

suspecting that the importation of counterfeit trademark or pirated copyright goods[14] may take place, to lodge an application in writing with competent authorities, administrative or judicial, for the suspension by the customs authorities of the release into free circulation of such goods. Members may enable such an application to be made in respect of goods which involve other infringements of intellectual property rights, provided that the requirements of this Section are met. Members may also provide for corresponding procedures concerning the suspension by the customs authorities of the release of infringing goods destined for exportation from their territories.

Article 52

Application

Any right holder initiating the procedures under Article 51 shall be required to provide adequate evidence to satisfy the competent authorities that, under the laws of the country of importation, there is *prima facie* an infringement of the right holder's intellectual property right and to supply a sufficiently detailed description of the goods to make them readily recognizable by the customs authorities. The competent authorities shall inform the applicant within a reasonable period whether they have accepted the application and, where determined by the competent authorities, the period for which the customs authorities will take action.

Article 53

Security or Equivalent Assurance

1. The competent authorities shall have the authority to require an applicant to provide a security or equivalent assurance sufficient to protect the defendant and the competent authorities and to prevent

---

[14] For the purposes of this Agreement:

(a) 'counterfeit trademark goods' shall mean any goods, including packaging, bearing without authorization a trademark which is identical to the trademark validly registered in respect of such goods, or which cannot be distinguished in its essential aspects from such a trademark, and which thereby infringes the rights of the owner of the trademark in question under the law of the country of importation;

(b) 'pirated copyright goods' shall mean any goods which are copies made without the consent of the right holder or person duly authorized by the right holder in the country of production and which are made directly or indirectly from an article where the making of that copy would have constituted an infringement of a copyright or a related right under the law of the country of importation.

abuse. Such security or equivalent assurance shall not unreasonably deter recourse to these procedures.

2. Where pursuant to an application under this Section the release of goods involving industrial designs, patents, layout-designs or undisclosed information into free circulation has been suspended by customs authorities on the basis of a decision other than by a judicial or other independent authority, and the period provided for in Article 55 has expired without the granting of provisional relief by the duly empowered authority, and provided that all other conditions for importation have been complied with, the owner, importer, or consignee of such goods shall be entitled to their release on the posting of a security in an amount sufficient to protect the right holder for any infringement. Payment of such security shall not prejudice any other remedy available to the right holder, it being understood that the security shall be released if the right holder fails to pursue the right of action within a reasonable period of time.

Article 54

Notice of Suspension

The importer and the applicant shall be promptly notified of the suspension of the release of goods according to Article 51.

Article 55

Duration of Suspension

If, within a period not exceeding 10 working days after the applicant has been served notice of the suspension, the customs authorities have not been informed that proceedings leading to a decision on the merits of the case have been initiated by a party other than the defendant, or that the duly empowered authority has taken provisional measures prolonging the suspension of the release of the goods, the goods shall be released, provided that all other conditions for importation or exportation have been complied with; in appropriate cases, this time limit may be extended by another 10 working days. If proceedings leading to a decision on the merits of the case have been initiated, a review, including a right to be heard, shall take place upon request of the defendant with a view to deciding, within a reasonable period, whether these measures shall be modified, revoked or confirmed. Notwithstanding the above, where the suspension of the release of goods is carried out or continued in accordance with a provisional judicial measure, the provisions of paragraph 6 of Article 50 shall apply.

Article 56

Indemnification of the Importer and of the Owner of the Goods

Relevant authorities shall have the authority to order the applicant to pay the importer, the consignee and the owner of the goods appropriate compensation for any injury caused to them through the wrongful detention of goods or through the detention of goods released pursuant to Article 55.

Article 57

Right of Inspection and Information

Without prejudice to the protection of confidential information, Members shall provide the competent authorities the authority to give the right holder sufficient opportunity to have any goods detained by the customs authorities inspected in order to substantiate the right holder's claims. The competent authorities shall also have authority to give the importer an equivalent opportunity to have any such goods inspected. Where a positive determination has been made on the merits of a case, Members may provide the competent authorities the authority to inform the right holder of the names and addresses of the consignor, the importer and the consignee and of the quantity of the goods in question.

Article 58

Ex Officio Action

Where Members require competent authorities to act upon their own initiative and to suspend the release of goods in respect of which they have acquired *prima facie* evidence that an intellectual property right is being infringed:

(a) the competent authorities may at any time seek from the right holder any information that may assist them to exercise these powers;

(b) the importer and the right holder shall be promptly notified of the suspension. Where the importer has lodged an appeal against the suspension with the competent authorities, the suspension shall be subject to the conditions, *mutatis mutandis*, set out at Article 55;

(c) Members shall only exempt both public authorities and officials from liability to appropriate remedial measures where actions are taken or intended in good faith.

Article 59

Remedies

Without prejudice to other rights of action open to the right holder and subject to the right of the defendant to seek review by a judicial authority, competent authorities shall have the authority to order the destruction or disposal of infringing goods in accordance with the principles set out in Article 46. In regard to counterfeit trademark goods, the authorities shall not allow the re-exportation of the infringing goods in an unaltered state or subject them to a different customs procedure, other than in exceptional circumstances.

Article 60

De Minimis Imports

Members may exclude from the application of the above provisions small quantities of goods of a non-commercial nature contained in travellers' personal luggage or sent in small consignments.

SECTION 5   CRIMINAL PROCEDURES

Article 61

Members shall provide for criminal procedures and penalties to be applied at least in cases of wilful trademark counterfeiting or copyright piracy on a commercial scale. Remedies available shall include imprisonment and/or monetary fines sufficient to provide a deterrent, consistently with the level of penalties applied for crimes of a corresponding gravity. In appropriate cases, remedies available shall also include the seizure, forfeiture and destruction of the infringing goods and of any materials and implements the predominant use of which has been in the commission of the offence. Members may provide for criminal procedures and penalties to be applied in other cases of infringement of intellectual property rights, in particular where they are committed wilfully and on a commercial scale.

PART IV ACQUISITION AND MAINTENANCE OF INTELLECTUAL PROPERTY RIGHTS AND RELATED *INTER PARTES* PROCEDURES

Article 62

1. Members may require, as a condition of the acquisition or maintenance of the intellectual property rights provided for under Sections 2 through 6 of Part II, compliance with reasonable procedures and formalities. Such procedures and formalities shall be consistent with the provisions of this Agreement.
2. Where the acquisition of an intellectual property right is subject to the right being granted or registered, Members shall ensure that the procedures for grant or registration, subject to compliance with the substantive conditions for acquisition of the right, permit the granting or registration of the right within a reasonable period of time so as to avoid unwarranted curtailment of the period of protection.
3. Article 4 of the Paris Convention (1967) shall apply *mutatis mutandis* to service marks.
4. Procedures concerning the acquisition or maintenance of intellectual property rights and, where a Member's law provides for such procedures, administrative revocation and *inter partes* procedures such as opposition, revocation and cancellation, shall be governed by the general principles set out in paragraphs 2 and 3 of Article 41.
5. Final administrative decisions in any of the procedures referred to under paragraph 4 shall be subject to review by a judicial or quasi-judicial authority. However, there shall be no obligation to provide an opportunity for such review of decisions in cases of unsuccessful opposition or administrative revocation, provided that the grounds for such procedures can be the subject of invalidation procedures.

PART V DISPUTE PREVENTION AND SETTLEMENT

Article 63

Transparency

1. Laws and regulations, and final judicial decisions and administrative rulings of general application, made effective by a Member pertaining to the subject matter of this Agreement (the availability, scope,

acquisition, enforcement and prevention of the abuse of intellectual property rights) shall be published, or where such publication is not practicable made publicly available, in a national language, in such a manner as to enable governments and right holders to become acquainted with them. Agreements concerning the subject matter of this Agreement which are in force between the government or a governmental agency of a Member and the government or a governmental agency of another Member shall also be published.

2. Members shall notify the laws and regulations referred to in paragraph 1 to the Council for TRIPS in order to assist that Council in its review of the operation of this Agreement. The Council shall attempt to minimize the burden on Members in carrying out this obligation and may decide to waive the obligation to notify such laws and regulations directly to the Council if consultations with WIPO on the establishment of a common register containing these laws and regulations are successful. The Council shall also consider in this connection any action required regarding notifications pursuant to the obligations under this Agreement stemming from the provisions of Article 6ter of the Paris Convention (1967).

3. Each Member shall be prepared to supply, in response to a written request from another Member, information of the sort referred to in paragraph 1. A Member, having reason to believe that a specific judicial decision or administrative ruling or bilateral agreement in the area of intellectual property rights affects its rights under this Agreement, may also request in writing to be given access to or be informed in sufficient detail of such specific judicial decisions or administrative rulings or bilateral agreements.

4. Nothing in paragraphs 1, 2 and 3 shall require Members to disclose confidential information which would impede law enforcement or otherwise be contrary to the public interest or would prejudice the legitimate commercial interests of particular enterprises, public or private.

Article 64

Dispute Settlement

1. The provisions of Articles XXII and XXIII of GATT 1994 as elaborated and applied by the Dispute Settlement Understanding shall apply to consultations and the settlement of disputes under this Agreement except as otherwise specifically provided herein.

2. Subparagraphs 1(b) and 1(c) of Article XXIII of GATT 1994 shall not apply to the settlement of disputes under this Agreement for a

period of five years from the date of entry into force of the WTO Agreement.

3. During the time period referred to in paragraph 2, the Council for TRIPS shall examine the scope and modalities for complaints of the type provided for under subparagraphs 1(b) and 1(c) of Article XXIII of GATT 1994 made pursuant to this Agreement, and submit its recommendations to the Ministerial Conference for approval. Any decision of the Ministerial Conference to approve such recommendations or to extend the period in paragraph 2 shall be made only by consensus, and approved recommendations shall be effective for all Members without further formal acceptance process.

PART VI   TRANSITIONAL ARRANGEMENTS

Article 65

Transitional Arrangements

1. Subject to the provisions of paragraphs 2, 3 and 4, no Member shall be obliged to apply the provisions of this Agreement before the expiry of a general period of one year following the date of entry into force of the WTO Agreement.

2. A developing country Member is entitled to delay for a further period of four years the date of application, as defined in paragraph 1, of the provisions of this Agreement other than Articles 3, 4 and 5.

3. Any other Member which is in the process of transformation from a centrally-planned into a market, free-enterprise economy and which is undertaking structural reform of its intellectual property system and facing special problems in the preparation and implementation of intellectual property laws and regulations, may also benefit from a period of delay as foreseen in paragraph 2.

4. To the extent that a developing country Member is obliged by this Agreement to extend product patent protection to areas of technology not so protectable in its territory on the general date of application of this Agreement for that Member, as defined in paragraph 2, it may delay the application of the provisions on product patents of Section 5 of Part II to such areas of technology for an additional period of five years.

5. A Member availing itself of a transitional period under paragraphs 1, 2, 3 or 4 shall ensure that any changes in its laws, regulations and practice made during that period do not result in a lesser degree of consistency with the provisions of this Agreement.

Article 66

Least-Developed Country Members

1. In view of the special needs and requirements of least-developed country Members, their economic, financial and administrative constraints, and their need for flexibility to create a viable technological base, such Members shall not be required to apply the provisions of this Agreement, other than Articles 3, 4 and 5, for a period of 10 years from the date of application as defined under paragraph 1 of Article 65. The Council for TRIPS shall, upon duly motivated request by a least-developed country Member, accord extensions of this period.
2. Developed country Members shall provide incentives to enterprises and institutions in their territories for the purpose of promoting and encouraging technology transfer to least-developed country Members in order to enable them to create a sound and viable technological base.

Article 67

Technical Cooperation

In order to facilitate the implementation of this Agreement, developed country Members shall provide, on request and on mutually agreed terms and conditions, technical and financial cooperation in favour of developing and least-developed country Members. Such cooperation shall include assistance in the preparation of laws and regulations on the protection and enforcement of intellectual property rights as well as on the prevention of their abuse, and shall include support regarding the establishment or reinforcement of domestic offices and agencies relevant to these matters, including the training of personnel.

PART VII INSTITUTIONAL ARRANGEMENTS; FINAL PROVISIONS

Article 68

Council for Trade-Related Aspects of Intellectual Property Rights

The Council for TRIPS shall monitor the operation of this Agreement and, in particular, Members' compliance with their obligations hereunder, and shall afford Members the opportunity of consulting on matters relating to the trade-related aspects of intellectual property rights. It shall carry out such other responsibilities as assigned to it by the Members, and it shall, in particular, provide any assistance requested by them in the context of dispute settlement procedures. In carrying out its functions, the Council for TRIPS may consult with and seek information from any source it deems appropriate. In consultation with WIPO, the Council shall seek to establish, within one year of its first meeting, appropriate arrangements for cooperation with bodies of that Organization.

Article 69

International Cooperation

Members agree to cooperate with each other with a view to eliminating international trade in goods infringing intellectual property rights. For this purpose, they shall establish and notify contact points in their administrations and be ready to exchange information on trade in infringing goods. They shall, in particular, promote the exchange of information and cooperation between customs authorities with regard to trade in counterfeit trademark goods and pirated copyright goods.

Article 70

Protection of Existing Subject Matter

1. This Agreement does not give rise to obligations in respect of acts which occurred before the date of application of the Agreement for the Member in question.

2. Except as otherwise provided for in this Agreement, this Agreement gives rise to obligations in respect of all subject matter existing at the date of application of this Agreement for the Member in question, and which is protected in that Member on the said date, or which meets or comes subsequently to meet the criteria for protection under the terms of this Agreement. In respect of this paragraph and paragraphs 3 and 4, copyright obligations with respect to existing works shall be solely determined under Article 18 of the Berne Convention (1971), and obligations with respect to the rights of producers of phonograms and performers in existing phonograms shall be determined solely under Article 18 of the Berne Convention (1971) as made applicable under paragraph 6 of Article 14 of this Agreement.

3. There shall be no obligation to restore protection to subject matter which on the date of application of this Agreement for the Member in question has fallen into the public domain.

4. In respect of any acts in respect of specific objects embodying protected subject matter which become infringing under the terms of legislation in conformity with this Agreement, and which were commenced, or in respect of which a significant investment was made, before the date of acceptance of the WTO Agreement by that Member, any Member may provide for a limitation of the remedies available to the right holder as to the continued performance of such acts after the date of application of this Agreement for that Member. In such cases the Member shall, however, at least provide for the payment of equitable remuneration.

5. A Member is not obliged to apply the provisions of Article 11 and of paragraph 4 of Article 14 with respect to originals or copies purchased prior to the date of application of this Agreement for that Member.

6. Members shall not be required to apply Article 31, or the requirement in paragraph 1 of Article 27 that patent rights shall be enjoyable without discrimination as to the field of technology, to use without the authorization of the right holder where authorization for such use was granted by the government before the date this Agreement became known.

7. In the case of intellectual property rights for which protection is conditional upon registration, applications for protection which are pending on the date of application of this Agreement for the Member in question shall be permitted to be amended to claim any enhanced protection provided under the provisions of this Agreement. Such amendments shall not include new matter.

8. Where a Member does not make available as of the date of entry into force of the WTO Agreement patent protection for pharmaceutical and agricultural chemical products commensurate with its obligations under Article 27, that Member shall:

    (a) notwithstanding the provisions of Part VI, provide as from the date of entry into force of the WTO Agreement a means by which applications for patents for such inventions can be filed;

    (b) apply to these applications, as of the date of application of this Agreement, the criteria for patentability as laid down in this Agreement as if those criteria were being applied on the date of filing in that Member or, where priority is available and claimed, the priority date of the application; and

(c) provide patent protection in accordance with this Agreement as from the grant of the patent and for the remainder of the patent term, counted from the filing date in accordance with Article 33 of this Agreement, for those of these applications that meet the criteria for protection referred to in subparagraph (b).

9. Where a product is the subject of a patent application in a Member in accordance with paragraph 8(a), exclusive marketing rights shall be granted, notwithstanding the provisions of Part VI, for a period of five years after obtaining marketing approval in that Member or until a product patent is granted or rejected in that Member, whichever period is shorter, provided that, subsequent to the entry into force of the WTO Agreement, a patent application has been filed and a patent granted for that product in another Member and marketing approval obtained in such other Member.

Article 71

Review and Amendment

1. The Council for TRIPS shall review the implementation of this Agreement after the expiration of the transitional period referred to in paragraph 2 of Article 65. The Council shall, having regard to the experience gained in its implementation, review it two years after that date, and at identical intervals thereafter. The Council may also undertake reviews in the light of any relevant new developments which might warrant modification or amendment of this Agreement.

2. Amendments merely serving the purpose of adjusting to higher levels of protection of intellectual property rights achieved, and in force, in other multilateral agreements and accepted under those agreements by all Members of the WTO may be referred to the Ministerial Conference for action in accordance with paragraph 6 of Article X of the WTO Agreement on the basis of a consensus proposal from the Council for TRIPS.

Article 72

Reservations

Reservations may not be entered in respect of any of the provisions of this Agreement without the consent of the other Members.

Article 73

Security Exceptions

Nothing in this Agreement shall be construed:

(a) to require a Member to furnish any information the disclosure of which it considers contrary to its essential security interests; or

(b) to prevent a Member from taking any action which it considers necessary for the protection of its essential security interests;

   (i) relating to fissionable materials or the materials from which they are derived;

  (ii) relating to the traffic in arms, ammunition and implements of war and to such traffic in other goods and materials as is carried on directly or indirectly for the purpose of supplying a military establishment;

 (iii) taken in time of war or other emergency in international relations; or

(c) to prevent a Member from taking any action in pursuance of its obligations under the United Nations Charter for the maintenance of international peace and security.

~

Annex 2
Provisions of the Paris Convention for the Protection of Industrial Property (1967)[†] referred to in the TRIPS Agreement[*]

Table of Contents

[†] Paris Convention for the Protection of Industrial Property of 20 March, 1883, as revised at Brussels on 14 December 1900, at Washington on 2 June 1911, at The Hague on 6 November 1925, at London on 2 June 1934, at Lisbon on 31 October 1958, and at Stockholm on 14 July 1967, and as amended on 28 September 1979.

[*] *[WTO Secretariat note] The provisions reproduced herein are referred to in Article 2.1 and in other provisions of the TRIPS Agreement. This volume uses the titles that the International Bureau of WIPO has given to them to facilitate their identification. The Table of Contents is added for the convenience of the reader. Neither the titles nor the Table of Contents appear in the signed (French) text.*

Article 1

[Establishment of the Union; Scope of Industrial Property]

(1) The countries to which this Convention applies constitute a Union for the protection of industrial property.

(2) The protection of industrial property has as its object patents, utility models, industrial designs, trademarks, service marks, trade names,

indications of source or appellations of origin, and the repression of unfair competition.

(3) Industrial property shall be understood in the broadest sense and shall apply not only to industry and commerce proper, but likewise to agricultural and extractive industries and to all manufactured or natural products, for example, wines, grain, tobacco leaf, fruit, cattle, minerals, mineral waters, beer, flowers, and flour.

(4) Patents shall include the various kinds of industrial patents recognized by the laws of the countries of the Union, such as patents of importation, patents of improvement, patents and certificates of addition, etc.

Article 2

[National Treatment for Nationals of Countries of the Union]

(1) Nationals of any country of the Union shall, as regards the protection of industrial property, enjoy in all the other countries of the Union the advantages that their respective laws now grant, or may hereafter grant, to nationals; all without prejudice to the rights specially provided for by this Convention. Consequently, they shall have the same protection as the latter, and the same legal remedy against any infringement of their rights, provided that the conditions and formalities imposed upon nationals are complied with.

(2) However, no requirement as to domicile or establishment in the country where protection is claimed may be imposed upon nationals of countries of the Union for the enjoyment of any industrial property rights.

(3) The provisions of the laws of each of the countries of the Union relating to judicial and administrative procedure and to jurisdiction, and to the designation of an address for service or the appointment of an agent, which may be required by the laws on industrial property are expressly reserved.

Article 3

[Same Treatment for Certain Categories of Persons as for Nationals of Countries of the Union]

Nationals of countries outside the Union who are domiciled or who have real and effective industrial or commercial establishments in the territory of one of the countries of the Union shall be treated in the same manner as nationals of the countries of the Union.

Article 4

[A to I. Patents, Utility Models, Industrial Designs, Marks, Inventors' Certificates: Right of Priority. – G. Patents: Division of the Application]

A.– (1) Any person who has duly filed an application for a patent, or for the registration of a utility model, or of an industrial design, or of a trademark, in one of the countries of the Union, or his successor in title, shall enjoy, for the purpose of filing in the other countries, a right of priority during the periods hereinafter fixed.

(2) Any filing that is equivalent to a regular national filing under the domestic legislation of any country of the Union or under bilateral or multilateral treaties concluded between countries of the Union shall be recognized as giving rise to the right of priority.

(3) By a regular national filing is meant any filing that is adequate to establish the date on which the application was filed in the country concerned, whatever may be the subsequent fate of the application.

B.– Consequently, any subsequent filing in any of the other countries of the Union before the expiration of the periods referred to above shall not be invalidated by reason of any acts accomplished in the interval, in particular, another filing, the publication or exploitation of the invention, the putting on sale of copies of the design, or the use of the mark, and such acts cannot give rise to any third-party right or any right of personal possession. Rights acquired by third parties before the date of the first application that serves as the basis for the right of priority are reserved in accordance with the domestic legislation of each country of the Union.

C.– (1) The periods of priority referred to above shall be twelve months for patents and utility models, and six months for industrial designs and trademarks.

(2) These periods shall start from the date of filing of the first application; the day of filing shall not be included in the period.

(3) If the last day of the period is an official holiday, or a day when the Office is not open for the filing of applications in the country where protection is claimed, the period shall be extended until the first following working day.

(4) A subsequent application concerning the same subject as a previous first application within the meaning of paragraph (2), above, filed in the same country of the Union, shall be considered as the first application, of which the filing date shall be

the starting point of the period of priority, if, at the time of filing the subsequent application, the said previous application has been withdrawn, abandoned, or refused, without having been laid open to public inspection and without leaving any rights outstanding, and if it has not yet served as a basis for claiming a right of priority. The previous application may not thereafter serve as a basis for claiming a right of priority.

D.– (1) Any person desiring to take advantage of the priority of a previous filing shall be required to make a declaration indicating the date of such filing and the country in which it was made. Each country shall determine the latest date on which such declaration must be made.

(2) These particulars shall be mentioned in the publications issued by the competent authority, and in particular in the patents and the specifications relating thereto.

(3) The countries of the Union may require any person making a declaration of priority to produce a copy of the application (description, drawings, etc.) previously filed. The copy, certified as correct by the authority which received such application, shall not require any authentication, and may in any case be filed, without fee, at any time within three months of the filing of the subsequent application. They may require it to be accompanied by a certificate from the same authority showing the date of filing, and by a translation.

(4) No other formalities may be required for the declaration of priority at the time of filing the application. Each country of the Union shall determine the consequences of failure to comply with the formalities prescribed by this Article, but such consequences shall in no case go beyond the loss of the right of priority.

(5) Subsequently, further proof may be required.

Any person who avails himself of the priority of a previous application shall be required to specify the number of that application; this number shall be published as provided for by paragraph (2), above.

E.– (1) Where an industrial design is filed in a country by virtue of a right of priority based on the filing of a utility model, the period of priority shall be the same as that fixed for industrial designs

(2) Furthermore, it is permissible to file a utility model in a country by virtue of a right of priority based on the filing of a patent application, and vice versa.

F.– No country of the Union may refuse a priority or a patent application on the ground that the applicant claims multiple priorities, even if they originate in different countries, or on the ground that an application claiming one or more priorities contains one or more elements that were not included in the application or applications whose priority is claimed, provided that, in both cases, there is unity of invention within the meaning of the law of the country.

With respect to the elements not included in the application or applications whose priority is claimed, the filing of the subsequent application shall give rise to a right of priority under ordinary conditions.

G.– (1) If the examination reveals that an application for a patent contains more than one invention, the applicant may divide the application into a certain number of divisional applications and preserve as the date of each the date of the initial application and the benefit of the right of priority, if any.

(2) The applicant may also, on his own initiative, divide a patent application and preserve as the date of each divisional application the date of the initial application and the benefit of the right of priority, if any. Each country of the Union shall have the right to determine the conditions under which such division shall be authorized.

H.– Priority may not be refused on the ground that certain elements of the invention for which priority is claimed do not appear among the claims formulated in the application in the country of origin, provided that the application documents as a whole specifically disclose such elements.

I.– (1) Applications for inventors' certificates filed in a country in which applicants have the right to apply at their own option either for a patent or for an inventor's certificate shall give rise to the right of priority provided for by this Article, under the same conditions and with the same effects as applications for patents.

(2) In a country in which applicants have the right to apply at their own option either for a patent or for an inventor's certificate, an applicant for an inventor's certificate shall, in accordance with the provisions of this Article relating to patent applications, enjoy a right of priority based on an application for a patent, a utility model, or an inventor's certificate.

Article 4bis

[Patents: Independence of Patents Obtained for the Same Invention in Different Countries]

(1) Patents applied for in the various countries of the Union by nationals of countries of the Union shall be independent of patents obtained for the same invention in other countries, whether members of the Union or not.

(2) The foregoing provision is to be understood in an unrestricted sense, in particular, in the sense that patents applied for during the period of priority are independent, both as regards the grounds for nullity and forfeiture, and as regards their normal duration.

(3) The provision shall apply to all patents existing at the time when it comes into effect.

(4) Similarly, it shall apply, in the case of the accession of new countries, to patents in existence on either side at the time of accession.

(5) Patents obtained with the benefit of priority shall, in the various countries of the Union, have a duration equal to that which they would have, had they been applied for or granted without the benefit of priority.

Article 4ter

[Patents: Mention of the Inventor in the Patent]

The inventor shall have the right to be mentioned as such in the patent.

Article 4^{quater}

[Patents: Patentability in Case of Restrictions of Sale by Law]

The grant of a patent shall not be refused and a patent shall not be invalidated on the ground that the sale of the patented product or of a product obtained by means of a patented process is subject to restrictions or limitations resulting from the domestic law.

Article 5

[A. Patents: Importation of Articles; Failure to Work or Insufficient Working; Compulsory Licenses.– B. Industrial Designs: Failure to Work; Importation of Articles. – C. Marks: Failure to Use; Different Forms; Use by Co-proprietors. – D. Patents, Utility Models, Marks, Industrial Designs: Marking]

A.– (1) Importation by the patentee into the country where the patent has been granted of articles manufactured in any of the countries of the Union shall not entail forfeiture of the patent.

(2) Each country of the Union shall have the right to take legislative measures providing for the grant of compulsory licenses to prevent the abuses which might result from the exercise of the exclusive rights conferred by the patent, for example, failure to work.

(3) Forfeiture of the patent shall not be provided for except in cases where the grant of compulsory licenses would not have been sufficient to prevent the said abuses. No proceedings for the forfeiture or revocation of a patent may be instituted before the expiration of two years from the grant of the first compulsory license.

(4) A compulsory license may not be applied for on the ground of failure to work or insufficient working before the expiration of a period of four years from the date of filing of the patent application or three years from the date of the grant of the patent, whichever period expires last; it shall be refused if the patentee justifies his inaction by legitimate reasons. Such a compulsory license shall be non-exclusive and shall not be transferable, even in the form of the grant of a sub-license, except with that part of the enterprise or goodwill which exploits such license.

(5) The foregoing provisions shall be applicable, mutatis mutandis, to utility models.

B.– The protection of industrial designs shall not, under any circumstance, be subject to any forfeiture, either by reason of failure to work or by reason of the importation of articles corresponding to those which are protected.

C.– (1) If, in any country, use of the registered mark is compulsory, the registration may be cancelled only after a reasonable period, and then only if the person concerned does not justify his inaction.

(2) Use of a trademark by the proprietor in a form differing in elements which do not alter the distinctive character of the mark in the form in which it was registered in one of the countries of the Union shall not entail invalidation of the registration and shall not diminish the protection granted to the mark.

(3) Concurrent use of the same mark on identical or similar goods by industrial or commercial establishments considered as co-proprietors of the mark according to the provisions of the domestic law of the country where protection is claimed shall not prevent registration or diminish in any way the protection

granted to the said mark in any country of the Union, provided that such use does not result in misleading the public and is not contrary to the public interest.

D.– No indication or mention of the patent, of the utility model, of the registration of the trademark, or of the deposit of the industrial design, shall be required upon the goods as a condition of recognition of the right to protection.

Article 5 ^{bis}

[All Industrial Property Rights: Period of Grace for the Payment of Fees for the Maintenance of Rights; Patents: Restoration]

(1) A period of grace of not less than six months shall be allowed for the payment of the fees prescribed for the maintenance of industrial property rights, subject, if the domestic legislation so provides, to the payment of a surcharge.

(2) The countries of the Union shall have the right to provide for the restoration of patents which have lapsed by reason of non-payment of fees.

Article 5 ^{ter}

[Patents: Patented Devices Forming Part of Vessels, Aircraft, or Land Vehicles]

In any country of the Union the following shall not be considered as infringements of the rights of a patentee:

1. the use on board vessels of other countries of the Union of devices forming the subject of his patent in the body of the vessel, in the machinery, tackle, gear and other accessories, when such vessels temporarily or accidentally enter the waters of the said country, provided that such devices are used there exclusively for the needs of the vessel;

2. the use of devices forming the subject of the patent in the construction or operation of aircraft or land vehicles of other countries of the Union, or of accessories of such aircraft or land vehicles, when those aircraft or land vehicles temporarily or accidentally enter the said country.

Article 5 ^{quater}

[Patents: Importation of Products Manufactured by a Process Patented in the Importing Country]

When a product is imported into a country of the Union where there exists a patent protecting a process of manufacture of the said product, the patentee shall have all the rights, with regard to the imported product, that are accorded to him by the legislation of the country of importation, on the basis of the process patent, with respect to products manufactured in that country.

Article 5^{quinquies}

[Industrial Designs]

Industrial designs shall be protected in all the countries of the Union.

Article 6

[Marks: Conditions of Registration; Independence of Protection of Same Mark in Different Countries]

(1) The conditions for the filing and registration of trademarks shall be determined in each country of the Union by its domestic legislation.
(2) However, an application for the registration of a mark filed by a national of a country of the Union in any country of the Union may not be refused, nor may a registration be invalidated, on the ground that filing, registration, or renewal, has not been effected in the country of origin.
(3) A mark duly registered in a country of the Union shall be regarded as independent of marks registered in the other countries of the Union, including the country of origin.

Article 6bis

[Marks: Well-Known Marks]

(1) The countries of the Union undertake, ex officio if their legislation so permits, or at the request of an interested party, to refuse or to cancel the registration, and to prohibit the use, of a trademark which constitutes a reproduction, an imitation, or a translation, liable to create confusion, of a mark considered by the competent authority of the country of registration or use to be well known in that country as being already the mark of a person entitled to the benefits of this Convention and used for identical or similar goods. These provisions shall also apply when the essential part of the mark

constitutes a reproduction of any such well-known mark or an imitation liable to create confusion therewith.

(2) A period of at least five years from the date of registration shall be allowed for requesting the cancellation of such a mark. The countries of the Union may provide for a period within which the prohibition of use must be requested.

(3) No time limit shall be fixed for requesting the cancellation or the prohibition of the use of marks registered or used in bad faith.

Article 6ter

[Marks: Prohibitions concerning State Emblems, Official Hallmarks, and Emblems of Intergovernmental Organizations]

(1) *(a)* The countries of the Union agree to refuse or to invalidate the registration, and to prohibit by appropriate measures the use, without authorization by the competent authorities, either as trademarks or as elements of trademarks, of armorial bearings, flags, and other State emblems, of the countries of the Union, official signs and hallmarks indicating control and warranty adopted by them, and any imitation from a heraldic point of view.

(b) The provisions of subparagraph *(a)*, above, shall apply equally to armorial bearings, flags, other emblems, abbreviations, and names, of international intergovernmental organizations of which one or more countries of the Union are members, with the exception of armorial bearings, flags, other emblems, abbreviations, and names, that are already the subject of international agreements in force, intended to ensure their protection.

(c) No country of the Union shall be required to apply the provisions of subparagraph *(b)*, above, to the prejudice of the owners of rights acquired in good faith before the entry into force, in that country, of this Convention. The countries of the Union shall not be required to apply the said provisions when the use or registration referred to in subparagraph *(a)*, above, is not of such a nature as to suggest to the public that a connection exists between the organization concerned and the armorial bearings, flags, emblems, abbreviations, and names, or if such use or registration is probably not of such a nature as to mislead the public as to the existence of a connection between the user and the organization.

(2) Prohibition of the use of official signs and hallmarks indicating control and warranty shall apply solely in cases where the marks in which they are incorporated are intended to be used on goods of the same or a similar kind.

(3) *(a)* For the application of these provisions, the countries of the Union agree to communicate reciprocally, through the intermediary of the International Bureau, the list of State emblems, and official signs and hallmarks indicating control and warranty, which they desire, or may hereafter desire, to place wholly or within certain limits under the protection of this Article, and all subsequent modifications of such list. Each country of the Union shall in due course make available to the public the lists so communicated.

Nevertheless such communication is not obligatory in respect of flags of States.

(b) The provisions of subparagraph *(b)* of paragraph (1) of this Article shall apply only to such armorial bearings, flags, other emblems, abbreviations, and names, of international intergovernmental organizations as the latter have communicated to the countries of the Union through the intermediary of the International Bureau.

(4) Any country of the Union may, within a period of twelve months from the receipt of the notification, transmit its objections, if any, through the intermediary of the International Bureau, to the country or international intergovernmental organization concerned.

(5) In the case of State flags, the measures prescribed by paragraph (1), above, shall apply solely to marks registered after November 6, 1925.

(6) In the case of State emblems other than flags, and of official signs and hallmarks of the countries of the Union, and in the case of armorial bearings, flags, other emblems, abbreviations, and names, of international intergovernmental organizations, these provisions shall apply only to marks registered more than two months after receipt of the communication provided for in paragraph (3), above.

(7) In cases of bad faith, the countries shall have the right to cancel even those marks incorporating State emblems, signs, and hallmarks, which were registered before November 6, 1925.

(8) Nationals of any country who are authorized to make use of the State emblems, signs, and hallmarks, of their country may use them even if they are similar to those of another country.

(9) The countries of the Union undertake to prohibit the unauthorized use in trade of the State armorial bearings of the other countries of the Union, when the use is of such a nature as to be misleading as to the origin of the goods.

(10) The above provisions shall not prevent the countries from exercising the right given in paragraph (3) of Article 6^{quinquies}, Section B, to refuse or to invalidate the registration of marks incorporating, without authorization, armorial bearings, flags, other State emblems, or official signs and hallmarks adopted by a country of the Union, as well as the distinctive signs of international intergovernmental organizations referred to in paragraph (1), above.

Article 6^{quater}

[Marks: Assignment of Marks]

(1) When, in accordance with the law of a country of the Union, the assignment of a mark is valid only if it takes place at the same time as the transfer of the business or goodwill to which the mark belongs, it shall suffice for the recognition of such validity that the portion of the business or goodwill located in that country be transferred to the assignee, together with the exclusive right to manufacture in the said country, or to sell therein, the goods bearing the mark assigned.

(2) The foregoing provision does not impose upon the countries of the Union any obligation to regard as valid the assignment of any mark the use of which by the assignee would, in fact, be of such a nature as to mislead the public, particularly as regards the origin, nature, or essential qualities, of the goods to which the mark is applied.

Article 6^{quinquies}

[Marks: Protection of Marks Registered in One Country of the Union in the Other Countries of the Union]

A. – (1) Every trademark duly registered in the country of origin shall be accepted for filing and protected as is in the other countries of the Union, subject to the reservations indicated in this Article. Such countries may, before proceeding to final registration, require the production of a certificate of registration in the country of origin, issued by the competent authority. No authentication shall be required for this certificate.

(2) Shall be considered the country of origin the country of the Union where the applicant has a real and effective industrial or commercial establishment, or, if he has no such establishment within the Union, the country of the Union where he has his domicile, or, if he has no domicile within the Union but is a national of a country of the Union, the country of which he is a national.

B. – Trademarks covered by this Article may be neither denied registration nor invalidated except in the following cases:

1. when they are of such a nature as to infringe rights acquired by third parties in the country where protection is claimed;

2. when they are devoid of any distinctive character, or consist exclusively of signs or indications which may serve, in trade, to designate the kind, quality, quantity, intended purpose, value, place of origin, of the goods, or the time of production, or have become customary in the current language or in the bona fide and established practices of the trade of the country where protection is claimed;

3. when they are contrary to morality or public order and, in particular, of such a nature as to deceive the public. It is understood that a mark may not be considered contrary to public order for the sole reason that it does not conform to a provision of the legislation on marks, except if such provision itself relates to public order.

This provision is subject, however, to the application of Article 10bis.

C. – (1) In determining whether a mark is eligible for protection, all the factual circumstances must be taken into consideration, particularly the length of time the mark has been in use.

(2) No trademark shall be refused in the other countries of the Union for the sole reason that it differs from the mark protected in the country of origin only in respect of elements that do not alter its distinctive character and do not affect its identity in the form in which it has been registered in the said country of origin.

D. – No person may benefit from the provisions of this Article if the mark for which he claims protection is not registered in the country of origin.

E. – However, in no case shall the renewal of the registration of the mark in the country of origin involve an obligation to renew the registration in the other countries of the Union in which the mark has been registered.

F. – The benefit of priority shall remain unaffected for applications for the registration of marks filed within the period fixed by Article 4, even if registration in the country of origin is effected after the expiration of such period.

Article 6^{sexies}

[Marks: Service Marks]

The countries of the Union undertake to protect service marks. They shall not be required to provide for the registration of such marks.

Article 6^{septies}

[Marks: Registration in the Name of the Agent or Representative of the Proprietor Without the Latter's Authorization]

(1) If the agent or representative of the person who is the proprietor of a mark in one of the countries of the Union applies, without such proprietor's authorization, for the registration of the mark in his own name, in one or more countries of the Union, the proprietor shall be entitled to oppose the registration applied for or demand its cancellation or, if the law of the country so allows, the assignment in his favor of the said registration, unless such agent or representative justifies his action.

(2) The proprietor of the mark shall, subject to the provisions of paragraph (1), above, be entitled to oppose the use of his mark by his agent or representative if he has not authorized such use.

(3) Domestic legislation may provide an equitable time limit within which the proprietor of a mark must exercise the rights provided for in this Article.

Article 7

[Marks: Nature of the Goods to which the Mark is Applied]

The nature of the goods to which a trademark is to be applied shall in no case form an obstacle to the registration of the mark.

Article 7bis

[Marks: Collective Marks]

(1) The countries of the Union undertake to accept for filing and to protect collective marks belonging to associations the existence of

which is not contrary to the law of the country of origin, even if such associations do not possess an industrial or commercial establishment.

(2) Each country shall be the judge of the particular conditions under which a collective mark shall be protected and may refuse protection if the mark is contrary to the public interest.

(3) Nevertheless, the protection of these marks shall not be refused to any association the existence of which is not contrary to the law of the country of origin, on the ground that such association is not established in the country where protection is sought or is not constituted according to the law of the latter country.

Article 8

[Trade Names]

A trade name shall be protected in all the countries of the Union without the obligation of filing or registration, whether or not it forms part of a trademark.

Article 9

[Marks, Trade Names: Seizure, on Importation, etc., of Goods Unlawfully Bearing a Mark or Trade Name]

(1) All goods unlawfully bearing a trademark or trade name shall be seized on importation into those countries of the Union where such mark or trade name is entitled to legal protection.

(2) Seizure shall likewise be effected in the country where the unlawful affixation occurred or in the country into which the goods were imported.

(3) Seizure shall take place at the request of the public prosecutor, or any other competent authority, or any interested party, whether a natural person or a legal entity, in conformity with the domestic legislation of each country.

(4) The authorities shall not be bound to effect seizure of goods in transit.

(5) If the legislation of a country does not permit seizure on importation, seizure shall be replaced by prohibition of importation or by seizure inside the country.

(6) If the legislation of a country permits neither seizure on importation nor prohibition of importation nor seizure inside the country, then, until such time as the legislation is modified accordingly, these measures shall be replaced by the actions and remedies available in such cases to nationals under the law of such country.

Article 10

[False Indications: Seizure, on Importation, etc., of Goods Bearing False Indications as to their Source or the Identity of the Producer]

(1) The provisions of the preceding Article shall apply in cases of direct or indirect use of a false indication of the source of the goods or the identity of the producer, manufacturer, or merchant.

(2) Any producer, manufacturer, or merchant, whether a natural person or a legal entity, engaged in the production or manufacture of or trade in such goods and established either in the locality falsely indicated as the source, or in the region where such locality is situated, or in the country falsely indicated, or in the country where the false indication of source is used, shall in any case be deemed an interested party.

Article 10bis

[Unfair Competition]

(1) The countries of the Union are bound to assure to nationals of such countries effective protection against unfair competition.

(2) Any act of competition contrary to honest practices in industrial or commercial matters constitutes an act of unfair competition.

(3) The following in particular shall be prohibited:
1. all acts of such a nature as to create confusion by any means whatever with the establishment, the goods, or the industrial or commercial activities, of a competitor;
2. false allegations in the course of trade of such a nature as to discredit the establishment, the goods, or the industrial or commercial activities, of a competitor;
3. indications or allegations the use of which in the course of trade is liable to mislead the public as to the nature, the manufacturing process, the characteristics, the suitability for their purpose, or the quantity, of the goods.

Article 10ter

[Marks, Trade Names, False Indications, Unfair Competition: Remedies, Right to Sue]

(1) The countries of the Union undertake to assure to nationals of the other countries of the Union appropriate legal remedies effectively to repress all the acts referred to in Articles 9, 10, and 10bis.

(2) They undertake, further, to provide measures to permit federations and associations representing interested industrialists, producers, or merchants, provided that the existence of such federations and associations is not contrary to the laws of their countries, to take action in the courts or before the administrative authorities, with a view to the repression of the acts referred to in Articles 9, 10, and 10bis, in so far as the law of the country in which protection is claimed allows such action by federations and associations of that country.

Article 11

[Inventions, Utility Models, Industrial Designs, Marks: Temporary Protection at Certain International Exhibitions]

(1) The countries of the Union shall, in conformity with their domestic legislation, grant temporary protection to patentable inventions, utility models, industrial designs, and trademarks, in respect of goods exhibited at official or officially recognized international exhibitions held in the territory of any of them.

(2) Such temporary protection shall not extend the periods provided by Article 4. If, later, the right of priority is invoked, the authorities of any country may provide that the period shall start from the date of introduction of the goods into the exhibition.

(3) Each country may require, as proof of the identity of the article exhibited and of the date of its introduction, such documentary evidence as it considers necessary.

Article 12

[Special National Industrial Property Services]

(1) Each country of the Union undertakes to establish a special industrial property service and a central office for the communication to the public of patents, utility models, industrial designs, and trademarks.

(2) This service shall publish an official periodical journal. It shall publish regularly:
   (a) the names of the proprietors of patents granted, with a brief designation of the inventions patented;
   (b) the reproductions of registered trademarks.
   . . .

Article 19

[Special Agreements]

It is understood that the countries of the Union reserve the right to make separately between themselves special agreements for the protection of industrial property, in so far as these agreements do not contravene the provisions of this Convention.

. . .

~

Annex 3
Provisions of the Berne Convention for the Protection of Literary and Artistic Works (1971)[†] referred to in the TRIPS Agreement[*]

Table of Contents

---

† Berne Convention for the Protection of Literary and Artistic Works of 9 September 1886, completed at Paris on 4 May 1896, revised at Berlin on 13 November 1908, completed at Berne on 20 March 1914, revised at Rome on 2 June 1928, at Brussels on 26 June 1948, at Stockholm on 14 July 1967, and at Paris on 24 July 1971, and amended on 28 September 1979.

* [WTO Secretariat note] The provisions reproduced herein are referred to in Article 9.1 and in other provisions of the TRIPS Agreement. This volume uses the titles that the International Bureau of WIPO has given to each Article and the Appendix to facilitate their identification. The Table of Contents is added for the convenience of the reader. Neither the titles nor the Table of Contents appear in the signed text of the Convention.

. . .

APPENDIX

SPECIAL PROVISIONS REGARDING DEVELOPING COUNTRIES

Article IV	Provisions Common to Licenses Under Articles II and III: 1. and 2. Procedure; 3. Indication of author and title of work; 4. Exportation of copies; 5. Notice; 6. Compensation
Article V	Alternative Possibility for Limitation of the Right of Translation: 1. Regime provided for under the 1886 and 1896 Acts; 2. No possibility of change to regime under Article II; 3. Time limit for choosing the alternative possibility
Article VI	Possibilities of Applying, or Admitting the Application of, Certain Provisions of the Appendix Before Becoming Bound by It: 1. Declaration; 2. Depository and effective date of declaration

The countries of the Union, being equally animated by the desire to protect, in as effective and uniform a manner as possible, the rights of authors in their literary and artistic works,

Recognizing the importance of the work of the Revision Conference held at Stockholm in 1967,

Have resolved to revise the Act adopted by the Stockholm Conference, while maintaining without change Articles 1 to 20 and 22 to 26 of that Act.

Consequently, the undersigned Plenipotentiaries, having presented their full powers, recognized as in good and due form, have agreed as follows:

Article 1

[Establishment of a Union]

The countries to which this Convention applies constitute a Union for the protection of the rights of authors in their literary and artistic works.

Article 2

[Protected Works: 1. 'Literary and artistic works'; 2. Possible requirement of fixation; 3. Derivative works; 4. Official texts; 5. Collections; 6. Obligation to protect; beneficiaries of protection; 7. Works of applied art and industrial designs; 8. News]

(1) The expression 'literary and artistic works' shall include every production in the literary, scientific and artistic domain, whatever may be the mode or form of its expression, such as books, pamphlets and other writings; lectures, addresses, sermons and other works of the same nature; dramatic or dramatico-musical works;

choreographic works and entertainments in dumb show; musical compositions with or without words; cinematographic works to which are assimilated works expressed by a process analogous to cinematography; works of drawing, painting, architecture, sculpture, engraving and lithography; photographic works to which are assimilated works expressed by a process analogous to photography; works of applied art; illustrations, maps, plans, sketches and three-dimensional works relative to geography, topography, architecture or science.

(2) It shall, however, be a matter for legislation in the countries of the Union to prescribe that works in general or any specified categories of works shall not be protected unless they have been fixed in some material form.

(3) Translations, adaptations, arrangements of music and other alterations of a literary or artistic work shall be protected as original works without prejudice to the copyright in the original work.

(4) It shall be a matter for legislation in the countries of the Union to determine the protection to be granted to official texts of a legislative, administrative and legal nature, and to official translations of such texts.

(5) Collections of literary or artistic works such as encyclopaedias and anthologies which, by reason of the selection and arrangement of their contents, constitute intellectual creations shall be protected as such, without prejudice to the copyright in each of the works forming part of such collections.

(6) The works mentioned in this Article shall enjoy protection in all countries of the Union. This protection shall operate for the benefit of the author and his successors in title.

(7) Subject to the provisions of Article 7(4) of this Convention, it shall be a matter for legislation in the countries of the Union to determine the extent of the application of their laws to works of applied art and industrial designs and models, as well as the conditions under which such works, designs and models shall be protected. Works protected in the country of origin solely as designs and models shall be entitled in another country of the Union only to such special protection as is granted in that country to designs and models; however, if no such special protection is granted in that country, such works shall be protected as artistic works.

(8) The protection of this Convention shall not apply to news of the day or to miscellaneous facts having the character of mere items of press information.

Article 2bis

[Possible Limitation of Protection of Certain Works: 1. Certain speeches; 2. Certain uses of lectures and addresses; 3. Right to make collections of such works]

(1) It shall be a matter for legislation in the countries of the Union to exclude, wholly or in part, from the protection provided by the preceding Article political speeches and speeches delivered in the course of legal proceedings.

(2) It shall also be a matter for legislation in the countries of the Union to determine the conditions under which lectures, addresses and other works of the same nature which are delivered in public may be reproduced by the press, broadcast, communicated to the public by wire and made the subject of public communication as envisaged in Article 11bis(1) of this Convention, when such use is justified by the informatory purpose.

(3) Nevertheless, the author shall enjoy the exclusive right of making a collection of his works mentioned in the preceding paragraphs.

Article 3

[Criteria of Eligibility for Protection: 1. Nationality of author; place of publication of work; 2. Residence of author; 3. 'Published' works; 4. 'Simultaneously published' works]

(1) The protection of this Convention shall apply to:
  (a) authors who are nationals of one of the countries of the Union, for their works, whether published or not;
  (b) authors who are not nationals of one of the countries of the Union, for their works first published in one of those countries, or simultaneously in a country outside the Union and in a country of the Union.

(2) Authors who are not nationals of one of the countries of the Union but who have their habitual residence in one of them shall, for the purposes of this Convention, be assimilated to nationals of that country.

(3) The expression 'published works' means works published with the consent of their authors, whatever may be the means of manufacture of the copies, provided that the availability of such copies has been such as to satisfy the reasonable requirements of the public, having regard to the nature of the work. The performance of a dramatic, dramatico-musical, cinematographic or musical work, the public

recitation of a literary work, the communication by wire or the broadcasting of literary or artistic works, the exhibition of a work of art and the construction of a work of architecture shall not constitute publication.

(4) A work shall be considered as having been published simultaneously in several countries if it has been published in two or more countries within thirty days of its first publication.

Article 4

[Criteria of Eligibility for Protection of Cinematographic Works, Works of Architecture and Certain Artistic Works]

The protection of this Convention shall apply, even if the conditions of Article 3 are not fulfilled, to:

(a) authors of cinematographic works the maker of which has his headquarters or habitual residence in one of the countries of the Union;

(b) authors of works of architecture erected in a country of the Union or of other artistic works incorporated in a building or other structure located in a country of the Union.

Article 5

[Rights Guaranteed: 1. and 2. Outside the country of origin; 3. In the country of origin; 4. 'Country of origin']

(1) Authors shall enjoy, in respect of works for which they are protected under this Convention, in countries of the Union other than the country of origin, the rights which their respective laws do now or may hereafter grant to their nationals, as well as the rights specially granted by this Convention.

(2) The enjoyment and the exercise of these rights shall not be subject to any formality; such enjoyment and such exercise shall be independent of the existence of protection in the country of origin of the work. Consequently, apart from the provisions of this Convention, the extent of protection, as well as the means of redress afforded to the author to protect his rights, shall be governed exclusively by the laws of the country where protection is claimed.

(3) Protection in the country of origin is governed by domestic law. However, when the author is not a national of the country of origin

of the work for which he is protected under this Convention, he shall enjoy in that country the same rights as national authors.

(4) The country of origin shall be considered to be:

(a) in the case of works first published in a country of the Union, that country; in the case of works published simultaneously in several countries of the Union which grant different terms of protection, the country whose legislation grants the shortest term of protection;

(b) in the case of works published simultaneously in a country outside the Union and in a country of the Union, the latter country;

(c) in the case of unpublished works or of works first published in a country outside the Union, without simultaneous publication in a country of the Union, the country of the Union of which the author is a national, provided that:

(i) when these are cinematographic works the maker of which has his headquarters or his habitual residence in a country of the Union, the country of origin shall be that country, and

(ii) when these are works of architecture erected in a country of the Union or other artistic works incorporated in a building or other structure located in a country of the Union, the country of origin shall be that country.

Article 6

[Possible Restriction of Protection in Respect of Certain Works of Nationals of Certain Countries Outside the Union: 1. In the country of the first publication and in other countries; 2. No retroactivity; 3. Notice]

(1) Where any country outside the Union fails to protect in an adequate manner the works of authors who are nationals of one of the countries of the Union, the latter country may restrict the protection given to the works of authors who are, at the date of the first publication thereof, nationals of the other country and are not habitually resident in one of the countries of the Union. If the country of first publication avails itself of this right, the other countries of the Union shall not be required to grant to works thus subjected to special treatment a wider protection than that granted to them in the country of first publication.

(2) No restrictions introduced by virtue of the preceding paragraph shall affect the rights which an author may have acquired in respect of a work published in a country of the Union before such restrictions were put into force.

(3) The countries of the Union which restrict the grant of copyright in accordance with this Article shall give notice thereof to the Director General of the World Intellectual Property Organization (hereinafter designated as 'the Director General') by a written declaration specifying the countries in regard to which protection is restricted, and the restrictions to which rights of authors who are nationals of those countries are subjected. The Director General shall immediately communicate this declaration to all the countries of the Union.

Article 6bis

[Moral Rights: 1. To claim authorship; to object to certain modifications and other derogatory actions; 2. After the author's death; 3. Means of redress]

(1) Independently of the author's economic rights, and even after the transfer of the said rights, the author shall have the right to claim authorship of the work and to object to any distortion, mutilation or other modification of, or other derogatory action in relation to, the said work, which would be prejudicial to his honor or reputation.

(2) The rights granted to the author in accordance with the preceding paragraph shall, after his death, be maintained, at least until the expiry of the economic rights, and shall be exercisable by the persons or institutions authorized by the legislation of the country where protection is claimed. However, those countries whose legislation, at the moment of their ratification of or accession to this Act, does not provide for the protection after the death of the author of all the rights set out in the preceding paragraph may provide that some of these rights may, after his death, cease to be maintained.

(3) The means of redress for safeguarding the rights granted by this Article shall be governed by the legislation of the country where protection is claimed.

Article 7

[Term of Protection: 1. Generally; 2. For cinematographic works; 3. For anonymous and pseudonymous works; 4. For photographic works and works of applied art; 5. Starting date of computation; 6. Longer terms; 7. Shorter terms; 8. Applicable law; 'comparison' of terms]

(1) The term of protection granted by this Convention shall be the life of the author and fifty years after his death.

(2) However, in the case of cinematographic works, the countries of the Union may provide that the term of protection shall expire fifty years after the work has been made available to the public with the consent of the author, or, failing such an event within fifty years from the making of such a work, fifty years after the making.

(3) In the case of anonymous or pseudonymous works, the term of protection granted by this Convention shall expire fifty years after the work has been lawfully made available to the public. However, when the pseudonym adopted by the author leaves no doubt as to his identity, the term of protection shall be that provided in paragraph (1). If the author of an anonymous or pseudonymous work discloses his identity during the above-mentioned period, the term of protection applicable shall be that provided in paragraph (1). The countries of the Union shall not be required to protect anonymous or pseudonymous works in respect of which it is reasonable to presume that their author has been dead for fifty years.

(4) It shall be a matter for legislation in the countries of the Union to determine the term of protection of photographic works and that of works of applied art in so far as they are protected as artistic works; however, this term shall last at least until the end of a period of twenty-five years from the making of such a work.

(5) The term of protection subsequent to the death of the author and the terms provided by paragraphs (2), (3) and (4) shall run from the date of death or of the event referred to in those paragraphs, but such terms shall always be deemed to begin on the first of January of the year following the death or such event.

(6) The countries of the Union may grant a term of protection in excess of those provided by the preceding paragraphs.

(7) Those countries of the Union bound by the Rome Act of this Convention which grant, in their national legislation in force at the time of signature of the present Act, shorter terms of protection than those provided for in the preceding paragraphs shall have the right to maintain such terms when ratifying or acceding to the present Act.

(8) In any case, the term shall be governed by the legislation of the country where protection is claimed; however, unless the legislation of that country otherwise provides, the term shall not exceed the term fixed in the country of origin of the work.

Article 7bis

[Term of Protection for Works of Joint Authorship]

The provisions of the preceding Article shall also apply in the case of a work of joint authorship, provided that the terms measured from the death of the author shall be calculated from the death of the last surviving author.

Article 8

[Right of Translation]

Authors of literary and artistic works protected by this Convention shall enjoy the exclusive right of making and of authorizing the translation of their works throughout the term of protection of their rights in the original works.

Article 9

[Right of Reproduction: 1. Generally; 2. Possible exceptions; 3. Sound and visual recordings]

(1) Authors of literary and artistic works protected by this Convention shall have the exclusive right of authorizing the reproduction of these works, in any manner or form.

(2) It shall be a matter for legislation in the countries of the Union to permit the reproduction of such works in certain special cases, provided that such reproduction does not conflict with a normal exploitation of the work and does not unreasonably prejudice the legitimate interests of the author.

(3) Any sound or visual recording shall be considered as a reproduction for the purposes of this Convention.

Article 10

[Certain Free Uses of Works: 1. Quotations; 2. Illustrations for teaching; 3. Indication of source and author]

(1) It shall be permissible to make quotations from a work which has already been lawfully made available to the public, provided that their making is compatible with fair practice, and their extent does not exceed that justified by the purpose, including quotations from newspaper articles and periodicals in the form of press summaries.

(2) It shall be a matter for legislation in the countries of the Union, and for special agreements existing or to be concluded between them, to permit the utilization, to the extent justified by the purpose, of literary or artistic works by way of illustration in publications, broadcasts or sound or visual recordings for teaching, provided such utilization is compatible with fair practice.

(3) Where use is made of works in accordance with the preceding paragraphs of this Article, mention shall be made of the source, and of the name of the author if it appears thereon.

Article 10bis

[Further Possible Free Uses of Works: 1. Of certain articles and broadcast works; 2. Of works seen or heard in connection with current events]

(1) It shall be a matter for legislation in the countries of the Union to permit the reproduction by the press, the broadcasting or the communication to the public by wire of articles published in newspapers or periodicals on current economic, political or religious topics, and of broadcast works of the same character, in cases in which the reproduction, broadcasting or such communication thereof is not expressly reserved. Nevertheless, the source must always be clearly indicated; the legal consequences of a breach of this obligation shall be determined by the legislation of the country where protection is claimed.

(2) It shall also be a matter for legislation in the countries of the Union to determine the conditions under which, for the purpose of reporting current events by means of photography, cinematography, broadcasting or communication to the public by wire, literary or artistic works seen or heard in the course of the event may, to the extent justified by the informatory purpose, be reproduced and made available to the public.

Article 11

[Certain Rights in Dramatic and Musical Works: 1. Right of public performance and of communication to the public of a performance; 2. In respect of translations]

(1) Authors of dramatic, dramatico-musical and musical works shall enjoy the exclusive right of authorizing:
  (i) the public performance of their works, including such public performance by any means or process;

(ii) any communication to the public of the performance of their works.

(2) Authors of dramatic or dramatico-musical works shall enjoy, during the full term of their rights in the original works, the same rights with respect to translations thereof.

Article 11*bis*

[Broadcasting and Related Rights: 1. Broadcasting and other wireless communications, public communication of broadcast by wire or rebroadcast, public communication of broadcast by loudspeaker or analogous instruments; 2. Compulsory licenses; 3. Recording; ephemeral recordings]

(1) Authors of literary and artistic works shall enjoy the exclusive right of authorizing:
   (i)   the broadcasting of their works or the communication thereof to the public by any other means of wireless diffusion of signs, sounds or images;
   (ii) any communication to the public by wire or by rebroadcasting of the broadcast of the work, when this communication is made by an organization other than the original one;
   (iii) the public communication by loudspeaker or any other analogous instrument transmitting, by signs, sounds or images, the broadcast of the work.

(2) It shall be a matter for legislation in the countries of the Union to determine the conditions under which the rights mentioned in the preceding paragraph may be exercised, but these conditions shall apply only in the countries where they have been prescribed. They shall not in any circumstances be prejudicial to the moral rights of the author, nor to his right to obtain equitable remuneration which, in the absence of agreement, shall be fixed by competent authority.

(3) In the absence of any contrary stipulation, permission granted in accordance with paragraph (1) of this Article shall not imply permission to record, by means of instruments recording sounds or images, the work broadcast. It shall, however, be a matter for legislation in the countries of the Union to determine the regulations for ephemeral recordings made by a broadcasting organization by means of its own facilities and used for its own broadcasts. The preservation of these recordings in official archives may, on the ground of their exceptional documentary character, be authorized by such legislation.

Article 11ter

[Certain Rights in Literary Works: 1. Right of public recitation and of communication to the public of a recitation; 2. In respect of translations]

(1) Authors of literary works shall enjoy the exclusive right of authorizing:
  (i) the public recitation of their works, including such public recitation by any means or process;
  (ii) any communication to the public of the recitation of their works.
(2) Authors of literary works shall enjoy, during the full term of their rights in the original works, the same rights with respect to translations thereof.

Article 12

[Right of Adaptation, Arrangement and Other Alteration]

Authors of literary or artistic works shall enjoy the exclusive right of authorizing adaptations, arrangements and other alterations of their works.

Article 13

[Possible Limitation of the Right of Recording of Musical Works and Any Words Pertaining Thereto: 1. Compulsory licenses; 2. Transitory measures; 3. Seizure on importation of copies made without the author's permission]

(1) Each country of the Union may impose for itself reservations and conditions on the exclusive right granted to the author of a musical work and to the author of any words, the recording of which together with the musical work has already been authorized by the latter, to authorize the sound recording of that musical work, together with such words, if any; but all such reservations and conditions shall apply only in the countries which have imposed them and shall not, in any circumstances, be prejudicial to the rights of these authors to obtain equitable remuneration which, in the absence of agreement, shall be fixed by competent authority.
(2) Recordings of musical works made in a country of the Union in accordance with Article 13(3) of the Conventions signed at Rome on

June 2, 1928, and at Brussels on June 26, 1948, may be reproduced in
that country without the permission of the author of the musical work
until a date two years after that country becomes bound by this Act.

(3) Recordings made in accordance with paragraphs (1) and (2) of this
Article and imported without permission from the parties concerned into a country where they are treated as infringing recordings
shall be liable to seizure.

Article 14

[Cinematographic and Related Rights: 1. Cinematographic adaptation
and reproduction; distribution; public performance and public communication by wire of works thus adapted or reproduced; 2. Adaptation of
cinematographic productions; 3. No compulsory licenses]

(1) Authors of literary or artistic works shall have the exclusive right of
authorizing:
 (i) the cinematographic adaptation and reproduction of these
 works, and the distribution of the works thus adapted or
 reproduced;
 (ii) the public performance and communication to the public by
 wire of the works thus adapted or reproduced.

(2) The adaptation into any other artistic form of a cinematographic
production derived from literary or artistic works shall, without
prejudice to the authorization of the author of the cinematographic
production, remain subject to the authorization of the authors of
the original works.

(3) The provisions of Article 13(1) shall not apply.

Article 14bis

[Special Provisions Concerning Cinematographic Works: 1. Assimilation
to 'original' works; 2. Ownership; limitation of certain rights of certain
contributors; 3. Certain other contributors]

(1) Without prejudice to the copyright in any work which may have
been adapted or reproduced, a cinematographic work shall be protected as an original work. The owner of copyright in a cinematographic work shall enjoy the same rights as the author of an original
work, including the rights referred to in the preceding Article.

(2) (a) Ownership of copyright in a cinematographic work shall be a
matter for legislation in the country where protection is claimed.

(b) However, in the countries of the Union which, by legislation, include among the owners of copyright in a cinematographic work authors who have brought contributions to the making of the work, such authors, if they have undertaken to bring such contributions, may not, in the absence of any contrary or special stipulation, object to the reproduction, distribution, public performance, communication to the public by wire, broadcasting or any other communication to the public, or to the subtitling or dubbing of texts, of the work.

(c) The question whether or not the form of the undertaking referred to above should, for the application of the preceding subparagraph *(b)*, be in a written agreement or a written act of the same effect shall be a matter for the legislation of the country where the maker of the cinematographic work has his headquarters or habitual residence. However, it shall be a matter for the legislation of the country of the Union where protection is claimed to provide that the said undertaking shall be in a written agreement or a written act of the same effect. The countries whose legislation so provides shall notify the Director General by means of a written declaration, which will be immediately communicated by him to all the other countries of the Union.

(d) By 'contrary or special stipulation' is meant any restrictive condition which is relevant to the aforesaid undertaking.

(3) Unless the national legislation provides to the contrary, the provisions of paragraph (2)*(b)* above shall not be applicable to authors of scenarios, dialogues and musical works created for the making of the cinematographic work, or to the principal director thereof. However, those countries of the Union whose legislation does not contain rules providing for the application of the said paragraph (2)*(b)* to such director shall notify the Director General by means of a written declaration, which will be immediately communicated by him to all the other countries of the Union.

Article 14*ter*

['Droit de suite' in Works of Art and Manuscripts: 1. Right to an interest in resales; 2. Applicable law; 3. Procedure]

(1) The author, or after his death the persons or institutions authorized by national legislation, shall, with respect to original works of art and original manuscripts of writers and composers, enjoy the

inalienable right to an interest in any sale of the work subsequent to the first transfer by the author of the work.

(2) The protection provided by the preceding paragraph may be claimed in a country of the Union only if legislation in the country to which the author belongs so permits, and to the extent permitted by the country where this protection is claimed.

(3) The procedure for collection and the amounts shall be matters for determination by national legislation.

Article 15

[Right to Enforce Protected Rights: 1. Where author's name is indicated or where pseudonym leaves no doubt as to author's identity; 2. In the case of cinematographic works; 3. In the case of anonymous and pseudonymous works; 4. In the case of certain unpublished works of unknown authorship]

(1) In order that the author of a literary or artistic work protected by this Convention shall, in the absence of proof to the contrary, be regarded as such, and consequently be entitled to institute infringement proceedings in the countries of the Union, it shall be sufficient for his name to appear on the work in the usual manner. This paragraph shall be applicable even if this name is a pseudonym, where the pseudonym adopted by the author leaves no doubt as to his identity.

(2) The person or body corporate whose name appears on a cinematographic work in the usual manner shall, in the absence of proof to the contrary, be presumed to be the maker of the said work.

(3) In the case of anonymous and pseudonymous works, other than those referred to in paragraph (1) above, the publisher whose name appears on the work shall, in the absence of proof to the contrary, be deemed to represent the author, and in this capacity he shall be entitled to protect and enforce the author's rights. The provisions of this paragraph shall cease to apply when the author reveals his identity and establishes his claim to authorship of the work.

(4) *(a)* In the case of unpublished works where the identity of the author is unknown, but where there is every ground to presume that he is a national of a country of the Union, it shall be a matter for legislation in that country to designate the competent authority which shall represent the author and shall be entitled to protect and enforce his rights in the countries of the Union.

(b) Countries of the Union which make such designation under the terms of this provision shall notify the Director General by means of a written declaration giving full information concerning the authority thus designated. The Director General shall at once communicate this declaration to all other countries of the Union.

Article 16

[Infringing Copies: 1. Seizure; 2. Seizure on importation; 3. Applicable law]

(1) Infringing copies of a work shall be liable to seizure in any country of the Union where the work enjoys legal protection.
(2) The provisions of the preceding paragraph shall also apply to reproductions coming from a country where the work is not protected, or has ceased to be protected.
(3) The seizure shall take place in accordance with the legislation of each country.

Article 17

[Possibility of Control of Circulation, Presentation and Exhibition of Works]

The provisions of this Convention cannot in any way affect the right of the Government of each country of the Union to permit, to control, or to prohibit, by legislation or regulation, the circulation, presentation, or exhibition of any work or production in regard to which the competent authority may find it necessary to exercise that right.

Article 18

[Works Existing on Convention's Entry Into Force: 1. Protectable where protection not yet expired in country of origin; 2. Non-protectable where protection already expired in country where it is claimed; 3. Application of these principles; 4. Special cases]

(1) This Convention shall apply to all works which, at the moment of its coming into force, have not yet fallen into the public domain in the country of origin through the expiry of the term of protection.

(2) If, however, through the expiry of the term of protection which was previously granted, a work has fallen into the public domain of the country where protection is claimed, that work shall not be protected anew.

(3) The application of this principle shall be subject to any provisions contained in special conventions to that effect existing or to be concluded between countries of the Union. In the absence of such provisions, the respective countries shall determine, each in so far as it is concerned, the conditions of application of this principle.

(4) The preceding provisions shall also apply in the case of new accessions to the Union and to cases in which protection is extended by the application of Article 7 or by the abandonment of reservations.

Article 19

[Protection Greater than Resulting from Convention]

The provisions of this Convention shall not preclude the making of a claim to the benefit of any greater protection which may be granted by legislation in a country of the Union.

Article 20

[Special Agreements Among Countries of the Union]

The Governments of the countries of the Union reserve the right to enter into special agreements among themselves, in so far as such agreements grant to authors more extensive rights than those granted by the Convention, or contain other provisions not contrary to this Convention. The provisions of existing agreements which satisfy these conditions shall remain applicable.

Article 21

[Special Provisions Regarding Developing Countries: 1. Reference to Appendix; 2. Appendix part of Act]

(1) Special provisions regarding developing countries are included in the Appendix.

(2) Subject to the provisions of Article 28(1)(b), the Appendix forms an integral part of this Act.

. . .

APPENDIX [SPECIAL PROVISIONS REGARDING DEVELOPING COUNTRIES]

Article I

[Faculties Open to Developing Countries: 1. Availability of certain faculties; declaration; 2. Duration of effect of declaration; 3. Cessation of developing country status; 4. Existing stocks of copies; 5. Declarations concerning certain territories; 6. Limits of reciprocity]

(1) Any country regarded as a developing country in conformity with the established practice of the General Assembly of the United Nations which ratifies or accedes to this Act, of which this Appendix forms an integral part, and which, having regard to its economic situation and its social or cultural needs, does not consider itself immediately in a position to make provision for the protection of all the rights as provided for in this Act, may, by a notification deposited with the Director General at the time of depositing its instrument of ratification or accession or, subject to Article V(1)(c), at any time thereafter, declare that it will avail itself of the faculty provided for in Article II, or of the faculty provided for in Article III, or of both of those faculties. It may, instead of availing itself of the faculty provided for in Article II, make a declaration according to Article V(1)(a).

(2) (a) Any declaration under paragraph (1) notified before the expiration of the period of ten years from the entry into force of Articles 1 to 21 and this Appendix according to Article 28(2) shall be effective until the expiration of the said period. Any such declaration may be renewed in whole or in part for periods of ten years each by a notification deposited with the Director General not more than fifteen months and not less than three months before the expiration of the ten-year period then running.

(b) Any declaration under paragraph (1) notified after the expiration of the period of ten years from the entry into force of Articles 1 to 21 and this Appendix according to Article 28(2) shall be effective until the expiration of the ten-year period then running. Any such declaration may be renewed as provided for in the second sentence of subparagraph (a).

(3) Any country of the Union which has ceased to be regarded as a developing country as referred to in paragraph (1) shall no longer be entitled to renew its declaration as provided in paragraph (2), and,

whether or not it formally withdraws its declaration, such country shall be precluded from availing itself of the faculties referred to in paragraph (1) from the expiration of the ten-year period then running or from the expiration of a period of three years after it has ceased to be regarded as a developing country, whichever period expires later.

(4) Where, at the time when the declaration made under paragraph (1) or (2) ceases to be effective, there are copies in stock which were made under a license granted by virtue of this Appendix, such copies may continue to be distributed until their stock is exhausted.

(5) Any country which is bound by the provisions of this Act and which has deposited a declaration or a notification in accordance with Article 31(1) with respect to the application of this Act to a particular territory, the situation of which can be regarded as analogous to that of the countries referred to in paragraph (1), may, in respect of such territory, make the declaration referred to in paragraph (1) and the notification of renewal referred to in paragraph (2). As long as such declaration or notification remains in effect, the provisions of this Appendix shall be applicable to the territory in respect of which it was made.

(6) *(a)* The fact that a country avails itself of any of the faculties referred to in paragraph (1) does not permit another country to give less protection to works of which the country of origin is the former country than it is obliged to grant under Articles 1 to 20.

    (b) The right to apply reciprocal treatment provided for in Article 30(2)*(b)*, second sentence, shall not, until the date on which the period applicable under Article I(3)expires, be exercised in respect of works the country of origin of which is a country which has made a declaration according to Article V(1)*(a)*.

Article II

[Limitations on the Right of Translation: 1. Licenses grantable by competent authority; 2. to 4. Conditions allowing the grant of such licenses; 5. Purposes for which licenses may be granted; 6. Termination of licenses; 7. Works composed mainly of illustrations; 8. Works withdrawn from circulation; 9. Licenses for broadcasting organizations]

(1) Any country which has declared that it will avail itself of the faculty provided for in this Article shall be entitled, so far as works published in printed or analogous forms of reproduction are concerned, to substitute for the exclusive right of translation provided for in

Article 8 a system of non-exclusive and non-transferable licenses, granted by the competent authority under the following conditions and subject to Article IV.

(2) *(a)* Subject to paragraph (3), if, after the expiration of a period of three years, or of any longer period determined by the national legislation of the said country, commencing on the date of the first publication of the work, a translation of such work has not been published in a language in general use in that country by the owner of the right of translation, or with his authorization, any national of such country may obtain a license to make a translation of the work in the said language and publish the translation in printed or analogous forms of reproduction.

(b) A license under the conditions provided for in this Article may also be granted if all the editions of the translation published in the language concerned are out of print.

(3) *(a)* In the case of translations into a language which is not in general use in one or more developed countries which are members of the Union, a period of one year shall be substituted for the period of three years referred to in paragraph (2)*(a)*.

(b) Any country referred to in paragraph (1) may, with the unanimous agreement of the developed countries which are members of the Union and in which the same language is in general use, substitute, in the case of translations into that language, for the period of three years referred to in paragraph (2)*(a)* a shorter period as determined by such agreement but not less than one year. However, the provisions of the foregoing sentence shall not apply where the language in question is English, French or Spanish. The Director General shall be notified of any such agreement by the Governments which have concluded it.

(4) *(a)* No license obtainable after three years shall be granted under this Article until a further period of six months has elapsed, and no license obtainable after one year shall be granted under this Article until a further period of nine months has elapsed

(i) from the date on which the applicant complies with the requirements mentioned in Article IV(1), or

(ii) where the identity or the address of the owner of the right of translation is unknown, from the date on which the applicant sends, as provided for in Article IV(2), copies of his application submitted to the authority competent to grant the license.

(b) If, during the said period of six or nine months, a translation in the language in respect of which the application was made is published by the owner of the right of translation or with his authorization, no license under this Article shall be granted.

(5) Any license under this Article shall be granted only for the purpose of teaching, scholarship or research.

(6) If a translation of a work is published by the owner of the right of translation or with his authorization at a price reasonably related to that normally charged in the country for comparable works, any license granted under this Article shall terminate if such translation is in the same language and with substantially the same content as the translation published under the license. Any copies already made before the license terminates may continue to be distributed until their stock is exhausted.

(7) For works which are composed mainly of illustrations, a license to make and publish a translation of the text and to reproduce and publish the illustrations may be granted only if the conditions of Article III are also fulfilled.

(8) No license shall be granted under this Article when the author has withdrawn from circulation all copies of his work.

(9) *(a)* A license to make a translation of a work which has been published in printed or analogous forms of reproduction may also be granted to any broadcasting organization having its headquarters in a country referred to in paragraph (1), upon an application made to the competent authority of that country by the said organization, provided that all of the following conditions are met:

> (i) the translation is made from a copy made and acquired in accordance with the laws of the said country;
>
> (ii) the translation is only for use in broadcasts intended exclusively for teaching or for the dissemination of the results of specialized technical or scientific research to experts in a particular profession;
>
> (iii) the translation is used exclusively for the purposes referred to in condition (ii) through broadcasts made lawfully and intended for recipients on the territory of the said country, including broadcasts made through the medium of sound or visual recordings lawfully and exclusively made for the purpose of such broadcasts;
>
> (iv) all uses made of the translation are without any commercial purpose.

(b) Sound or visual recordings of a translation which was made by a broadcasting organization under a license granted by virtue of this paragraph may, for the purposes and subject to the conditions referred to in subparagraph (a) and with the agreement of that organization, also be used by any other broadcasting organization having its headquarters in the country whose competent authority granted the license in question.

(c) Provided that all of the criteria and conditions set out in subparagraph (a) are met, a license may also be granted to a broadcasting organization to translate any text incorporated in an audio-visual fixation where such fixation was itself prepared and published for the sole purpose of being used in connection with systematic instructional activities.

(d) Subject to subparagraphs (a) to (c), the provisions of the preceding paragraphs shall apply to the grant and exercise of any license granted under this paragraph.

Article III

[Limitation on the Right of Reproduction: 1. Licenses grantable by competent authority; 2. to 5. Conditions allowing the grant of such licenses; 6. Termination of licenses; 7. Works to which this Article applies]

(1) Any country which has declared that it will avail itself of the faculty provided for in this Article shall be entitled to substitute for the exclusive right of reproduction provided for in Article 9 a system of non-exclusive and non-transferable licenses, granted by the competent authority under the following conditions and subject to Article IV.

(2) (a) If, in relation to a work to which this Article applies by virtue of paragraph (7), after the expiration of

    (i) the relevant period specified in paragraph (3), commencing on the date of first publication of a particular edition of the work, or

    (ii) any longer period determined by national legislation of the country referred to in paragraph (1), commencing on the same date,

copies of such edition have not been distributed in that country to the general public or in connection with systematic instructional activities, by the owner of the right of reproduction or with his authorization, at a price reasonably related to that normally charged in the country for comparable works, any national of such country may obtain a license to reproduce and publish such edition at that or a lower price for use in connection with systematic instructional activities.

(b) A license to reproduce and publish an edition which has been distributed as described in subparagraph (a) may also be granted under the conditions provided for in this Article if, after the expiration of the applicable period, no authorized copies of that edition have been on sale for a period of six months in the country concerned to the general public or in connection with systematic instructional activities at a price reasonably related to that normally charged in the country for comparable works.

(3) The period referred to in paragraph (2)(a)(i) shall be five years, except that

  (i) for works of the natural and physical sciences, including mathematics, and of technology, the period shall be three years;

  (ii) for works of fiction, poetry, drama and music, and for art books, the period shall be seven years.

(4) (a) No license obtainable after three years shall be granted under this Article until a period of six months has elapsed

  (i) from the date on which the applicant complies with the requirements mentioned in Article IV(1), or

  (ii) where the identity or the address of the owner of the right of reproduction is unknown, from the date on which the applicant sends, as provided for in Article IV(2), copies of his application submitted to the authority competent to grant the license.

(b) Where licenses are obtainable after other periods and Article IV(2) is applicable, no license shall be granted until a period of three months has elapsed from the date of the dispatch of the copies of the application.

(c) If, during the period of six or three months referred to in subparagraphs (a) and (b), a distribution as described in paragraph (2)(a) has taken place, no license shall be granted under this Article.

(d) No license shall be granted if the author has withdrawn from circulation all copies of the edition for the reproduction and publication of which the license has been applied for.

(5) A license to reproduce and publish a translation of a work shall not be granted under this Article in the following cases:
   (i) where the translation was not published by the owner of the right of translation or with his authorization, or
   (ii) where the translation is not in a language in general use in the country in which the license is applied for.

(6) If copies of an edition of a work are distributed in the country referred to in paragraph (1) to the general public or in connection with systematic instructional activities, by the owner of the right of reproduction or with his authorization, at a price reasonably related to that normally charged in the country for comparable works, any license granted under this Article shall terminate if such edition is in the same language and with substantially the same content as the edition which was published under the said license. Any copies already made before the license terminates may continue to be distributed until their stock is exhausted.

(7) (a) Subject to subparagraph (b), the works to which this Article applies shall be limited to works published in printed or analogous forms of reproduction.
   (b) This Article shall also apply to the reproduction in audio-visual form of lawfully made audio-visual fixations including any protected works incorporated therein and to the translation of any incorporated text into a language in general use in the country in which the license is applied for, always provided that the audio-visual fixations in question were prepared and published for the sole purpose of being used in connection with systematic instructional activities.

Article IV

[Provisions Common to Licenses Under Articles II and III: 1. and 2. Procedure; 3. Indication of author and title of work; 4. Exportation of copies; 5. Notice; 6. Compensation]

(1) A license under Article II or Article III may be granted only if the applicant, in accordance with the procedure of the country concerned, establishes either that he has requested, and has been denied, authorization by the owner of the right to make and publish the translation or to reproduce and publish the edition, as the case may be, or that, after due diligence on his part, he was unable to find the owner of the right. At the same time as making the request, the

applicant shall inform any national or international information center referred to in paragraph (2).

(2) If the owner of the right cannot be found, the applicant for a license shall send, by registered airmail, copies of his application, submitted to the authority competent to grant the license, to the publisher whose name appears on the work and to any national or international information center which may have been designated, in a notification to that effect deposited with the Director General, by the Government of the country in which the publisher is believed to have his principal place of business.

(3) The name of the author shall be indicated on all copies of the translation or reproduction published under a license granted under Article II or Article III. The title of the work shall appear on all such copies. In the case of a translation, the original title of the work shall appear in any case on all the said copies.

(4) *(a)* No license granted under Article II or Article III shall extend to the export of copies, and any such license shall be valid only for publication of the translation or of the reproduction, as the case may be, in the territory of the country in which it has been applied for.

   (b) For the purposes of subparagraph *(a)*, the notion of export shall include the sending of copies from any territory to the country which, in respect of that territory, has made a declaration under Article I(5).

   (c) Where a governmental or other public entity of a country which has granted a license to make a translation under Article II into a language other than English, French or Spanish sends copies of a translation published under such license to another country, such sending of copies shall not, for the purposes of subparagraph *(a)*, be considered to constitute export if all of the following conditions are met:

   (i) the recipients are individuals who are nationals of the country whose competent authority has granted the license, or organizations grouping such individuals;

   (ii) the copies are to be used only for the purpose of teaching, scholarship or research;

   (iii) the sending of the copies and their subsequent distribution to recipients is without any commercial purpose; and

   (iv) the country to which the copies have been sent has agreed with the country whose competent authority has granted the license to allow the receipt, or distribution, or both, and the Director General has been notified of the agreement by the Government of the country in which the license has been granted.

(5) All copies published under a license granted by virtue of Article II or Article III shall bear a notice in the appropriate language stating that the copies are available for distribution only in the country or territory to which the said license applies.

(6) *(a)* Due provision shall be made at the national level to ensure

(i) that the license provides, in favour of the owner of the right of translation or of reproduction, as the case may be, for just compensation that is consistent with standards of royalties normally operating on licenses freely negotiated between persons in the two countries concerned, and

(ii) payment and transmittal of the compensation: should national currency regulations intervene, the competent authority shall make all efforts, by the use of international machinery, to ensure transmittal in internationally convertible currency or its equivalent.

(b) Due provision shall be made by national legislation to ensure a correct translation of the work, or an accurate reproduction of the particular edition, as the case may be.

Article V

[Alternative Possibility for Limitation of the Right of Translation: 1. Regime provided for under the 1886 and 1896 Acts; 2. No possibility of change to regime under Article II; 3. Time limit for choosing the alternative possibility]

(1) *(a)* Any country entitled to make a declaration that it will avail itself of the faculty provided for in Article II may, instead, at the time of ratifying or acceding to this Act:

(i) if it is a country to which Article 30(2)*(a)* applies, make a declaration under that provision as far as the right of translation is concerned;

(ii) if it is a country to which Article 30(2)*(a)* does not apply, and even if it is not a country outside the Union, make a declaration as provided for in Article 30(2)*(b)*, first sentence.

(b) In the case of a country which ceases to be regarded as a developing country as referred to in Article I(1), a declaration

made according to this paragraph shall be effective until the date on which the period applicable under Article I(3) expires.

(c) Any country which has made a declaration according to this paragraph may not subsequently avail itself of the faculty provided for in Article II even if it withdraws the said declaration.

(2) Subject to paragraph (3), any country which has availed itself of the faculty provided for in Article II may not subsequently make a declaration according to paragraph (1).

(3) Any country which has ceased to be regarded as a developing country as referred to in Article I(1) may, not later than two years prior to the expiration of the period applicable under Article I(3), make a declaration to the effect provided for in Article 30(2)(b), first sentence, notwithstanding the fact that it is not a country outside the Union. Such declaration shall take effect at the date on which the period applicable under Article I(3) expires.

Article VI

[Possibilities of Applying, or Admitting the Application of, Certain Provisions of the Appendix Before Becoming Bound by It: 1. Declaration; 2. Depository and effective date of declaration]

(1) Any country of the Union may declare, as from the date of this Act, and at any time before becoming bound by Articles 1 to 21 and this Appendix:

(i) if it is a country which, were it bound by Articles 1 to 21 and this Appendix, would be entitled to avail itself of the faculties referred to in Article I(1), that it will apply the provisions of Article II or of Article III or of both to works whose country of origin is a country which, pursuant to (ii) below, admits the application of those Articles to such works, or which is bound by Articles 1 to 21 and this Appendix; such declaration may, instead of referring to Article II, refer to Article V;

(ii) that it admits the application of this Appendix to works of which it is the country of origin by countries which have made a declaration under (i) above or a notification under Article I.

(2) Any declaration made under paragraph (1) shall be in writing and shall be deposited with the Director General. The declaration shall become effective from the date of its deposit.

~

Annex 4
Provisions of the International Convention for the Protection of Performers, Producers of Phonograms and Broadcasting Organizations (the Rome Convention) (1961)[†] referred to in the TRIPS Agreement[*]

Table of Contents

[†] Done at Rome on 26 October 1961.

[*] *[WTO Secretariat note] There is no general obligation in the TRIPS Agreement to comply with substantive provisions of the Rome Convention. However, the Rome Convention is referred to in Articles 1.3, 2.2, 3.1, 4(b) and 14.6 of the TRIPS Agreement. This volume uses the titles that the International Bureau of WIPO has given to Articles to facilitate their identification. The Table of Contents is added for the convenience of the reader. Neither the titles nor the Table of Contents appear in the signed text of the Convention.*

Article 1

[Safeguard of Copyright Proper]

Protection granted under this Convention shall leave intact and shall in no way affect the protection of copyright in literary and artistic works. Consequently, no provision of this Convention may be interpreted as prejudicing such protection.

Article 2

[Protection given by the Convention. Definition of National Treatment]

1. For the purposes of this Convention, national treatment shall mean the treatment accorded by the domestic law of the Contracting State in which protection is claimed:
   (a) to performers who are its nationals, as regards performances taking place, broadcast, or first fixed, on its territory;
   (b) to producers of phonograms who are its nationals, as regards phonograms first fixed or first published on its territory;
   (c) to broadcasting organisations which have their headquarters on its territory, as regards broadcasts transmitted from transmitters situated on its territory.
2. National treatment shall be subject to the protection specifically guaranteed, and the limitations specifically provided for, in this Convention.

Article 3

[Definitions: (a) Performers; (b) Phonogram; (c) Producers of Phonograms; (d) Publication; (e) Reproduction; (f) Broadcasting; (g) Rebroadcasting]

For the purposes of this Convention:

(a) 'performers' means actors, singers, musicians, dancers, and other persons who act, sing, deliver, declaim, play in, or otherwise perform literary or artistic works;

(b) 'phonogram' means any exclusively aural fixation of sounds of a performance or of other sounds;

(c) 'producer of phonograms' means the person who, or the legal entity which, first fixes the sounds of a performance or other sounds;

(d) 'publication' means the offering of copies of a phonogram to the public in reasonable quantity;

(e) 'reproduction' means the making of a copy or copies of a fixation;

(f) 'broadcasting' means the transmission by wireless means for public reception of sounds or of images and sounds;

(g) 'rebroadcasting' means the simultaneous broadcasting by one broadcasting organisation of the broadcast of another broadcasting organisation.

Article 4

[Performances Protected. Points of Attachment for Performers]

Each Contracting State shall grant national treatment to performers if any of the following conditions is met:

(a) the performance takes place in another Contracting State;

(b) the performance is incorporated in a phonogram which is protected under Article 5 of this Convention;

(c) the performance, not being fixed on a phonogram, is carried by a broadcast which is protected by Article 6 of this Convention.

Article 5

[Protected Phonograms: 1. Points of Attachment for Producers of Phonograms; 2. Simultaneous Publication; 3. Power to Exclude Certain Criteria]

1. Each Contracting State shall grant national treatment to producers of phonograms if any of the following conditions is met:

   (a) the producer of the phonogram is a national of another Contracting State (criterion of nationality);

   (b) the first fixation of the sound was made in another Contracting State (criterion of fixation);

   (c) the phonogram was first published in another Contracting State (criterion of publication).

2. If a phonogram was first published in a non-contracting State but if it was also published, within thirty days of its first publication, in a Contracting State (simultaneous publication), it shall be considered as first published in the Contracting State.

3. By means of a notification deposited with the Secretary-General of the United Nations, any Contracting State may declare that it will not apply the criterion of publication or, alternatively, the criterion of fixation. Such notification may be deposited at the time of ratification, acceptance or accession, or at any time thereafter; in the last case, it shall become effective six months after it has been deposited.

Article 6

[Protected Broadcasts: 1. Points of Attachment for Broadcasting Organizations; 2. Power to Reserve]

1. Each Contracting State shall grant national treatment to broadcasting organisations if either of the following conditions is met:
   (a) the headquarters of the broadcasting organisation is situated in another Contracting State;
   (b) the broadcast was transmitted from a transmitter situated in another Contracting State.
2. By means of a notification deposited with the Secretary-General of the United Nations, any Contracting State may declare that it will protect broadcasts only if the headquarters of the broadcasting organisation is situated in another Contracting State and the broadcast was transmitted from a transmitter situated in the same Contracting State. Such notification may be deposited at the time of ratification, acceptance or accession, or at any time thereafter; in the last case, it shall become effective six months after it has been deposited.

. . .

Article 10

[Right of Reproduction for Phonogram Producers]

Producers of phonograms shall enjoy the right to authorise or prohibit the direct or indirect reproduction of their phonograms.

. . .

Article 12

[Secondary Uses of Phonograms]

If a phonogram published for commercial purposes, or a reproduction of such phonogram, is used directly for broadcasting or for any communication to the public, a single equitable remuneration shall be paid by the user to the performers, or to the producers of the phonograms, or to both. Domestic law may, in the absence of agreement between these parties, lay down the conditions as to the sharing of this remuneration.

Article 13

[Minimum Rights for Broadcasting Organisations]

Broadcasting organisations shall enjoy the right to authorise or prohibit:

(a) the rebroadcasting of their broadcasts;
(b) the fixation of their broadcasts;
(c) the reproduction:
    (i) of fixations, made without their consent, of their broadcasts;
    (ii) of fixations, made in accordance with the provisions of Article 15, of their broadcasts, if the reproduction is made for purposes different from those referred to in those provisions;
(d) the communication to the public of their television broadcasts if such communication is made in places accessible to the public against payment of an entrance fee; it shall be a matter for the domestic law of the State where protection of this right is claimed to determine the conditions under which it may be exercised.

Article 14

[Minimum Duration of Protection]

The term of protection to be granted under this Convention shall last at least until the end of a period of twenty years computed from the end of the year in which:

(a) the fixation was made – for phonograms and for performances incorporated therein;
(b) the performance took place – for performances not incorporated in phonograms;
(c) the broadcast took place – for broadcasts.

Article 15

[Permitted Exceptions: 1. Specific Limitations; 2. Equivalents with Copyright]

1. Any Contracting State may, in its domestic laws and regulations, provide for exceptions to the protection guaranteed by this Convention as regards:

    (a) private use;

    (b) use of short excerpts in connexion with the reporting of current events;

    (c) ephemeral fixation by a broadcasting organisation by means of its own facilities and for its own broadcasts;

    (d) use solely for the purposes of teaching or scientific research.

2. Irrespective of paragraph 1 of this Article, any Contracting State may, in its domestic laws and regulations, provide for the same kinds of limitations with regard to the protection of performers, producers of phonograms and broadcasting organisations, as it provides for, in its domestic laws and regulations, in connection with the protection of copyright in literary and artistic works. However, compulsory licences may be provided for only to the extent to which they are compatible with this Convention.

. . .

Article 19

[Performers' Rights in Films]

Notwithstanding anything in this Convention, once a performer has consented to the incorporation of his performance in a visual or audio-visual fixation, Article 7 shall have no further application.

. . .

~

Annex 5
Provisions of the Treaty on Intellectual Property in Respect of Integrated Circuits (1989) ('Washington Treaty')[†] referred to in the TRIPS Agreement[*]

Table of Contents

[†] Done at Washington, D.C., on 26 May 1989.

[*] *[WTO Secretariat note] The provisions reproduced herein are referred to in Article 35 and in other provisions of the TRIPS Agreement.*

343

. . .

Article 2

Definitions

For the purposes of this Treaty:

    (i) 'integrated circuit' means a product, in its final form or an inter-
mediate form, in which the elements, at least one of which is an
active element, and some or all of the interconnections are inte-
grally formed in and/or on a piece of material and which is
intended to perform an electronic function,

    (ii) 'layout-design (topography)' means the three-dimensional dispos-
ition, however expressed, of the elements, at least one of which is
an active element, and of some or all of the interconnections of an
integrated circuit, or such a three-dimensional disposition prepared for an integrated circuit intended for manufacture,

    (iii) 'holder of the right' means the natural person who, or the legal
entity which, according to the applicable law, is to be regarded as
the beneficiary of the protection referred to in Article 6,

    (iv) 'protected layout-design (topography)' means a layout-design
(topography) in respect of which the conditions of protection
referred to in this Treaty are fulfilled,

    (v) 'Contracting Party' means a State, or an Intergovernmental Organ-
ization meeting the requirements of item (x), party to this Treaty,

    (vi) 'territory of a Contracting Party' means, where the Contracting Party
is a State, the territory of that State and, where the Contracting Party
is an Intergovernmental Organization, the territory in which the
constituting treaty of that Intergovernmental Organization applies,

    (vii) 'Union' means the Union referred to in Article 1,

    (viii) 'Assembly' means the Assembly referred to in Article 9,

    (ix) 'Director General' means the Director General of the World Intel-
lectual Property Organization,

    (x) 'Intergovernmental Organization' means an organization consti-
tuted by, and composed of, States of any region of the world,
which has competence in respect of matters governed by this
Treaty, has its own legislation providing for intellectual property
protection in respect of layout-designs (topographies) and binding on all its member States, and has been duly authorized, in
accordance with its internal procedures, to sign, ratify, accept,
approve or accede to this Treaty.

Article 3

The Subject Matter of the Treaty

(1) *[Obligation to Protect Layout-Designs (Topographies)]*

(a) Each Contracting Party shall have the obligation to secure, throughout its territory, intellectual property protection in respect of layout-designs (topographies) in accordance with this Treaty. It shall, in particular, secure adequate measures to ensure the prevention of acts considered unlawful under Article 6 and appropriate legal remedies where such acts have been committed.

(b) The right of the holder of the right in respect of an integrated circuit applies whether or not the integrated circuit is incorporated in an article.

(c) Notwithstanding Article 2(i), any Contracting Party whose law limits the protection of layout-designs (topographies) to layout-designs (topographies) of semiconductor integrated circuits shall be free to apply that limitation as long as its law contains such limitation.

(2) *[Requirement of Originality]*

(a) The obligation referred to in paragraph (1)(a) shall apply to layout-designs (topographies) that are original in the sense that they are the result of their creators' own intellectual effort and are not commonplace among creators of layout-designs (topographies) and manufacturers of integrated circuits at the time of their creation.

(b) A layout-design (topography) that consists of a combination of elements and interconnections that are commonplace shall be protected only if the combination, taken as a whole, fulfills the conditions referred to in subparagraph (a).

Article 4

The Legal Form of the Protection

Each Contracting Party shall be free to implement its obligations under this Treaty through a special law on layout-designs (topographies) or its law on copyright, patents, utility models, industrial designs, unfair competition or any other law or a combination of any of those laws.

Article 5

National Treatment

(1) *[National Treatment]*

Subject to compliance with its obligation referred to in Article 3(1)*(a)*, each Contracting Party shall, in respect of the intellectual property protection of layout-designs (topographies), accord, within its territory

>   (i) to natural persons who are nationals of, or are domiciled in the territory of, any of the other Contracting Parties, and

>   (ii) to legal entities which or natural persons who, in the territory of any of the other Contracting Parties, have a real and effective establishment for the creation of layout-designs (topographies) or the production of integrated circuits,

the same treatment that it accords to its own nationals.

(2) *[Agents, Addresses for Service, Court Proceedings]*

Notwithstanding paragraph (1), any Contracting Party is free not to apply national treatment as far as any obligations to appoint an agent or to designate an address for service are concerned or as far as the special rules applicable to foreigners in court proceedings are concerned.

(3) *[Application of Paragraphs (1) and (2) to Intergovernmental Organizations]*

Where the Contracting Party is an Intergovernmental Organization, 'nationals' in paragraph (1) means nationals of any of the States members of that Organization.

Article 6

The Scope of the Protection

(1) *[Acts Requiring the Authorization of the Holder of the Right]*

>   *(a)* Any Contracting Party shall consider unlawful the following acts if performed without the authorization of the holder of the right:

>   (i) the act of reproducing, whether by incorporation in an integrated circuit or otherwise, a protected layout-design (topography) in its entirety or any part thereof, except the act of reproducing any part that does not comply with the requirement of originality referred to in Article 3(2),

    (ii) the act of importing, selling or otherwise distributing for commercial purposes a protected layout-design (topography) or an integrated circuit in which a protected layout-design (topography) is incorporated.

   (b) Any Contracting Party shall be free to consider unlawful also acts other than those specified in subparagraph (a) if performed without the authorization of the holder of the right.

(2) *[Acts Not Requiring the Authorization of the Holder of the Right]*

   (a) Notwithstanding paragraph (1), no Contracting Party shall consider unlawful the performance, without the authorization of the holder of the right, of the act of reproduction referred to in paragraph (1)(a)(i) where that act is performed by a third party for private purposes or for the sole purpose of evaluation, analysis, research or teaching.

   (b) Where the third party referred to in subparagraph (a), on the basis of evaluation or analysis of the protected layout-design (topography) ('the first layout-design (topography)'), creates a layout-design (topography) complying with the requirement of originality referred to in Article 3(2) ('the second layout-design (topography)'), that third party may incorporate the second layout-design (topography) in an integrated circuit or perform any of the acts referred to in paragraph (1) in respect of the second layout-design (topography) without being regarded as infringing the rights of the holder of the right in the first layout-design (topography).

   (c) The holder of the right may not exercise his right in respect of an identical original layout-design (topography) that was independently created by a third party.

   . . .

(4) *[Sale and Distribution of Infringing Integrated Circuits Acquired Innocently]*

Notwithstanding paragraph (1)(a)(ii), no Contracting Party shall be obliged to consider unlawful the performance of any of the acts referred to in that paragraph in respect of an integrated circuit incorporating an unlawfully reproduced layout-design (topography) where the person performing or ordering such acts did not know and had no reasonable ground to know, when acquiring the said integrated circuit, that it incorporates an unlawfully reproduced layout-design (topography).

(5) *[Exhaustion of Rights]*

Notwithstanding paragraph (1)*(a)*(ii), any Contracting Party may consider lawful the performance, without the authorization of the holder of the right, of any of the acts referred to in that paragraph where the act is performed in respect of a protected layout-design (topography), or in respect of an integrated circuit in which such a layout-design (topography) is incorporated, that has been put on the market by, or with the consent of, the holder of the right.

Article 7

Exploitation; Registration; Disclosure

(1) *[Faculty to Require Exploitation]*

Any Contracting Party shall be free not to protect a layout-design (topography) until it has been ordinarily commercially exploited, separately or as incorporated in an integrated circuit, somewhere in the world.

(2) *[Faculty to Require Registration; Disclosure]*

> *(a)* Any Contracting Party shall be free not to protect a layout-design (topography) until the layout-design (topography) has been the subject of an application for registration, filed in due form with the competent public authority, or of a registration with that authority; it may be required that the application be accompanied by the filing of a copy or drawing of the layout-design (topography) and, where the integrated circuit has been commercially exploited, of a sample of that integrated circuit, along with information defining the electronic function which the integrated circuit is intended to perform; however, the applicant may exclude such parts of the copy or drawing that relate to the manner of manufacture of the integrated circuit, provided that the parts submitted are sufficient to allow the identification of the layout-design (topography).
>
> *(b)* Where the filing of an application for registration according to subparagraph *(a)* is required, the Contracting Party may require that such filing be effected within a certain period of time from the date on which the holder of the right first exploits ordinarily commercially anywhere in the world the layout-design (topography) of an integrated circuit; such period shall not be less than two years counted from the said date.

(c) Registration under subparagraph *(a)* may be subject to the payment of a fee.

. . .

Article 12

Safeguard of Paris and Berne Conventions

This Treaty shall not affect the obligations that any Contracting Party may have under the Paris Convention for the Protection of Industrial Property or the Berne Convention for the Protection of Literary and Artistic Works.

. . .

Article 16

Entry Into Force of the Treaty

. . .

(3) *[Protection of Layout-Designs (Topographies) Existing at Time of Entry Into Force]*

Any Contracting Party shall have the right not to apply this Treaty to any layout-design (topography) that exists at the time this Treaty enters into force in respect of that Contracting Party, provided that this provision does not affect any protection that such layout-design (topography) may, at that time, enjoy in the territory of that Contracting Party by virtue of international obligations other than those resulting from this Treaty or the legislation of the said Contracting Party.

. . .

~

Annex 6
Declaration on the TRIPS Agreement
and Public Health[†]

Adopted on 14 November 2001

1. We recognize the gravity of the public health problems afflicting many developing and least-developed countries, especially those resulting from HIV/AIDS, tuberculosis, malaria and other epidemics.

2. We stress the need for the WTO Agreement on Trade-Related Aspects of Intellectual Property Rights (TRIPS Agreement) to be part of the wider national and international action to address these problems.

3. We recognize that intellectual property protection is important for the development of new medicines. We also recognize the concerns about its effects on prices.

4. We agree that the TRIPS Agreement does not and should not prevent Members from taking measures to protect public health. Accordingly, while reiterating our commitment to the TRIPS Agreement, we affirm that the Agreement can and should be interpreted and implemented in a manner supportive of WTO Members' right to protect public health and, in particular, to promote access to medicines for all.

   In this connection, we reaffirm the right of WTO Members to use, to the full, the provisions in the TRIPS Agreement, which provide flexibility for this purpose.

5. Accordingly and in the light of paragraph 4 above, while maintaining our commitments in the TRIPS Agreement, we recognize that these flexibilities include:

   (a) In applying the customary rules of interpretation of public international law, each provision of the TRIPS Agreement shall be read in the light of the object and purpose of the Agreement as expressed, in particular, in its objectives and principles.

[†] Document WT/MIN(01)/DEC/2.

(b) Each Member has the right to grant compulsory licences and the freedom to determine the grounds upon which such licences are granted.

(c) Each Member has the right to determine what constitutes a national emergency or other circumstances of extreme urgency, it being understood that public health crises, including those relating to HIV/AIDS, tuberculosis, malaria and other epidemics, can represent a national emergency or other circumstances of extreme urgency.

(d) The effect of the provisions in the TRIPS Agreement that are relevant to the exhaustion of intellectual property rights is to leave each Member free to establish its own regime for such exhaustion without challenge, subject to the MFN and national treatment provisions of Articles 3 and 4.

6. We recognize that WTO Members with insufficient or no manufacturing capacities in the pharmaceutical sector could face difficulties in making effective use of compulsory licensing under the TRIPS Agreement. We instruct the Council for TRIPS to find an expeditious solution to this problem and to report to the General Council before the end of 2002.

7. We reaffirm the commitment of developed-country Members to provide incentives to their enterprises and institutions to promote and encourage technology transfer to least-developed country Members pursuant to Article 66.2. We also agree that the least-developed country Members will not be obliged, with respect to pharmaceutical products, to implement or apply Sections 5 and 7 of Part II of the TRIPS Agreement or to enforce rights provided for under these Sections until 1 January 2016, without prejudice to the right of least-developed country Members to seek other extensions of the transition periods as provided for in Article 66.1 of the TRIPS Agreement. We instruct the Council for TRIPS to take the necessary action to give effect to this pursuant to Article 66.1 of the TRIPS Agreement.

~

Annex 7
Implementation of Paragraph 6 of the Doha Declaration on the TRIPS Agreement and Public Health[†]

Decision of 30 August 2003[*]

The General Council,

Having regard to paragraphs 1, 3 and 4 of Article IX of the Marrakesh Agreement Establishing the World Trade Organization ('the WTO Agreement');

Conducting the functions of the Ministerial Conference in the interval between meetings pursuant to paragraph 2 of Article IV of the WTO Agreement;

Noting the Declaration on the TRIPS Agreement and Public Health (WT/MIN(01)/DEC/2) (the 'Declaration') and, in particular, the instruction of the Ministerial Conference to the Council for TRIPS contained in paragraph 6 of the Declaration to find an expeditious solution to the problem of the difficulties that WTO Members with insufficient or no manufacturing capacities in the pharmaceutical sector could face in making effective use of compulsory licensing under the TRIPS Agreement and to report to the General Council before the end of 2002;

Recognizing, where eligible importing Members seek to obtain supplies under the system set out in this Decision, the importance of a rapid response to those needs consistent with the provisions of this Decision;

Noting that, in the light of the foregoing, exceptional circumstances exist justifying waivers from the obligations set out in paragraphs (f) and (h) of Article 31 of the TRIPS Agreement with respect to pharmaceutical products;

[†] Document WT/L/540 and Corr.1.

[*] *Secretariat note for information purposes only and without prejudice to Members' legal rights and obligations:* This Decision was adopted by the General Council in the light of a statement read out by the Chairman, which can be found in JOB(03)/177. This statement will be reproduced in the minutes of the General Council to be issued as WT/GC/M/82.

Decides as follows:

1. For the purposes of this Decision:
   (a) 'pharmaceutical product' means any patented product, or product manufactured through a patented process, of the pharmaceutical sector needed to address the public health problems as recognized in paragraph 1 of the Declaration. It is understood that active ingredients necessary for its manufacture and diagnostic kits needed for its use would be included[1];
   (b) 'eligible importing Member' means any least-developed country Member, and any other Member that has made a notification[2] to the Council for TRIPS of its intention to use the system as an importer, it being understood that a Member may notify at any time that it will use the system in whole or in a limited way, for example only in the case of a national emergency or other circumstances of extreme urgency or in cases of public non-commercial use. It is noted that some Members will not use the system set out in this Decision as importing Members[3] and that some other Members have stated that, if they use the system, it would be in no more than situations of national emergency or other circumstances of extreme urgency;
   (c) 'exporting Member' means a Member using the system set out in this Decision to produce pharmaceutical products for, and export them to, an eligible importing Member.
2. The obligations of an exporting Member under Article 31(f) of the TRIPS Agreement shall be waived with respect to the grant by it of a compulsory licence to the extent necessary for the purposes of production of a pharmaceutical product(s) and its export to an eligible importing Member(s) in accordance with the terms set out below in this paragraph:
   (a) the eligible importing Member(s)[4] has made a notification[2] to the Council for TRIPS, that:

---

[1] This subparagraph is without prejudice to subparagraph 1(b).

[2] It is understood that this notification does not need to be approved by a WTO body in order to use the system set out in this Decision.

[3] Australia, Austria, Belgium, Canada, Denmark, Finland, France, Germany, Greece, Iceland, Ireland, Italy, Japan, Luxembourg, the Netherlands, New Zealand, Norway, Portugal, Spain, Sweden, Switzerland, the United Kingdom and the United States.

[4] Joint notifications providing the information required under this subparagraph may be made by the regional organizations referred to in paragraph 6 of this Decision on behalf

    (i) specifies the names and expected quantities of the product(s) needed[5];

  (ii) confirms that the eligible importing Member in question, other than a least-developed country Member, has established that it has insufficient or no manufacturing capacities in the pharmaceutical sector for the product(s) in question in one of the ways set out in the Annex to this Decision; and

 (iii) confirms that, where a pharmaceutical product is patented in its territory, it has granted or intends to grant a compulsory licence in accordance with Article 31 of the TRIPS Agreement and the provisions of this Decision[6];

(b) the compulsory licence issued by the exporting Member under this Decision shall contain the following conditions:

    (i) only the amount necessary to meet the needs of the eligible importing Member(s) may be manufactured under the licence and the entirety of this production shall be exported to the Member(s) which has notified its needs to the Council for TRIPS;

  (ii) products produced under the licence shall be clearly identified as being produced under the system set out in this Decision through specific labelling or marking. Suppliers should distinguish such products through special packaging and/or special colouring/shaping of the products themselves, provided that such distinction is feasible and does not have a significant impact on price; and

 (iii) before shipment begins, the licensee shall post on a website[7] the following information:

    – the quantities being supplied to each destination as referred to in indent (i) above; and

    – the distinguishing features of the product(s) referred to in indent (ii) above;

---

of eligible importing Members using the system that are parties to them, with the agreement of those parties.

[5] The notification will be made available publicly by the WTO Secretariat through a page on the WTO website dedicated to this Decision.

[6] This subparagraph is without prejudice to Article 66.1 of the TRIPS Agreement.

[7] The licensee may use for this purpose its own website or, with the assistance of the WTO Secretariat, the page on the WTO website dedicated to this Decision.

(c) the exporting Member shall notify[8] the Council for TRIPS of the grant of the licence, including the conditions attached to it.[9] The information provided shall include the name and address of the licensee, the product(s) for which the licence has been granted, the quantity(ies) for which it has been granted, the country(ies) to which the product(s) is (are) to be supplied and the duration of the licence. The notification shall also indicate the address of the website referred to in subparagraph (b) (iii) above.

3. Where a compulsory licence is granted by an exporting Member under the system set out in this Decision, adequate remuneration pursuant to Article 31(h) of the TRIPS Agreement shall be paid in that Member taking into account the economic value to the importing Member of the use that has been authorized in the exporting Member. Where a compulsory licence is granted for the same products in the eligible importing Member, the obligation of that Member under Article 31(h) shall be waived in respect of those products for which remuneration in accordance with the first sentence of this paragraph is paid in the exporting Member.

4. In order to ensure that the products imported under the system set out in this Decision are used for the public health purposes underlying their importation, eligible importing Members shall take reasonable measures within their means, proportionate to their administrative capacities and to the risk of trade diversion to prevent re-exportation of the products that have actually been imported into their territories under the system. In the event that an eligible importing Member that is a developing country Member or a least-developed country Member experiences difficulty in implementing this provision, developed country Members shall provide, on request and on mutually agreed terms and conditions, technical and financial cooperation in order to facilitate its implementation.

5. Members shall ensure the availability of effective legal means to prevent the importation into, and sale in, their territories of products produced under the system set out in this Decision and diverted

---

[8] It is understood that this notification does not need to be approved by a WTO body in order to use the system set out in this Decision.

[9] The notification will be made available publicly by the WTO Secretariat through a page on the WTO website dedicated to this Decision.

to their markets inconsistently with its provisions, using the means already required to be available under the TRIPS Agreement. If any Member considers that such measures are proving insufficient for this purpose, the matter may be reviewed in the Council for TRIPS at the request of that Member.

6. With a view to harnessing economies of scale for the purposes of enhancing purchasing power for, and facilitating the local production of, pharmaceutical products:

    (i) where a developing or least-developed country WTO Member is a party to a regional trade agreement within the meaning of Article XXIV of the GATT 1994 and the Decision of 28 November 1979 on Differential and More Favourable Treatment Reciprocity and Fuller Participation of Developing Countries (L/4903), at least half of the current membership of which is made up of countries presently on the United Nations list of least-developed countries, the obligation of that Member under Article 31(f) of the TRIPS Agreement shall be waived to the extent necessary to enable a pharmaceutical product produced or imported under a compulsory licence in that Member to be exported to the markets of those other developing or least-developed country parties to the regional trade agreement that share the health problem in question. It is understood that this will not prejudice the territorial nature of the patent rights in question;

    (ii) it is recognized that the development of systems providing for the grant of regional patents to be applicable in the above Members should be promoted. To this end, developed country Members undertake to provide technical cooperation in accordance with Article 67 of the TRIPS Agreement, including in conjunction with other relevant intergovernmental organizations.

7. Members recognize the desirability of promoting the transfer of technology and capacity building in the pharmaceutical sector in order to overcome the problem identified in paragraph 6 of the Declaration. To this end, eligible importing Members and exporting Members are encouraged to use the system set out in this Decision in a way which would promote this objective. Members undertake to cooperate in paying special attention to the transfer of technology and capacity building in the pharmaceutical sector in the work to be undertaken pursuant to Article 66.2 of the TRIPS Agreement,

paragraph 7 of the Declaration and any other relevant work of the Council for TRIPS.

8. The Council for TRIPS shall review annually the functioning of the system set out in this Decision with a view to ensuring its effective operation and shall annually report on its operation to the General Council. This review shall be deemed to fulfil the review requirements of Article IX:4 of the WTO Agreement.

9. This Decision is without prejudice to the rights, obligations and flexibilities that Members have under the provisions of the TRIPS Agreement other than paragraphs (f) and (h) of Article 31, including those reaffirmed by the Declaration, and to their interpretation. It is also without prejudice to the extent to which pharmaceutical products produced under a compulsory licence can be exported under the present provisions of Article 31(f) of the TRIPS Agreement.

10. Members shall not challenge any measures taken in conformity with the provisions of the waivers contained in this Decision under subparagraphs 1(b) and 1(c) of Article XXIII of GATT 1994.

11. This Decision, including the waivers granted in it, shall terminate for each Member on the date on which an amendment to the TRIPS Agreement replacing its provisions takes effect for that Member. The TRIPS Council shall initiate by the end of 2003 work on the preparation of such an amendment with a view to its adoption within six months, on the understanding that the amendment will be based, where appropriate, on this Decision and on the further understanding that it will not be part of the negotiations referred to in paragraph 45 of the Doha Ministerial Declaration (WT/MIN(01)/DEC/1).

ANNEX

Assessment of Manufacturing Capacities in the Pharmaceutical Sector

Least-developed country Members are deemed to have insufficient or no manufacturing capacities in the pharmaceutical sector.

For other eligible importing Members insufficient or no manufacturing capacities for the product(s) in question may be established in either of the following ways:

(i) the Member in question has established that it has no manufacturing capacity in the pharmaceutical sector;
OR

(ii) where the Member has some manufacturing capacity in this sector, it has examined this capacity and found that, excluding any capacity owned or controlled by the patent owner, it is currently insufficient for the purposes of meeting its needs. When it is established that such capacity has become sufficient to meet the Member's needs, the system shall no longer apply.

~

Annex 8
Amendment of the TRIPS Agreement[†]

Decision of 6 December 2005

The General Council;

Having regard to paragraph 1 of Article X of the Marrakesh Agreement Establishing the World Trade Organization ('the WTO Agreement');

Conducting the functions of the Ministerial Conference in the interval between meetings pursuant to paragraph 2 of Article IV of the WTO Agreement;

Noting the Declaration on the TRIPS Agreement and Public Health (WT/MIN(01)/DEC/2) and, in particular, the instruction of the Ministerial Conference to the Council for TRIPS contained in paragraph 6 of the Declaration to find an expeditious solution to the problem of the difficulties that WTO Members with insufficient or no manufacturing capacities in the pharmaceutical sector could face in making effective use of compulsory licensing under the TRIPS Agreement;

Recognizing, where eligible importing Members seek to obtain supplies under the system set out in the proposed amendment of the TRIPS Agreement, the importance of a rapid response to those needs consistent with the provisions of the proposed amendment of the TRIPS Agreement;

Recalling paragraph 11 of the General Council Decision of 30 August 2003 on the Implementation of Paragraph 6 of the Doha Declaration on the TRIPS Agreement and Public Health;

Having considered the proposal to amend the TRIPS Agreement submitted by the Council for TRIPS (IP/C/41);

Noting the consensus to submit this proposed amendment to the Members for acceptance;

[†] Document WT/L/641.

Decides as follows:

1. The Protocol amending the TRIPS Agreement attached to this Decision is hereby adopted and submitted to the Members for acceptance.
2. The Protocol shall be open for acceptance by Members until 1 December 2007 or such later date as may be decided by the Ministerial Conference.
3. The Protocol shall take effect in accordance with the provisions of paragraph 3 of Article X of the WTO Agreement.

ATTACHMENT

Protocol Amending the TRIPS Agreement

Members of the World Trade Organization;

Having regard to the Decision of the General Council in document WT/L/641, adopted pursuant to paragraph 1 of Article X of the Marrakesh Agreement Establishing the World Trade Organization ('the WTO Agreement');

Hereby agree as follows:

1. The Agreement on Trade-Related Aspects of Intellectual Property Rights (the 'TRIPS Agreement') shall, upon the entry into force of the Protocol pursuant to paragraph 4, be amended as set out in the Annex to this Protocol, by inserting Article 31*bis* after Article 31 and by inserting the Annex to the TRIPS Agreement after Article 73.
2. Reservations may not be entered in respect of any of the provisions of this Protocol without the consent of the other Members.
3. This Protocol shall be open for acceptance by Members until 1 December 2007 or such later date as may be decided by the Ministerial Conference.
4. This Protocol shall enter into force in accordance with paragraph 3 of Article X of the WTO Agreement.
5. This Protocol shall be deposited with the Director-General of the World Trade Organization who shall promptly furnish to each Member a certified copy thereof and a notification of each acceptance thereof pursuant to paragraph 3.
6. This Protocol shall be registered in accordance with the provisions of Article 102 of the Charter of the United Nations.

Done at Geneva this sixth day of December two thousand and five, in a single copy in the English, French and Spanish languages, each text being authentic.

ANNEX TO THE PROTOCOL AMENDING THE TRIPS AGREEMENT

Article 31 *bis*

1. The obligations of an exporting Member under Article 31(f) shall not apply with respect to the grant by it of a compulsory licence to the extent necessary for the purposes of production of a pharmaceutical product(s) and its export to an eligible importing Member(s) in accordance with the terms set out in paragraph 2 of the Annex to this Agreement.

2. Where a compulsory licence is granted by an exporting Member under the system set out in this Article and the Annex to this Agreement, adequate remuneration pursuant to Article 31(h) shall be paid in that Member taking into account the economic value to the importing Member of the use that has been authorized in the exporting Member. Where a compulsory licence is granted for the same products in the eligible importing Member, the obligation of that Member under Article 31(h) shall not apply in respect of those products for which remuneration in accordance with the first sentence of this paragraph is paid in the exporting Member.

3. With a view to harnessing economies of scale for the purposes of enhancing purchasing power for, and facilitating the local production of, pharmaceutical products: where a developing or least-developed country WTO Member is a party to a regional trade agreement within the meaning of Article XXIV of the GATT 1994 and the Decision of 28 November 1979 on Differential and More Favourable Treatment Reciprocity and Fuller Participation of Developing Countries (L/4903), at least half of the current membership of which is made up of countries presently on the United Nations list of least-developed countries, the obligation of that Member under Article 31(f) shall not apply to the extent necessary to enable a pharmaceutical product produced or imported under a compulsory licence in that Member to be exported to the markets of those other developing or least-developed country parties to the regional trade agreement that share the health problem in question. It is understood that this will not prejudice the territorial nature of the patent rights in question.

4. Members shall not challenge any measures taken in conformity with the provisions of this Article and the Annex to this Agreement under subparagraphs 1(b) and 1(c) of Article XXIII of GATT 1994.

5. This Article and the Annex to this Agreement are without prejudice to the rights, obligations and flexibilities that Members have under the provisions of this Agreement other than paragraphs (f) and (h) of Article 31, including those reaffirmed by the Declaration on the TRIPS Agreement and Public Health (WT/MIN(01)/DEC/2), and to their interpretation. They are also without prejudice to the extent to which pharmaceutical products produced under a compulsory licence can be exported under the provisions of Article 31(f).

ANNEX TO THE TRIPS AGREEMENT

1. For the purposes of Article 31*bis* and this Annex:

   (a) 'pharmaceutical product' means any patented product, or product manufactured through a patented process, of the pharmaceutical sector needed to address the public health problems as recognized in paragraph 1 of the Declaration on the TRIPS Agreement and Public Health (WT/MIN(01)/DEC/2). It is understood that active ingredients necessary for its manufacture and diagnostic kits needed for its use would be included[1];

   (b) 'eligible importing Member' means any least-developed country Member, and any other Member that has made a notification[2] to the Council for TRIPS of its intention to use the system set out in Article 31*bis* and this Annex ('system') as an importer, it being understood that a Member may notify at any time that it will use the system in whole or in a limited way, for example only in the case of a national emergency or other circumstances of extreme urgency or in cases of public non-commercial use. It is noted that some Members will not use the system as importing Members[3] and that some other Members have stated that, if they use the system, it would be in no more than situations of national emergency or other circumstances of extreme urgency;

---

[1] This subparagraph is without prejudice to subparagraph 1(b).

[2] It is understood that this notification does not need to be approved by a WTO body in order to use the system.

[3] Australia, Canada, the European Communities with, for the purposes of Article 31*bis* and this Annex, its member States, Iceland, Japan, New Zealand, Norway, Switzerland, and the United States.

(c) 'exporting Member' means a Member using the system to produce pharmaceutical products for, and export them to, an eligible importing Member.

2. The terms referred to in paragraph 1 of Article 31*bis* are that:

(a) the eligible importing Member(s)[4] has made a notification[2] to the Council for TRIPS, that:

   (i) specifies the names and expected quantities of the product(s) needed[5];

   (ii) confirms that the eligible importing Member in question, other than a least-developed country Member, has established that it has insufficient or no manufacturing capacities in the pharmaceutical sector for the product(s) in question in one of the ways set out in the Appendix to this Annex; and

   (iii) confirms that, where a pharmaceutical product is patented in its territory, it has granted or intends to grant a compulsory licence in accordance with Articles 31 and 31*bis* of this Agreement and the provisions of this Annex[6];

(b) the compulsory licence issued by the exporting Member under the system shall contain the following conditions:

   (i) only the amount necessary to meet the needs of the eligible importing Member(s) may be manufactured under the licence and the entirety of this production shall be exported to the Member(s) which has notified its needs to the Council for TRIPS;

   (ii) products produced under the licence shall be clearly identified as being produced under the system through specific labelling or marking. Suppliers should distinguish such products through special packaging and/or special colouring/shaping of the products themselves, provided that such distinction is feasible and does not have a significant impact on price; and

---

[4] Joint notifications providing the information required under this subparagraph may be made by the regional organizations referred to in paragraph 3 of Article 31*bis* on behalf of eligible importing Members using the system that are parties to them, with the agreement of those parties.

[5] The notification will be made available publicly by the WTO Secretariat through a page on the WTO website dedicated to the system.

[6] This subparagraph is without prejudice to Article 66.1 of this Agreement.

    (iii) before shipment begins, the licensee shall post on a website[7] the following information:
- the quantities being supplied to each destination as referred to in indent (i) above; and
- the distinguishing features of the product(s) referred to in indent (ii) above;

  (c) the exporting Member shall notify[8] the Council for TRIPS of the grant of the licence, including the conditions attached to it.[9] The information provided shall include the name and address of the licensee, the product(s) for which the licence has been granted, the quantity(ies) for which it has been granted, the country(ies) to which the product(s) is (are) to be supplied and the duration of the licence. The notification shall also indicate the address of the website referred to in subparagraph (b)(iii) above.

3. In order to ensure that the products imported under the system are used for the public health purposes underlying their importation, eligible importing Members shall take reasonable measures within their means, proportionate to their administrative capacities and to the risk of trade diversion to prevent re-exportation of the products that have actually been imported into their territories under the system. In the event that an eligible importing Member that is a developing country Member or a least-developed country Member experiences difficulty in implementing this provision, developed country Members shall provide, on request and on mutually agreed terms and conditions, technical and financial cooperation in order to facilitate its implementation.

4. Members shall ensure the availability of effective legal means to prevent the importation into, and sale in, their territories of products produced under the system and diverted to their markets inconsistently with its provisions, using the means already required to be available under this Agreement. If any Member considers that such measures are proving insufficient for this purpose, the matter may be reviewed in the Council for TRIPS at the request of that Member.

---

[7] The licensee may use for this purpose its own website or, with the assistance of the WTO Secretariat, the page on the WTO website dedicated to the system.

[8] It is understood that this notification does not need to be approved by a WTO body in order to use the system.

[9] The notification will be made available publicly by the WTO Secretariat through a page on the WTO website dedicated to the system.

5. With a view to harnessing economies of scale for the purposes of enhancing purchasing power for, and facilitating the local production of, pharmaceutical products, it is recognized that the development of systems providing for the grant of regional patents to be applicable in the Members described in paragraph 3 of Article 31*bis* should be promoted. To this end, developed country Members undertake to provide technical cooperation in accordance with Article 67 of this Agreement, including in conjunction with other relevant intergovernmental organizations.

6. Members recognize the desirability of promoting the transfer of technology and capacity building in the pharmaceutical sector in order to overcome the problem faced by Members with insufficient or no manufacturing capacities in the pharmaceutical sector. To this end, eligible importing Members and exporting Members are encouraged to use the system in a way which would promote this objective. Members undertake to cooperate in paying special attention to the transfer of technology and capacity building in the pharmaceutical sector in the work to be undertaken pursuant to Article 66.2 of this Agreement, paragraph 7 of the Declaration on the TRIPS Agreement and Public Health and any other relevant work of the Council for TRIPS.

7. The Council for TRIPS shall review annually the functioning of the system with a view to ensuring its effective operation and shall annually report on its operation to the General Council.

APPENDIX TO THE ANNEX TO THE TRIPS AGREEMENT

Assessment of Manufacturing Capacities in the Pharmaceutical Sector

Least-developed country Members are deemed to have insufficient or no manufacturing capacities in the pharmaceutical sector.

For other eligible importing Members insufficient or no manufacturing capacities for the product(s) in question may be established in either of the following ways:

(i) the Member in question has established that it has no manufacturing capacity in the pharmaceutical sector;

or

(ii) where the Member has some manufacturing capacity in this sector, it has examined this capacity and found that, excluding any capacity owned or controlled by the patent owner, it is currently insufficient for the purposes of meeting its needs. When it is established that such capacity has become sufficient to meet the Member's needs, the system shall no longer apply.

~

Annex 9
Extension of the Transition Period under Article 66.1 of the TRIPS Agreement for Least-Developed Country Members for Certain Obligations with Respect to Pharmaceutical Products[†]

Decision of the Council for TRIPS of 27 June 2002

The Council for Trade-Related Aspects of Intellectual Property Rights (the 'Council for TRIPS'),

Having regard to paragraph 1 of Article 66 of the TRIPS Agreement;

Having regard to the instruction of the Ministerial Conference to the Council for TRIPS contained in paragraph 7 of the Declaration on the TRIPS Agreement and Public Health (WT/MIN(01)/DEC/2) (the 'Declaration');

Considering that paragraph 7 of the Declaration constitutes a duly motivated request by the least-developed country Members for an extension of the period under paragraph 1 of Article 66 of the TRIPS Agreement;

Decides as follows:

1. Least-developed country Members will not be obliged, with respect to pharmaceutical products, to implement or apply Sections 5 and 7 of Part II of the TRIPS Agreement or to enforce rights provided for under these Sections until 1 January 2016.
2. This decision is made without prejudice to the right of least-developed country Members to seek other extensions of the period provided for in paragraph 1 of Article 66 of the TRIPS Agreement.

———————

[†] Document IP/C/25.

~

Annex 10
Extension of the Transition Period under Article 66.1 for Least-Developed Country Members[†]

Decision of the Council for TRIPS of 29 November 2005

The Council for Trade-Related Aspects of Intellectual Property Rights (the 'Council for TRIPS'),

Having regard to paragraph 1 of Article 66 of the TRIPS Agreement (the 'Agreement');

Recalling that, unless extended, the transition period granted to least-developed country Members under Article 66.1 of the Agreement will expire on 1 January 2006;

Having regard to the request from least-developed country Members of the World Trade Organization (the 'WTO'), dated 13 October 2005, for an extension of their transition period under Article 66.1 of the Agreement contained in document IP/C/W/457;

Recognizing the special needs and requirements of least-developed country Members, the economic, financial and administrative constraints that they continue to face, and their need for flexibility to create a viable technological base;

Recognizing the continuing needs of least-developed country Members for technical and financial cooperation so as to enable them to realize the cultural, social, technological and other developmental objectives of intellectual property protection;

Decides as follows:

[†] Document IP/C/40.

I

Extension of the transition period under Article 66.1 of the Agreement for least-developed country Members

1. Least-developed country Members shall not be required to apply the provisions of the Agreement, other than Articles 3, 4 and 5, until 1 July 2013, or until such a date on which they cease to be a least-developed country Member, whichever date is earlier.

II

Enhanced technical cooperation for least-developed country Members

2. With a view to facilitating targeted technical and financial cooperation programmes, all the least-developed country Members will provide to the Council for TRIPS, preferably by 1 January 2008, as much information as possible on their individual priority needs for technical and financial cooperation in order to assist them taking steps necessary to implement the TRIPS Agreement.

3. Developed country Members shall provide technical and financial cooperation in favour of least-developed country Members in accordance with Article 67 of the Agreement in order to effectively address the needs identified in accordance with paragraph 2.

4. In order to assist least-developed country Members to draw up the information to be presented in accordance with paragraph 2, and with a view to making technical assistance and capacity building as effective and operational as possible, the WTO shall seek to enhance its cooperation with the World Intellectual Property Organization and with other relevant international organizations.

III

General provisions

5. Least-developed country Members will ensure that any changes in their laws, regulations and practice made during the additional transitional period do not result in a lesser degree of consistency with the provisions of the TRIPS Agreement.

6. This Decision is without prejudice to the Decision of the Council for TRIPS of 27 June 2002 on 'Extension of the Transition Period under Article 66.1 of the TRIPS Agreement for Least-Developed Country

Members for Certain Obligations with respect to Pharmaceutical Products' (IP/C/25), and to the right of least-developed country Members to seek further extensions of the period provided for in paragraph 1 of Article 66 of the Agreement.

———————

INDEX